Rule and Conflict in an Early Medieval Society

Ottonian Saxony

K. J. Leyser

INDIANA UNIVERSITY PRESS
Bloomington and London

Library of Congress catalog card number: 79–5471
ISBN 0–253–17525–9

Filmset in VIP 10 on 11pt Times
Manufactured in Great Britain

131488

Contents

List of Illustrations   iv
Preface   v
Abbreviations   vii
Introduction   1

I Otto I and his Saxon Enemies   9
  1 The Roots of Discord   9
  2 The Later Conflicts   23
  3 Otto I and Count Liuthar of Walbeck   32
  4 The Aftermath of Rebellion   43

II The Women of the Saxon Aristocracy   49
  5 Survival and Inheritance   49
  6 The Saxon Nunneries   63

III Sacral Kingship   75
  7 The Carolingian Inheritance in Tenth-Century East Francia   77
  8 The Ottonians as Sacral Kings   83
  9 Lay Nobles and Sacrosanct Rulers   92
10 The *Vicarius Christi* and Justice   98

Epilogue   109
Appendix: MS. John Rylands Library, 88   113
Bibliography   125
Notes   143
Index   181

Illustrations

Maps 1 and 2 appears on pages ix and x.
Plates I-IV appear between pages 108 and 109.
The genealogical table appears between pages 91 and 92.

To Henrietta

Preface

The three studies presented here have a common theme. They grew out of another book on the Saxon nobility as a ruling class which is not far from completion. Many years' work has gone into both these attempts to look at the genesis of the German kingdom and the formation of its society in the tenth and eleventh centuries in a new way. My debts to friends and scholars who encouraged me and gave me opportunities to work in German libraries, archives, learned institutes and historical seminars are manifold and spread over nearly two decades. I am grateful to the British Academy for travel grants, to Professors Karl Jordan and Hans Eberhard Mayer of the University of Kiel who had me to lecture there on the women of the Saxon aristocracy, to Professors Theodor Schieffer, Carl-Richard Brühl and Peter Classen who invited me to speak on kingship at Cologne, Giessen and Heidelberg. I owe a special debt of gratitude to Professor Josef Fleckenstein, Director at the Max-Planck-Institut für Geschichte, who enabled me to stay and work there for some weeks as a guest, to benefit from countless lively and stimulating discussions and to address a circle of distinguished medievalists under the auspices of Professor Hermann Heimpel. To him and Professors Reinhard Wenskus and Hans Goetting I feel grateful for interest and advice and it will be at my peril where I have not followed it. Without the offprints and copies of books which they and many others so generously gave and sent me, it would have been difficult to work on tenth-century Eastern Saxony in an Oxfordshire village. It would have been impossible but for the patience and understanding of the Librarians of Magdalen College and the History Faculty Library, who allowed me to borrow volumes of the *Monumenta Germaniae Historica* for very long periods indeed. For the best possible facilities to study early episcopal and private charters I stand indebted to Professor W. Heinemeyer and his institute at Marburg. The plates from the Aachen Gospel and the Regensburg Sacramentary I owe to the kindness and help of Dr Henry Mayr-Harting of St Peter's College. For vi

the photograph from the Sacramentary I am also very grateful to the Bavarian State Library at Munich and I should like to thank warmly Professor L. Küppers, the *Custos* of the Essen Minster's Treasury, for letting me have several pictures of the Processional Cross. Lastly I want to record my largest debt of all: to Henrietta and Conrad, Ottoline, Crispin and Matilda Leyser who for many years cheerfully put up with the moody and temperamental ups and downs of work on a lonely subject.

Islip, 10.X.1978
Karl Leyser

Abbreviations

AESC	*Annales Économies Sociétés Civilisations*
AKG	*Archiv für Kulturgeschichte*
AQ	*Annales Quedlinburgenses*
AS	*Annalista Saxo*
ASA	Association of Social Anthropologists of the Common-wealth
Ausgewählte Quellen	*Ausgewählte Quellen zur Deutschen Geschichte des Mittelalters Freiherr vom Stein-Gedächtnisausgabe*
AUF	*Archiv für Urkundenforschung*
BEHE	*Bibliothèque de l'École des Hautes Études*
BJRL	*Bulletin of the John Rylands Library*
CDA	*Codex Diplomaticus Anhaltinus*, ed. O. von Heinemann (Dessau, 1867–73)
DA	*Deutsches Archiv für Erforschung des Mittelalters*
EHR	*English Historical Review*
FSI	*Istituto Storico Italiano Fonti per la storia d'Italia*
HZ	*Historische Zeitschrift*
MGH	*Monumenta Germaniae Historica*
D	Diploma
DD·	Diplomata
DH I	Heinrici I. diploma
DO I	Ottonis I. diploma
DO II	Ottonis II. diploma
DO III	Ottonis III. diploma
DH II	Heinrici II. diploma, etc.
SS	*Scriptorum Tomus*
SRG	*Scriptores Rerum Germanicarum in usum scholarum ex Monumentis Germaniae Historicis separatim editi*
NS	Nova Series
MIÖG	*Mitteilungen des Instituts für Österreichische Geschichtsforschung*

Ergbd.	*Ergänzungsband*
NF	*Neue Folge*
P & P	*Past and Present*
Philol.-Histor.	
Klasse	*Philologisch-Historische Klasse*
RI II	J. F. Böhmer, *Regesta Imperii II Sächsisches Haus 919–1024*
RI II, 1	*Die Regesten des Kaiserreichs unter Heinrich I. und Otto I. 919–973*, neubearbeitet von E. von Ottenthal mit Ergänzungen von H. Kaminsky (Hildesheim, 1967)
RI II, 2	*Die Regesten des Kaiserreiches unter Otto II. 955 (973)–983*, neubearbeitet von H. L. Mikoletzky (Graz, 1950)
RI II, 3	*Die Regesten des Kaiserreiches unter Otto III. 980 (983)–1002*, neubearbeitet von M. Uhlirz (in two parts, Graz, Cologne, 1956, 1957)
RI II, 4	*Die Regesten des Kaiserreiches unter Heinrich II. 1002–1024*, neubearbeitet von J. F. Graff (Vienna, Cologne, Graz, 1971)
RI II, 5	*Papstregesten 911-1024*, bearbeitet von H. Zimmermann (Vienna, Cologne, Graz, 1969)
SB	*Sitzungsberichte*
Studien und Vorarbeiten	*Studien und Vorarbeiten zum Historischen Atlas Niedersachsens*
TRHS	*Transactions of the Royal Historical Society*
UB	*Urkundenbuch*
VSWG	*Vierteljahrschrift für Sozial- und Wirtschaftsgeschichte*
Vorträge und Forschungen	*Vorträge und Forschungen Herausgegeben vom Konstanzer Arbeitskreis für mittelalterliche Geschichte*
WBG	*Wissenschaftliche Buchgesellschaft*
ZRG	*Zeitschrift der Savigny-Stiftung für Rechtsgeschichte*
Kanon. Abt.	*Kanonistische Abteilung*
GA	*Germanistische Abteilung*

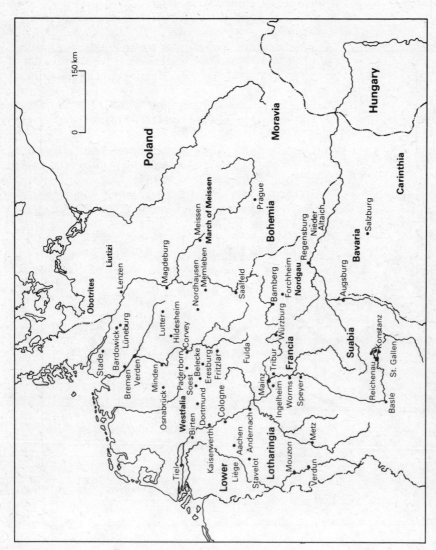

Map 1: Ottonian Germany

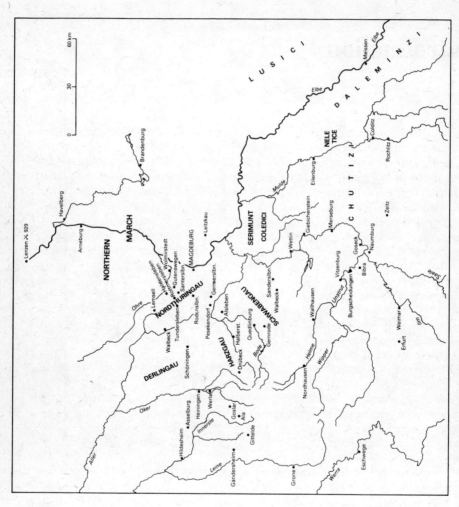

Map 2: Eastern Saxony in the Tenth Century

Introduction

The world of the tenth century is, or ought to be, strange to us, much stranger than that of the twelfth with its lyrical, individualistic, witty and rationalizing traits. Its kings, clerks, poets and women, even its saints, were beginning to have more in common with us than they did with their Carolingian and Ottonian forbears. Abelard, Walter Map, John of Salisbury, the Archpoet and Walther von der Vogelweide can be understood on many levels, some of them very demanding and dominated by exacting philological disciplines and critical methodology, others ruled by imagination and sensitiveness alone. Widukind of Corvey and his contemporaries cannot be understood like that. And if we ask wherein the strangeness of the tenth century lay or what was the reason for it, the answer must be the heroic mould of its values and norms set in the harsh necessities and unashamed ferocity of its conflicts and their objects. The society which experienced these dichotomies, this dissonance between what we might be tempted to call, in our language, fact and value, was not unaware of them but its historians' and homilists' difficulties were different from ours. The underlying theme of this book is the relationship between the very tangible conflicts and the norms, aiming to find the flashpoints where both can be illuminated in terms of one another. This is not to attempt to classify conflicts anthropologically but rather to employ anthropological insights sparingly, to understand the history of the Saxon empire at its native centres of gravity a little better and to explain the changes which slowly turned it into a reluctant German one, with conflicts of a new kind.

In September 937, little over a year after succeeding his father, Otto I set about endowing his new monastic foundation in Magdeburg, dedicated to the holy martyrs St Maurice and St Innocent. On the 21st and 27th of that month and on 11 October he gave the new congregation of monks their first diplomata, conferring lavish gifts: his *curtis* at Magdeburg—he had more than one—with all the localities west of the Elbe in the Nordthüringau which belonged to it and owed services, whosesoever fief they might now be. Over thirty places were named and already the diploma spoke also of rents and taxes on sales in the barely subjected *pagi* east of the river. The third diploma added scores of *familiae* of Slavs, *liti*, *coloni* and slaves, mostly again settled in the same region, but it bestowed also some more lands in a more distant area. The human beings were given to St Maurice with the exclusive rights to all the dues and services they owed, their tenures and chattels.¹ The world of the Ottonian emperors emerges suddenly, without any warning, ready made, crowded and organized. Magdeburg's early diplomata unfold a large landscape, relatively well settled west of the Elbe and with profitable exactions to the east of it, counts with the characteristic names of Thietmar, Christan, Gero and Wichmann, and evidence of markets, tolls and trade.

An element of optical illusion is necessarily part of this vision. Magdeburg had been an important frontier station of Charlemagne's Saxony where trade in contraband—merchandise that might be useful to hostile Slav tribes—was checked and controlled. A special *missus* supervised the merchants wanting to visit the Slavs and enforced the Thionville Capitulary of 805 against the sale of arms and hauberks.² Bardowick and Erfurt were other centres of inspection and it seems that the Thionville ordinance remained alive, at least in the authoritative and much-copied legal collection of Louis the Pious's reign, the work of Abbot Ansegis. Two fortresses and a church dedicated to St Stephan were the core of Carolingian Magdeburg. The Nordthüringau is occasionally mentioned in the ninth century, in the *Traditiones Corbeienses* for instance, since the distant Weser monastery received gifts there which it sometimes sought to exchange for more conveniently sited estates.³ In the avalanche of placenames engulfing us in Otto's earliest diplomata for St Maurice, not every one is new. A slow but steady enlargement of settlement in the Börde, Magdeburg's western hinterland, lay behind the emergence of the Ottonian town, with its massive resources, building activities and communities of clerical consumers. It was a fertile, open region, not so troubled by the density of forest which divided areas of settlement from one another elsewhere. Communications were somewhat easier, not least of all thanks to the River Elbe itself. That so many vills were attached to and served the royal *curtis* suggests an administrative organization to collect dues and rents. The *civitas*, for so Magdeburg was called in Otto's diploma of 21 September 937, was already the centre of a large district and dominated its economy. The mention of *beneficia*, 'benefices' (fiefs), in the same royal grant, points to a close military following, a group of dependant *milites*, in this region. It could have been built up by Henry I, of whom it was said that he left no notable man in Saxony unrewarded with fiefs and offices. It may well have come into existence earlier, well before the Liudolfings began to rule as kings, just as they had implanted a body of their vassals in Thuringia whom they also provided with 'benefices' there.

Magdeburg belonged to the dower of Queen Edith, Otto I's Anglo-Saxon wife. How had the Liudolfings acquired it? Was it part of the Carolingian fisc which they seem to have taken over quietly, as if by the leave of the late ninth-century Carolingian rulers; that is to say, was it the fruit of their close relations and affinity with Louis the Younger (876–82) and Arnolf (887–99)? Most likely, yes. In two successive generations daughters of the leading East Saxon family married Carolingian kings. Before 874 Liudolf's daughter, Liudgard, became the wife of Louis the Younger and in 897 the Emperor Arnolf himself made his son, King Zwentibold of Lotharingia, marry Duke Otto's sister, Oda. This was seen as an act of prudent management by which it might be hoped to safeguard the interests of the *stirps regia*, not to mention those of the Liudolfings. The second marriage alliance already wore something of the air almost of a tradition, a system. Here as elsewhere royal tasks in a remote and threatened region, together with the wealth to shoulder them, fell into the hands of a well-placed family more by the consent of the Carolingians than by usurpation.

There is little to prepare us for the inner conflicts of Ottonian Saxony and the feuds of its nobles. The segmentation of the tenth century was a function of Liudolfing kingship in its native habitat. We do not know what enemies the Liudolfings had to overcome to force themselves to the leading place in East Saxony nor do we know much about the feuds in the Saxon aristocracy under Carolingian rule. Occasionally the Fulda Annals and their continuations, the most important chronicle of the East Frankish kingdom during the second half of the ninth century, mention such things. In 872 a Saxon and Thuringian host was dispatched against the Morawians by Louis the German but the king did not come himself to lead it, with disastrous results 'because they could not agree with one another'.[4] We know that there were counts in this army. In 882 again we hear of a *civile bellum* between Saxons and Thuringians at the instigation of a Count Egino and the Babenberg Poppo who presided over Thuringia in defence against the Slavs. Egino was a Frank but like others must have had a Saxon following.[5] The rich and varied literature of the *Translations*, the accounts of the miracles wrought by the saints' relics recently brought into Saxony, sometimes allows us to see how the new judicial institutions, the comital courts, could be used to further revenges by procuring unjust judgments and savage penalties. During the fraternal conflicts in the Carolingian house after Louis the Pious's death, both Lothar and Louis the German were able to muster Saxon noble adherents, who were thus pitted against one another although Louis soon had the better of these alignments. Later, when Saxony had become Louis the Younger's share of the East Frankish kingship, he could raise support there when he wanted to rebel against the loss of some of his *beneficia* elsewhere. On the whole this evidence is meagre.

The Regensburg Continuation of the Fulda Annals tells us that in 887 the Saxons deserted Charles III 'more solito' ('after their fashion'); but they did not desert the Carolingians as such.[6] They preferred, like most others, to bow to Arnolf of Carinthia and to make him their king. The Regensburg Continuator's prejudice agains the Saxons' reliability and loyalty is not borne out by their actual conduct. For various reasons they adhered to and supported the Carolingians as long as that was possible. For one, their military resources and equipment in the ninth century were not yet sufficient to sustain the whole weight of the pressures on their frontiers. Danes, Obotrites, Sorbs and Daleminzi, the last two between the Saale and the Elbe, when striking against the Frankish *Reich* usually struck at Saxony and Thuringia first. The Slav peoples had been patronized by the Carolingians in their aggressive decades and throughout the ninth century the East Frankish rulers sought to maintain vestiges and more than vestiges of this relationship. Some measure of dependance was expected and enforced but it could only be done by direct royal intervention, backed by forces raised in Francia or the Rhineland strengthening the Saxon hosts.

Conventional wisdom has it that, after 852 when Louis the German came to Saxony and held a great assembly at Minden and from there proceeded eastwards, no Carolingian king visited Saxony again until Arnolf appeared briefly at Corvey before warring against the Obotrites in 889. Louis the German's progress had a twofold purpose.[7] There were royal possessions to be reclaimed by judgment but, above all, Louis came as kings were wont and meant to come, to remedy the injustices of men who had suffered at the hands of evil and deceitful judges. It would be dangerous to translate the term *causas populi* ('the cases of the people'), which he came to hear, as the suits of non-nobles against their betters, as some scholars have done. Usually the *populus* that acted, elected bishops, chose kings or deserted them were nobles and their followings, little hierarchies in which again the nobler and better born held pride of place. The evil and sly judges mentioned by Rudolf of Fulda are important because they reveal the shortcomings and malpractices in the new secular institutions that the Frankish conquerors had brought to Saxony—the comital courts. The masters who now presided in these courts were leading members of the Saxon aristocracy, the Ekbertines, the Hessi clan, the Billungs, the Liudolfings and a few others. That is why their forbears had espoused the Frankish cause. It furnished them with new and much more sweeping powers of government over their own kind and the lower castes than they had possessed before. Rudolf's exposé is supported by the miracles which accompanied the translations of the saints. Their arrival and *signa*, mostly cures, are one of the main themes of Saxon, ninth-century history. They were the most dynamic element in the Christian cult of the day. Bishops, abbots and lay princes imported West Frankish and Roman relics to build up and enhance their churches and new family sanctuaries as centres of worship. Against the blindings inflicted in the courts and countless other misfortunes, including failure in a feud, the saints offered remedies, perhaps, and certainly consolations more enduring than a rarely visiting Carolingian ruler could offer. They became part of the locality which bishop and count controlled.

For it is true that after Louis's progress in 852 this type of royal visit ceased, although it did not mean that Carolingian kings and princes no longer came to Saxony. The assumption that they stayed away overlooks their important and continuing role in the campaigns against the Slavs, be it to exact hostages for good behaviour and tribute or to counter-attack in retribution of their raids. There were campaigns in 856, 858, 862, 867 and 869. Each of these expeditions led Louis the Younger and two—those of 856 and 862—his father, back into Saxony, where the Carolingians were joined by the Saxon host. We must not forget that this, the *exercitus*, was, or had become, the most important institution of secular stem society. It brought together warriors from a much wider region than the comital pleas and, since royal court days in Saxony were so rare and older provincial assemblies had been forbidden, the host had a political and judicial as well as military face. Men fulfilled their obligations and showed their mettle 'domi militiaque' ('at home and in the field'). Widukind of Corvey and others found here a classical phrase which could be used to describe something familiar to their audience, an accepted routine. During the 850s and 860s, the Slav wars and the Saxon participation in Carolingian hosts against the Morawians and at Andernach against Charles the Bald in 876 maintained their relationships and contacts with their kings. They furnished troops also for the Elsloo campaign of 882 and the battle at the Dyle in 891. It would be mistaken to think that the later Carolingian East Frankish kings allowed their Saxon *fideles* to drift away and had no use or need for their services.

Nonetheless, from about 870 onwards the rulers met their commitments on the Saxon frontiers less often by campaigning in person and more frequently by sending capable commanders like the Babenberg Count Heinrich or even bishops, like Archbishop Liutbert of Mainz and Arn of Würzburg. Despite some severe defeats and heavy casualties, it seems that towards the end of the century Saxon hosts were slowly gaining the upper hand against Danes and Slavs. Long before he succeeded his father as duke in Saxony, Henry, the future king, was able to carry the burden of offensive war against the Daleminzi—the Slavs between the Elbe and the Mulde—on his own. In 856 Louis the German himself had had to take the field against this enemy. The northeastwards shift in the centre of gravity of the East Frankish kingdom, which was the very essence of Ottonian rule, had already begun.

The Regensburg Continuator's sour judgment on the Saxons during the Carolingian crisis of 887–8 is belied by another source, albeit of a very different kind. It is of Saxon origin, a poem of over 2,600 verses, recording and appraising the deeds of Charlemagne and most of all his labours to subdue and then convert the Saxons to Christianity. Charlemagne is here extolled not just because he conquered so many peoples whose very names remained unknown to the Romans, but because he gained countless souls for God when he made the Saxons abjure their pagan rites. He is likened to the Apostles: nobody came so near to them as he did. On the day of judgment he would be attended by throngs of Saxons, whom his invasion and mission had wrested from the clutches of Satan and saved, however brutal and sanguinary the methods employed—and the author did not conceal these ugly features of the Saxon wars. The Poeta Saxo, as he is called, wrote between 888 and 891, perhaps at Corvey.[8] We do not know who he was. For the most part he versified Charlemagne's wars and other deeds from the later text of the *Frankish Royal Annals* and from Einhard. His lines echo these sources all too faithfully. Once, however, and on a very important topic, he departed from them with a story of which he is the earliest and most detailed reporter. Later Saxon historiography, the Quedlinburg Annals, the Halberstadt episcopal *Gesta*, the Saxon Annalist and a forged Charlemagne diploma in Adam of Bremen, contain the core of the poet's tale but they lack his fullness and elaboration. In 803, 'that noble year', he tells us, Charlemagne and his Franks met the entire Saxon nobility at Salz on the Frankish Saale to conclude a formal treaty of peace and settle their future relationships after thirty-three years of fighting. The poet gave what he thought were the terms of this pact in full: the Saxons must forsake the heathen cults they had practised hitherto, obey the bishops and their clergy and offer them the tithes ordained by divine law. On the other hand they would not have to pay any (degrading) tribute to the Frankish kings and were to enjoy the freedom (*honor libertatis*) of living under their own customary laws but with judges and royal *missi* imposed by Charlemagne. This meant the introduction of the comital constitution which had in fact been brought to Saxony over twenty years earlier. The authority of Einhard's *Life of Charlemagne* is cited if any one doubted the veracity of the poet's account. Those of his readers who followed up the reference and consulted Einhard would have been disappointed. He did not set out these very specific and detailed peace terms, but in the Poeta Saxo they were not only accepted but became the basis on which the Saxons associated with the Franks in future and swore fealty to Charlemagne, his sons and heirs. It was a *foedus* which the Saxons decided to keep for all times and, the author insists, they had not changed it ever since.[9]

The entire Saxon nobility concluded this fictional treaty according to the *Poeta* and we can therefore say that it reflected something of its latter-day views, attitudes and historical consciousness. This is how Saxon nobles in the late ninth century were meant to understand their past and their present. The riches of Gaul and rewards hitherto unknown to their poor ancestors had become theirs as a consequence of this compact and the poet even mentioned them—precious garments, silver and wine.[10] He wanted his audience to share his love, reverence and gratitude for Charlemagne's mission. His sense of indebtedness included, it is true, a personal concern. Writing, learning and the beginnings of a literate culture had come to Saxony only because Charlemagne had come and imposed his will. The poet was the very self-conscious exponent of this new dimension yet he felt that he spoke for all, not only for himself, in cultivating the emperor's deeds in Saxony and their lasting benefits.

In the fifth book of his work he turned to his own times and addressed a prayer of intercession to the ancestor of the Carolingians, Bishop Arnulf of Metz, on behalf of his name-sake, Arnolf of Carinthia, now East Frankish king. He compared the former security and ascendancy of Francia to the miseries and losses of the day, the devastations wrought by the savage heathen *gentes*. Yet Arnolf had the qualities of his great-great-grandfather, Charlemagne. He was magnanimous, clement and hard at work to restore and revive the *Reich*, calling the Franks back into action and the other stems back to arms. Only it would take time. What had collapsed could not be rebuilt in a day. Arnolf had that all-pervasive quality of *virtus* from which salvation could be hoped. If this was written not long before the battle of the Dyle in 891, where a large host under the king stormed a Viking camp successfully, it reveals a mood of returning and mounting confidence.[11]

Whoever the Poeta Saxo and his circle were, his is an important Saxon voice from the last decades of East Frankish Carolingian rule and there is none to contradict him. It was of course an aristocratic voice. We must listen to it carefully and note the almost obsequious provincialism which speaks from the accomplished verse of the poet's text. The Saxons' attachment to the Carolingian house was to be grounded on the inestimable gain of belief. They now belonged to the *populus christianus*. Churches and monasteries were gleaming where heathen sanctuaries had once stood. Charlemagne, moreover, had bestowed other, tangible, advantages and rewards to which the author's own generation of Saxon nobles were, as he reminded them, heirs. The idea that anyone but a Carolingian could hold the kingship had not yet struck the Poeta or the audience he addressed as a serious possibility, although it was beginning to happen elsewhere. A strain of anxiety can be heard, though, in his prayer that the Carolingian line should not fail. Louis the Child was not yet born when he wrote. Our author seems to convey a sense of satisfaction with the *status quo* despite its dangers. What happened in 911—the rejection of the West Frankish Carolingian, Charles the Simple, and the election of Conrad I—is almost surprising in the light of the poet's message. It suggests that sheer necessity, rather than deliberate choice or a new sense of identity, lay behind the acceptance of a non-Carolingian ruler. It was different only when the Liudolfings themselves entered upon the succession in 919 and so gave their Saxon followers the opportunities and prospects which nearness to an aggressive and enterprising kingship had always brought in its wake. Here lies the opening of our theme.

I   Otto I and his Saxon Enemies

1

The Roots of Discord

To become and to remain masters of their *Reich*, the Ottonians had to be masters in their homeland Saxony. A bare glance at their itineraries shows how much of their yearly stint of ruling or, to use the words of the Quedlinburg Annalist, 'pleasing the pious with mildness and frightening the wicked with stern judgment', depended on their Saxon *palatia*, *curtes* and ecclesiastical strongholds.[1] From there they set out and there they returned whatever enterprise was afoot. With Otto I's victories over some of the Conradine clan in Rhenish Francia, Hessen and Western Saxony, it is true, Frankfurt and Ingelheim were added to the bases on which his itinerancy pivoted. Later, a Saxon lord in Otto III's following is known to have held a *mansus* in the upper vill of Ingelheim so that he had a pied-à-terre there and in general, Otto III, once past his minority, showed a marked preference for Aachen.[2] But even this does not detract from the importance of Saxony, for here Ottonian kingship developed something like a military and fiscal system, which grew out of the conquest of the Slav peoples beyond the Elbe-Saale line and survived to some extent the great setback of 983. Huge reserves of land, an annual flow of tributes, a primitive kind of *fiefs-rentes* to reward the *milites* and a belt of fortresses which the lay nobles and bishops had to garrison by a duty roster, in other words castle-guard, were at their disposal in the East Saxon marches.[3] Moreover, the labour services and dues of the peasant population had been harnessed to the building and upkeep of these fortresses. Elsewhere the authority of the Saxon rulers was less intense and wielded more or less infrequently. In times of trouble it could happen that Otto I was denied both the material and the ritual supports of kingship, the *servitia* to feed him and his marching train and the solemn receptions and crown-wearings which proclaimed his God-given rightful role. In 953 when the rising of Liudolf, Otto's son and Duke Conrad of Lotharingia, his son-in-law, was already fermenting, the king did not dare to keep Easter in Ingelheim lest his enemies should suddenly attack him there. He had lived through the dangers of a *coup-de-main* during a royal Easter court once before. Turning to Mainz instead, he was kept waiting outside the city and somewhat reluctantly served by the archbishop. When he moved to Aachen in order to manifest his kingship at the right place where it had so solemnly begun in 936, he discovered that nothing had been prepared for him. He then returned to Saxony where, as Widukind of Corvey so well expressed it, 'he found the king again in his own *patria* whom he had nearly lost in Francia.'[4] In Widukind's eyes, Saxony was the true fountain-head of Otto's rule, especially in a time of crisis.

Yet it is difficult to think of a time between 936 and 973 when Otto had no enemies in his stemland and when these enemies were not stirring. There are references to *civilia bella* already in Henry I's reign, both in Widukind and, more explicitly, in Ruotger's *Life of Archbishop Brun of Cologne*. Now when Widukind spoke of civil wars he meant, it seems, Henry I's clashes with the South German dukes and he appears to set off these wars against external ones; but sometimes his 'civil discords' were inner-Saxon feuds.[5] Ruotger, when he extolled Brun's ancestry and especially his father, said that at his accession Henry I found grave dissension 'inter cives' and even among kinsmen (*cognatos*), all of which his *virtus* and *industria*, qualities borrowed from Cicero, overcame.[6] Here we stumble at once over the roots of the Ottonians' difficulties in their Saxon home—their kinship and close neighbourhood with most of the other East Saxon and some leading Engern and Thuringian family groups of nobles. This kinship entailed also the relationship of *co-hereditas*, mutual expectations of inheriting land and sharing in the division of patrimonies as they fell vacant on the death of joint kindred. To give an example: it would be difficult to know why Otto II, in 975, gave back to Bishop Liudolf of Osnabrück (967–78) parcels of land and *hereditas* in Applerbeck, Heessen and Lingen which the bishop had first given him *in proprium*, if in the diploma which set out this transaction Liudolf was not called 'consanguineus noster'. Through his mother, Ald-burg, he belonged to the *stirps Widukindi*, the posterity of Charlemagne's foremost Saxon enemy and from whom Queen Mathilda, Otto II's grand-mother, was also thought to be descended. At the same time the prelate's father, also called Liudolf, must have sprung from the ninth-century Liudolfings, a very large family group.[7] Perhaps the re-grant of his own land protected the bishop against the claims of other kinsmen. The Ottonians in the tenth century were engaged in more than one such transaction.

A system of primogeniture envisages one great moment in the life of the eldest son when he will inherit his main fortune and rank. All his time up to then was a preparation for it. In a family structure where partibility and *co-hereditas* rule descent, there is no such commanding moment, no such polarity. The death of his father might be but one event in a chain of inheritances, which mortality among kin could throw into the lap of an individual. Thus, the death of the mother, an aunt, a brother, nephew, uncle or cousin might be as important for amassing a fortune as the death of the male parent.[8] Conversely, the individual was rarely the only participant in the devolution of an inheritance. Under these conditions it is not difficult to see why dissension between *cognati* was, if anything, the rule and concord the exception among the wealthier families of the aristocracy in early medieval Germany and, in tenth-century Saxony, not least of all. For here in particular new wealth, new forms of military power and lordship, for instance the margraviates of the eastern frontier, were not only bitterly contested between families but also upset the equilibrium within them. Among the poorer nobles and the *liberi* it was probably different. They lived throughout in the ambit of their kinsfolk. When landed resources were scarce and did not afford much room for manoeuvre, co-operation was essential to make ends meet. Great wealth combined with a large following and high office fostered a different kind of family and different attitudes.

We must now seek to identify the quarrels among kinsmen, the 'gravissimae inter cognatos dissensiones' which Henry I was said to have encountered when he became king. His father, Duke Otto, had taken over the Liudolfing *ducatus* in East Saxony and the defence of the frontiers which was its chief raison d'être only in 880, when an elder brother of his called Brun fell in a disastrous encounter with the Danes.[9] Two bishops, twelve counts and eighteen royal vassals in Saxony were killed with him. Henry I and Otto I were thus descendants of a younger brother. They reached out towards kingship and 'magnum latumque imperium' while the posterity of Brun and Count Liudolf who died in defeat remained, as it were, in the ranks.[10] Widukind again reveals the unease of this situation when he wrote: 'Brun perished and left the *ducatus* to his younger brother who however was superior to him in every virtue.'[11] The Corvey writer felt the need to justify and explain the relative positions of the two descent groups. Counts named Liudolf and Brun appeared in Otto I's diplomata twice (942 and ?965) and their *comitatus* lay in the Derlingau, where the Liudolfing clan as a whole had been much at home in the ninth century and the Ottonians possessed a great many estates in the tenth.[12] There is at least a hint that some of these cousins of kings resented their relative obscurity and especially the men whom Otto I preferred to them when he chose his representatives along the Slav frontiers.

The holder of a permanent command fighting a continuous war against the Slav tribes could summon armies and lead his fellow nobles and equals, thus rising above them. The appointment of Hermann Billung as *princeps militiae* against the Slav Redarii in 936 angered his peers and they were not appeased when he won victories on the king's first campaign. Hermann's advancement, in the first place, alienated his brother Wichmann and gave rise to a deep feud in the Billung kin, which can be traced throughout the reigns of the first two Ottos and the minority of the third. It also offended a young man called Ekkard, the son of a Liudolf. The manner in which Widukind narrates these details suggests that he expected his audience to know who these men were. Ekkard collected a small band of warriors from the whole host and, breaking a royal order, crossed the morass which lay between the Saxon camp and the enemy fortress and attacked. He and all his eighteen companions were surrounded and perished. It is not far-fetched to connect Ekkard or rather his father, Liudolf, with the ninth-century bearers of this name and so also with the count who fell in 880.[13] Finally, in 1002, a Count Brun, neighbour and bitter enemy of Bishop Bernward of Hildesheim, made a fleeting bid for the royal succession after Otto III's death.[14]

It is probable that some of the Brunones, as they came to be called later, took part in the murderous assault of Henry against his brother Otto I in 941.[15] We do not know for certain whether they sided with the king's son Liudolf in 953–5 or with the attacks on Otto II's and Otto III's kingship. Perhaps it was not worth their while to attach themselves to any member of the rival descent group, Henry I's posterity. There is no such uncertainty about the elder Wichmann and his two sons Wichmann and Ekbert. He, for a time, and they, for most of their lives, joined every enemy of Hermann Billung and Otto they could find and the sons were prepared to carry on the struggle on their own in league with the Slavs or Hugh the Great, if for a time they could not find any allies at home. The implacability of the elder Wichmann's descendants was nursed not only by unsatisfied claims to patrimony but also by the very fact that they were closer kin to Otto than their uncle Hermann. For their mother was a sister of Henry I's wife, Mathilda, and they belonged to the royal *consanguinitas* and were therefore entitled to expect more advancement and greater *honores* than others. In the last part of his *Saxon History* Widukind returned to the theme *bellum civile* and told the story of the younger Wichmann's final struggles and tragic end. He has Otto I recognize the justice of his cousin's aspirations and it was only the emperor's long-delayed return from Italy after 962 which tried Wichmann's patience too far.[16] As late as 984 his brother Ekbert held a fortress, Ala, much treasure and a royal princess, Otto II's daughter Adelheid, as a valuable pawn for Henry the Wrangler.[17] The clerical Billungs did not hold themselves aloof from these feuds. A third son of the elder Wichmann, Brun, bishop of Verden, not only excommunicated Herman Billung but in 973 would not even allow him to be buried in the house monastery, St Michael's Lüneburg, which the duke had founded and richly endowed with lands and treasure.[18] We shall have more to say about this cleavage in the Saxon family that did best out of the Ottonian regime.

Henry I not only inherited enmities which he then in turn bequeathed to his successors, he also generated some of his own. His first wife Hatheburg brought him a rich and valuable inheritance in and about Merseburg.[19] In 909, however, he sent her away in order to be able to marry Mathilda, who was of the large and powerful Immeding clan even if she was praised above all for being of the *stirps Widukindi*. Mathilda had useful possessions in Engern and the Osnabrück region and above all she conveyed to her husband valuable and badly needed connections in Westfalian Saxony and Lower Lotharingia.[20] Hatheburg, however, had given him a son, Thangmar. It is odd that Henry's repudiation of his first wife did not there and then plunge him into difficulties, especially as he seems to have kept the Merseburg lands. Part of the reason may have been that Hatheburg had been *vidua velata* at the time of her match and that it was the marriage rather than its abrupt end which earned Henry censures, particularly from the bishop of Halberstadt.[21] It is true also that her father, Erwin, had no sons who might have avenged the slight and he himself was deceased by 909. On the other hand Hatheburg had very powerful relations through her mother, none other than the man whom Widukind called 'secundus a rege', Count Siegfried. We know now that he was a brother of Margrave Gero and related also to the Asigs and Esicos who at various times in the tenth and early eleventh centuries appear as counts in the Merseburg region.[22] Henry seems to have struck a bargain with this clan and no doubt they had their share of the inheritance but there remained Thangmar, his son. Adalbert of St Maximin in his chronicle described him bluntly as the offspring of a concubine—as in the judgment of the church he was; but among the Saxon lay nobility of the early tenth century his claims could not be dismissed so lightly.[23] He had a *legatio*, a command with a *heribannus* against the Slav Redarii but, when in 937 Siegfried, the 'secundus a rege' and 'comes Merseburgensis' died, his countships and frontier command went to Gero.[24] Thangmar had been provided for by Henry I and he received his share of the lands and treasures the king distributed to his sons; but his mother's inheritance eluded him and here is another startling example of the importance of maternal kin in this society. Thangmar was the son of a duke's son who had risen to kingship, but he rebelled against his half-brothers, Otto and Henry, and the Gero kin because he had been cheated of his mother's *praedium* and the leading position in the southeastern marches of Saxony which should have gone with it—as he saw it. Instead Merseburg and its fortress came into the possession of the young Henry and it is not surprising that Thangmar later singled him out for revenge.

So far kinship and the thwarted expectations of co-heirs seem to lie behind reports of unrest in Saxony in Henry I's time. There is only one such report, recorded by Thietmar of Merseburg, which bore a more general, let us say 'political', character. In Book I of his *Chronicon*, devoted to the first Saxon king, the bishop wrote: 'If he plundered [committed robbery] in his own kingdom, as many say he did, may the merciful God forgive him.'[25] What might Henry's robberies in his own kingdom have been? It has been thought that Thietmar here received a tradition which accused the king of seizing church treasures in order to pay tributes to the Hungarians.[26] Yet the context in which this passage occurs suggests something quite different. Thietmar has just described how Henry built Meissen and coerced the inhabitants of a Lusatian fort. It is tempting to think of the labour services he commandeered in Saxony, and perhaps the garrisons of his *urbes* did not always treat the surrounding countryside more gently than did Henry IV's notorious Suabian knights 140 years later. We know also that Henry I maintained a band of outlaw warriors at Merseburg, and Thietmar may have found this less praiseworthy than did Widukind of Corvey.[27]

Lastly, we must remember the mutual oaths which the Saxon warriors swore before joining battle against the coalition of northern Slav tribes at Lenzen in 929. They promised to help their *duces* and one another. A *bellum publicum* was a rare event and feuds were frequent and many; they threatened the cohesion of hosts which the king did not lead himself and even those which he did command.[28]

The course of events during the early crisis years of Otto I's regime is complex. Thangmar's attack on his half-brothers was only one of several, at first disjointed, risings, which however soon merged and combined. He joined his forces with those of the Frankish Duke Eberhard, who in turn disposed of a large Saxon following though some of his Saxons were fighting to break the vassalage they owed him. Between them, Thangmar and Eberhard captured the young Henry at Belecke on the Mohne in Westfalia. When Otto marched westwards he found Thangmar alone, occupying the Eresburg near the Saxon-Hessian border whence he raided the countryside. Thangmar was struck down by one of Henry's *milites* who had joined Otto's host to fight for his lord. Only to a modern historian would his death appear as an obviously fortunate event in Otto's struggle for his kingship and his lordship over Saxony. Widukind and Thietmar were only too anxious to exculpate him, to show him anxious to avenge his kinsman and punish the perpetrator of the deed.[29] It was not only the social gulf between the *miles* and the prince that troubled them but also the certainty that Otto had to bear the responsibility for the sacrilegious act. The slaying must have made new enemies for him among Thangmar's connections in the nobility. It is at least possible that the conspiracy against Margrave Gero and Otto early in 941, the most purely Saxon rising against the king, was fanned by the smouldering resentments left behind by Thangmar's death. These were matters on which Widukind, if he knew them, preferred to keep silent.

However, Otto's most dangerous enemy in Saxony during these years was his younger brother Henry. Brun, the third of King Henry's sons by Mathilda, had been destined for the church from childhood. The nobility were accustomed to designate some of their children for the secular clergy or for religion almost from birth but this had not been at all usual for the legitimate male offspring of the Carolingians. Only the children of concubines, like Drogo and Hugh, were provided for in this way and even this was not a rule.[30] Charles the Bald, it is true, did have two of his sons by Ermintrude tonsured. One of them was lame and unsuited for secular life, the other, Karlmann, revolted and pressed for his share of kingship in no uncertain fashion.[31] Here the Ottonians were compelled to follow a different course. In 936 Brun, aged about eleven, lived in the care of Bishop Balderich of Utrecht, almost certainly a kinsman of Queen Mathilda's. He was thus far away from Eastern Saxony and in any case too young to intervene effectively, but it is noteworthy that one stream of tradition reaching Thietmar of Merseburg implicated him too in machinations against his eldest brother.[32]

Henry and Otto had been enemies ever since childhood, 'ab infantia', according to the author of the second *Vita Mathildis*. As Henry was born in 920 or 921 and *infantia* ended with the seventh year, their antagonism must have been very real throughout Henry I's later years when the succession question was being settled as far as it could be.[33] When the king died the young Henry was of age and on the scene. Already during Otto I's coronation rites at Aachen it had been felt necessary to keep him under some form of honourable arrest in Saxony where Count Siegfried, the 'secundus a rege', was in charge of him. Widukind presents his temporary custody of the stemland and of Henry as if it had been Siegfried's coronation office, like the services of the dukes at Otto's feast after his sacring.[34] It is not surprising that Henry later joined hands with the enemies of Siegfried's brother and successor, Margrave Gero. Fundamentally his hostility and determined attempts on Otto's life sprang from an anomaly in the Liudolfings' position in the *Reich*, an anomaly which by the inherited traditions of East Frankish Carolingian kingship hit him particularly hard. Henry I's patrimony and treasures could be and were divided among his sons but his royal dignity and *imperium* could not be. The East Frankish Carolingians, following the ways of Charlemagne and Louis the Pious, had provided kingships for their sons, Louis the German by partitioning his *Reich* into a Bavarian, Franco-Saxon and Suabian portion in 865. The settlement was to come into effect fully after his death. The emperor Arnolf worked hard to secure Lotharingia and Italy for his two illegitimate sons, Zwentibold and Ratold, while the East Frankish succession was to be reserved for the lawful Louis the Child. In 895 Zwentibold received Lotharingia as king from his father and with the *collaudatio* of the magnates.[35]

When Henry I began to order his house in 929 the situation was quite different. Now the Bavarian Luitpolding duke, the Conradines in Francia and Suabia and Giselbert in Lotharingia were far too powerful and kinglike themselves to allow the Liudolfings, aspiring to become a new *stirps regia*, to do what Louis and Arnolf had done.[36] They were scarcely willing to relinquish those Carolingian fiscs which they had come to control. There was thus no room, no adequate material base, for a shared kingship any longer and this remains the most compelling reason why only one of Henry I's sons could hope to succeed him as king.[37] Much has been written about the rise of undivided rule and individual succession in the post-Carolingian, East Frankish kingdom. Some scholars have come to see in this phenomenon a conscious change in the constitution, a new awareness of the advantages of unity and indeed the progress of the Christian idea of kingship among the ruling men.[38] On another view it expressed the community of the Germanic peoples in the East Frankish kingdom and, more still, was 'both the presupposition and the consequence of the genesis of a German people'.[39] It is not denied that the necessities and interests of the moment played their part, but what underlay them is in danger of being overlooked. Here we must turn to a famous passage in the *Chronicon* of Regino of Prüm. When Regino, himself a Frankish aristocrat, wanted to explain the troubles, the 'magnos bellorum motus' which broke out in Italy, France and Burgundy after the death of Charles III in 888, he dwelt on the parity of the princes who were now contending for fragments of the great Carolingian inheritance.[40] Modern historians would be wise to take Regino's explanation to heart. After 888 the shapes and structures of the post-Carolingian *regna* remained fluid for some decades because, as he said, nobody among the Frankish princes so surpassed the others that they would submit to him. This means that not the end of Carolingian partitions but the very survival of the larger *regna* as such must be accounted for. Here, perhaps, is room for speculation about new solidarities or new powers of political abstraction. It has also been stressed that indivisibility triumphed not only in East Francia but likewise in the west, in Burgundy and Italy.[41] Yet it is not difficult to show that the situation in these kingdoms in many ways resembled that of East Francia, the future

Germany. In France too, powerful if precarious duchies and other inter-
mediate forces confronted a threatened kingship. The later West Frankish
Carolingians gave up dividing their kingdom among themselves—Lothar's
brother Charles complained that he had received nothing—because they
could no longer afford to. The Burgundian kings had never been able to
afford it. In 936, the predicament Regino had seen so clearly three decades
earlier still held the Saxon Ottonians in its grip. They had not yet overcome
the 'aequalitas generositatis, dignitatis et potentiae' of their kind although in
a few years they, and they alone, succeeded in amassing an empire (for
purposes not so very different from those of the eighth-century Carolingians) which enabled them to do so.

The young Henry, therefore, could only secure his share in what had
become, at least for his family, indivisible by murdering his brother Otto or
winning away his Saxon supports and entering into alliances with the Frankish and Lotharingian dukes who had become Otto's men at Aachen in 936.
He tried to do all three. There is no need to explain his actions by ideas
imported into tenth- and eleventh-century German historiography from
Byzantium, perhaps through Liudprand of Cremona. Henry, so Liudprand
and the later of the two *Lives* of Queen Mathilda intimated, was born after
his father had become a king, 'in regali solio natus', while Otto was not.[42] We
cannot know for certain whether such arguments were voiced during the
struggle for Henry I's succession, which began while he was still alive. If they
were, they only reinforced Henry's claims without being of their essence.
The idea of porphyrogenesis might enable him to assert that, since he could
not be king together with his brother, he had a better right to individual
succession than Otto.

The tradition, moreover, of kingship shared within a *stirps regia* was by no
means extinct in Ottonian house historiography. It died more slowly than
the practice.[43] When Hrotsvitha of Gandersheim dwelt reverently on the
offspring of Queen Mathilda's marriage with Henry I she wrote:

> The triune deity gave them three sons and so provided for the fortunate
> people lest after the venerable King Henry's death evil men should seize
> the governance of the kingdom but that these three, born of the royal line,
> should *rule* their father's kingdom in concord and peace although differ-
> ent honours would be destined for them, two subject to the *ruling* one [my
> italics].

The dilemma is evident from the uses made of the word *regnare*. The poetess
employed it both for the joint rule of the three brothers and the rule of Otto
over his nearest blood relations.[44]

When Henry collected his Saxon following about him at Saalfeld in 939,
Widukind called him 'magnus ac potens maiestate et potestate regali'.[45] Otto
never punished his brother for his relentless attacks on his kingship, as if he
recognized the indefeasible justice of his claims. Once he had been reconciled to him and established him in the Bavarian duchy he did what he could
to make his position as regal as possible. Near the end of Book II of his *Saxon
History*, Widukind extolled the new peace and concord between the two

brothers—how they advanced the *res publicae* together, fought enemies
with one mind and presided over their people (*cives*) with paternal power.⁴⁶
The vocabulary of Roman public life, which Widukind liked, here helped
him to create the impression of shared rule and parity. Bohemia and later the
march of Verona were subjected to Henry. It is quite possible that Byzantine
embassies sent to the *Reich* in search of a bride for Constantine
Pophyrogenitus's son, Romanus, addressed Henry, whose daughter was the
only candidate available, as king.⁴⁷ The Bavarian Liudolfings never forgot
their regal claims and sought to make them good in three further risings,
until in 1002 they at last succeeded because Otto III left no sons. The
tradition of their quasi-regal authority in Bavaria was still alive in the
eleventh century when the biographer of St Godehard wrote of Henry's son,
Henry the Wrangler: 'qui eandem provinciam acsi regali dominatione sibi
vendicabat.'⁴⁸ It should be remembered also that Archbishop Brun of
Cologne in 953 became no ordinary duke in the *regnum Lotharii* and his
position too, especially after Henry of Bavaria's death in 955, had near-regal
characteristics.⁴⁹ The Carolingian custom of kingship divided among
brothers still haunted the second generation of the new *stirps regia*.

The chief battle ground for Henry's bid to seize his elder brother's place
was Saxony, for here alone he had his share of Henry I's *palatia*, *curtes*,
treasures, fortresses, vassals and warbands. Without these he could neither
challenge Otto nor appear as even an equal to the Lotharingian and Frankish dukes whom he hoped to win over, although they, quite clearly, aimed at
little less than kingship themselves. The struggles of 938–9, with their
vertiginous ups and downs, have been vividly described by Widukind, who
saw in their outcome a divine justification of Otto's rule. Henry's most
important military assets in Saxony and Thuringia were his fortresses.
They lay as far apart as Belecke and Dortmund in Westfalia and
Burgscheidungen, Saalfeld and Merseburg close to the southeastern Slav
marches. Yet he was persuaded by his Saxon supporters to leave them
behind well garrisoned and to join Duke Giselbert of Lotharingia, now
openly hostile to Otto. To be known to favour fraternal discord was dangerous, as Thangmar's companions had learned to their cost in 938. Widukind's
hint at wirepullers and instigators of strife in the following of princes leads us
to the very heart of these conflicts.⁵⁰ That he reveals to us here a social reality
and not only a moral is proved by the many echoes of this theme in Ottonian
historiography. We hear something about over-zealous vassals, 'seducers' of
their lords and of feuds between rival gangs in Hrotsvitha, Ruotger, Liudprand and even the laconic Adalbert of St Maximin.⁵¹ A segmented aristocratic military society needed the enmities in the royal kin to fight its own
and did what it could to fan them.

When Henry and Giselbert were defeated at Birten on the Lower Rhine in
March 939 a Thuringian noble, Count Dedi, spread the rumour among the
commanders of Henry's strongholds in the east that their lord had died. He
had in fact been wounded. They surrendered at once to the king, which
brought Henry back to the scene but too late. Otto followed and besieged
him for two months in Merseburg, one of his last two remaining *urbes*. When

he surrendered he was given thirty days to leave Saxony with all those of his vassals who would go with him rather than submit to the king and profit from the pardon he offered.[52] Otto's main aim seems to have been to get his brother out of the stemland and persuade as many of his *milites* as possible to come into his own following. The struggle for the *Reich* was in the first place a struggle for Saxony and the loyalty of Saxon nobles, fought out inside the Liudolfing family. The prosopography of these loyalties for the most part escapes us. It has already been mentioned that some of the Frankish Duke Eberhard's Saxon vassals, quite early in Otto's reign, refused to recognize their obligations.[53] One of these was an important man called Bruning, with a castle at Helmern (near Warburg). We also know that at the same time, in 937, fighting broke out between Henry's and Eberhard's men. Later a certain Brunicho can be shown to have forfeited lands in Thuringia and a Count Bruning and his son Amelung lost fiefs near Helmern, suggesting that they had suffered penalties for their share in one or more of Henry's risings.[54]

Without his Saxon bases and warriors Henry could not count for much among Otto's enemies outside Saxony. Later, Widukind mentioned, he took his revenge on Count Dedi, who was handed over to him for punishment in 953 for complicity in Liudolf's rising.[55] Otto soon forgave his brother and assigned a few Saxon fortresses to him again. In June 940 Henry can be found sponsoring two royal grants, usually a sign of favour and solidarity, but the attempt to establish him in Lotharingia failed ignominiously and this may have quickened his last and most desperate effort to destroy Otto with the help of another Saxon conspiracy in the following year.[56] With this we shall deal later. The Bavarian Liudolfings never lost their connections with certain Saxon nobles, though consistency in these adherences from generation to generation was perhaps the exception rather than the rule.[57] Duke Henry's son and successor, known as the Wrangler, had important Saxon followers when he rose against Otto II. Their names stand out among the Bavarian ones on a list of accomplices who were excommunicated together with their lord outside Regensburg in July 976. They included Margrave Günther of Merseburg and his son Ekkehard, the later margrave of Meissen and one of Otto III's foremost and most favoured lay lords. Two years later, after Henry's last vain attempt against his cousin, Count Ekbert, whom we have already met as an enemy of Otto I, shared his lot—detention and exile.[58]

The Bavarian Liudolfings also kept a stake in the family's Saxon patrimony. The evidence is scanty and disparate but worth surveying. Sometime after 954 Gerberga, the daughter of the elder Henry, became abbess of Gandersheim.[59] Her father had been made duke of Bavaria in 947 or 948 but it is perhaps significant that a year later he sponsored a grant to one of Otto I's *fideles* in Saxony and that the land given lay 'in confinio Mersapurag', the march of Merseburg—Henry's share of the paternal inheritance and his chief stronghold in the war of 939.[60] When his son, the 'Wrangler', lost his Bavarian duchy in 978 and surrendered into the custody of Bishop Folcmar of Utrecht, a Saxon, his wife Gisela had to reside in

Merseburg. Otto II can be found staying there only once during his entire reign and that was in 974. The duchess thus may have been provided for in her father-in-law's erstwhile possession and her husband's pied à terre in Saxony.[61] The next piece of evidence is less ambiguous. In 984, when Henry was forced to negotiate with the Saxon lords who adhered to the infant Otto III, they offered to let him keep Merseburg, Frohse and Walbeck for the time being. Then they allowed him to depart with his followers and it was at Merseburg that he rejoined his wife and decided to abandon his quest for the kingship.[62] The future emperor Henry II received a good part of his clerical education in the cathedral close of Hildesheim. That Merseburg later became the Saxon *palatium* he frequented more often than any other again suggests that it had been closely connected with the Bavarian Liudolfings for much of the tenth century. He stayed there no less than twenty-six times.[63] In Saxony it was really his home.

We must now turn to Otto's son Liudolf and his connections in the Saxon aristocracy. Like his uncle and enemy, Liudolf had important lands and rights in Eastern Saxony and notably in the newly gained Slav *pagi* between the Saale and the Mulde. It was customary to endow the sons of kings and princes early and to give them military responsibilities so that they could learn their dangerous calling in good time and gain the fidelity and confidence of their following. The expectations of life were too short and the risks of a wholly inexperienced successor too great for sons to wait until their fathers' deaths for their entire inheritance. They entered upon part of it sooner, besides any lands which might fall to them on the deaths of other kinsmen. They needed estates and subjects also to contract marriages and set up house, although in the *stirps regia* this did not always happen immediately. When Liudolf married Ida, the only daughter and heiress of the Conradine Duke Hermann of Suabia, Hrotsvitha tells us that his father kept him and his daughter-in-law in his company as he marched through the *Reich*. He could thus show them to the nobles as their future king and queen. Otto did here for his son what his father had done for him when he married the Anglo-Saxon princess, Edith, King Aethelstan's half-sister.[64] Each region visited took part in the royal wedding and the Ottonians used these important events in their family to propagate their kingship among their Frankish, Lotharingian and Suabian *fideles* and to appear to share its gains with their Saxons.

Otto I had been schooled in the Slav wars in his father's lifetime, just as Henry I as a young man had been given a frontier command against the Daleminzi, the Slavs near Meissen, by his father Duke Otto. At one time it must have been intended that Liudolf should undergo the same experience but then his great match called him away to his father-in-law's Frankish and Suabian spheres of lordship. Yet Liudolf kept important Saxon connections, strongholds and vassals. When Duke Hermann took him to see his future inheritance in the south and they visited the abbeys of Suabia, St Gallen, Pfäfers and Einsiedeln, he had a considerable Saxon following in his company. In the *Liber Memorialis* of Pfäfers there is an impressive entry headed by Liudolf and Duke Hermann and below them names familiar from the

East Saxon and Thuringian frontier like Ricdag, Thietmar, Siegfried and Burckhard.[65] It seems, moreover, that the young prince tried to attract some of his father's closest adherents to his interest. In July 951 Otto confirmed a gift of three Slav marches in Serimunt to Margrave Gero, which the margrave had originally been given by Liudolf. The *narratio* of the royal diploma set out that the king had at first donated the whole region to his son whose grant, *per manum* though lawful, evidently needed Otto's sanction. In the dispositive clause Liudolf's role was reduced to that of sponsor and Otto became the real donor.[66] Serimunt lay just south of the Elbe-Saale junction, close to the southeastern *pagi* of Saxony and the northeastern ones of Thuringia. It is not surprising therefore to find leading Thuringian nobles like Count Dedi, whom we have already met, and Wilhelm (of Weimar) implicated in Liudolf's rising. When the young prince returned prematurely from his father's first Italian expedition with much loss of face and standing, he hurried to Saalfeld, 'the place of evil council', as Widukind wrote, for here Henry had assembled his supporters in 939.[67] In the Ottonian *Reich* even a rebellion had to begin with the right rituals and in the right setting. Liudolf kept Christmas in regal style at Saalfeld and men like Dedi and Wilhelm may have joined him there and begun to plot the rising for reasons of their own which cannot now be traced.

The rising of Liudolf and his brother-in-law, Duke Conrad of Lotharingia, was in the first place a family conflict brought about by Otto's second marriage. Adelheid, the daughter of King Rudolf of Burgundy and widow of Lothar of Italy, joined him in Pavia towards the end of 951. The wealth and *honor* of the Italian kingdom could now become his by right. Their first child, a boy, was born late in 952. Liudolf's place in the royal house deteriorated at once and his future seemed far less secure. For a time his wife, Ida, had held the position of a queen at Otto's court as they moved about the *Reich* with him in 948.[68] He himself was later described by Hrotsvitha as 'regni sociatus in aula', almost his father's partner in kingship. The stability of early medieval kingdoms, that of the Ottonians no less than of the Carolingians and of Wessex, was threatened by these second marriages of their rulers. Here it was above all Duke Henry of Bavaria who could draw advantage from the altered family situation by supporting his brother's new wife and so secure his share of the Italian booty, the marches of Aquilea and Verona. It is not surprising that Duke Conrad, who had been left with a garrison in Pavia when Otto returned home from his first Italian expedition, should have attempted to reconcile King Berengar II with his Saxon conqueror and seek his reinstatement. Nor is it surprising that Liudolf, who had gained nothing from the venture of 951–2, should have stood with Conrad when the latter was rebuffed and could not have Berengar admitted to Otto's presence for three days at the Magdeburg court of late April 952—a sign that Adelheid and Henry were hostile and their influence predominant. Loss of face as much as any other motif drew the younger men together against the king's brother. We must note also how Widukind explained the uncle-nephew feud: Liudolf was deprived of maternal support and this made him vulnerable.[69]

In the East Frankish crisis of 937–9, the family conflicts of the Liudolfings were only part of the wider enmities which set the leading Bavarian, Lotharingian and Frankish princes in motion to challenge the Ottonians as a *stirps regia*. In 953–4 the Liudolfing family quarrel sucked up all other inflammable matter into its blaze. This was the measure of Otto I's achievement so far. For the war against his father Liudolf assembled a splendid band of youthful followers, made up of Saxon, Frankish, Suabian and Bavarian nobles.[70] In this way he, the *frondeur*, did as much to foster new unities within his heterogeneous entourage as the king did in his. Brun of Cologne's biographer, Ruotger, had nothing but words of admiration for this military elite, if only it had not been infested by the contagion of their mutual oaths.[71] We know that the Saxon contingent in Liudolf's *comitatus* and band of warriors played an important part in the war up to its very end, especially in the prolonged fighting round Regensburg. What is more, quite soon after the outbreak of trouble when things began to go badly for the king and his brother Henry, Liudolf succeeded in winning over new adherents from the Saxon *Hochadel*. The brothers, Wichmann and Ekbert, were persuaded to change sides. The war now spread to Saxony whence the king drew most of his reinforcements. The nephews of Queen Mathilda came over to Liudolf as the bitter enemies of their paternal uncle, Herman Billung, whom they accused, probably not without good reason, of pilfering their inheritance and treasures after the death of the elder Wichmann in 944.[72] The rifts in the royal house gave them an opening hitherto not available. Just as Otto supported his brother against his son he also stood by Duke Hermann against the latter's nephews. It was a war between generations over inheritances and expectations.

Wichmann and Ekbert began by harassing Duke Hermann in 953. The case and the duke's complaints against them were heard by Otto during his brief stay in Saxony, perhaps early in 954, and they failed.[73] It is significant that the king did not punish the brothers then but kept Wichmann with him under a kind of honourable arrest. Later he evaded control and rejoined Ekbert in Saxony. Thinking themselves to be in the right despite the adverse verdict found against them, the brothers now warred against their royal cousin as much as against their uncle, but were driven out of the fortresses they had seized.[74] The fighting, both in Saxony and elsewhere, revolved round fortresses and cities, the centres where wealth, dues and tribute accumulated and could be stored.[75] Wichmann's and Ekbert's next steps were not in the least unusual for tenth-century Saxon princes with wrongs to avenge. They entered into a compact with two Obotrite 'sub-reguli', as Widukind contemptuously called them, and so greatly enhanced the scope of the war.[76] Before long they were judged *hostes publici*, but only they, not the other Saxons who had joined the compact; they were to be forgiven if they returned. Probably these were Wichmann's and Ekbert's men so that once again Otto hoped to suborn loyalties and thus isolate his enemies and kinsmen as he had done in his brother's case in 939. Yet there may have been other malcontents of higher rank, of whom Widukind said nothing. The familial character of these conflicts shaped their treacherous course. Vassals and followers who stood by their rebel lords to the last had usually no reason to bless themselves for their fidelity.[77]

Wichmann's and Ekbert's kinship to Queen Mathilda opened doors for them in times of need. They could flee to Duke Hugh the Great in 955 when even Sclavania was no longer safe after Otto's crushing victory over the Obotrites and other Slav tribes. Their sister Hathui, moreover was married to Margrave Gero's son, Siegfried. Gero fought on Otto's side throughout the troubles of 954 and 955 but it is significant that he and Siegfried secured Wichmann's restoration to the king's grace, to peace and part of his lands three years later.[78] In 963 the margrave gave Wichmann at least temporary shelter when he was again in serious trouble.[79] In the same year, moreover, Gero and Wichmann collaborated in attacking Miesco of Poland, Wichmann with his companions and Slav allies, the margrave with his.[80] Hermann Billung and Gero were rivals, each with his own clientèle among the Slav rulers and tribes.[81] Count Wichmann as a roving exile, but with friends and sympathizers in Saxony, remained dangerous both to his royal cousin and his representative in the stemland. He moved about with a warband which followed him into Sclavania, against Miesco of Poland and on raids into Saxony. Treasure and arms may have been more important to these men than the firm anchorage of land, though it seems that Wichmann's associates became restless during his last year and they lacked horses. His military aid mattered to the Slav forest kings in their internecine wars and he could probably support his force by demanding and receiving tribute in return, just like the margraves. Wichmann died fighting with the Slavs of Wollin against Miesco of Poland in 967, after fourteen years of intermittent but often savage conflict with Duke Hermann and Otto who, so Widukind wrote, wanted to be as a father to him.[82]

We can catch a glimpse of the savagery not only from the pages of Widukind but also from a diploma of Otto I, given in 959, in which he granted the lands of a certain Wulfhard, the son of Wulfhard, to Hermann Billung's foundation at Lüneburg. Wulfhard must have been one of Wichmann's companions, and that his *hereditas* should be given to St Michael's suggests that he was a kinsman. The possessions had been adjudged to the king because, so the diploma recited, 'Wulfhard with others who were at that time seen to be our enemies, inflicted great strife on us and on our faithful so much so that he set fire to a fortress in our kingdom with the church and all the other buildings inside it.'[83] We do not know which stronghold Wulfhard burnt down. Predatory warfare and acts of devastation were endemic along the Slav frontier and quickly spread inland during times of unrest and crisis. The pages of Thietmar, moreover, are full of outrages and incidents of gang warfare in Saxony in times of peace. There is no reason to think that they were uncommon in Otto I's reign.

2
The Later Conflicts

Neither the king's great victory over the Magyars at the Lech nor his rout of the Slavs at the Recknitz nor even the death of Wichmann silenced all opposition to his regime in Saxony. The evidence for it after 955 is harder to come by and to interpret but by no means negligible. Let us begin with a difficult case. In 944 one of Henry's vassals, called Billing, received back all his lands which he had lost by judgment, almost certainly for taking part in the rising of 941 with his lord. Henry himself must have been restored once more to some of his Saxon *hereditas* before he succeeded to the Bavarian duchy in 947–8. By 952, however, Billing had become Otto's *miles*, a clear indication that the king took over and absorbed at least a good part of his brother's Saxon following and interests when Henry departed to Bavaria. In the same year, in 958 and again in 961, the king and his vassal exchanged much land and Billing evidently enjoyed his new lord's favour. He was described as 'dilectus' and 'nobis dilectus' in the diplomata recording the exchanges. These built up his holdings on the eastern confines of Thuringia and across the Saale in the Slav *pagus* of Neletice, where he had become count before 958.[1] These eastward shifts in general were an important element in the rise of certain margravial families during the decades of Saxon military expansion. In 966, however, some of Count Billing's acquisitions by exchange were granted by the emperor to St Maurice, Magdeburg, and the earlier arrangements declared cancelled and revoked.[2] Two years later Otto gave Billing's monastic foundation, Bibra, in Eastern Thuringia (northwest of Naumburg) to Magdeburg, claiming that he had built it on imperial fisc.[3] Billing may have held *in beneficium* or perhaps Otto meant by this no more than that the lands he gave to him in exchange had never properly become his own.

Between the vassal's advancement and his dubious end lies the privilege of protection and exemption which he received for his monastery from Pope John XII, dated 25 April 963. It was addressed to the count and his abbot and under its terms Bibra was to be subject only to the jurisdiction of Rome.[4] Whereas John XII's privilege for Gernrode of 961, now lost, had been requested expressly at Otto's wish, the Bibra privilege was asked for and granted without any reference to the emperor, except in the date.[5] This too is important, for it points to a time when relations between the pope and Otto I were deteriorating and John XII had already begun to look far and wide for allies against the emperor. A rebellion on the Saxon frontier would have been useful, forcing him to go home. Billing's unlicensed *traditio* of his monastery could therefore be regarded as a suspect act. This raises the question, what could have estranged the count from his lord? Shortly before Otto set off for his Roman expedition in August 961 he gave to St Maurice, Magdeburg, the entire *pagus* of Neletice with its most important castle, the Giebichenstein, and all appurtenances 'for the sustenance of the clerks and monks'. The large gift was a solemn and fitting offering for his own, his mother's, his kingdom's, his queen's and his son's welfare on the eve of a hazardous undertaking. The grant was repeated in 965 when Otto returned to Saxony and the whole *census* of honey due from the area was added as a further endowment.[6] Count Billing's opportunities in Neletice must have been severely curtailed. New gains were now scarcely possible except as *beneficia* from Magdeburg.

There were, however, other reasons for the quashed exchange and the grant of Bibra to Magdeburg. Billing had funded the transaction of 952 out of the *hereditas* of his wife. Otto gave the lands he received, like so much else, to St Maurice in 953, but he and the monks could have been confronted eventually by serious difficulties from her *co-heredes*.[7] There is evidence also that the emperor kept lands he withdrew from Magdeburg in his own hands rather than pass them back to Billing or his wife's heirs.[8] According to the Corvey Annals, a *fidelis* Billing died in 968 but, even if the confiscation of Bibra was posthumous, the loss of four burgwards in 966 which had formed part of the exchange in 952, further diminished and stunted Billing's position in Neletice.[9] We can only guess who his enemies were: the papal privilege must have offended Otto I's son, Archbishop William of Mainz, in whose diocese the monastery lay and if Billing took part in the rising of 941, he cannot have been a friend of Margrave Gero against whom it was in part aimed. A powerful man in Eastern Thuringia, Billing may have hoped for a higher position in the marches than Otto allowed him to hold. Nothing was permitted to stand in the way of his great ecclesiastical foundation. Yet all this is speculative and, despite the fine run of diplomata, significantly preserved or transmitted through the archives of the see of Magdeburg, his relations with the emperor remain somewhat elusive. It is worth noting that many of the texts mentioning Billing make a point of stressing his vassalage. He was 'vassallus', 'miles', 'vassallus et comes'.

Another hint that all opposition was not silenced comes from one of Thietmar's stories. In 969 Gero, the brother of Margrave Thietmar of Serimunt and one of Otto I's *capellani*, was elected by the clergy and people of Cologne to be their archbishop. Yet the emperor in Italy did not want to give him the staff because he was enraged with his brother, the margrave, 'for many kinds of reason'.[10] The bishop of Merseburg does not tell us what they were. In a diploma of 965 granting him a vill, Thietmar was called 'fidelis comes'.[11] The young Otto II (and his mother) sponsored this gift. On

7 May 973, less than a month after his father's death, Otto gave Thietmar a large tract of land in the Slav *pagus* of Coledizi (Colditz) 'as a reward for his most faithful services which he frequently rendered to our father . . . and to us'. This *passus* of the diploma and its date suggest that the young emperor hastened to compensate Thietmar for setbacks suffered under the previous regime.[12] He was evidently anxious to exonerate him from the taint of disloyalty. In Otto II's reign the margrave, who died in 978, stood in high favour and had the marches of Merseburg and Meissen added to his command. Here it must be recalled that he was the nephew of the great Gero, whose death in 965 vacated a huge inheritance from which his heirs hoped to gain much more than they got. Gero's dispositions in favour of the nunnery he founded at Gernrode, in honour of the Virgin and St Peter and as a home for his daughter-in-law, Hathui, were protected and enforced by Otto I, who gained by them.[13] Another kinsman of Gero's who succeeded him in a section of his huge command, Margrave Hodo, was equally at odds with the distant emperor. In 972 he gathered a host, attacked Miesco of Poland and suffered a costly defeat. Widukind called Miesco an 'amicus imperatoris', which was why Wichmann the younger had attacked him, not for the first time, in 967. Thietmar of Merseburg, our main source for Hodo's ill-fated campaign, described the Polish duke as the emperor's liegeman (*fidelis*) who duly paid his tribute. Otto responded from Italy by ordering both sides to remain at peace until he could come and judge between them.[14] Hodo, too, enjoyed Otto II's favour, having been his military tutor.

We may conclude that after 965 Gero's kin became restive and, like Wichmann, struck at Miesco of Poland who was in the emperor's *fidelitas* and *amicitia*. Historians have rightly warned us not to exaggerate the seriousness of this and other rifts such as the hostility between the count of Stade and Hermann Billung.[15] They have, however, misjudged their character. They have seen in these incidents evidence chiefly for the strains which the *Italienpolitik* of the Ottonians placed upon their *Reich* north of the Alps and especially their homeland Saxony.[16] Yet they were part of a continuing situation, and absence, as we shall see, especially when the old emperor summoned his son to his side, had even some advantages. The strains were real enough but of a different kind. Widukind allows us to know that the emperor's instructions, sent to the Saxon counts from somewhere near Capua in 968, were made public and then set aside by the stem meeting at Werla.[17] They could not be carried out. With all his panegyric of Otto's world-wide *potentiae maiestas*, Widukind does not quite conceal his unease about the dangers which too much extension of empire, 'dilatatio imperii', might bring.[18] Not long before Otto returned—and perhaps hastening his pace—there were rumours of many Saxons wanting to rebel. Even a false report of the emperor's death could be very dangerous.[19] Poor communications bred fear and insecurity and of these Widukind is more than once a sombre witness.[20]

Political historians may easily overlook how precarious Otto I's regime remained despite all his successes. Contemporaries were less purblind. In a letter which Archbishop William of Mainz sent to Pope Agapitus II in

October 955, he dwelt on the theme of discord in the Liudolfing family, within other kins and neighbourhoods. The recent victory at the Lech, which Widukind, Ruotger, Adalbert of St Maximin, not to mention the poet of the *Modus Ottinc*, acclaimed more or less panegyrically as a unique triumph, was seen here only as an escape from even worse than the existing disasters. The lament on discord culminates in the outcry, 'the king has no chance of ruling.' This meant he could not fulfil his primary task to protect bishops and churches and they had suffered and were suffering severe losses in goods and person. Archbishop William had reasons of his own for pessimism and he himself bitterly opposed his father's plans for Magdeburg; but it must be remembered that the buoyancy and optimism of Widukind and others had the advantage of hindsight and against them this letter, written not long after Otto's victory, carries weight.[21]

A year later Liudolf went to Italy. This was to be his sphere of action and lordship once he had driven out King Berengar II and his son Adalbert, who had used the recent troubles in the Saxon *Reich* to regain their rough control. Liudolf took with him the same band of companions, including no doubt Saxons whom he had refused to sacrifice to his father's anger. Their mutual oaths still stood, according to Widukind, and Italy offered rich opportunities to compensate them for their losses. The invasion succeeded and treasure was amassed but on 6 September 957 Liudolf died of malaria.[22] At this time his own son, called Otto, was only three years old at the most and the other Otto, his half-brother, perhaps not yet two. Henry of Bavaria had died in 955 leaving behind a son aged four. Whatever plans Otto I had made for the succession after Liudolf's rising and submission, his death now greatly exposed and weakened the *stirps regia*. The king, so Widukind summed up, committed his *imperium* to God who had so far guided it.[23] Human prudence failed in such a situation. Unlike his father in 929, Otto could not order his house, his succession or his kingdoms at this moment, although it was high time he did so. Next year he fell ill and, had he succumbed, the Liudolfings would have faced their first minority crisis. Not surprisingly Otto II was elected, anointed and crowned in 961 before his father set out on his second Italian expedition. Contemporaries again were grateful when he returned safely in 965 and worried about him while he was away. Queen Mathilda, his mother, founded another nunnery to strengthen her prayers on his behalf and for the well-being of her house in general.[24] These actions reflect a state of anxiety and insecurity which becomes understandable, given the poor expectations of life for warring kings and their nobles. The dangers of the Italian climate and the treacherousness of the Romans were serious additional risks.

The emperor's homecoming in 965 for the moment banished these apprehensions but even then, if we can trust the text of a contemporary Halberstadt charter, the *pax regni* was seen as a fitful and uncertain boon. In July 965 Bishop Bernhard of Halberstadt, at Otto's behest, granted to Gandersheim the tithes of four recently acquired vills. In return Abbess Gerberga conceded that two cartloads of wine from the nunnery's Rhenish possessions were to be given annually to the canons of Halberstadt. It is the last clause in the charter recording this transaction which must be considered here: 'If, however, no wine is available, be it through any civil discord [*quod absit*] or crop failure, then four marks by weight should be paid instead.'[25] Otto I had returned triumphantly from Italy as *imperator augustus* and just held what was perhaps the most imposing court of his entire reign at Cologne, gathering his family and *fideles* about him before journeying home to Saxony where he spent the rest of the summer. If, therefore, this passage is authentic, its author and the parties to the bargain regarded a *discidium regni* as an evil no less likely than the periodic droughts and harvest calamities.

The charter, as we have it, has been exposed convincingly as a forgery of the late twelfth century, but based on a genuine original of Bishop Bernhard's.[26] The bargain between Halberstadt and Gandersheim was really struck. Only the last clause is thought to have been interpolated on the grounds that a *discidium regni* was so improbable at this moment and all too real in 1198.[27] We have already seen that internal rifts, or rather the fear of them, troubled the well-wishers of the Ottonians at all times. The phrase *discidium regni*, moreover, was familiar and none other than Adalbert of St Maximin, the future archbishop of Magdeburg, a bystander at the transaction of 965, used it in the chronicle he was perhaps already writing. He has the dying King Conrad I admonish his kinsmen and the Frankish princes in 919 to beware of strife in the election of his successor and then order them to choose the Saxon Henry.[28] We cannot dismiss *discidium regni* from the authentic text of 965 lightly, though the four marks by weight are another matter. There had been rifts in the Liudolfing family and there might be again.

From what has been said, it is clear that the Ottonian rulers were inevitably partners to the feuds of their greater Saxon nobles and these again were drawn inescapably into the conflicts within the Liudolfing kin. The open-ended family groups and existing bonds of affinity and *co-hereditas* did not end when the Ottonians began their royal and imperial ascent. Often it is very difficult to say why a noble like Count Henry of Stade (died *c*. 976), Thietmar of Merseburg's maternal grandfather, was called *consanguineus imperatoris*, or the unpopular Saxon bishop of Cambrai, (956–7), Berengar, who is even described as 'Ottonis imperatoris proxime consanguineus'.[29] The Ottonian rulers were not unaware of these constricting ties and fitfully sought to plan for their diminution. After Otto I had fallen out with his son-in-law, Conrad the Red, the ancestor of the Salians, he did not rely henceforth mainly on his bishops, as the textbooks would have it.[30] He merely made sure that his next surviving daughter, Mathilda, should be an abbess rather than marry. Of Otto II's daughters only one, Mathilda, married and this happened during her brother's minority when the Ottonian house lacked the firm control of a *senior*.[31] Feuds and rifts broke out as much within as between the aristocratic family groups whose frontiers are so difficult to define. Defeating and then outliving the agnates in his own generation and also the offspring from his first marriage and a son-in-law, Otto in the end mastered and dominated his own family. Before that it had been deeply divided over the kingship and the Liudolfing lands. As we have seen, he had to defend part of the patrimony against his half-brother, the crown against his brother and, it must be remembered, also against his mother. For a time Mathilda openly favoured Henry. At least one of her Lotharingian blood relations, Ansfried, opposed her son between 940 and 942 and was imprisoned before being reconciled.[32] Other kins did not differ from the Liudolfings. The Billungs, the Brunones, the family of Margrave Gero, of Dedi and of the Frankish Conradines, whose lands and influence stretched far into southwestern Saxony, were all rent by divisions. Nor must we be surprised therefore that alliances between the *primores*, the men who had precariously gathered much lordship, lands, treasure and following about them, shifted so rapidly during the most formative years of the Ottonian *Reich*.

To understand this fluidity we must look once more at the early trials of Otto I's young regime. In 938 the Conradine Gebhard, a son of Duke Hermann of Suabia's brother Udo, was killed when Duke Eberhard together with Thangmar attacked Belecke. Eberhard and Udo were cousins but, so Widukind wrote, 'because of this killing the leaders of the Franks were divided.'[33] He meant the Conradine family, for Udo, another cousin, Conrad, and, above all, Duke Hermann now sided with Otto against their own kinsman and won the battle of Andernach for him in 939 when the king was in extreme danger. On the other hand, Otto's brother Henry made peace with his captor Eberhard and concluded an alliance with him in preparation for his own stroke. In 938 also some of Eberhard's vassals killed a certain Dedi outside the gates of Laar, a fortress near Meschede in Westfalia. On hearing this Wichmann the Elder, Otto's bitter enemy ever since the advancement of his own brother Hermann to a permanent command against the northeastern Slavs, made his peace with the king and did not rebel again.[34] We do not know what his connections with the slain man were but a *Dedi comes* appears in the *necrologium* of the Billung house monastery, St Michael's, Lüneburg. The second duke, Bernhard (973–1011), and his wife, Hildegard, gave an estate to the abbey for the express purpose of endowing an anniversary for among others a *Dedi senior*, seemingly of Duke Hermann's and the elder Wichmann's generation.[35]

In Widukind, our chief source, these alignments and realignments are prompted by the violent deaths of kinsmen or *amici* in the gang-warfare of the great. To explain the character and incidence of these recurrent disturbances in the Saxon centres of the Ottonian *Reich*, it is tempting to turn to the equilibrium and conflict theories which social anthropologists have developed and hotly debated in studying the political tensions of pre-industrial and pre-colonial societies.[36] They fall into two categories: first of all that in which conflicts express shared aspirations and a common system of values, so that even rebellions recurring at fairly regular intervals stand for continuity, equilibrium and cohesion in, for instance, certain African states, As against this, there are conflicts which arise from contradictions in the social and political structure, affecting the shape of the structure itself. It would be foolhardy to apply either of these models strictly and exclusively to the Ottonian polity of the tenth century, but faintly and fitfully they light up some of its contours.

Between 938 and 1002 all the major upheavals in the homeland of the Saxon dynasty had one common characteristic: disaffected nobles with very few exceptions rose only when a member of the royal house equally resentful collected and led them or could be inveigled to do so. We have seen how equivocal Otto I's treatment of the participants in Henry's and Wichmann's risings was. To those who would desert their lords in time he offered pardons. Those who stayed with them to the bitter end suffered for their fidelity.[37] We shall have more to say about punishment. Here it is enough to note once more how much the feuds in the royal family served to channel those of the nobles. That was in part their function and explains why, during the rising of Liudolf and Conrad, Otto I demanded again and again that the instigators in their *comitatus* must be handed over to him. Widukind and Ruotger agreed here in their account of the conflict, and the homily which Ruotger has Brun address to his nephew finally turned on this point.[38] Since Liudolf refused to surrender his companions, the fighting continued and this was in the end the only reason why he fought and refused to submit. Ruotger, it seems, and Brun himself saw the conflict as one in which the prince was acting against his own best interests. He is warned against his followers and allies who were really enemies of the Liudolfings and only using him as a pawn.[39] We hear much about Liudolf's duties as a son and little about the *Reich*. The familial note predominated even though a principle, the fidelity and duties of followers, had been raised. These East Frankish risings of the tenth century still bore some resemblance to the revolts of Carolingian princes in the eighth. The speedy surrender of Henry's castellans and *milites* on the false rumour of his death recalls the instant submission of Karlmann's *primates* to his brother Charles in 771.[40] In each case a hard core of followers who could not hope for favour or forgiveness stood by their lord or his widow and offspring and fled with them. The Frankish nobles who, on their pilgrimages to Rome kept on visiting the older Karlmann, Pippin's brother, hoping perhaps that their former lord would emerge to head their discontent, furnish another example.[41]

Conversely, it is possible to say that, when no Liudolfing prince was available, able and willing to take the lead, rebellions hung fire. The Saxon unrest and disaffection smouldering under the surface in 972, on the eve of Otto's homecoming after years of absence, did not erupt because there was no Ottonian prince in Saxony to mobilize against the old emperor. It is true that Henry (the Wrangler), his brother's son and successor in Bavaria, was of age, but it seems as if he was still serving his military apprenticeship on the eastern marches of Bavaria and that he had not yet enough connection and credit in Saxony to be followed and trusted there, nor must the influence of his mother, the Duchess Judith, be dismissed too soon. Even so Henry did not escape suspicion; yet in October 972 we find him in Otto I's company sponsoring the renewal of a grant to the see of Passau—a sign that all was well between them.[42] The old emperor, moreover, had arranged to have his own son with him in Italy. In 967 he ordered the young king to come south to

be crowned and sacred emperor by Pope John XIII on Christmas Day. Otto
II was born in 955 and approaching his majority, that is to say his fifteenth
year. Early in 968, it is true, his father planned to send him home again but in
the company of the Empress Adelheid, and he himself wanted to follow after
a short detour to destroy the Saracen colony at Fraxinetum.[43] It does not
seem as if his father wished to leave him out of his sight for long. All this
depended, however, on a settlement with the Byzantines, who were not so
soon appeased over Otto's invasion of their South Italian sphere of clientage. Otto II remained in Italy, usually by his father's side. He could not
therefore become the focus of aristocratic family feuds in Saxony and this
may well have been one of the reasons for keeping him in the south. His
Byzantine bride, for whom his father had been negotiating since 967, only
arrived in April 972, but this alone does not explain his five-year stay. There
is some evidence that, despite all his *honores* and his position as *conregnans*,
the young Otto, who also uttered diplomata in his own name, felt discon-
tented and deprived of real lordship—as indeed he was.[44] It comes from a
famous anecdote in Ekkehart IV's *Casus Sancti Galli*, written, it is true,
towards the middle of the eleventh century. The incident belongs to the two
Ottos' visit to St Gallen on Ascension Day 972, on their way back from Italy.
The old emperor stood alone in the nave of the church and dropped his stick
to test the discipline of the monks. When this was mentioned to his son he is
related to have said: 'We marvel that the staff fell when he grips his *Reich* so
firmly. For the kingdoms he has gained he has held like a lion and to me, his
son, he has not given even one particle of them.' Ekkehart's account of the
persons present is full of confusions and the story itself belongs to a monastic
repertoire with echoes elsewhere, but even so it retains and reflects something of the young Otto's anomalous situation under his father's gaunt
authority.[45]

Thietmar of Merseburg reported that towards the end of Otto III's reign
the Saxon princes, 'nostri duces et comites', began to conspire against the
emperor with the connivance of some bishops.[46] The circumstances were not
unlike those of Otto I's last years (too much friendship being shown to
Polish dukes), but on this occasion there were more than rumours or, at any
rate, Thietmar knew more than Widukind had known. The malcontents
turned for help to Duke Henry IV of Bavaria, the son of the 'Wrangler' and
future king. He refused to give them any. Nothing could prove more start-
lingly that the leadership of a Liudolfing was felt to be necessary to rouse,
hold together and legitimize a revolt. Here a descendant of King Henry I, whose
father and grandfather had headed groups of Saxon lords against the three
Ottos, was available, but he gave no countenance to the emperor's enemies.
For the moment they were at a loss, but Otto III died soon afterwards at
Paterno, north of Rome and under Henry II the situation changed markedly.

The very nature of the inner Saxon conflicts of the tenth century thus
helped to maintain a certain equilibrium and cohesion in the stemland and,
as the horizons of the Ottonian family circle grew larger, even in the other
regna of their *Reich*. We are dealing mainly with kinsmen's and in-laws'
quarrels. In Saxony these were, however, aggravated by the growing impor-

tance of the great *honores* like the Billung duchy, the margraviates of the eastern frontier and the office of count palatine. Their permanence created new interests and a smaller group of leading princes who rose above their peers, not least of all their own wider kin. They generated both more and new kinds of conflict, but Saxon aristocratic rebellions against the king as such, without the participation of any member of the *stirps regia*, were a development of the eleventh century. The first symptoms appeared in the reign of Henry II, who had no sons and whose brother was made a bishop after taking part in Henry of Schweinfurt's rising of 1003.[47] The change in the style and character of Saxon unrest, however, was not merely fortuitous. The want of an effective rival in the *stirps regia* coincided with more deep-seated causes of trouble and alienation: the king's blatant appeal to his prelates to use their fortunes to endow poor sees like Paderborn, Hamburg and Merseburg, at the expense of their lay heirs, and his unequivocal support for prelates who encroached upon the always unstable *hereditates* of lay nobles, especially their shaky hold over proprietary monasteries. The Billungs were among the first to suffer and the first to rebel.[48] Henry also backed the synodal sentences of bishops against offending margraves and their *milites*, and their fines and penances could be heavy. We shall have more to say about the emperor's dealings with some of the families of the southeastern marches.[49] Yet it was only when the Ottonians, the male descent from Henry I, failed in 1024 and a new royal house entered Saxony, to lay hands on their still very large landed possessions, fiscal resources and rights of lordship, that the equilibrium of familial relations collapsed altogether and a far more disruptive conflict began to build up.

3
Otto I and Count Liuthar of Walbeck

By far the most serious aristocratic plot Otto I had to face in Saxony took shape early in 941.[1] It seems to have had more general causes. During the disturbances of the previous years the collection of tribute among the Slavs had broken down and the *milites*, the East Saxon warrior nobles placed under Margrave Gero's command, remained unrewarded and indeed unpaid. Tribute in all its forms was the indispensable economic base for an expanding military society. Without it, the more important men along the eastern frontier could not maintain their followings. As Otto stood by his frontier commander, they were ready to listen to his brother's promises. Henry, we must recall, had some of his fortresses restored to him so that he was once again a force to reckon with in Saxony.[2] Where he stayed after his discomfiture in Lotharingia is not known, but messengers between him and the East Saxons passed freely during the winter of 940–1. Perhaps some of Thangmar's friends were, as has been suggested, among the malcontents and they had much to avenge.[3] Gero held a *legatio*, a frontier command, which Thangmar had claimed as his own. Some of the *milites* placed under the margrave were perhaps altogether opposed to him. That they should now accept Henry as their leader and future king need not surprise us. Before long most of the frontier warriors had been won over to the plan of the conspiracy. It was a simple one. Henry was to come to Otto's Easter court at Quedlinburg, the king would be killed and he crowned. Otto, when he was warned secretly, shortly before the feast, met the threat with all his iron nerve which contemporaries came to know, fear and admire so much. He kept Easter with the sacred solemnities exalting kingship but had himself closely guarded and so outfaced the conspirators. It is possible that the Ottonian kings employed Slav bodyguards about their persons.[4]

Next day Otto unleashed a relentless pursuit against the conspirators. Henry, so Widukind wrote, fled the kingdom (by which he meant Saxony) but he had to give himself up or was caught and imprisoned, not very harshly, at Ingelheim. This was the only constraint he ever suffered. Archbishop Frederick of Mainz, who seems to have been implicated, cleared himself by taking the sacraments as an ordeal. The East Saxon lords, however, Otto ordered to be arrested or killed if they resisted. Those caught rather than slain were executed or banished *secundum leges*. These penalties hit the leading men rather than their rank-and-file following. The Quedlinburg Annals and, following them, Thietmar, record some of their names and perhaps some half-explored Saxon *necrologium* may yet tell us something more about their associations. One of them, called Bacco, has been noticed in a large group-entry in the *Liber Memorialis* of Reichenau.[5] Here he stands close to members of Gero's family and the Brunones, with their Liudolfing names, are also represented. Once again the deep divisions within these fluid families are exposed, but Bacco's strange name suggests that he was perhaps not a kinsman but one of the nobler vassals who suffered after the failure of the *coup*. The *Libri Memoriales* may record social relations other than kinship among the thousands of laymen and women who found a place there.

Widukind wrote one of his finest heroic epitaphs about another of the conspirators, Erich, who died fighting his assailants. Erich's son Hildiward was about eighteen years old at the time of the insurrection.[6] Later he became provost and then bishop of Halberstadt but he had been schooled at St Gallen.[7] It is at least possible that this was a form of temporary exile and that the young Hildiward did not altogether escape the consequences of his father's offence, even if he was not implicated himself. In general, treasonable clerks and even bishops could not count on immunity in the tenth-century *Reich*. Hildiward must have been allowed to return, or at any rate he found a secure place at Halberstadt under Bishop Bernhard (923–68). In the Ottonian world it was not unusual for reigning bishops to nurse and designate their own successors and in Thietmar's *Chronicon* Hildiward had been so marked out by his lord.[8] Elected by clergy and people at Halberstadt— and Thietmar cared about elections—he was also received and 'constituted' bishop by Duke Hermann Billung, standing in Otto's place, before a Saxon stem meeting at Werla.[9] The emperor played, therefore, less than his full part in Hildiward's promotion but he accepted it nonetheless and summoned him to Ravenna.[10] There he took his homage and gave him the staff with the startling words, 'take here the price for your father.'[11] The bishopric became the wergild which the emperor paid for the slain man to his son. Thietmar, to whom we owe this story, was Hildiward's parishioner before he joined the clerical *familia* of Magdeburg and the bishop had baptized and confirmed him. The high aristocracy knew its diocesans and the anecdote did not have to travel very far. Banter between kings and bishops-elect was not unusual but this had a serious, even grim, undertone and it reveals once again the domestic atmosphere of Ottonian rule in Saxony.[12] The king did not regard himself as exempt from the social obligations which bound his nobles nor is he seen standing outside the ring of feud and revenge.

Thietmar of Merseburg had special reasons for dwelling on Hildiward's investiture, with its sinister echo from the past. His own paternal grandfather, Liuthar, had been one of the conspirators of 941 and the *Chronicon* therefore enables us for once to follow the consequences and traditions of a conflict between Otto I and a family of Saxon nobles in far greater detail.

Thietmar's work is in some part a memoir, not only of his episcopal and clerical brethren and predecessors but also of his princely lay kin. He began to keep weekly notes already as a Magdeburg clerk, in the compulsive and timeless way of great writers of memoirs—though we must not confuse his purposes with those of a modern diarist. To write about his forbears and his contemporaries, whether they were in the church or in lay estate, was for the bishop of Merseburg a duty, an office he felt he had to perform as a mediator to ensure that the men and women he mentioned and he himself were remembered and prayed for. He was unique in applying himself to the episcopal tasks of instruction and the care of souls of the living and the dead by writing a commemorative historical work.

Thietmar is our only first-hand source for Count Liuthar's share in the rising of 941. He does not tell us why he joined it but the counts of Walbeck were one of the foremost families in the confined space west of Magdeburg where so many of the leading Ottonian nobles were at home. They had at that time not been chosen for a *legatio* (a permanent command on the frontier), but were obliged to obey the military summons of their neighbours and rivals to fight the Slav wars. Thietmar's paternal great-grandfather, also called Liuthar, was killed at the battle of Lenzen in 929, where a *legatus*, Bernhard, gave the orders, almost certainly an ancestor of the Margrave Dietrich who, after Gero's death in 965 and probably even earlier, held the Northern March.[13] In 953 Dietrich had resisted Liudolf's persuasions to come over to his side, unlike the younger Wichmann and his brother Ekbert. Dietrich and his house were favoured, the Walbeckers were not. This is what Thietmar wrote:

> My grandfather Liuthar took part in the plot and he [Otto I] would gladly have destroyed him but he had to bow to the advice of the princes who were his intimates [at the time]. Thereupon he sent him as a prisoner to Bavaria into the custody of Count Berthold [of the Bavarian Nordgau], having seized and widely distributed all his property. So matters stood for a whole year and then he gained the king's grace and all his possessions with a large sum of money and land in Santersleben and Gutenswegen.[14]

The first *Monumenta* edition of Thietmar, by Lappenberg, appeared in 1839. A new translation into German followed in 1848. Its author, M. Laurent, and his revisors and successors, J. Strebitzki in 1878, W. Wattenbach (1892), R. Holtzmann (1938) and most recently W. Trillmich, have all taken this last passage to mean that Count Liuthar was not only restored to his own but also received, as a mark of reconciliation and to compensate him for his losses, a large amount of money and two manors.[15] Their interpretation of the final sentence, moreover, only endorses that already found in the earliest of all Thietmar translations, made by Georg Hahn. His German version of the *Chronicon* appeared in 1606. Johann Friederich Ursinus whose rendering, published in 1790, was thought to be a great improvement on Hahn's, here did not dissent from his predecessor.[16] In as far as they have taken notice of the passage, historians, beginning with Heinrich Meibom the Elder (1555–1625) have followed the translators. Only Mrs Schölkopf, in her study of the tenth-century Saxon counts, preferred to regard the two estates as allods which were given back to Liuthar after a year, but Thietmar's text gives no countenance to this interpretation.[17]

There is, however, something odd and surprising about this dénouement. Liuthar was in Otto's eyes as guilty as the other leading figures of the conspiracy and the king wanted to see him executed. He was spared only because powerful men among the *familiares* intervened on his behalf. Otto did as much justice as he dared but it was never cheap. There is a story in the Saxon Annalist of the twelfth century that in 952, as news of his return from Italy spread in the north, everyone settled with his adversary as quickly as possible by agreement out of court so that he should find nothing to judge.[18] Here, however, a culprit who had nearly forfeited his life and was, as a milder punishment, disseized and exiled for a year, is thought to have been given a large present of treasure and two estates as well, both of them lying close to other important possessions of his family.

At this point we must ask how his contemporaries judged Otto I, or rather, how the writers of his and the next two generations reflected on his kingship and with what qualities they saw it endowed. The role and character of a king in early medieval societies and later ones demanded and were thought to demand the power to frighten. When the Quedlinburg Annalist described Henry II's rule as 'pleasing the pious with mildness and frightening the wicked with stern judgment', he was only echoing a formula from some coronation *ordo* which accompanied the delivery of the sceptre and staff, the insignia of judgment and correction.[19] Liudprand of Cremona, in his *Antapodosis* (begun in 958), apostrophized Otto I in the same vein: the northern and western parts of the world, he said, were ruled by his power, pacified by his wisdom, gladdened by his faith and frightened by the severity of his just judgment.[20] There is an unmistakable stress mark on this last quality. Both contemporaries and writers, who could compare the later Ottonians with Otto the Great, were in no doubt about the terror he could inspire and the frequency and danger of his *ira*. Widukind's complex characterization must occupy us last but there are enough indications elsewhere. Otto's *ira* against Liudolf's followers is the concrete theme of the encounter between uncle and nephew in Ruotger's *Life of Brun*.[21] Richer of St Remi spoke of Otto's 'levis furor', which persuaded Hugh the Great in 943 to make peace with his lord, King Louis IV.[22] Thietmar of Merseburg extols his maternal grandfather, Count Henry of Stade, because he knew how to placate the emperor when he was in a rage better than any other prince. He has Otto flare up with indignation when he heard of the regal reception Archbishop Adalbert had given to Duke Hermann Billung in Magdeburg.[23] Otto's demand in 953, that his son and son-in-law must hand over the instigators of their plots, was prompted by wrath, 'ira dictante', Thietmar felt.[24] Brun of Querfurt in his *Life of St Adalbert*, written in 1004, accused Otto II of having destroyed the peace which his father's terror had given to the church. In his panegyrical lament for the old emperor, 'migrans migravit Otto Pius, Otto rigidus, fluxa gubernare doctus', our attention is held by 'rigidus'. It sums up much. Brun, moreover, placed a wholly positive value on this royal terror.[25]

Lastly, Widukind. If the person of Charlemagne in Einhard's biography embodied *magnanimitas* and *animositas* as its ruling norms, Otto the Great's central quality in Widukind is thought to be *clementia*. Both men shared *constantia*.[26] *Clementia* in Widukind carries partly classical and partly Christian accents. It was a ruler's virtue *par excellence*, which Otto personified, and yet Widukind is not quite at ease with his leniency. After Book II of the *res gestae Saxonicae* it disappears and instead the king is said to show a harsher face towards his enemies.[27] Moreover, just as Charlemagne's *magnanimitas* in Einhard sometimes stood for the need to make concessions so Otto's *clementia* in Widukind covered a multitude of expediencies and involuntary constraints.[28] Not all acts of treachery could be avenged: there were too many of them. We have already seen that the king's forbearance towards his brother, which could be presented as nearly superhuman *clementia*, had another meaning. Too much custom and right were on Henry's side. The Liudolfings had to learn to live with an indivisible kingship. It was a difficult lesson. Where, however, Otto had used the 'terror of his royal discipline' against Saxons, it can be seen that Widukind was very anxious to excuse him. He mentioned that a certain Dietrich and three of his cousins who had joined Thangmar were condemned and hanged under Frankish law.[29] Yet it is by no means certain that they were Franks rather than Saxons; on the contrary, would Widukind have troubled to mention the chief culprit's name if he had been of the Rhine-Frankish aristocracy? The ruthless repression of the 941 conspiracy came about, so Widukind explained, 'most of all by the council of the Franks', Count Udo, Duke Hermann (of Suabia) and the Salian Conrad.[30] At that time, he wrote apologetically, they had great influence with Otto, as if cutting down or executing Saxon nobles were, so to speak, un-Saxon activities. Thus, what Widukind had to say about the king's dealings with his defeated enemies strengthens rather than weakens the judgment of later writers. The *clementia* theme in Book II of the *Saxon History* served as a palliative. Thietmar, who depended on the *res gestae Saxonicae* for his account of Otto I's times, ignored it and praised the emperor and his circle of princes for other qualities. Like Brun of Querfurt, the bishop of Merseburg looked back on his reign as a golden age. *Ira* was a sin but Thietmar felt that Otto as a ruler could not help committing many sins.[31]

This stark impression of Otto I's regime, which became a Saxon historical tradition handed down to the twelfth century (whence it passed into the *Kaisersage*), is immeasurably strengthened by the evidence of his diplomata.[32] They show that his path was indeed strewn with the victims of his relentless purposes. There are at least 27 grants of forfeited lands extant from his reign, more than for all the other Ottonians, including Henry II, counted together.[33] Five of these distributed the large possessions of a single enemy, Count Guntram; he was condemned before Otto I himself at Augsburg in August 952 'because the same Guntram appeared as a rebel against our royal power', which was equated with the *res publica* in the context. No chronicle mentions what the 'perfidy of his offence' had been, but he probably stood in the way of the new interests and connections Otto acquired in Suabia and Alsace after his marriage with the Burgundian Adelheid in 951.[34] What happened to Liuthar of Walbeck's lands, albeit only for a year, had its parallels elsewhere. In four cases, estates forfeited by judgment were after a rather longer period restored to their former owners; but one of these was now 'a servant of God' at Einsiedeln, having been condemned to death and then pardoned for his misdeed.[35] His lands there- fore fell to the monastery before long. In another instance, two thirds of a Main-Frankish *proprietas* were granted to the Saxon convent of Drübeck where the culprit's sister was a nun. The king allowed her a life interest in half the lands for her maintenance.[36] All the regions of the *Reich* north of the Alps were represented in these grants of forfeited estate—Saxony, Suabia, Francia, Bavaria, the Nordgau, Lotharingia and even Carinthia. Otto's success in stretching his influence over unsettled, disputed and peripheral regions in the west and the south may be measured by these gifts of es- cheated lands and the fact that diplomata disposing of them in distant Alsace and Switzerland were uttered in East Saxony.[37] Judicial proceedings in local courts or before the itinerant king and his assembly of *optimates* sanctioned all these forfeitures. Not every one of them atoned for acts of major rebel- lion. We hear of mere 'latrocinia et malefacta' but often enough the narra- tive clauses of the diplomata were quite explicit. We have already mentioned the Saxon Wulfhard, 'who with others . . . at that time our enemies' burnt down a castle and the church inside it. In 959 we hear also of a Frankish noble, Ernst, who lost his patrimony 'quia nobis maxime contrarius extitit'. It is not difficult to identify him with one of Liudolf Frankish partisans in 954 whom Widukind mentioned.[38]

The 27 diplomata exhaust neither the number nor the scope of forfeitures, royal confiscations, re-grants and transfers. We know of others from narra- tive sources but the two great waves of unrest and trouble, those of 937–41 and 953–5, have clearly left their traces in the extant royal documents. This evidence is especially important for the aftermath of the second upheaval, the wars between Otto and his brother on one side, against Liudolf, Conrad and their mixed following on the other. Since Otto wanted the leading men, 'those who promoted plots', delivered to him for punishment, as we have seen he deepened and aggravated the crisis.[39] It was against the grain of loyalties and the mutual obligations between great men and their noble companions, as Widukind and many others felt. To return to our anthro- pological models—here lay a real threat to conventions which upheld equilibrium, yet Otto threatened to impose new attitudes without a corres- ponding change of institutions. Widukind did not openly criticize the king as Thietmar was to do but he lamented the tragic conflict which Otto's chal- lenge to the segmented society had provoked. The clash of principles was to him a trick of the devil's which meant it was intractable, if not insoluble.[40] By insisting, Otto recalled and pressed for a political discipline, less articulate than Charlemagne's great oaths-takings, under which *fidelitas* to the king as a quasi-religious duty overrode that of followers to their lords. It was a principle which never came to be clearly established in the *Reich* as it was to be in the garrison feudalism of Norman England, although there are some traces of it during the troubles of Otto II's reign and in Conrad II's struggles with his stepson, Duke Ernst of Suabia.[41] The immediate question, however, is whether Liudolf's and Duke Conrad's men were in fact punished. The *diplomata* granting away the former lands of Saxon and Frankish nobles between 959 and 961 prove that a good many of them were. Retribution began to hit the Lotharingians in 956 when Otto held two *placita* with them, the first to exact hostages from their fortress towns, the second to take heavy fines in treasure.[42] Liudolf's companions, too, must have suffered spoliation. When he submitted finally to his father in December 954, he lost his duchy and his Suabian vassals, but this did not mean that he became landless and an important group of his sworn followers still remained with him. Sending him to Italy with them in 956 thus relieved their neighbourhoods and *patriae* of dangerous claims and pressures. Hrotsvitha of Gandersheim was not altogether mistaken when she spoke of the Italian enterprise as a hard exile.[43] Otto I failed to shift the boundary marks of principle permanently but he was able to exact much revenge and retribution and so enhance the menace of his *terror*.

The king's own acts and the traditions about them which began to form even in his lifetime have been surveyed in some detail because together they point to his style of ruling so unambiguously and forcefully. It is time now to return to Liuthar of Walbeck and the rising of 941. There are strong grounds for looking at the Thietmar passage (II. 21) again and asking whether it will really bear the sense which translators and historians from at least the early seventeenth century onwards have placed upon it. Let us first of all look at the history of the text. The matter of the rising and its aftermath was of course transcribed into the Corvey version of the *Chronicon*, now preserved in a manuscript of the Royal Library at Brussels.[44] It originated about the year 1120, although the extant copy was made in the fourteenth century. At Corvey, Thietmar's text underwent much change, and was smoothed, added to and annotated. The bishop's sentence about his grandfather's complicity and penalties was touched up in a way which might suggest that Liuthar had been condemned to a year's exile rather than to exile at the king's pleasure, until he succeeded in regaining the royal grace perhaps by the renewed intervention of powerful men including his own jailer, Count Berthold.[45] The whole incident was also transcribed, like so much else, by the mid-twelfth century author known as the Saxon Annalist, who incorporated all the best known Saxon historical writings of the tenth and eleventh centuries into his own work and some that have not come down to us independently.[46] The Saxon Annalist carried the story of Count Liuthar under the year 943. The Magdeburg Annals, compiled perhaps a little later, also embody it in their groundwork but they place it, as Thietmar had done, by way of a digression after the account of Bishop Hildiward's investiture in 968.[47] Both these versions however stand closer to Thietmar's original text than to the Corvey recension of it and drop the latter's newly imported verb, *exiliare*. How they interpreted their model we don't know.

Have the translators and the historians following in their footsteps not seriously misunderstood Thietmar's sentence? Do his words not invite a radically different rendering, namely, 'then he [Liuthar] regained the king's grace and all his possessions with the help of much money and the land at Santersleben and Gutenswegen', that is by a hefty fine in treasure and land? The most obvious and serious objection to this translation is its inconsistency. If Liuthar had to offer the king treasure and lands he would have regained less than all his possessions, but if we consider what was at stake and the element of haggling and bargaining behind so many judicial procedures this should not weigh unduly. It is legitimate to question the current translation not merely on general grounds but also on the strength of the discovery that not all the adapters and users of Thietmar's text understood his phrase, in the sense that Liuthar gained not only restoration but also compensation and new favours. Let us turn for a moment to the foremost Saxon vernacular history of the later fourteenth century, the so-called *Magdeburger Schöppenchronik*. Its author, the secretary of the Magdeburg *scabini*, drew his copious material about Otto I's life and times for the most part from the Saxon Annalist or a similar compilation, and we duly find the story of Count Liuthar again in the context of Hildiward's visit to Otto in Italy. Here we read: 'And he also wanted to have Count Liuthar killed but the princes intervened for him. The emperor took away all his property and sent him prisoner to Bavaria. He was imprisoned for one year. Then the emperor's grace was procured for him in such a way that he gave much money and ransomed himself with it and the farms of Santersleben and Gutenswegen.'[48] The sense of this is ambiguous. It could mean that Liuthar had to give both money and the lands to be forgiven, but it could also mean that he redeemed both himself and the two named estates by a heavy cash payment. Of these translations, however, the second one makes less than good sense because Liuthar had many more estates to regain than just Santersleben and Gutenswegen; and in the very same sentence the author proceeds to tell his readers how the count founded a collegiate church at Walbeck with the tenth part of his entire inheritance to make amends for his offence against the emperor. Whichever rendering is preferred, they both differ strikingly from that adopted by more recent translators. In Konrad Bote's late-medieval, popular and illustrated *Saxon Chronicle* in Low German we find the story again, strangely altered, under the year 969.[49] Here Liuthar lost much money, had to surrender the use of his land at Santersleben and endow the house of canons for protecting the rebel Erich (Bishop Hildiward's father). Neither the author of the *Magdeburger Schöppenchronik* nor Konrad Bote had any first-hand knowledge of Thietmar's *Chronicon,* but drew from the ever more turbid stream of transmission which sprang from the twelfth-century compilers. The first printed edition of the *Chronicon* appeared in 1580.[50] Meibom the Elder and his editors could therefore dismiss the story they found in Konrad Bote's *Saxon Chronicle* and in Johannes Pomarius's High German version of it.[51] They preferred to believe Thietmar himself, but did they understand him aright?

To find out what the bishop of Merseburg wanted to say about his ancestor's troubles with Otto I, we too must consult his *Chronicon*, and only by looking at his habits as a writer can we comprehend him as a family historian. Thietmar's style was, according to his editor, Robert Holtzmann, 'somewhat rough and unkempt in manner . . . sometimes not easy to understand'.[52] Despite his erudition, the Latin he wrote was wilful, crotchety and jarring but all the same arresting, and this precisely gives his work its personal strength and intimacy, for all his concern with the care of souls, episcopal instruction and the wrongs done to his see. It was all of a single cast and his individuality stands out among the historians of the tenth and early eleventh century. Compared with him, Widukind was heroic, sonorous but remote, Adalbert of St Maximin rather cold, and Liudprand of Cremona, who also took his preaching seriously, was more ostentatious, more anxious to please and more many-sided than his later Saxon colleague and also far less self-critical. Thietmar's usages were often odd and when he wrote, 'then he [Liuthar] acquired the king's grace and all his property again with a large sum of money and land in Santersleben and Gutenswegen', it is worth investigating how he employed the word *acquirere* and whether there are other passages in the *Chronicon* which can help us to decipher this one. He used the verb often enough, usually in the sense 'to acquire', 'to get', 'to secure'. Archbishop Giselher of Magdeburg, for instance, secured a countship for his protégé, Count Dedi, or the garrison of Meissen were out getting fodder for their horses.[53] There is, however, another chapter in which Thietmar described a situation not unlike that of 941, and once more the conspirator who fell foul of an Ottonian king was a member of his own family, in this case his cousin Werner. In 1013 Henry II learned that Werner together with Ekkehard, the brother of Margrave Hermann of Meissen, had paid an unlicensed visit to the court of the king's great enemy, Duke Boleslas Chrobry of Poland, had spoken seditiously and often received the duke's messengers in secret. Both men were summoned and when they did not come, their possessions were seized (here Thietmar used almost the same words as in II. 21), and they stood accused of contumacy.[54] Werner had acted in the time-honoured way of a Saxon noble whose enemies had got the better of him. In 1009 he had lost the margraviate of the Northern March to the old rivals and near neighbours of his house, now represented by Bernhard, the son of Margrave Dietrich, whom we have already met. 'In the end', Thietmar wrote, 'my cousin bought the king's grace and the right to live peacefully on his lands [as against having to go into exile] with an estate and with gold.'[55] There is nothing equivocal about this. Werner had to surrender both—money and estate. In form as well as in content this passage stands very close to the one relating the events of 942, only Thietmar here used the verb *comparare* (to purchase) in order to describe the costly business of regaining the king's grace.

We can, however, go further. In 1012 the see of Magdeburg fell vacant for the second time, after the very brief episcopate of Archbishop Walthard. Henry II saw to it that his *capellanus*, the Saxon Gero, became Walthard's successor. Though archbishop-elect, Gero was evidently not yet a member of the Magdeburg clerical community—he had been a canon of Hildesheim—or perhaps he only wanted to win the goodwill of his clerks who had to accept and to elect him as the king's choice. At any rate, almost his first act was to acquire the fellowship of his canons by the gift of ten *mansus*. There is no question that Gero parted with the lands but Thietmar here expressed this without employing the preposition *cum*. He wrote: 'communionem fratrum X mansis acquirens'.[56] However, the closest parallel to II. 21 for the use of *cum* in conjunction with *acquirere*, meaning 'to secure' or 'gain' something by means of an expenditure, occurs in another snippet of family history. In 1003 Thietmar's uncle, Margrave Liuthar, died suddenly at Cologne. His widow Godila rose to the crisis and secured the march and the *beneficium* that went with it for their ill-fated son Werner, with a money payment of 200 marks, in effect a relief.[57] 'Wirinhario beneficium patris et marcam cum ducentorum precio talentorum acquisivit', Thietmar wrote, and we are entitled to interpret his sentence about Count Liuthar's way out of trouble in 941–2 in the same way. He secured restitution by a heavy fine and the surrender of two estates. It is true that Thietmar can also use *cum* and *acquirere* together in a cumulative sense, 'to gain one object and another', but there is a strong balance of probability against it in this case.[58] To make it stronger still it is worth glancing briefly at the marginalia in the Corvey version of the *Chronicon*, the annotations which have come down to us in the fourteenth-century copy now in Brussels. The annotator drew attention to the kinship between the author and the conspirator and then he exclaimed: 'How many estates his guilt cost him!' This would not make much sense if they had all been restored and two new *curtes* as well as treasure added by royal favour after a year's exile.[59]

Count Liuthar died in 964 leaving two sons, one also called Liuthar, the future margrave of the Northern March, the other, Count Siegfried, Thietmar's father. The partition of the inheritance led to a certain crystallization of the family into two branches, but it did not yet go very far and the early death of Siegfried in 991 concentrated authority and control in the hands of the margrave for some years.[60] The collegiate church at Walbeck was shared and served as a mausoleum for both branches, although Margrave Liuthar was by his own wish buried in Cologne. For some reason both he and Count Siegfried had important links with the Rhenish metropolis.[61] Thietmar's clergy did not in any way exclude him from the division of his father's and mother's inheritances. It was his wealth and the hope that he would bestow some of it on the relatively poor see of Merseburg which recommended his candidature for the bishopric to the prudent piety of Henry II.[62] Thietmar's brothers and his uncle do not seem to have parcelled up and so fragmented individual *curtes*, for we find the bishop possessed a number of entire 'manors' which he mentions casually in the *Chronicon*. Certain important centres, Walbeck and the fortress of Wolmirstedt, where the river Ohre flowed into the old course of the Elbe, were at times but not always held or used in common and as always the *co-heredes* retained a close interest in the portions held by their brothers and cousins. Some of Thietmar's *curtes* lay a good distance away from Walbeck, as for instance Heeslingen (near Zeven) which he can only have inherited through his mother, Kunigunde, of the family of the counts of Stade. Santersleben and Gutenswegen, on the other hand, were situated near the core of the Walbeckers possessions in the Magdeburg Börde, the fertile and well-settled area west of the town which made its rise possible. In this countryside Thietmar possessed the *curtis* of Gross-Rottmersleben, his mother Nord-Germersleben and his brother Count Henry, Tundersleben.[63] There they also rubbed shoulders with other leading East Saxon noble clans who shared the profits of empire in Sclavania and elsewhere. The Ottonians themselves had enormous holdings in the Nordthüringau, the *pagus* of the Börde, and Magdeburg itself had been the dowry of Queen Edith, Otto the Great's first wife. By 941 the foundation of the monastery of St Maurice, the future archbishopric, was already under way. The first huge endowments had been made and cultivated land in this region was becoming scarcer. Otto I needed what he had for his great ecclesiastical enterprise, and the surrender of two estates by an exiled rebel seeking to make his peace would usefully replenish the king's resources.[64]

4

The Aftermath of Rebellion

The Walbeck family thus lost much treasure and two estates from the core of
their holdings in the Nordthüringau, thanks to Count Liuthar's dabbling in
Henry's rising. There is no evidence of his ever regaining favour with Otto I.
He appears as *comes* only once in a diploma of questionable authenticity. Its
source, a *notitia*, could even have pre-dated the conspiracy.[1] His second son,
Siegfried, was one of those who joined Margrave Hodo's unauthorized
expedition against Miesco of Poland. Thietmar wrote apologetically that his
father was young and not yet married and perhaps no special motif should be
read into this escapade.[2] Not many Saxon nobles of his age and situation
resisted the call of a military adventure they deemed to be profitable. Service
in the following of an established man of power and authority was the way to
gain experience for those who had prospects of their own. It was the
common lot of those who had few or none.

We seldom know who baptized and confirmed the children of counts and
margraves. Occasionally their godfathers are mentioned but it is noticeable
that Thietmar, the grandson of a rebel, received these offices from the son of
one, Bishop Hildiward.[3] Liuthar the younger and his brother did not join
Henry the Wrangler's assault on Otto II's kingship. On the contrary, it seems
that the 'reversionary interest', so familiar to English historians of the
eighteenth century, made them welcome to Otto the Great's successor as
was also the case with Margrave Thietmar of Serimunt.[4] Liuthar owed his
marriage to Godila, who came from a Westfalian comital family and was a
cousin of Bishop Wicfried of Verdun (959–83), to the good offices of Otto
II.[5] The Walbeck brothers may have held back also because their Franco-
Bavarian affinity, of whom more must be said later, profited by the
emperor's redistribution of power in Bavaria in 976.[6]

Otto II's death at the age of twenty-eight at once changed all this. Henry
the Wrangler was freed, became the rightful guardian of the infant Otto III
and soon sought to thrust his charge aside while remaining in control of his
person. Among the Wrangler's Saxon followers and supporters were Counts
Liuthar and Siegfried, who now joined the son of their father's chosen lord and
king. Thietmar does not tell us expressly that they attended Henry's Easter

court at Quedlinburg in 984, where his kingship was ritually inaugurated with oaths and *laudes*. In any case, many of those present were not the Wrangler's friends but withdrew to take part in a rival assembly which met at the Asselburg some 75 kilometres away. There they made plans to save Saxony and the kingship for the infant Otto III. What matters is that the Walbeck brothers were not of this company. Thietmar has recorded the names of sixteen leading participants, headed by Duke Bernhard. His own next of kin were conspicuously absent and in this indirect fashion he reveals the lines of division in the Saxon higher aristocracy.[7] Behind each margrave and group of counts we must see the ranks of their more and less important vassals, a cluster of small armies, ready to strike and plunder. Neither the feuds of the past nor the unsatisfied claims of the present were forgotten. The leading Slav princes, Miesco of Poland, Boleslas II of Bohemia and Mistui, the ruler of the Obotrites, who all became Henry's men at Quedlinburg, were part of this network of *amicitiae*, clientage and enmities which cut across ethnic frontiers.[8]

Henry had to abandon his attempt on the kingship, not least because his Saxon opponents were too numerous, formidable and determined and they succeeded in concerning him in a dangerous military situation on their own ground, the southeastern marches. He had to surrender the young Otto III to the two empresses and his aunt, the Abbess Mathilda of Quedlingburg, at Rohr towards the end of June 984. The final submission at Frankfurt a year later is presented by the Quedlinburg Annalist as an act of penance, of undemanding, contrite self-humiliation, but the conditions of his surrender were very different from those he had to accept in 978, when he went into exile and could be replaced in Bavaria by another Liudolfing, Liudolf's son Otto.[9] It is remarkable how much Otto II also in his own family relied on the descendants of his father's enemies. By 985, however, Henry was the senior male representative of them all. Immense though the influence of Theophanu, Adelheid and Mathilda of Quedlinburg was in holding the Ottonian *regna* together, the Wrangler's restoration to the *ducatus* over Bavaria was necessary not only for the sake of peace. His followers elsewhere had to be treated with consideration and respect. The women and men who ruled Otto III's minority could not imitate the *terror regius* of his grandfather. An old *frondeur* like Count Ekbert, the younger Wichmann's brother, and the Thuringian Count Wilhelm seem to have made their peace on terms which gave them some consolation for their life-long *gravamina*. Liuthar of Walbeck at last achieved his family's ambition and received the margraviate of the Northern March sometime after 985, when Margrave Dietrich died, and his son Bernhard was passed over until Werner of Walbeck fell from grace in 1009.[10] According to one tradition, which characteristically went back to Thietmar, the excesses of Dietrich's rule had set off the shock wave of the Slav rising in 983, destroying Saxon lordship in Brandenburg and further north for a long time to come.[11] Lastly, Count Siegfried, the chronicler's father, also found a place in the minority regime. He served the Empress Theophanu faithfully 'domi miliciaeque'. The classical phrase was a commonplace to Widukind and Thietmar but it meant at least that Siegfried not only took part in the expeditions against the Slavs and Boleslas of Bohemia but also followed the empress's itineration from time to time.[12] However, the connection between the family and the descendants of Duke Henry I of Bavaria did not break off. In 1002 Liuthar was the first Saxon lord to seek out the duke's grandson at Bamberg, to help him win supporters in Saxony in return for the promise of restoring a kinsman to a countship from which he had been removed by Otto III.[13]

It can be said, therefore, that from the beginning of Otto I's reign, if not before, until the second decade of the eleventh century, the horizons of the Walbeck family were set in their enmity and rivalry with the house of Margrave Dietrich, the counts of Haldensleben as they came to be called. Haldensleben, one of their residences and strongholds, lay only a few miles away from the possessions of Liuthar and Siegfried in the Nordthüringau, not quite half way between their Walbeck and Wolmirstedt centres. For long periods hostility simmered under the surface to flare up suddenly like summer lightning. Thietmar, to whom we owe most of what we know about these relationships, is sometimes a little reticent about his own kin. Yet even his bare hints are revealing. When he tells the story of Count Gero of Alsleben, who in 979 was destroyed by his enemies, Archbishop Adalbert of Magdeburg and Margrave Dietrich, exploiting the device of a charge followed by a judicial duel, he also mentions that his father and uncle were given custody of the accused man. It was not usual to commit high aristocratic prisoners to their worst enemies on such occasions and most likely the Walbeck counts felt sympathy for Gero or were at least neutral.[14]

The Walbeck and Haldensleben feud was not obsessive like some. Both family groups had other interests and wider, far-flung connections. Rivalry and clashes did not exclude some elusive kinship between them—Thietmar mentioned a *consanguineus* and Magdeburg friend called Bernhard—or even tears wept when the enemy lay dying.[15] They were, however, the monotonous constant of this aristocracy, which in the tenth century still controlled almost everything—the subject populations of the less free and the unfree in the old Saxon *pagi* and the conquered Slav settlements of the marches, their security, police, religious, cultural and economic lifelines.

It would be a mistake to think that the conspiracy of 941 and Otto I's reprisals were all loss to Thietmar's ancestor. Liuthar had spent a year in the keeping of Count Berthold of Schweinfurt and their relationships were or became friendly rather than hostile. Sometime after 942 he gave his daughter Eila in marriage to his former jailer.[16] Only the circumstances of this alliance were unusual. Marriages between leading families of the Saxon nobility and those of Bavaria, Suabia, Francia, the Lower Rhine, the counts of Flanders and Slav rulers were not uncommon in the tenth century and became more frequent in the eleventh, although the tradition and the prestige-building character of these alliances across hundreds of miles went back to the Carolingian and pre-Carolingian past.[17] The Ottonians themselves achieved much of their *dilatatio imperii* and vastly increased their wealth by marrying into the Conradine and Luitpolding families established in Francia, Suabia and Bavaria, not to mention the Italian rights of

Adelheid. Their Saxon nobles could not be imposed as a *Reichsvolk*, a ruling people, on the stem magnates of the south but a few of them followed the Liudolfings' example and intermarried with them. We do not hear that they always needed Ottonian patronage, as Count Liuthar had done, in order to form matrimonial alliances with aristocratic families outside Saxony or even outside the *Reich*. Their landed wealth, treasures and military manpower made Saxon margraves and counts of the tenth and eleventh century more than equal partners, who could choose brides and marry off their daughters well. Carolingian Saxony had been dominated mainly by Franco-Saxon alliances.[18] Nobles from the Middle Rhine established themselves there by marriages and, among Francophil Saxon lords, Frankish brides were sought after as elsewhere. But with the exception of a few outstanding families, especially the Liudolfings themselves, the Saxons had not yet, even by the year 900, wholly shaken off the character of a *gens subacta*, a people subject to the Franks. At the Synod of Tribur in 895 we meet with the case of a Frankish *nobilis* who had repudiated his Saxon wife after more than fifteen years of fertile marriage. The synodal judgment and decree with their publicity and solemnity evidently sought to discourage others from doing the same.[19]

In the *Reich* which Otto I's survivals and victories bequeathed to his successors, the 'exogamous' alliances of the Saxon aristocracy were spread more evenly among Lotharingian, Bavarian, Suabian and Rhine-Frankish partners. They also assumed a new role for they began to foster solidarities between powerful families across stem boundaries, quite independently from those created by the royal *iter*, the imperial chapel, the bishops' synods and the mixed following attending a Liudolfing king or prince. The beginnings of the *regnum Teutonicum* owed something to this closer network of kinship, acquaintance and interests, which their success enabled Saxon princely families to form outside their stem area.[20] Here again Thietmar allows us the deepest insights. His maternal grandfather, Count Henry of Stade (died 976), married a daughter of the Conradine Count Udo, the brother of Duke Hermann of Suabia.[21] We have met Udo already as Otto I's staunch friend and supporter during the emergencies of 939 and 941. Thietmar felt keenly his blood relationship with this large and, in his day, still foremost Rhine-Frankish family. They, and of course the descendants of Count Berthold of the Bavarian Nordgau, belonged to his personal world and so entered his memorial. When they stood out and rebelled against Henry II, he reflected on the rights and wrongs of their conduct with deep concern about their earthly and eternal welfare.[22] The kings' journeys through the *Reich*, judging, rewarding and punishing, thus came to be matched gradually by a competing skein of communications becoming denser and more complex with time. Its profound importance and implications are summed up for us, unwittingly, by Brun, the historian of the Saxon wars against Henry IV. Writing in 1082 he has the South German princes say to their king, who begged them for quick armed help against the Saxons after his flight from the Harzburg: 'They would on no account fight against innocent men, Christians and their own kin.'[23] Much but not all of this must be read as polemical rhetoric. The *cognatio*, however, was real. The new and the old conflicts dividing the *Reich* were linked by this development.

Largely thanks to Thietmar, it has been possible to follow one rising and feud through their lesser and larger implications over three generations. Their *imperium* on the whole gave the Saxon higher nobles what they wanted but it did not solve all their problems and created more besides. One of these to be mentioned in passing was a chronic shortage of well-equipped and trained mounted warriors to sustain the ubiquitous wars of Otto I's reign. Widukind referred to it four times.[24] Native kingship itself was new to Saxony. It could not, as we have seen, transcend the endemic strains within and between noble families but rather added to them. One of these additions presents a paradox. The crowned ruler was now much nearer than he had been in the ninth century and yet he had to become more remote. Let us return to the subject of indivisibility. One of the consequences of the reluctant change to impartible rule was the new singularity of the king, his isolation even in his own family as against the almost gregarious kingship of the Carolingians and their predecessors. It made possible and indeed necessary a further growth of institutional ideas, of kingship seen as an office in abstract and super-personal terms and it also endowed its ancient sacral garb with new functions. These must occupy us later. Before they do, we have to turn to another area of conflict in early medieval Saxony which slowly poisoned the relationships between kings and lay lords. Its source lay in the very make-up of aristocratic families, the frequent imbalance between men and women which favoured the influence and authority of women, not least of all in the Ottonian family itself. This in turn gave rise to serious clashes over inheritances. By the early eleventh century these ranged the rulers, their bishops, abbots and abbesses against resentful, land-hungry lay nobles.

II The Women of the Saxon Aristocracy

5

Survival and Inheritance

The deeds of Otto I were sung by a woman, Hrotsvitha of Gandersheim, and Widukind of Corvey dedicated his *Res Gestae Saxonicae* to Mathilda, the emperor's daughter. If his work was, as some think, an Ottonian house history, the individual emperors, with the exception of Henry II and Hrotsvitha's panegyric of Otto, had no biographers of their own.[1] Their womenfolk fared almost better or at least no worse. Of Queen Mathilda, Henry I's wife, we possess two *vitae* and the Empress Adelheid had an *epitaphium* from the pen of none less than Odilo of Cluny who presented her as the examplar of cardinal Cluniac virtues—*discretio* and *caritas*. The memory and sanctity of these dowagers could be appealed to and conjured with. In times of crisis the Empresses Theophanu and Adelheid held a large and heterogeneous circle of clerical and lay princes together and, in their Saxon *patria*, Mathilda, the abbess of Quedlinburg, Otto I's daughter, Sophia and Adelheid, the children of Otto II, were looked up to with awe and veneration. Mathilda could be left in charge when her nephew, the last of the Ottos, went to Rome in 997 and she was able to allay, if not to quell, dangerous feuds among the leading East Saxon nobles of these years.[2] A slight offered to Sophia and Adelheid by Margrave Ekkehard of Meissen during the interregnum of 1002 was the plausible cause for his murder.[3] The mere presence of the two sisters enhanced the aura of the court of their second cousin, Henry II, and when in November 1024 they came to meet the newly anointed Salian king, Conrad II, at Vreden in Westfalia, he could be fairly sure of a friendly welcome in Saxony beyond.

More surprising still are the influence, prestige and even authority of Ottonian dowagers and princesses in the church. The entries of the emperors' daughters into religion were great occasions of state. In 966 when the eleven-year-old Mathilda was blessed in and elected abbess, not one bishop, as was the custom, but all the archbishops and bishops of the *Reich*, according to one report, took part in her *velatio*, in the presence of the emperor, his wife, his mother, the young Otto II and all the greater East Saxon nobility of both sexes. The bishops had been specially summoned.[4] Sophia, at much the same age and in the same situation, had thus a good precedent when she wanted an archbishop rather than her diocesan to veil her, and so unleashed over forty years of strife between Mainz and Hildesheim.[5] The old Empress Adelheid with her grandson in 996 summoned a *conventus* of bishops to secure the future of her monastic foundation, Selz. The decretum of the Synod of Dortmund in 1005, which imposed obligations of prayer and almsgiving for the commemoration of the bishops present and also regulated a number of fasts, was promulgated by Henry II in the first place, followed by his queen, Kunigunde.[6] The authority of other great ladies in Saxon society equalled that of the most respected prelates and lay lords. Hathui, abbess of Gernrode, Liudgard of Elten, not to mention her notorious sister Adela, were centres of little aristocratic worlds. They had noble kinsmen and vassals to serve them. The widows of counts and margraves could on occasion handle the dangers of a succession on behalf of their sons no less well than did the empress on behalf of hers.[7] A notable number of Saxon and Lower Rhenish illuminated manuscripts and processional crosses of the Ottonian period and the eleventh century were created for and commissioned by women. The Essen treasures, the cross made for the abbess of Borghorst, the Svenhilda Evangelia, also from Essen, in the John Rylands Library, the Hitda Codex in Darmstadt (from Meschede) may serve as certain examples and the famous Gospel Book named after Quedlinburg, now in the Pierpont Morgan Library, may well have been at the nunnery since the middle of the tenth century.[8]

The families of the early medieval German aristocracy (and not only of the German) have been described recently as large agnatic and cognatic associations, to use the language of social anthropologists, of bilineal, undifferentiated descent. This meant that the individuals who belonged to them might derive their rights, duties and possessions as much from their maternal as their paternal ancestry.[9] Large groups of kinsmen rather than conjugal families seem to stand in the foreground, at least in one kind of source—the *Libri Memoriales* of the South German monasteries, St Gallen, Reichenau and Pfäfers—and on their pages aristocratic Saxon visitors, warriors or pilgrims, often had themselves and their kin inscribed to benefit from the prayers of the community. Yet the *Libri Memoriales* may mislead us. The equality of patrilineal and matrilineal connections is not always supported by all the other evidence. In eight generations of Charlemagne's descendants, for instance, the names of the men have been transmitted much better than those of the women.[10] The wives of some outstanding Saxon lords in the tenth century are barely known to us and their origins have remained obscure. In the *Lex Saxonum* noble women enjoyed the same compensations as the men but the *paternum genus* had *tutela* over the widow of one of their own deceased.[11] Men in high secular positions, dukes, counts, margraves and the like, strove to consolidate their fortunes and their families in order to secure as much as possible for their direct descendants to the detriment of their wider kin. Early medieval kinship structures must remain obscure until we have understood the conditions which underlay them and these again must be looked for not so much in the aristocracy's self-awareness, as has been done recently, but in its situation—its hard, dangerous and unhealthy mode of existence, its short expectations of life.[12] In the pages that follow an attempt will be made to show why women occupied such a high place in the history and culture of the Ottonian *Reich* despite the fragility and the levity of their sex, which clerical writers in the patristic tradition imputed to them as a matter of course.

Modern demographers would find the tenth-century German aristocracy an ungrateful subject. The straw to make the bricks of statistical analysis is not to be found. We cannot raise cohorts of sufficient size and consistency to make sound statements about nuptiality, fertility and mortality. These are the three headings under which important segments of less remote aristocratic societies have been studied in recent years, for instance, the ducal families of England, Scotland and Ireland from 1330 to 1954 and the *ducs et pairs* of the *ancien régime* in France from 1650 to 1799.[13] T. H. Hollingsworth, C. Lévy and L. Henry, the authors of these pilot-ventures, characteristically chose closed circles as their subjects, for the English dukedoms and the French *duchés-pairies* had this in common: they were both created by royal letters patent, originally for princes of the blood and then for other favoured subjects. No such sharply delineated frontiers exist for the Ottonian nobles and, although their *primores*, their dukes, margraves, counts palatine and counts, were anxious enough to transmit their honours to their sons and consolidate their families round themselves, mortality and the vagaries of royal favour often dealt harshly with these attempts. The leading men, the bishops and princes of the Saxon *Reich* were closely interrelated and within their families they formed temporary ascendancies round which their lesser kinsmen and vassals could rally but without much assurance of continuity. Too often there were no sons to succeed fathers, no brothers in lay estate, uncles and nephews, or, conversely, there were too many. These ruling strata, therefore, did not constitute what demographers have called a universe, a clearly definable and limited area of sampling. When T. H. Hollingsworth attempted to survey the 'British', by which he meant the English, Scottish and Irish, and United Kingdom peerage as a whole, he had to begin in the 1560s rather than 1330, the date of the first duke's birth.[14] We are dealing with data 'not chosen but presented to the demographer', not a 'completely defined population' but only a 'more vaguely limited quasi-random sample'.[15] Behind the handful of men and women portrayed in the narrative sources and royal diplomata as acting, governing and fighting, there are hundreds, perhaps thousands, of other *nobiles* who remain obscure and unknown to us. Even counts may never be mentioned in a single royal diploma.[16] Here the *Libri Memoriales*, the *Traditiones* of Corvey and Fulda, must serve as a warning.

Of the Saxon nobles in the tenth century, the men who fought the prolonged wars of conquest against the Slavs and followed the Ottonian rulers on their more distant enterprises as far as southern Italy, we possess only stray scraps of evidence to answer questions about their nuptuality and the fertility of their marriages. In general girls became wives early. Thietmar of Merseburg whose *Chronicon* is, as we have seen, a memorial for the living and the dead of his own family, its endlessly ramifying connections in the

Saxon and Frankish aristocracy and his contemporaries among the Magdeburg *alumni*, occasionally has something to tell us about these matters. When his uncle Liuthar made his good match with the Emperor Otto II's help, his bride, Godila, was barely thirteen years old and probably less.[17] For at that age she bore him his son Werner, who was to cause the bishop of Merseburg so much anxiety. Thirteen years old was also Hathui, the daughter of Count Wichman the Elder, when she married Siegfried, the son of Margrave Gero.[18] They had no surviving children. Whether Mathilda, Otto II's daughter, married the future Count Palatine Ezzo at the age of fourteen must remain uncertain for, although it appears that she was born in summer 978, Thietmar did not mention the date of her wedding which, he wrote, displeased many.[19]

We know a little more about the high incidence of infant mortality. Einhard said of Charlemagne that he was singularly fortunate to lose only two sons and one daughter in his own lifetime.[20] These were adults and he did not trouble to mention the deaths of one son and two daughters in infancy. Among the Liudolfings, every generation from that of Duke Liudolf in the mid-ninth century until 979, Otto II's time, suffered premature losses. Only in the case of Henry I's marriages have none been recorded. Duke Liudolf had eleven children of whom four died in tender years.[21] His son Otto lost two boys so that Henry I, as Thietmar so well expressed it, came to a vacant inheritance. It is not known how old his predeceased brothers were but they disappeared before founding families and households of their own.[22] Otto I and his second wife Adelheid lost two sons before they reached the age of five and Otto II a baby girl.[23] Otto III died before he married and Henry II's union with Kunigunde remained childless. With the coming of the Salians infant mortality once more depleted each generation: Conrad II, Henry III and Henry IV all lost sons and daughters of very young years and the dynasty ended with another childless marriage.[24] It is unlikely that the nobility fared much better with their offspring.

All these remain fragments. There is however one demographic feature to be observed in early Saxon aristocratic society which can be traced more clearly—the respective expectations of life for adult men and women. In collecting materials for the history of the leading kins in the tenth and early eleventh centuries, it would be difficult and rather purblind not to notice the surprising number of matrons who outlived their husbands, sometimes by several decades and sometimes more than one, their brothers and even their sons. The examples are so numerous and widespread both in charters of gift and in narrative sources that they ask aloud to be collected. They can be studied and help to explain something important about the history of the Ottonian and early Salian ruling class and its culture. Let us begin with instances from the Liudolfing family and their connections by marriage, not only because the evidence is more readily available, especially dates of birth, but also because the activities and tastes of their surviving women differed from those of other Saxon noble women in degree rather than in kind. Liudolf, the first to hold a foremost position in eastern Saxony, died in 866, his wife Oda in 913 at the age, it is thought, of 107.[25] Only one of her large family, a daughter named Christina, abbess of Gandersheim, survived her. Oda outlived the greatest of her sons, Duke Otto, by six months and Widukind called him 'iam gravior' at the time of Louis the Child's death in 911 to explain to his readers why he should not be the East Frankish king. In dividing up the ages of man, most medieval writers regarded *gravitas* as a distinct period and set it against *senium* or *senectus*. If Widukind weighed his words carefully Duke Otto would have been between fifty and sixty years old at the time.[26] The same Otto *dux*, Henry I's father, had a daughter named Oda after her grandmother. First she married King Zwentibold of Lotharingia, the bastard son of the Emperor Arnold, who perished in 900, and almost immediately afterwards she was taken to wife by one of his enemies, Count Gerhard, who fell in a battle against the Hungarians in 910.[27] Oda herself lived into the 950s, surviving her brother Henry, the king, by at least fifteen years. Queen Mathilda, the second wife of Henry I, died in 968, thirty-two years after her husband, thirteen years after her second son, Duke Henry of Bavaria, and three after her third, Archbishop Brun of Cologne. She survived also her grandson, Archbishop William of Mainz, who had come to visit her when she lay in her last illness at Quedlinburg.[28]

Mathilda's daughter Gerberga was born before her husband had become king. In 929 she was married to Duke Giselbert of Lotharingia, who drowned in the Rhine at the battle of Andernach in 939 fighting against Otto I's Frankish allies. She was carried off by Louis d'Outremer who used the troubles of the Ottonians to enlarge his foothold and following in Lotharingia. Gerberga, however, lost her second husband in 954 when he gave chase to a wolf he met on his way from Laon to Reims. He was thrown from his horse and died of his injuries. His wife outlived him by fifteen years.[29] Her sister Hathui was allied to Hugh the Great (died 956) and, if Sigebert of Gembloux is right, she was alive nine years after the Capetian duke's death.[30] In the next generation Otto I's wife, Edith, King Athelstan's half-sister, died in 946 and so is an exception to the trend, but the Burgundian Adelheid whom he married in 951 outlived him by twenty-six years and her first husband Lothar, king of Italy, by forty-nine.[31] Judith, the wife of Otto I's brother, Duke Henry of Bavaria, died sometime after 985, over thirty years later than her husband.[32] In the next generation only two of Adelheid's children lived to adulthood, Otto II and Mathilda, the abbess of Quedlinburg. Although she attained only her forty-fourth year and died a few months before her mother in 999, she outlived her brother, the emperor, by about fifteen years.[33] The emperor's wife, Theophanu, even though she too died prematurely young, still saw her little son, Otto III, through the first eight years of his minority. The offspring of Queen Edith, Liudgard and Liudolf, both died young in the 950s, Liudgard even before her brother but Liudolf's wife Ida, the daughter and heiress of Duke Hermann of Suabia, had a widowhood of nearly thirty years.[34] Of her children, Duke Otto of Suabia and Bavaria died in 982 at Lucca, worn out by the disastrous campaign of his cousin, the Emperor Otto II, against the Saracens in Calabria. His sister lived a more sedentary life as abbess of Essen where she ended her days in 1011.[35] Duke Henry of Bavaria's daughter Hadwig survived her husband, Duke Burkhard II of Suabia, by twenty-one years, though not her brother, Duke Henry the Wrangler. She was, however, at least ten years older than he but at the same time much younger than Burkhard. The oldest sister, Gerberga, abbess of Gandersheim, survived them both.[36] In August 994, shortly after reaching his majority at the age of fourteen, Otto III gave his sister Sophia the great *curtis* of Eschwege on condition that if she died before him it was to revert to the king's *hereditas*.[37] It did not usually fall out in this way: Otto died in 1002, Sophia, abbess of Gandersheim and later also Essen, in 1039. Her sister Adelheid, abbess of Quedlinburg, Gernrode, Frohse, Vreden and in the end also Gandersheim, ended her life very much on the far side of sixty in 1045. Mathilda, the only one of Otto II's daughters who married, died in 1025 outlived by her husband the Count Palatine Ezzo.[38]

This is only a selection. In the six generations of Liudolfings beginning with the mid-ninth century *princeps*, Liudolf, and his wife and ending with Otto III, Henry II and Robert the Pious, wives outlived husbands thirty-four times and only thirteen times did they not. Among the same group of persons, 149 in all, one sister or several survived all their brothers fourteen times while a brother or brothers were the last to die only nine times.[39] Wives were not always much younger than husbands when they married but it was more often so than not and this would explain the almost three to one chance they had of outliving their men. The brides of thirteen or even twelve, of whom we have already encountered several, were not in the least unusual.[40] A girl was regarded as nubile when she reached that age. In his *Antapodosis* Liudprand of Cremona tells a story which neatly confirms this. When Otto I wanted to draw into his web of family alliances the Luitpolding Berthold, who had just overthrown a nephew as Duke of Bavaria, he offered him the hand of his recently widowed sister Gerberga if he could gain possession of her person. If this did not work out, he had in his keeping Gerberga's daughter by Duke Giselbert, 'almost of marriageable age' (*fere iam nubilem*) and Berthold could have her instead.[41] As Gerberga had married the duke of Lotharingia in 929, probably in December, her daughter, called Alberada, could not have been born much before the end of the following year at the earliest.[42] According to Liudprand, Otto I's offer was made almost immediately after the battle of Andernach, fought on 2 October 939. Alberada was therefore only nine years old at the time. Duke Berthold preferred the young girl, whom the historian now called 'not yet marriageable' (*nondum nubilem*), but the implication was that he would not have had long to wait. In the end neither match came to fruition because Gerberga, as we have seen, became the wife of the West Frankish king, Louis IV, and her daughter Alberada was returned to her to marry Count Ragenold of Roucy a few years later.[43]

Among the sisters who survived all their brothers in our sample, we may note already that abbesses counted for a great deal. It could be objected that in presenting these figures no allowance has been made for birth intervals. In the case of a large family, like the progeny of the ninth-century *princeps* Liudolf and his wife Oda, this is not immaterial. Yet Christina, the daughter who survived all her brothers and sisters, was almost certainly not the youngest child, although she must have been born a few years after her brother Otto, the duke, who died in 912. In all too many cases the year and sometimes even the exact order of births remain matters for conjecture. It is, however, striking that the children of the Ottonian rulers in the tenth century were born in quick succession to one another and that child-bearing ceased altogether before the mother even reached the age of thirty. Henry I's and Mathilda's five surviving offspring were born between 912 and 925 when the queen was about twenty-nine years old.[44] During her brief marriage to King Lothar of Italy (947–50), Adelheid gave him a daughter. All the four children of her second marriage were born between 951 and 956 when she was twenty-five.[45] The births of Otto II's and Theophanu's family of five fell between the years 975 and 980. She may even have been a little older than her husband but counted less than thirty years when her only son, Otto III, was safely delivered.[46] The three sisters who outlived him by more than two, three and four decades respectively, were thus all his seniors by birth. The same is true of Gerberga, the abbess of Gandersheim (died 1001), Henry the Wrangler's first-born sister.[47] Years older than her brother, she outlived him.

The descendants of Liudolf and Oda in the male and female line form thus a fairly accessible group, whether they were regal, ducal or only comital, like Alberada's husband. It is impossible to know as much about other great Saxon families, but here too elderly widows and spinsters abound. Thietmar of Merseburg, who wrote of nearly all his kinsmen and kinswomen and whose *Chronicon* is interspersed with reminiscences of his childhood and youth, learnt his letters at the knees of an aged great-aunt in Quedlinburg who died in 991.[48] Her sister, the bishop's grandmother, ended her days in the same year, twenty-seven years after her husband, Count Liuthar of Walbeck.[49] Her daughter Eila, Thietmar's aunt (died 1015), outlived the bishop's father by twenty-four years and his uncle, Margrave Liuthar, by twelve.[50] Her husband, Count Berthold of Schweinfurt, had died in 980.[51] Both the brothers, Margrave Liuthar (died 1003) and Count Siegfried (died 991), left widows behind them and Godila eventually shocked Thietmar by her second and uncanonical marriage.

Let us now look at the descendants of Duke Hermann Billung. One of his daughters, Swanehild (died 1014), outlived not only both her brothers, Duke Bernhard I (died 1011) and Count Liudger (died 1011), but also her two husbands, Margrave Thietmar (died 979) and Margrave Ekkehard of Meissen (died 1002), although her two sisters had died before 1011. One of these, Imma, had been abbess of Herford, the other, Mathilda, at any rate outlived two husbands, Count Baldwin III of Flanders (died 962) and Count Godfrey of Verdun (died after 995).[52] Among the offspring of Count Wichmann the Elder, Hermann Billung's brother, none proved as long lived as his daughter Hathui. The wife of Margrave Gero's son, Siegfried, who died to his father's bitter grief in 959, Hathui as abbess of Gernrode enjoyed the bulk of the great margrave's fortune and survived until 1014, long after all her brothers had perished.[53] Let us recall that Count Wichmann the

Younger was killed in 967 after a brief life of ceaseless struggle against his uncle, Duke Hermann and Otto I.[54] Count Ekbert died in 994. It has been thought that Hathui had two sisters, Friderun and the Countess Imma, the foundresses and mistresses of the nunnery of Kemnade, who were still alive in 1025.[55] Much more likely, however, is that the two women were the daughters of the younger Wichmann on whose inheritance the convent was raised. We know from Widukind of Corvey that Wichmann was married and for his daughters to enjoy their father's forfeited estates in this way was not at all unusual. Even if they were born between 957 and 963 rather than before 944, when the older Wichmann died, they would still have been very old in 1025.[56] We find another example in the family of Bishop Bernward of Hildesheim; his maternal aunt, Rothgard, who was abbess of Hilwarts-hausen until 1006 while her brother, Bishop Folcmar of Utrecht, had died in 991.[57]

When Thietmar, in a famous passage, deplored the ill-consequences that must hit the Saxons when their ruling family failed to produce male heirs, he voiced the perennial anxieties of all aristocracies.[58] At this time not only the Billungs but also the counts, later called 'of Stade', the Ekkehardine mar-graves of Meissen, the Dedis and Fredericks of Eilenburg, the Northeims, the Bernhards and Dietrichs who lorded it in the Northern March and some others, were relatively well sustained and did not lack men, sons or nephews, who survived to replace their ancestors. Some tenth-century Saxon families, however, can hardly be identified except through the lavish religious founda-tions of their womenfolk. The Lady Helmburg, who has given genealogists so many headaches, had lost her husband and sons by 955 when she set about founding the nunnery of Fischbeck under Otto I's protection.[59] In 970 she can be found presiding over Hilwartshausen, another house to whose endowment she contributed much land.[60] Of her daughters two, if not three, were alive in 1003. Her kinswoman and perhaps sister, Aeddila, who took the lead in the foundation of Hilwartshausen, had lost her husband and two sons by 960. Her daughters, Berthild and Emma, seem to have settled in the house and the latter became abbess and was still alive in 990.[61] The survivor of a childless marriage, Marcswith and her kinswoman Emma in 940 began to found the nunnery of Schildesche in Westfalia. In an admittedly late *Vita*, she is called 'unica heres' of her *parentes*.[62]

If our impression is correct, and it cannot be much more than an impres-sion, it is worth while asking the question, what could have tilted the prospects of survival in favour of women in the Saxon aristocracy of the tenth and eleventh centuries? For it was by no means a universal rule. Many general population studies of late antiquity, the middle ages and the early modern period firmly point to the opposite conclusion: that women fared much worse than men, especially during the child-bearing age. The evidence comes from many quarters and is of many kinds.[63] Even the practice of infanticide to reduce the number of girls in the peasant households of the Paris basin during the ninth century cannot be ruled out.[64] However, when we turn to look at comparable closed populations, the life expectations of women in some of the sub-groups studied by demographers were better than those of the men in the same group and this not only in the modern epoch. Women, for instance, did better than men in the Genevan bourgeoisie for most of the time from the sixteenth to the twentieth century and considerably better among the ruling families of Europe from the early sixteenth to the mid-nineteenth century.[65] Hollingsworth, in his survey of the English dukes, found that in the cohort of 1337 to 1479, after the heavy toll of infant mortality, the number of surviving males dropped most severely between the ages of twenty and forty. This was followed by a still very heavy loss in the span from the fortieth to the sixtieth year. By contrast, more duchesses and women of ducal stock reached the age of twenty and quite disproportionately more that of forty, and twice as many as the men attained their sixtieth year of life.[66] Violence presents itself as the ready reason for this difference.[67] Scanning the pages of Widukind, Thietmar of Merseburg, the Lüneburg and Fulda *necrologia*, it would not be difficult to show that the Saxon aristocracy of the tenth and early eleventh centuries, especially the leading kins, lost heavily in the wars and feuds into which they so readily plunged. It was the price they paid for their eminence and success. Even the more long lived and continuous families survived only precariously and with severe losses. In the case of the Billungs, calamities struck not only Count Wichmann the Younger but also the descendants of his brother Ekbert and likewise the brothers of Dukes Bernhard I and Bernhard II. Ekbert's son, usually known as Count Wichmann III, was murdered in 1016.[68] He left an infant boy, who died young. Duke Bernhard I's brother, Count Liudger, was outlived by his widow, Emma, by twenty-seven years. It is doubtful whether they had any sons but their daughter, mentioned by Adam of Bremen, for some reason incurred the Emperor Conrad II's displeasure.[69] Duke Bernhard II's brother, Count Thietmar, perished in a judicial duel while his only son, Thietmar or Thiemo, disappeared in exile because he had avenged his father.[70]

The ancestors of the Wettins, too, survived only in the teeth of disaster. In 1009 Count Dedi was murdered by Thietmar of Merseburg's cousin, Werner. His son Dietrich received his father's fiefs and burgwards but Dedi's brother, Frederick, died in 1017 with only three daughters. His nephew succeeded to the Eilenburg but in 1034 the vassals of Margrave Ekkehard II of Meissen murdered him in his bed. They had entered his house on the pretence of paying their respects to their lord's brother-in-law. His son Dedi succeeded to the Eastern March and acquired a larger command still in 1046 when the Ekkehards died out; yet the future did not lie with his descendants but with those of a brother.[71]

The counts of Stade did not succeed one another deep into the twelfth century by an unbroken chain of filiation. In 994 a Viking force struck up the Elbe and was met by a Saxon host led by Count Henry and his brothers, Udo and Siegfried. They were defeated, captured and Udo killed. We know the details of this much-recorded episode especially thanks to Thietmar, for the counts were his maternal uncles and the calamity threatened to engulf him too. At this time Thietmar was a young clerk in the Magdeburg cathedral community. To ransom the prisoners the whole family had to club together;

Otto III helped out too and so did the neighbours. No less than seven thousand marks were raised but as usual not handed over in one lump sum. Count Henry was allowed to go but his only son became a hostage in his place and Count Siegfried, who had no sons, was to be released for one of the boys of his sister Kunigunde and so Thietmar was in the end chosen. He went on his dangerous errand in lay costume when tragedy cut short his journey to the raiders. Count Siegfried succeeded in escaping by inebriating his guards but his deliverance brought vengeance on the hostages still in the Vikings' hands. They were horribly mutilated and left to be picked up by their appalled relatives. Thietmar was lucky not to have been among them. As a result of this catastrophe, Count Henry lost his only son and never had another and it was his brother, Count Siegfried, as yet childless, who entered upon the lordship and honours of the family.[72]

Great nobles were killed by their rivals, by their own *milites* and even by what Thietmar called 'servilis presumptio'.[73] Above all the Slav and Polish wars took a heavy toll, not only after the great rising of 983 but even long before this decisive reverse during the decades when the *legati* and margraves had been the attackers and royal campaigns reinforced their efforts. The *necrologia* of Merseburg and Lüneburg record the names of important casualties quite frequently with the laconic addition 'et multi alii occisi'.[74] Nor should the losses of the long-distance expeditions to Italy and France be underrated. The Roncevaux of the Ottonian emperors was the battle at Capo Colonne in 982 against the Saracen emir of Sicily, Abu al Qasim, where Otto II lost a whole host of Saxon lords, a Thietmar, a Burkhard, a Dedi and a Gunther, not to mention others, from the Fulda *necrologium*.[75] Count Brun of Arneburg died in France on the 978 expedition.[76] It could be thought that the wars on the eastern frontiers and against Bohemia for the most part engaged only the East Saxon lords and their armies and that the Italian expeditions too drew only a few hundred nobles from Saxony into their vortex. Yet they always included important men from the leading strata, bishops, counts and their followings, and fighting may have been the least dangerous feature of these journeys. In Italy disease was even more treacherous and it struck the hosts from the north very soon. The greater nobles lived not unlike their kings. They too were restlessly itinerant and the short careers of Liudolf, Duke Henry, Otto II, Otto III and Henry III should warn us not to expect much longer working lives from their princes. The empresses sometimes shared the exertions and fatigues of these long journeys in dangerous climates but the wives of the nobles for the most part escaped them. The example of Hidda, Margrave Christian's widow, who in 969 pilgrimaged to Jerusalem and died there, was not yet widely followed.[77]

If women therefore had better chances of survival, it was inevitable that much land should accumulate in their possession even if the customs of inheritance placed them below the men in order of expectation. The *Lex Saxonum* prescribed that a deceased father or mother should leave their *hereditas* to the son and not to the daughter. If there were no sons but only daughters, then all was to go to them.[78] This meant at least that they had the advantage over their parents' brothers. When Hessi, one of the most Francophil of the Saxon *nobilissimi*, died as a monk in Fulda in 804, only daughters survived him. According to the ninth-century life of the anchoress Liutbirg, they inherited all his wealth although it is at least possible that Hessi had a powerful brother or nephew, Count Bernhard.[79] On the other hand, when the Wettin Count Frederick (died 1017) wanted to leave as much of his *predium* as possible to his three daughters, he made over his chief seat, the Eilenburg, to his nephew Dietrich, Count Dedi's son, 'because he was his heir and it could not be done lawfully in any other way', that is to say, without his consent and goodwill.[80]

In the *Landrecht* of the *Sachsenspiegel* the position of women as heiresses is not unambiguous, although they seem to be less categorically at a disadvantage compared with the *Lex*. Here too it is stated that the son should take the inheritance of his father, mother, brothers and sisters in preference to a daughter and only if there were no sons should the daughter succeed.[81] Yet elsewhere it seems that women, even those who remained unmarried in their father's house, could expect a share, for instance when an inheritance accrued from relatives other than parents, brothers or sisters.[82] We must note also that women in the *Sachsenspiegel* enjoyed much better terms when their only brother was a clerk. In that case, they took half the inheritance as well as half the mother's furnishings known as the *rade*.[83] The *hereditas* of a wife, moreover, did not become the property of her husband although it passed into his seisin.[84] It devolved separately from his own to sons, daughters or other heirs. Fathers and, if they were no longer alive, mothers took over the inheritance of the dying childless son with more right than his brother.[85] The situations set out in the *Landrecht* in many ways echo and resemble the practices of the Saxon aristocracy in the tenth century, and to them we must now turn.

It was very common to endow sons with *hereditas* in the parents' lifetime and so set them up, usually in separate households. This enabled them not only to marry but also to prove themselves in action, so that they could succeed to *honores* and take command of vassals in good time. An untried count or lord was no more secure than an untried king. In East Saxony it can be seen very clearly how newly conquered lands during the tenth century enabled favoured nobles to endow their sons with the king's help so that their own *hereditas* was not unduly diminished.[86] The custom of *Abschichtung*, of parents parting with estate to their children in their own lifetime, may explain why fathers and mothers became the heirs of their own offspring. Now as wives outlived their husbands more often than not, the more common way in which the rule applied was that mothers were the heiresses of their own sons. In some *traditiones* we find the mother of the donor cited as 'heres justissima' and in this case we can assume that she had outlived her husband and that her son had as yet no offspring.[87] A particularly stark case was that of Count Dodicho, who sometime between 1015 and 1020 made over his whole *predium* with all its useful rights and eight mills, excepting only a number of *ministeriales homines* and women, to St Liborius and the church of Paderborn. It was one of Bishop Meinwerk's greatest coups as the maker of his see's fortune. Dodicho, whose countships stretched across several Westfalian *pagi*, was an uncomfortable neighbour. He had apparently ruined himself by his association with an apostate nun and by other excesses. Their illegitimate son was killed in a riding accident. In the charter recording the *traditio* of Count Dodicho's estate and the immense outlay for the benefit of his soul and future commemoration, his mother gave her consent in the first place as *heres primitiva*, and his brother, Count Sigebodo, assented next. He was not described as an heir and in a gift which he and his wife made to Paderborn about the same time the mother, Hildegunde, once again is called *heres* and consented.[88]

The narrative sources, the diplomata and the few and far between early episcopal and private charters, if they can be so called, contain plenty of evidence that women accumulated, transmitted and alienated predial estate in the tenth century as a matter of course. Thangmar, Henry I's son by his first marriage with Hathui, rose in arms because he had been defrauded of his maternal inheritance.[89] The widow Aeddila, who in 960 transferred four *curtes* to Otto I for the endowment of Hilwartshausen, had received them from the *hereditates* of her dying sons.[90] Three kinsmen, however, had been given their share before the gift was made. A remarkable and rare charter of the year 1003 tells the story of Helmburg and her four daughters. Two of the girls, Aethelwif and Marcswith, had many years ago entered Hilwartshausen while their sisters, Frideburg and Hildeburg, both still alive, belonged to Gandersheim, a hint perhaps of a family connection with the Liudolfings themselves. Sometime in 965 or 966 the four women and their mother Helmburg had been taken to Otto I's court at Grone by Count Adalbero, Bernward of Hildesheim's maternal grandfather. There Helmburg solemnly gave her *predium* in five vills, all situated in the Saxon Hessengau, to Hilwartshausen. Adalbero's presence as protector (*tutor*) and patron was no accident, for his daughter Rothgard, Bernward's aunt, was, as has already been mentioned, abbess there later. He and his kin must have had an interest in the lands and the foundation and belonged to the same family group. Helmburg's daughters, as the 1003 charter averred, could consent the more easily to their mother's munificence because already they all possessed *hereditas* in their own right from other quarters.[91] Already at the time of the *traditio*, then, they were very clearly the beneficiaries of survivorship.

Massive evidence for the extensive inheritances in the possession of noblewomen, including nuns, comes from the *Life of Bishop Meinwerk of Paderborn* and from the surviving *notitiae* of gifts which the *Vita* so often summarizes, for they were the surest source of the author, a twelfth-century monk of Abdinghof. Here women gave their lands to Paderborn in return for *precariae* and rents in money and kind for their sustenance, with the consent of their brothers or other heirs but sometimes even against the wishes and without the agreement of sons. Nuns of neighbouring houses like Geseke and Meinwerk's own sister Azela at Elten made *traditiones* in much the same form as laywomen, through their advocates and with the assent of their own heirs.[92] Moreover, when the bishop's mother, the ill-famed Countess Adela, died after 1021, his sister, the nun at Elten, received her half share of the remaining inheritance in the Low Countries.[93] It is worth noting that Count Dietrich, the elder brother in lay estate, was by then no longer alive. In the diocese of Paderborn also lay most of the huge inheritance which fell to Godesti, the daughter of Duke Bernhard Billung I. It was characteristically fragmented and lay scattered over more than sixty places. She was in addition abbess of Metelen and Herford and, as we shall see, became a foundress in her own right.[94]

Custom thus treated female heirs better than the *Lex Saxonum*, although it was far from uniform over the whole of the huge Saxon stem area, or even within its component regions. The rich harvest of evidence from Meinwerk's circle and connections can be enhanced from the pages of Thietmar. In 1012 Archbishop Walthard of Magdeburg, the son of Erp and Amulrada, knew that he was a dying man. He had two sisters, one also called Amulrada who became the mother of none less than Bishop Suitger of Bamberg, later Pope Clement II (died 1047). The other sister was a nun. From the *Traditiones Corbeienses*, however, we know that Walthard also had brothers, one called Liudolf who has been identified with the count often witnessing land transactions on Bishop Meinwerk's behalf, and another who entered religion at Corvey about the year 1000. Archbishop Walthard, as he felt his end to be drawing near, called his sister Amulrada and reminded her of a former promise: if she succeeded to his inheritance she should give one of his estates at Olvenstedt near Magdeburg to St Maurice, the cathedral church, for the sake of his soul. The sister acknowledged and reaffirmed her obligation and then the archbishop amidst tears said, as Thietmar reports: 'Do this and know for certain that I will not alienate anything else away from you, my sisters.' Here then the two women, the nun and Amulrada who had to be endowed for marriage, appear to have enjoyed a certain preference. Thietmar did not mention the brothers and there were other possible *heredes*, notably the Count Erp who appears frequently as a witness in Bishop Meinwerk's *notitiae*.[95]

It was not uncommon for single women to live in the household and under the protection of a clerical kinsman if they were not placed in a religious house. A tradition, found in the *History of the Bishops of Halberstadt*, related that Bishop Bernhard (923–68) and his sister had an identical vision of twelve starving poor sitting as doomsmen in the heavenly tribunal and so they felt urged to found an almshouse for the perpetual maintenance of twelve poor out of their patrimony, their *jus hereditarium*.[96] The parallel between the shared vision and the shared inheritance is striking. It suggests—and so do the examples of Bishop Meinwerk's and Archbishop Walthard's sisters—close bonds of interest and mutual expectations between noblewomen and their clerical brothers in the partition and devolution of estate, not unlike the legal maxims in the *Landrecht* of the *Sachsenspiegel*. This meant that when a prelate died, outlived by his sister, she stood to gain over his other heirs. It also meant that the lands of women living under the roof of a bishop, their brother, often went to enrich his see, enlarging existing foundations or helping to set up new ones. The tenth century saw a spate of these in all the episcopal sees of the *Reich*.

Enough has been said about the landed wealth which their better chances of survival and custom played into the hands of so many Saxon *dominae*. Yet it is also clear that the position of wealthy unmarried widows was insecure. They had to face the unremitting pressures and challenges of their *co-heredes*—their own and especially their husband's kin who did not acquiesce in their control of so much *predium*, enhanced as it was by dower-rights. Mathilda, Henry I's wife, was not allowed to enjoy peacefully the *curtes* and fortresses which her husband had made over to her in his house-order of 929. When Thietmar of Merseburg's father, Count Siegfried, died in 991, his uncle Margrave Liuthar, who shared in the inheritance, sought to drive out his sister-in-law Kunigunde altogether and she needed the help of the young king Otto III to be restored.[97] The Countess Adela, who certainly lacked neither spirits nor nerve, could not really make much headway in the fight for the inheritance of which she had been thwarted without a husband to act as her advocate.[98] Sometimes a wealthy woman lived under the emperor's special *mund* and needed it, as did Reinhilde of Beichlingen whom Count Werner, Thietmar's cousin, kidnapped in 1014.[99] The time-honoured royal duty to grant merciful protection to widows, solemnly proclaimed in the coronation ritual and the *ordines*, was real and the sermon with this admonition, which Wipo inserted into his account of Conrad II's sacring, no empty generality.[100]

6

The Saxon Nunneries

For a widow with much estate the foundation of a religious house was probably the best security she and her daughters could have against the importunity of their *co-heredes*. Historians have often noted the very large number of religious foundations for women in early medieval Saxony but they do not seem to have felt it necessary to account for this phenomenon. The constitutional arrangements which governed these houses, the immunity and advocacy clauses of their royal diplomata, have been studied in abundance but not the social needs which caused them to be founded and endowed.[1] For the period from 919 to 1024 at least thirty-six communities for noblewomen and *ingenuae* were brought to life and given land.[2] The tenth century here only continued what had already been done by the lay and the nascent clerical aristocracy of the ninth. The new dioceses of Westfalia and Engern led the way, Münster with Nottuln and Freckenhorst, Paderborn with Herford, Neuenheerse and Bödekken, and Minden with Wunstorf and Möllenbeck, to name only some, but the beginnings of renowned East Saxon foundations in the dioceses of Hildesheim and Halberstadt, Wendhausen, Lammspringe and Brunshausen, later moved to Gandersheim, belong to the same period. Their founders, the men and women of the Hessi-clan, Ricdag and the early Liudolfings, shared the ideas and proprietary interests of their Westfalian peers. No other institution of the Christian cult attracted the nobility, its mainstay in ninth-century Saxony, quite so much and took root so quickly. In the Ottonian period, as wealth from tribute, gifts, plunder and silver mining poured into East Saxony and more land in the Slav marches became available quickly, the flow of foundations, beginning with Quedlinburg in 936, rose markedly from about 960 onwards. Their geographical distribution demands attention. A large number of the East Saxon noble kins who shouldered the burdens and earned the rewards of the Ottonian ascendancy were at home in the diocese of Halberstadt where no less than fourteen nunneries rose between 936 and 1025 as against seven houses for men.[3] The figures were equally striking in the neighbouring see of Hildesheim where, out of six institutions set up between 973 and 1022 when Bishop Bernward died, four were intended for women.[4] With the coming of Bishop Godehard, however, a decided turn towards monasteries and collegiate churches can be observed. In the Engern diocese of Minden the tenth century added five nunneries to the two existing ones and not a single house for monks or canons.[5] Only in the see of Hamburg-Bremen and the new dioceses of Magdeburg, Merseburg, Meissen and Zeitz were founders less anxious to establish convents for women.[6] They stretched along many miles of insecure frontiers and two nunneries, Kalbe and Hillersleben, both in the see of Halberstadt, fell victims to the Slav counterblows of 983, having been sited too near the front line of the struggle.[7]

During the tenth and early eleventh centuries the Saxon nobles' and bishops' preference for endowing nunneries rather than houses for men was peculiar to their society. Other Germanic peoples, however, not least of all the Franks and Anglo-Saxons, had responded to conversion and the opportunities of forming communities for unmarried women in much the same way, albeit three centuries earlier. This prompts the question whether there was not some underlying common predicament in the pre-Christian beliefs and make-up of all three peoples to which the endowment of nunneries furnished a welcome and eagerly sought-after solution. Only a brief and speculative answer can be hazarded here. Marriages were costly and the presence of many unbetrothed girls in the houses of Anglo-Saxon, Frankish and Old Saxon nobles threatened their peace. Infanticide was not unknown even among the aristocracy.[8] Unmarried girls were exposed to the incestuous advances of their own kin. The children so begot brought more disorder and confusion to an already sufficiently confused situation in these large family groups. They counted when it came to sharing out scarce goods and landed resources. There was danger also from the intrusion of strangers and worst of all unequals, especially slaves. Savage penalties awaited the latter and the offending women but the former could saddle heads of families with unwanted feuds. There is evidence enough for all these calamities.[9] To read the penitentials of the early middle ages suggests that there was something like an unending promiscuity crisis in the habitations of the laity—noble, free and serf—and not the laity alone.[10] The foundation of religious houses for women shifted the burden of safeguarding and maintaining them within their own caste into another sphere. The new institutions transcended the problems they were meant to solve, with a host of positive new values. They also moved the necessity of punishing intolerable but all too frequent acts from one set of laws and agents towards another, at once exacting and flexible. It was a welcome transfer of responsibility and yet not, for the founders and their heirs, necessarily a loss of power.

The relatively late entry of the Old Saxons into the ambit of the church and their rapid advance to wealth and new lordship in the tenth century set them apart from their neighbours in the East Frankish *Reich*. They also enable us to study the development of their religious preferences much more closely. In the Upper Weser valley, the Thuringian and Hessian areas of the see of Mainz, the Saxon influence can be seen in the foundation of Hilwartshausen, Kaufungen, Wetter and Eschwege, but in the Rhine-Frankish dioceses of the province, in the Lotharingian bishoprics of Cologne, in Constance and in the province of Salzburg, monastic benefactors did not, or did no longer, share this predilection for endowing religious communities for women.[11] Only Augsburg in Suabia, with five nunneries raised between 924 and 1026, seems to be an exception. Moreover, the Saxon interest in founding them declined noticeably from the third decade of the eleventh century onwards and instead pious patronage turned towards the development of canonries and more abbeys for men, and this well before the new monastic reform movements entered Saxony in the wake of the great religious and secular crisis of the 1070s. Not a few of the nunneries founded during the Ottonian period fell on evil days in the twelfth century and invited drastic changes like the introduction of a strict Benedictine rule.[12] More significantly still, a considerable number were handed over by the bishops who controlled them to congregations of reformed monks or had their lands and rights annexed to new foundations for men. At Wimmelburg, a Halberstadt convent founded some time before 1038, this change from a nunnery to an abbey for monks took place within little more than a generation.[13] Kalbe, Schöningen, Hillersleben, Walsrode, Oldenstadt and Vitzenburg ceased to be abodes for the daughters and widows of Saxon nobles and henceforth accommodated canons or monks instead.[14] Kemnade was handed over to Corvey in 1147 and occupied by Benedictines but in 1194 nuns returned. Other convents like Steterburg, Heiningen, Stötterlingenburg and Heeslingen suffered far-reaching changes in their constitution when, during the twelfth century, provosts were thrust upon them who took charge of their ecclesiastical and secular administration.[15] The great spate of early medieval foundations for women in Saxony was thus unique, singular in time and in extent, and this makes it all the more compelling to investigate their origins and the situations that called them into existence.

Many of them were undoubtedly the work of masterful matrons. Already in Carolingian Saxony well-propertied women had been to the fore as foundresses, either alone or in conjunction with their clerical kinsmen.[16] In the tenth century Marcswith, Helmburg and Aeddila, whose *hereditates* and lordly management set up Schildesche, Fischbeck and Hilwartshausen, by no means stood alone. Queen Mathilda herself converted three of the five *civitates* which Henry I had given her in 929 into religious houses and of these, two—Quedlinburg and Nordhausen—were intended for nuns.[17] The two daughters of Count Wichmann the Younger, Friderun and the Countess Imma, as we have seen, took charge of Kemnade where Otto I allowed part of his enemy's estates to go.[18] They had inheritance of their own to add to the endowment. At Heiningen on the Oker, Hildesuit and her daughter Walburgis built a small house and poured their more modest fortune into their foundation.[19] They too may have been kinswomen of the Billungs. In the case of another nunnery, Vitzenburg, in the diocese of Halberstadt, the *narratio* of Otto III's diploma of 991 relates that a noble, called Brun, and his wife Adilint had built a church in their *civitas* Vitzenburg with the consent of their heirs, but the succession to the abbacy was reserved to Adilint's kin only and the advocacy over the house too was to go to the most senior member of the *maternum genus*. Evidently Adilint's *hereditas* formed the base of the endowment and Vitzenburg should be added to the list of houses which owed their existence to the initiative of a wealthy noblewoman.[20] It also furnishes a good example of the separate descent of maternal inheritance. At Steterburg, Friderun, the daughter and heiress of Count Altmann, found shelter as abbess of a small house into which she converted her fortune. Her kinsman, Bishop Bernward of Hildesheim, helped her.[21]

Borghorst, in the diocese of Münster, was founded by a widow, Bertha, in Otto I's time. Her daughter Hathui became, as daughters so often did, the first abbess, but it seems as if Bertha had been married twice, outlived both her husbands and used both their *predia* for the endowment of her nunnery. From the earliest possible date Borghorst in Westfalia had been placed under the protection of the archbishops of Magdeburg but this did not deter Bertha's daughter by her first husband, called Bertheida, from coming forward and claiming her father's inheritance against Archbisop Giselher and the nuns of Borghorst, immediately after her mother's death. Bertheida had sons to back her, though she too seems to have outlived her husband, who took no part in the settlement of the dispute. She won her case handsomely at Otto III's court in 989 and her story bears some resemblance to that of the Countess Adela whose father, Count Wichmann of Hamalant (died shortly after 973), had ignored her claims when he founded Elten for his other daughter, Liudgard.[22]

Of the tenth- and eleventh-century Saxon foundations for women, three owed their institution to the rulers' wives, Queen Mathilda and the Empress Kunigunde. At least nine were set up mainly by noblewomen with the lands of their inheritances and dowers.[23] Moreover, the abbesses of certain very august convents sometimes endowed subsidiary and dependant houses: Mathilda of Quedlinburg (Otto I's daughter) did so at St Andreas Walbeck and on the Münzenburg by Quedlinburg. Gerberga of Gandersheim added St Mary in the upper town to her empire and Sophia of Gandersheim St Cyriacus at Eschwege, which she may have founded before she succeeded Gerberga in 1002. Godesti of Herford raised a satellite endowment, Sancta Maria ad Crucem iuxta Herfordiam, in 1011 after a vision.[24] These subordinate houses served more than one purpose. In the first place they were rather less exclusive than the parent convents to which they remained subject. Some of them, moreover, St Andreas Walbeck, St Mary on the Münzenberg and St Mary at Gandersheim, were vowed to the Benedictine rule and in this way the governing foundations maintained permanent associations with the stricter and more arduous form of the religious life. It was a kind of holiness by proxy comparable to the vicarious piety of the tenth-century lay aristocracy in general. Yet there were also instances of noble ladies in the parent houses renouncing their comforts and converting to the rule of St Benedict in the much more modest endowments of the satellite institutions.[25]

Several houses, including two very distinguished ones, Elten and Gernrode, were founded by fathers who lost their sons prematurely and could therefore hope to be commemorated only in nunneries raised for a daughter or a daughter-in-law. Heeslingen-Zeven is another example. Lastly, it was not uncommon for bishops to use their patrimony at one and the same time on behalf of their church and their kinswomen by setting up a nunnery, which then remained the property of their see and under the perpetual control of their successors. Hadmersleben, Oldenstadt and Stötterlingen-burg are instances in the tenth and eleventh centuries, Nottuln (Münster) and Neuenheerse (Paderborn) in the ninth.[26]

In all these *primordia* the survival of women and the inevitable devolution of inheritances into their keeping played an important part. Now for their sex childbirth was probably the most dangerous hazard to health and life expectations, especially during the first fifteen years of marriage. This is no mere ratiocination but can be seen reflected in an important early eleventh-century source, the second and later *Life of Queen Mathilda*. The author, probably a nun's priest of Nordhausen, wrote just after the critical months of Henry II's advance to the kingship in 1002 and he set himself two tasks. First of all he wanted to legitimize and justify Henry's new dignity by appealing to the merits, the saintliness and therefore also the reputed prophecies of the king's great-grandmother Mathilda, the ancestress which the Bavarian Liudolfings had in common with the three Ottos. But he also wanted to raise the standing and esteem of Nordhausen in the order of the great Ottonian family foundations for women. Nordhausen was the last of Mathilda's religious enterprises and she did not live to see her work completed. It never achieved quite the distinction, the eminence, the nearness to the *stirps regia* of her first foundation, Quedlinburg. The sacral importance of royal tombs, which hallowed the churches where they stood, speaks vividly from the biographer's pages. They came second only to the relics of the saints them-selves and shared some of their religious power.[27] Mathilda, however, could not be buried at Nordhausen for she had to lie next to her husband at Quedlinburg, but the author of the second *vita* sought to make good this flaw in the nunnery's title-deeds and reputation by dwelling long and lovingly on other close connections between the locality and the foundress. There was the place in the church where Otto I had stood at mass before his final leave-taking from his mother, who then returned to kiss it. Above all, Mathilda had twice survived the perils of childbirth at Nordhausen. In his solemn farewell scene between mother and son, the author has his heroine remind the emperor that she had founded the nunnery not least of all in gratitude for her two safe confinements. Otto then once more promised to look after the house and to complete the endowment as his mother wished.[28] In the admittedly late foundation history of Schildesche, the pangs and dangers of childbirth are held up against the blessings of a life in religion. Perhaps it did attract the women, especially the young widows of the aristoc-racy, for this very reason if they had not been vowed to remain unmarried and live in a monastic foundation from the very beginning.[29] At any rate entry into a nunnery, and even the active and busy life of founding and running one, further enhanced the life expectancies of a good many nob-lewomen. Abbesses and their flock stood a sound chance of reaching a very ripe old age and thus the existence of so many foundations for women aggravated the situation which had in good measure brought about their endowment in the first place.

There were, of course, other types of foundations, where brothers and sisters or a whole group of kinsmen joined, for instance Gerbstedt and Drübeck in Halberstadt and Geseke in Westfalia.[30] They served as family mausolea and offered suitable provision and occupations for unmarried girls or widows while the advocacy and lordship remained with a senior kinsman, so that as long as there were heirs the endowment could maintain a certain polarity in ramifying families, a concentration of some lands at least and continuity of possession which checked the perennial partitions and splintering of inheritances. For reasons that will soon be apparent, the remedy often did not work. The internal economy of these houses reflected and underpinned also the order of things outside their walls—the bonds between the founders' kins and their vassals, their hangers-on and friends.

The essential feature and cornerstone of security for all these religious foundations of the nobility in the tenth century was the royal diploma of protection and immunity. Without it the mistresses of the nunneries, whether they became abbesses or simply ruled as proprietresses, could not hope to save their endowments against claims which sooner or later had to be faced. There is a legend in the Annalista Saxo that the brothers of the future Henry I, his *co-heredes*, wanted to strip the family monastery, Gandersheim, of 11,000 *mansus*. Henry, however, did not agree and was rewarded for his patient piety by succeeding to the whole inheritance before long.[31] In 963 Otto II, already an anointed king but under the guidance of his half-brother, Archbishop William of Mainz, confirmed his father's diploma for Hilwartshausen and took the convent into his *mundeburdium* and *defensio*. Hilwartshausen should be as other royal monasteries and it should never be owned or be liable to the kindred or the *pro-heredes* of the two sisters, Berthild and Emma, who were at this moment in charge.[32] Here the function of the royal protection and of becoming an *abbatia regalis* could not be made clearer: it was to banish the claims of kinsmen and to make the alienation of the land to religious uses permanent. The first generation of founders and foundresses usually succeeded in combining their own undiminished *proprietas* and power with the royal *defensio*. The two complemented rather than contradicted one another. Yet with the passing of this generation or the next, the special right and power diminished and dwindled away, especially where only one life stood between the founder's time and heirlessness. When the first abbess of Elten, Liudgard, died, her successor entered, as Otto III's diploma of 996 asserted, 'imperialis nostrae potestatis iure'.[33] Henry II's privilege for Kemnade decreed that the abbey was to be in the possession of Frederun and her sister, the Countess Imma, for as long as they lived. After their deaths, however, it should belong to the king's *ius publicum*.[34] It was the same with the lands and possessions of individual, well-propertied nuns. In the more aristocratic foundations it seems that most of the inmates had ample means of their own so that the common revenues could be used for the upkeep of the church, the services, hospitality and alms. For their time the nuns lived on the comfortable food rents which their *hereditates* or the *precariae* for which they alienated them brought in, and we must see the foundation and first endowment of these abbeys as a long process. Their corporate estate grew slowly as nuns died and their inheritances fell to the convent, if they had not made them over to others and their heirs could be kept at bay. In 958 Otto I bestowed a diploma on Meschede (on the Ruhr, diocese of Cologne) which provided in general that the possessions of deceased abbesses and of their flock should accrue to the house.[35] It could by no means be taken for granted that they would. Nothing shows more clearly the purpose of the royal intervention: it favoured the institution against the *heredes* of its individual members.

Hilwartshausen was not the only house founded by aristocratic survivors and heiresses or for their sake which, with all its endowments, became the king's. Elten and Gernrode from their very beginnings went the same way and so did Fischbeck and Kemnade, although their advocacies belonged to the long-lived Billung dukes. Alsleben (diocese of Halberstadt) came to the Ottonians because the women survivors of the founder, Count Gero, needed their protection, although the counts of Stade had an interest by marriage in the house.[36] In Drübeck and Vreden too the *Reich* had the better of complex and obscure hereditary rights. In 1014 Henry II gave Vreden to Adelheid of Quedlinburg although the church contained Billung family tombs. He also granted Schildesche to Bishop Meinwerk of Paderborn, with much counsel but all the same as if he was free to do so.[37] Altogether the bishops probably gained most by the royal diplomata confirming new foundations and granting them immunity and protection. Houses like Borghorst, Heiningen, Steterburg and Heeslingen were handed over to the lordship and patronage of favoured prelates, not necessarily the diocesans, at the very beginning of their existence. At Heeslingen the counts of Stade sought to assert themselves and Thietmar described how his maternal grandfather, Henry, with Otto I's help, imposed one of his daughters who had been nursed in the house as abbess when she was twelve years old. Archbishop Adaldag of Hamburg-Bremen, who protested then, prevailed in the end and Heeslingen became one of his see's proprietary monasteries. It had been endowed by a Count Hed, who placed it under the *mundeburdium* of the archbishop on condition that his daughter Wendilgard should be the first abbess and he himself *advocatus*. These offices were to be reserved for his kin for as long as suitable candidates within the third degree of affinity could be found in it. Hed, it should be remembered, had no sons. But in the diploma Archbishop Adaldag gained in 986, the very history of the foundation was obscured and we read no more about the count and his daughter. Instead the *narratio* of the diploma asserted that the archbishop's *antecessores* had built Heeslingen. This was ambiguous and could mean either his predecessors or his forbears. Adaldag had ruled Hamburg since 937 and for ten years before that served in Henry I's chapel. By 986 he was very much the sole survivor from the episcopate of Otto I's early years. An octogenarian or almost one, his *antecessores* were remote indeed in either sense. It is probable that the counts of Stade retained at least the advocacy over Heeslingen.[38] The ancient Westfalian houses for women now and again received imperial diplomata confirming their immunities, protection and rights of election and here the diocesans usually stood sponsors to the grants and sought to increase their influence.

In some of the foundations for and by women the lands intended for the endowment were first transferred to the king, who then granted them to the new religious house. This happened at Metelen in 889 and again at Hilwartshausen in 960, so that Otto I himself appeared as the donor in his son's diploma of 963.[39] At Borghorst too a *traditio* to the emperor preceded the transfer of the nunnery into the guardianship of the see of Magdeburg.[40] By switching themselves into the process of endowment, the emperors fulfilled their duty of protecting widows and orphans and furthering the service of God, but it was also very advantageous to them. The acquisition of important nunneries by the Ottonians and the workings of the royal *mundeburdium* in favour of bishops meant that much land was for ever alienated from the founders' *co-heredes*—nobles always in need to increase their patrimonies so that they could set up their own sons and marry at any rate some of their daughters. This did not, of course, follow only from the foundation of houses for women. The monasteries of Helmarshausen, Arneburg (diocese of Halberstadt) and Reepsholt (diocese of Hamburg), the latter however endowed by two sisters, also came into the possession of acquisitive prelates through royal help.[41] In the case of Nienburg on the Saale (diocese of Magdeburg) the Ottonian emperors added so much to the lands and rights of the monks that Henry II could assert an interest in the election of the abbot, although Margrave Gero, the son and nephew of the founders, Archbishop Gero of Cologne and Margrave Thietmar, was alive and active.[42] Yet the losses suffered by the nobles through the endowment of nunneries were the most important. While they have not escaped historians, they have been studied mostly as constitutional developments, aspects of the expanding *Reichskirche* up to the great crisis of reform and the emergence of a new kind of *abbatia libera* which sought to do away with lay proprietorship altogether.[43] The social reality and its implications have been ignored.

The causes of these very considerable dispossessions which the Saxon aristocracy had had to endure lay embedded in the porous subsoil of its own domesticity, the conflicting pressures within kins and, not least, in the advantages women enjoyed as survivors and sharers of inheritances. From a rather unusual charter for the nunnery of Ödingen in Westfalia it appears that the foundress, Gerberga, and her son, Count Hermann of Werl, were well aware of the risks they ran. Both Archbishop Heribert of Cologne and Otto III himself, in whose name the document was drafted, had to acquiesce in clauses with a certain edge against themselves in order to safeguard the advocacy and election of future abbesses for the heirs.[44] The large number and often lavish endowment of nunneries in Ottonian Saxony thus distorted the pattern of landholding and may have played some part in estranging Saxon nobles from their kings, an estrangement first noticeable—as has been said—in Henry II's reign, which became acute in Henry III's.[45] The rapid decline in the number of foundations for women from about 1020 onwards and the decay of many of the existing houses suggest not only that the need for them had been more than satisfied but also that the Saxon princes became somewhat less tolerant of wealthy widows disposing of great inheritances.[46] Instead they forced them to remarry and used their possessions to build up those competitive territorial lordships which the prolonged impotence of the later Salian emperors in Saxony made possible.

Little has been said so far about the mode of life in these religious communities for women, with their *lectio sacra* and *manuum operationes*, their numerous attendant priests and servants. The tenth- and eleventh-century Saxon convents varied greatly in wealth and importance. Some, like Heiningen and Steterburg, had to begin with endowments for only a few nuns, while others, Gernrode and Gerbstedt, were built and enriched with the spoils of the Slav wars won by great margraves and warriors like Gero and Ricdag of Meissen. It was not unusual for lands in the marches and tributary regions beyond the Saale and the Elbe to come into the possession of nunneries.[47] We rarely know the number of *sanctimoniales* even for the better documented houses, at the time of their beginnings and during their early decades. Abbess Gerberga's foundation, St Mary in the upper town of Gandersheim, provided for only thirty Benedictine nuns.[48] Alsleben was intended for thirty-four 'and more', according to Otto II's diploma, and these almost certainly followed the easier ways of the Aachen rule.[49] Essen, Quedlinburg and the parent convent at Gandersheim were somewhat larger and when a Gernrode source of 1275 asserted that the number of prebends there had always been twenty-four 'from the first institution', this information must be treated with caution.[50] We do not know how many *sanctimoniales* entered Gerbstedt when it was founded by Ricdag and his sister Eilsuit in 985, but during the last quarter of the eleventh century, after a reorganization, there were twenty-four. In 1118 Conrad of Wettin, later margrave of Meissen, aided by a reforming bishop, Reinhard of Halberstadt, and a cardinal legate, imposed a strict rule with a *professio*, rigorous enclosure and an Augustinian regular provost. From a late twelfth-century text in the form of a margravial charter, it appears that up to 120 nuns now subsisted on the endowment, which after some losses had been restored but not hugely augmented. Reform here meant, among other things, a more economical use of resources.[51]

In 916 there were sixty-two monks and children at Corvey.[52] It is possible that the most renowned houses for *sanctimoniales*, like Essen, Herford, Quedlinburg and Gandersheim, reached the same figures in all (including their clerks), but the majority were much smaller, although there were many more of them.[53] Great wealth did not necessarily always mean greater numbers. It simply enabled abbesses and their aristocratic flocks to live, build, commission manuscripts and other works of art more lavishly and sumptuously. An eleventh-century abbess of Borghorst, with the founders' family name Bertha, had one of the finest of the later Ottonian processional crosses made for her.[54] It contained two small fatimite crystal flasks which served as reliquaries. At Gernrode, where the founder had deposited an arm of St Cyriacus, Abbess Hathui ordered a new life of the saint to be written. His *patrocinium* had, by the end of the century, prevailed over the original dedication. Gero acquired the relic in Rome on one of his pilgrimages and the cult, which enjoyed a wide vogue in Saxony, found in Gernrode its greatest architectural setting. The *Life of St Cyriacus*, with a prologue addressed to Hathui, was written by an erudite Saxon priest, Nadda, and the warlike career he invented for the saint's father distinctly evoked that of Otto I's margrave. Gernrode, with its surviving pre-Romanesque church, begun c. 960, is thus an imposing monument to the most successful decade of the East Saxon assault upon Sclavania, the period of the most rapid *dilatatio imperii*. The convent also possessed a translation of the Psalter into Old Saxon.[55] For the most part, however, the aristocratic foundations could not match the royal ones in literary and artistic achievement.

The eagerness to found nunneries or allow them to be founded was the response of a very self-protective aristocratic caste to its predicaments, but it was also much more. Noblewomen held a special place in the new religious culture of the German north whether they became *ancillae Dei* and lived canonically or whether they endowed and ruled houses, without taking the veil, or remained mistresses of large households in the lay world. Their good works and prayers were felt to secure the successes of their menfolk, fathers, uncles, brothers, husbands and sons, in this life and they were responsible for the welfare of their souls in the next. The two *Vitae* of Queen Mathilda were as deeply concerned with this duty and its performance as was Thietmar in his *Chronicon*. Mathilda's prayers, pious works, endowments and personal sanctity secured Otto's safe return from his second Italian expedition and by them she expiated Henry I's sins as did Adelheid those of the emperor.[56] According to her biographers, one of the queen-dowager's last acts was to hand over to her grand-daughter, the thirteen-year-old Mathilda of Quedlinburg, a calendar with the names and obits of deceased Saxon lords, and she asked her to commemorate not only herself and Henry but all those whom she used to mention in her prayers.[57] Death thus did not sever the survivors from the departed and, as the young abbess inherited much of her grandmother's monastic empire and other lands, so she also took over her acts of remembrance and intercession for the dead. The *famulatus Dei* of nuns and their patronesses redeemed the necessarily sinful and cruel labours of emperors, dukes, margraves and counts.[58] Of Judith, the wife of Duke Henry of Bavaria, Thietmar wrote that she heard her husband's deathbed confession and made amends for all his sins that she knew or heard others speak of with tears and alms past telling.[59] She ended her days as a *sanctimonialis femina* in Niedermünster (Regensburg). To return to Thietmar's own kin, Godila, before she fell from grace and remarried, did what good she could for the soul of her first husband, Margrave Liuthar. Margrave Werner's wife, Liudgard, fasted in the cold, prayed and gave alms for him rather than for herself. She was, so the bishop wrote, 'the guardian of his life and soul' and this, 'animae . . . custodia', seems to sum up the noblewomen's acknowledged and prescribed religious obligations to whichever *ordo* in this life they belonged.[60] If we then turn to fiction, in the poem *Ruodlieb*, the hero's mother did what she could for Christ's poor, widows, orphans and pilgrims so that she should earn him success.[61]

It is often said that the twelfth century saw the first emancipation of women in our civilization and that they participated in its spiritual movements, whether orthodox or heretical, as never before. This view could be questioned. The piety of the tenth-century Saxon noblewomen fulfilled itself in action, in offices performed, alms given and works done. It was at once lordly and circumscribed but the foundresses, abbesses, nuns and women in general played a more essential role in the early Christian neighbourhoods and family foyers of their recently converted stemland than did their successors in the twelfth century. Nor must we underrate their share in the literary, artistic and architectural creativeness of their—the Ottonian—renaissance.

III Sacral Kingship

It was not without misgivings that I chose the word 'sacral' rather than 'sacred' or 'theocratic' to try to interpret the numenous aura of Ottonian and early Salian kingship. In doing so I followed the usage of many Continental scholars, by no means all fervent partisans of Germanic continuity. The very neutrality of the word offers a passport of access to the insights gained by social anthropologists studying similar problems in very dissimilar societies. Yet some scholars would banish 'sacral' when discussing the ever-public life of a post-Carolingian Christian king, who was to be looked up to as the minister of God, and they would employ it only to describe the pre-Christian vestiges, be they charisma, magic powers or blood-right and suchlike, which may still have adhered to him. The distinction seems to me to be over sharp and even a little wilful for the early middle ages. The sanctity of Queen Edith, Otto's wife, and Queen Mathilda, his mother, as presented by their panegyrists, was also part of their sacrality. To thrust the dead saint king against the living sacral king may mislead us by assuming a spurious clarity where there was often enough confusion.[1] A mysterious power also emanated from the tombs of royal and noble ancestors. The historian must account for these beliefs. He must also account for the aspect of the living ruler exalted to a sphere so near to God which he can still share with the small circle of bishops, clerks, monks and lay princes, who in their day gazed at Otto III's Gospel Book (now in Aachen) or at the figure of Henry II in the centre of a cross throning on his ancestral seat with the Holy Spirit above him.[2] Since this image of kingship became the subject of the most violent European religious and cultural upheaval before the Reformation, we must not allow the battle-cries of the late eleventh and twelfth centuries to deafen us prematurely.

7

The Carolingian Inheritance in Tenth-Century East Francia

In Thietmar of Merseburg's description of the battle at the Lech we read that Otto, after collecting his small army, comforted them thus when they were drawn up for battle: to those who would be slain he held out eternal rewards, to those who won through earthly advantages.[1] To requite service, and especially armed service, was one of the most important functions of early medieval kings and also of later ones. Let us remember how in 793 Charlemagne lavished gold, silver and silks on his bishops and counts merely because they had not taken part in the conspiracy of his son Pippin the previous year.[2] In Thietmar, this secular business of reward is enlarged upon. Here it was the king who consoled his men with the promise of salvation if they fell in the battle against the heathen, not, as was already customary in the ninth century, the popes and the bishops. It is not certain which bishops or indeed whether any bishops fought at the Lech in Otto's host.[3] In Thietmar's narrative, however, there was one present who on St Lawrence's Day, 10 August, gave the king the sacrament; this was St Udalrich of Augsburg, whom we know to have been in his besieged city during the action. In the Ottonian coronation *ordo*, the Mainz Pontifical of *c*. 960, the ruler appears as one who shared the episcopal *ministerium* and also as the mediator between clergy and people. Yet this partnership lay 'in exterioribus'.[4] His was the task of defending the church against its adversaries. Perhaps Thietmar's account of Otto I's exhortations and vows before he joined action with Christianity's most dangerous enemies went no further than that. Before the promise of rewards, he tells us, Otto alone had confessed his sins, as if for all, and had pledged the foundation of a see at Merseburg in honour of St Lawrence if Christ gave him life and victory by the martyr's intercessions.[5]

To the best of my knowledge, this passage has not been noticed for the purpose of studying the long prehistory of the Crusading movement. It introduces us also to the tasks and attributes of early medieval kingship and the ideas by which it had to be sustained. About these neither the writers of the tenth and eleventh centuries nor modern historians could be unanimous and here I do not want to add much to the ever-swelling torrent of literature on this subject. A brief sketch must suffice. The magical and sacral kingship of the migrating Germans was slowly christianized and its sacrality transformed.[6] In this process, the anointing of the Carolingians and the divine grace which they claimed for their rule were decisive steps. The new character which rulers acquired by their sacring and exhibited in their *laudes* and crown-wearings was transmitted to them by the bishops. As Carolingian kings failed to measure up to the tasks which the divine will had entrusted to them, their bishops felt called upon to admonish and harangue them. Whole councils, like that at Paris in 829, and tracts, like Jonas of Orleans's so-called *De Institutione Regia* (the title is d' Achéry's), were filled with this *admonitio* addressed to kings. In these texts it was not his ancestry but God who had given the kingdom to a ruler and he was earnestly asked to remember this and act accordingly. In the writings of Jonas or Hincmar we hear nothing about an inherent sacrality of the Carolingians and they were, if anything, warned against such presumption.[7] Theirs was a *ministerium*, they would be judged for it and their bishops could not preach its duties loudly enough in and out of season. Whether the *clericalis ordo* already stood outside the royal governance, whether the new sacrality of kings had been purchased at the high price of dependence on the episcopate who conferred it, as Professor Ullmann maintains, is another question.[8] The logic of the ritual and its implications must not be pressed too far. At the Synod of Tribur in 895, the emissaries of the bishops as usual lavished their exhortations on King Arnolf, but they also avowed that their churches were committed to him 'per regalem potestatem'. He was their helper but at the same time like a father and lord.[9].

Most of these ideas and their ambiguities about royal power in the *ecclesia* were therefore at home in the East Frankish kingdom towards the end of the ninth century and some of them could be found also in the ambience of the Ottonian and early Salian emperors. In the *ordo* of 960 which, as Carl Erdmann showed, drew on older West Frankish and East Frankish precepts, we see the metropolitan leading the crowned king to his seat and then enjoining upon him that it is his now not just by paternal succession but by the authority of God and this 'our present *traditio*', that is to say, the act of the bishops and the clergy.[10] The exaltation of the king came to entail ever greater expectations of righteousness and imposed gigantic duties. In the imperial Gospel Book at Aachen, Otto III appears crowned by the hand of God and seated in a mandorla normally reserved for the throning Christ. The Gospels, which in the form of a scroll he seems at once to receive and to dispense, represented a form of divine investiture. Nowhere is Christocentric kingship depicted so uncompromisingly as in this painting. The creation and display of such books partly renewed and partly enlarged upon royal coronation ceremonies as did the crown-wearings on feast days. Yet on the opposite page looking towards the enthroned ruler, the donor, the monk Liuthar, is ready with his homily: may God clothe the emperor's heart with this book—the Gospels. Liuthar also expected a reward.[11] Acts of self-humiliation had to accompany and legitimize the king's elevation to the role of Christ's vicar.

The tradition of the episcopal *admonitio* addressed to kings revived. It could take many forms—discreet and personal as was Bernward of Hildesheim's farewell advice to the young Otto III in 1001 not to throw himself headlong into every new enterprise and experience; or more public and pressing as in Brun of Querfurt's letter to Henry II (1008), imploring him to make peace with Boleslas Chrobry and abandon his sinful alliance with the heathen Liutizi. It turned almost into a tract on kingship with the sermon, in the pages of Wipo, which Archbishop Aribo of Mainz is made to deliver to Conrad II before his sacring.[12] It could rise to something like constitutional opposition in a situation of crisis and fear, as in the letter of Archbishop Werner of Magdeburg addressed to his episcopal colleagues in the royal camp after the battle of Homburg (9 June 1075), to which Brun gave such prominence in his *Book of the Saxon War*.[13] The bishops by the victor's side, Henry IV's men, were reminded that they possessed the *familiaritas regis*. It was a divine gift which they must use on behalf of those who needed help, here of course in the first place Archbishop Werner himself who had fought in arms against his royal lord. They must remind Henry that he stood in the place and bore the name of the king of Heaven who, in the Evangelist's words, came not to judge the world but to save it. For the sake of his own salvation, then, Henry should begin at last to imitate Christ by his deeds. Defeat had not intimidated Archbishop Werner's letter writer. His sharp polemic, however, stood within the tradition of sacral Christian kingship.[14] Kings were not infrequently reminded that there was a gulf between their sinful humanity and their character as the Lord's ordained representative on earth. Some of them, like Otto I, as we have seen, and Henry III, before and after their battles, professed and acted out this awareness.[15]

All the same, however, the ideas of the ninth century carried a very different inflexion in the Saxon and Salian *Reich*. Its kings were not failing like the later Carolingians; on the contrary, they rebuilt with interest what the crisis of the later ninth and early tenth centuries had destroyed. If Jonas of Orleans and Hincmar would fortify kings against all lay challengers but by that very act make them more answerable to their bishops' exhortations, the Ottonians and Salians were clearly understood to be masters of their prelates and this not only *de facto*, without title. In Thietmar of Merseburg, kings stood in the place of God whereas the bishops were by Christ's will *terrae principes*. It was therefore right that they and they alone should rule over their bishops and be able to appoint them, as against any other lay lord. Thietmar's concept, that kings stood in God's place and bishops in Christ's, was not new for this note had already been struck by Cathwulf in earlier Carolingian times (775).[16] In the more recent of the two *Lives* of Queen Mathilda (1002–3), the author addressed and congratulated Henry II, who was then still gathering belated adherences to his kingship and also facing his first trials. The biographer characteristically coupled his good wishes with an exhortation. He prayed that God's grace should be with Henry always and make him the epitome of justice 'to govern and rule the church faithfully'.[17] He did not think that to rule (*regere*) applied only to the *populus*. Brun of Querfurt wanted Henry II to be 'the pious and strict director of the church'.[18] When Abbot Ekbert of Tegernsee (1046–8) wrote to Henry III to win his goodwill and help—a famine and sterility had struck the estates—he called him 'governor of monks' and 'caput ecclesiae'. Abbot Siegfried, his successor, wrote in even greater alarm because a rumour of threatened subinfeudation had reached the monks, and here the emperor is addressed thus: 'you whom God has delegated as his *vicarius* in the church.'[19] On the ivory situla at Aachen, an emperor, Otto III or Henry II, is shown sitting to the left of St Peter, the Pope to his right, but the two archbishops and bishops and the abbot stand. In the sacramentary which Henry II gave to his foundation, Bamberg, he is crowned by Christ, invested with the Holy Lance and a sword by two angels and supported by two saint bishops, St Emmeram of Regensburg and St Udalrich of Augsburg.[20]

If the sacrosanctity of kings still came to them through the anointing and coronation performed by their archbishops—and we may ask whether it only came from that source—it sat more firmly upon them and made them more rather than less commanding with these very men. The voice of Anselm of Liège, who had his hero, Bishop Wazo, defy the emperor and attack the force and worth of his anointing, was as yet unusual in the circle to which he belonged, that of the cathedral clergy.[21] In the *Lives* of tenth- and eleventh-century bishops the emperor is always the *dominus* or *senior* even if the prelate had once been his *magister* and tutor. The third Otto, Henry II and the Salians often became canons in their cathedrals and royal collegiate churches like Charlemagne's foundation at Aachen. They made themselves thoroughly at home in the *Reichskirche* and were really its centre giving it what solidarity it possessed.[22]

We can and do dispute about the meaning of all these manifestations of early and high medieval kingship, but they do not exhaust our subject. For it is thought by a formidable body of scholars that they coexisted with the much older, archetypal and magical components of sacrality. This kind of kingship, or at least elements of it, were not dissolved by Christianity; on the contrary, they lived on to contaminate and compromise the new religion. Sacrality here stands for the charisma of the royal kin and its ancestry, the immanent magic force in kings from which their peoples—and not only Germanic ones—expected to derive their well-being and prosperity. We are moving towards the magnetic fields of the *Golden Bough* and Georges Dumezil. The king has it in him to give victory in war, good harvests, good weather and health. Even Alcuin can be called upon to testify to the enduring vitality of these beliefs. In a famous letter to a Northumbrian king he wrote: 'We read that the king's goodness equals the welfare of the whole people, victory of the host, mild climate, fertility, male offspring and health.'[23] Alcuin wanted to inculcate the qualities and self-restraints by which kings and their *ministri* might earn their salvation but he also knew what would make his audience listen. Even so the passage must not be read too far away from the homilies surrounding it.

Should the royal charisma fail—I cite Walter Schlesinger—'then all human efforts are in vain', and in later Scandinavian sources, as in Ammianus Marcellinus writing about fifth-century Burgundian kings, we read of luckless rulers being sacrificed or at least deposed.[24] Evidence for the enduring

reality of such beliefs has been found by the advocates of Germanic continuity in many tenth- and eleventh-century sources, in Widukind of Corvey
especially and his justification for the transfer of the kingship from the
Frankish Conradines to the Saxon Henry I. The dying Conrad I pronounces
his own family's want of *fortuna* and *mores*. These have passed to the Saxons
and their duke, and Widukind also endowed Henry's forbears with kingly
charisma so that he did not lack bloodright. Here he followed Einhard.
Einhard had poured scorn and ridicule on the long hair and ox-carts of the
last Merowingian but it was power, wealth, innate *virtus* and ancestry which
had made the Carolingians true kings, in the eyes of Charlemagne's biographer. He had nothing to say about anointing.[25]

Undertones of an archaic sacrality have also been noted in the feasts and
triumphs which followed Henry's and Otto's victories over the Magyars,
although Widukind was not slow to describe also their thanksgiving to God
by gifts to the churches and to the poor.[26] Nor is this all. The cult of some
surpassing ancestor, the deeply felt need to sanctify men and women of a
regal or princely family, the foundation of lordship on the memory of some
outstanding achievement, all these are met with in the historical and bio-
graphical literature of the early middle ages, not only in Einhard and
Widukind but also in the *Lives* of Queen Mathilda and in Wipo. It is true that
the identification of these themes often presents some difficulty, since
Widukind and Wipo drew on Sallust and the language of Roman public life
when they wrote about war and the secular polity, and we cannot always be
certain when or even whether they were transcribing age-old native traditions about kings into the idiom of classical Rome. Even Widukind's *fortuna
et mores* were taken from Sallust.[27] To complete this brief survey, the
scholars who have laid the most stress on the enduring force of charisma and
magic in kingship have thought that it was especially potent and always to be
reckoned with in the beliefs and attitudes of the subject rural population.[28]
Lastly, it is important to note that some scholars, especially Frantisek Grauss
and the East German, W. Baetke, have been very sceptical about the
existence of sacral kings descended from the gods among German peoples
before their conversion. It followed that any magic they possessed later
could not have stemmed from these origins.[29]

Now, whatever importance we attach to either the one or the other form
of sacrality in post-Carolingian kings, or a mixture of them both, we know of
it mainly through literary sources, liturgical texts, the *arengae* of diplomata,
insignia and the visual arts. How this sacrality acted in society and what its
functions were are questions more often deliberately evaded than asked.
The German scholar, Helmut Beumann, who broke away so decisively from
a purely positivistic assessment of early medieval historiography, met this
reproach by arguing with some ingenuity that historical writing in the middle
ages was after all itself a piece and part of medieval history. The historians,
let us say Einhard or Widukind of Corvey, 'wanted to engage in political
life', whatever that meant in their time and circumstances. 'We must
assume', he wrote, 'that the spiritual forces which we meet in this historiography, not only guided the author's pen but also influenced the course of

events.'[30] But how did they do this and should we rest content with the mere presupposition? The historical effectiveness of kingship, he reasoned, depended on the ideas contemporaries entertained about it.[31] Yet it is only too easy and very questionable indeed to mistake these ideas for the effects themselves. It is therefore necessary to try to trace the imprint of sacral kingship on society and to do so—it must be said—with much the same sources. The question to be tabled is this: what impression did the exalted and quasi-numenous image of the king make on those whose conduct it was meant to govern or at least influence? What did nobles or lesser men think of the *unctus domini* walking under the crown or rather, lest we should once again study only the relationship of ideas, how can we reconcile the awe-inspiring role which liturgy, architecture, art and the festive prose and verse of historical panegyric created for kings with their day-to-day struggles, their evident insecurity and the self-confidence of their enemies?

It may be objected that these questions were raised and in a large measure answered many years ago by Fritz Kern in a book of which the English title, *Kingship and Law*, conceals rather than unfolds the subject. 'Divine Grace and the Right of Resistance' was the theme of this fundamental study. Kern, however, for all his profound and wide insights, forced an anachronistic and speculative concept of state power, state consciousness and positive law on to the history of the German peoples of the earlier middle ages.[32] He wanted to classify and analyse legal and theocratic ideas rather than expose their infinite malleability in action. He laid down the distinction between the Germanic sacral and the Christian ministerial conception of kingship and he also distinguished between a Germanic and an ecclesiastical right of resistance. Much of this has remained common ground or at least the instinctive starting point for criticism. Kern's approach, legal and constitutional rather than strictly historical, compelled him to admit that it was often difficult to distinguish between different kinds and different aspects of revolt or to find the legal norms he postulated in a given situation. The end result of his distinctions was schematic. It did not matter to him whether the sources he used to demonstrate facets of kingship, or opposition to it, ranged from the Visigothic kingdom of Spain to the high and later middle ages.[33] On the whole he saw the 140 years from the arrival of the Liudolfings to the death of Henry III more as a trough between the papal and episcopal claims of the ninth century and the 'great turning point of Gregory VII', than as a distinctive and formative age.[34] Ottonian and Salian royal theology was not yet understood as a growing and changing body of ideas and habits. Last but not least, throughout this seminal book the two opposites, kingship by divine grace and the right of resistance, rest on themselves as fundamental, given immanencies. Their incompatibility was irreducible so that the medieval polity seemed to be governed chiefly by contradictions. If this is so, the question of what the function of the numenous face of kingship really was in the century and a half before the papal assault becomes even more pressing. It must also be asked whether the contradictions themselves remained the same throughout and whether the papacy must bear the lion's share of responsibility for the crisis of kingship in the *Reich*.

8

The Ottonians as Sacral Kings

In August 1073 the East Saxon princes with few exceptions rose against their lord, Henry IV, and advanced on the Harzburg with their forces. They hoped to corner him there and force him to concede their demands. The king prepared his escape while he had negotiations conducted by some of the bishops in his company and Berthold of Zähringen. On the night of 9 August he fled. According to one source, the Annals of Niederaltaich, he was ambushed by Otto of Northeim, who had a much larger number of men with him. But Otto, so the annalist wrote, did not presume to join battle with Henry, who had recognized him.[1] Why not? Was it the reverence which even enemies owed to their king, or calculation? It is important to remember that Henry and Otto could come to terms once more after the general surrender of the Saxon lords in the autumn of 1075. Otto was then entrusted with the management of the king's business in Saxony until the time came for him to change sides once more, under threats, if we are to believe Lampert of Hersfeld.[2] In 1081 only a miraculous fall from his horse prevented him crossing camps again and withdrawing from the planned election of Hermann of Salm.[3] Otto's position was ambiguous. He had been deposed from his Bavarian *ducatus* by Henry IV, but Welf IV who received it in his place not only gained by his downfall but also sent home his daughter whom he had married. The former duke's best chances of restitution and revenge may have been through the king. We do not know. The other sources for Henry's flight from the Harzburg make no mention of this nocturnal encounter but the Altaich annalist had a certain interest in Otto of Northeim, who for a time possessed the abbey as a *beneficium*. Later, Henry's enemies lost all reverence for him but we know that some of them, towards the close of the negotiations at Tribur in 1076, had a bad conscience because they had not been to see and greet him.[4] The answer to the question, why Otto failed to use his chance, must remain uncertain and this uncertainty hangs about the interpretation of a good many other examples. Let it be mentioned in passing that kings were sometimes described as having a very special gaze. Widukind wrote of Otto I's fiery glowing eyes which sent forth a gleam like a flash of lightning.[5]

The sacrality of kings was a complex phenomenon and its development and transformations did not follow a straightforward course. If in the ninth century it seemed to give way to the churchmen's ideas of kingship as a *ministerium*, the collapse of the Carolingian *Reich* perhaps gave it new life in the East Frankish regions. The loss of many useful connections between the highly developed old-Carolingian and West Frankish centres of culture and the underdeveloped eastern frontier may have prevented the rapid spread of such ideas in Saxony, which lay far away from the itinerary and normal resorts of even the East Frankish kings in the ninth century. These older and richer centres had been attacked, plundered and ravaged, many of them several times. Three Saxon bishops attended the Council of Mainz in 888 and all of them came to the Council of Tribur in 895 but none took part in the Synod of Hohenaltheim in 916, with its Pseudo-Isidorian background and bold attempts to defend both the king and the episcopate against treacherous attacks.[6] Without spiritual and material support from the west, the East Saxon churches remained obscure outposts of Christianity. The Ottonian kings rose at a time of military and cultural crisis in East Francia, which they gradually mastered, but they had to create and propagate their own sacrality in the process, whether it meant a more charismatic interpretation of divine grace or the renewal of West Frankish ecclesiastical traditions. This could not be done only with the help of historiography and panegyric, for both of these were, after all, backward looking. None of the greater Ottonian histories—Liudprand's *Antapodosis*, Widukind's *Res Gestae Saxonicae*, Adalbert's *Continuatio* of Regino of Prüm, Ruotger's *Life of Brun*, Hrotsvitha of Gandershaim's *Gesta Ottonis* or the first of the two biographies of Queen Mathilda—were written before 955 and most of them not before 962. In the *Miracles of St Wigbert*, a Hersfeld work of *c.* 936, we don't hear anything about Henry I's divine election or his innate *virtus*.[7] Neither his orders to build fortresses nor his support for a land-hungry *advocatus* secured him the goodwill of Hersfeld's saint.

Certainly the Ottonian historians played a part in the sacral ascent of the *stirps regia*. They interpreted the historical process as a manifestation of divine justice and in it successful kings were bearers of the divine will. Whatever constitutional historians have made of Otto I's struggles for his kingship between 937 and 941 and again in the crisis of 953–5, writers like Hrotsvitha, Widukind and Liudprand were unanimous in their response to the lucky outcome of these near disasters. Otto I was the 'potestas a Deo ordinata' saved again and again from his scheming and murderous enemies. Hrotsvitha declaimed how often God had preserved Otto and this in turn was a sign that he ruled by right as against anyone else.[8] To Liudprand, the victory which a small band of Otto's mounted warriors won over his brother Henry and Duke Giselbert of Lotharingia at Birten in 939 was a lesson to strengthen the faith of the weak. Here he made much of the victory-working power of the Holy Lance before which Otto had prayed when cut off from his men.[9] Widukind professed that it was above him to unfold the reasons for the great defection from Otto I at this time but, when some of the king's enemies, the Conradines, fell out among themselves in 938, it was again

God's will, 'Deo omnia ordinante'.[10] This mattered more than any 'political' explanation and the three writers were not interested in the secular reasons for Otto's survival and success. The *ordinatio Dei* dwelt not only in the person of the elect but also in events which helped his cause. Again when Duke Conrad of Lotharingia and Archbishop Frederick of Mainz abandoned Liudolf and his rising in 954 they joined 'God and the king'.[11] What is startling here and cannot be ignored is that this interpretation was shared by writers so different from one another as Hrotsvitha, Widukind and Liudprand.

It was given to Ottonian kings more than to ordinary men to feel the nearness of God and to interpret his purposes. If they had visions they had to be respected, however strange the result. There is a story in Thietmar of Merseburg that Otto I, having heard of an episcopal vacancy at Regensburg (940), went there and was warned in his sleep that he must give the see to the first person he met next day. Early in the morning Otto went with a small following to the monastery of St Emmeram and, of course, the first person he encountered was the monk porter, Gunther, who let him in. The monks had not expected his visit. Otto greeted the venerable *custos* and then asked him: 'Brother, what will you give me for the bishopric?' The old man must have thought he was joking and replied: 'My shoes'. Bishop, however, he became, by the advice of the clergy and people after Otto had explained his dream.[12] Now in Thietmar's story, Gunther was not as improbable and accidental a candidate for the see as the anecdote suggests. His brief episcopate had been prophesied by his predecessor Bishop Isingrim (930–40) and this form of legitimation or indeed designation was not at all unusual in the tenth century. Gunther was thus the God-willed successor and Thietmar told the light-hearted incident only to say something important about Otto I's regime. Heaven often revealed to the emperor what it wished to see done. The direct divine inspiration of his rule could scarcely be proclaimed in more forthright words. There was something miraculous rather than frivolous about this story.

How did the Ottonians create this spiritual power for themselves or how did it grow side by side with their following, their lands, their booty and ability to reward? Anointing alone cannot account for its character. Here a few passages in Widukind, which have hitherto not been looked at from this point of view, can help. In two places he spoke of the *regalis disciplina* and the *timor regalis disciplinae* which surrounded Henry I and Otto the Great.[13] Their *comitatus* had as yet to learn the distance which set a king apart from his warriors as against that between any other lord and his. He also pointed to Queen Mathilda who, for all her cares for the poor and redemptive piety, never forgot her regal dignity. What the author of the earlier *Vita Mathildis* criticized—her splendid attire—Widukind very deliberately praised.[14] More striking still is the personal inviolability and immunity of the Liudolfing family circle, despite all the crises and rebellions within it. Here the first two Ottos differed markedly from the Carolingians. Charlemagne, as has recently been shown, dealt ruthlessly with his nephews, his brother Karlmann's family, when they fell into his power and he barely spared the life of his son Pippin the Hunchback after the discovery of his plot in 792.[15] Pippin was thrust into Prüm, the family monastery. The year of his death, 811, coincided oddly with that of his half-brother and erstwhile rival, Karl. The *Divisio regnorum* of 806 contained a clause commanding the emperor's sons not to kill, mutilate, blind or cause to be tonsured against their will any of their nephews without a just investigation and hearing.[16] Louis the Pious did not break the letter, and perhaps not even the spirit, of this precept when he allowed his nephew Bernhard to be blinded in 818. By contrast, Liudolf and Conrad the Red (Otto's son-in-law) fared much better after their prolonged and very dangerous rising in 953–4. They lost their duchies but Conrad kept his patrimony and Frankish vassals.[17] For a short time after his submission late in 954, Liudolf may have been less fortunate but he regained his father's grace and soon also the goodwill of his uncle, Archbishop Brun. By the autumn of 955 he was campaigning with Otto against a coalition of Slav peoples in Mecklenburg. It seems that he still had his band of warlike followers when he was sent against Berengar II of Italy in 956, the very men whom he had not wanted to abandon to his father's anger.[18]

Widukind treated the clash, between Liudolf and Conrad on one side and the king and his brother Henry on the other, as a tragic conflict. He has Otto display a certain helplessness outside Mainz in 953 when Liudolf offered to submit. He could not nor did he know how to punish his son, whom Widukind certainly did not think blameless.[19] The war now broke out in earnest because Otto characteristically demanded that Liudolf and Conrad must surrender their noble followers and advisers, which the obligations of lordship forbade them to do. It could be argued that Liudolf was at this time still the king's only adult son and fit successor. There is however the even more startling impunity of his brother Henry, who suffered, as we saw, only a few months' custody for his fratricidal onslaught in 941. According to Beumann this betrays Otto's strong family feeling in a modern sense.[20] Now Otto had, as has been shown, many reasons for sparing Henry but one of them almost certainly was the necessity not to impair the royal dignity in his brother, although the latter was not and could not be king. Moreover, even as an enemy Henry brought to the Liudolfings important and valuable connections and channelled the activities of other enemies.

That all the sons of Henry I and Mathilda were to be thought of as men possessed of charisma is confirmed by a panegyrical hyperbole in Ruotger's *Life of Brun*. From the late ninth century onwards the Liudolfings had gained influential contacts in Lower Lotharingia and they were anxious to maintain these after their advance to kingship. In 929, when only four years old, Brun was sent by his father to Bishop Balderich of Utrecht to be brought up as a clerk. Utrecht had suffered badly at the hands of the Danes but the mere presence of the child was seen as a means to rebuild the shattered and dilapidated see. Though he was as yet unknowing ('inscius'), the *populus christianus* were through him freed from their worst enemies. The Viking raids ceased. Ruotger wrote the *Life* of the archbishop between 967 and 969 when Brun had died but Bishop Balderich was still alive and ruling his diocese.[21] Already Liudprand in his *Antapodosis*, written between 958 and

963, had picked up the Ottonian house tradition that Henry I had sent Brun to serve in the church of Utrecht for the sake of its restoration.²² We can here follow the growth of a sacral legend to fill the gap left by Brun's death in 965 and to strengthen the next generation of Ottonian rulers.

There remains the death of Thangmar, Otto's half-brother, who was killed in the chapel of the Eresburg after divesting himself of his golden necklace as a sign of surrender. The *miles* who struck him down from behind also seized the gold from the altar as booty. Thangmar was the son of a king but by a repudiated wife and, at the time of his birth (before 909), Henry had not yet succeeded even to his paternal inheritance. Although the oldest, he could not hope to rank equal with Otto, the first born of the marriage with Mathilda, but he held an important frontier command against the Slavs. His position in the Liudolfing family, seen as an aspiring *stirps regia*, faintly resembled that of Pippin the Hunchback in Charlemagne's house. He had to reckon not only with his exclusion from kingship, a lot he shared with his junior half-brothers, Henry and Brun, but also with being placed behind them after his father's death in 936. Within less than two years Thangmar became the relentless enemy of Mathilda's offspring, who dragged the young Henry captive in fetters 'like a wretched slave', yet even so Otto had to show that he was outraged by the sacrilegious killing in the chapel.²³ Widukind, who wrote so heroic and, for the Ottonians, almost embarrassing an account of the death, has the king speak a few words in his half-brother's praise. Yet it was done mainly to illustrate the theme of Otto's clemency and later the Corvey historian set off these few words against the long lament of Otto's own following on the night of 7 May 973, when they heard their lord had died.²⁴ For a mere *miles* to slay a royal kinsman and prince treacherously and then take the jewellery which expressed his rank was an enormity in itself which should have been punished there and then. A huge social gulf stretched between the killer and his victim. Whether the inviolability of Thangmar's person, even as an enemy, went any further is not clear.²⁵ His name appears in the great *necrologium* of Merseburg of the early eleventh century, into which Thietmar himself entered a few memorials.²⁶ In the *Chronicon*, moreover, Otto is reported to have avenged his half-brother, although Meginzo, the slayer, was but one of the casualties of the fight at Birten in 939.²⁷ Thangmar's personal circumstances are unknown—whether he was married and to whom and if any offspring survived him. It seems as if the sacrality which came to enfold the Ottonians, living and dead, left him out. Its very existence, however, must not be taken for granted too soon.

The acquisition of relics was already in Merowingian times a means to strengthen aristocratic lordship and to sanctify also the donors.²⁸ With the help of these wonder-working pledges (*pignora*) which assured the presence of the saints, aristocratic foundations could become important religious centres and they gave their fluctuating noble founding kins a chance to consolidate round their sanctuary. The shrines also bound the surrounding rural population more closely to their lords' power. The Saxon nobility in the ninth century learned of these advantages from its Frankish teachers. The Ottonians in the tenth developed their royal authority in their own *patria* not least of all by lavish gifts of relics. With the acquisition of the Holy Lance and the relics of St Maurice, a cult common to the whole kingdom, but located mainly in its new Saxon centre of gravity and the itinerant court chapel, seems to have been planned.[29] Now it is characteristic of rising dynasties in this period that they sought to acquire and make the *virtus* of especially exalted and martial saints their own—saints who would enhance the belief in the divine vocation of their clients and, above all, those that transmitted powers of victory. The possession of such relics encouraged and persuaded a king's military following to chance their future on his *imperium* and take risks for his sake. They, as it were, enhanced his political credit. Not only the Liudolfings but also the kings of Wessex and, imitating the emperors, the Arpads and the Piasts can be shown to have desired and possessed holy lances with their warlike associations.[30] The relics Otto I caused to be translated to Saxony must be compared with those King Athelstan received from Hugh the Great in 926, together with many other presents, when the duke sought the hand of one of his sisters in marriage. Among them was a sword of Constantine with a nail of the Cross, a lance of Charlemagne's and a banner of St Maurice. William of Malmesbury is our source for this transfer of a Carolingian hoard to the king of Wessex but he had a tenth-century panegyric to draw on and there were Athelstan's gifts to his own monastery to cite in support.[31] William's story and the poem behind it must be studied minutely, not only by art historians and the students of early medieval piety. For Athelstan's gain of these Carolingian relics and much other Carolingian treasure besides shows him on the way to becoming an imperial ruler well before the Ottonians, and one interested, moreover, in the same Christian warrior saint, St Maurice.

Here we must pause and note that, while Henry I, Otto and Athelstan found the transfer of relics to their kingdoms useful, Hugh the Great and Rudolf of Burgundy, who sold the Holy Lance to the Saxon king, did not mind letting them go. Liudprand of Cremona, who is our sole source for the acquisition of the lance, had of course to make it appear that Rudolf was unwilling or at any rate very reluctant to part with it.[32] Relics often changed functions, designations and interest when they changed hands and it is possible that among the return presents Hugh the Great received from Athelstan there were also relics. Later, Ottonian envoys to the court of Wessex brought the cult of St Ursula back with them from England.[33] All the same, it seems as if the expanding and aggressive aristocratic societies round the Liudolfings and Alfred's successors were more interested and influenced by these imported cults than the princes of Francia, fighting their long wars of attrition with the last Carolingians. Liudprand leaves us in no doubt that the possession of the lance was seen as a sign of divine favour and a guarantee of perpetual victory.

For the later Ottonians there is some evidence to prove, albeit not unambiguously, that their enhanced sacrality and charisma were real. Already as a six-year-old boy, Otto III was made to take the field against the Slavs of Lusatia. He can hardly have led his host but his presence gave it cohesion as only that of a king could. We are reminded of his grand-uncle Brun being sent to Utrecht at the age of four and the miraculous benefits which were later said to have attended his coming. It must be mentioned at once that the young Otto III's nominal leadership also ensured the participation and homage of Duke Miesco of Poland.[34] The same purpose, to make possible Duke Henry of Bavaria's and Duke Boleslas of Bohemia's suit of host, explains Otto's presence in the Slav campaign of 992, two years before his majority. This time the Polish duke, Miesco's successor, Boleslas Chrobry, did not come but he sent his contingents.[35] It was the young king's personal attendance, not the fidelity owed to him in principle, that bound these dangerous and powerful men to the Saxon army attempting to regain Brandenburg and some of the other Slav tribute lands lost in 983.

A more revealing hint for the charismatic functions of the Liudolfings can be pieced together from the evidence of the Quedlinburg Annals which were begun *c*. 1007–8 or a little earlier.[36] Under the year 995 they reported that the Princess Adelheid, Otto III's sister, already aged eighteen, entered the convent and was blessed in by Bishop Hildiward of Halberstadt in the presence of her brother and two archbishops. 'For the love of God' she spurned kings, princes and their courting messages, promising her treasures, mountains of gold and castles. Whether this was really her own decision must remain an open question. The annalist recorded that 994 and 995 had been disastrous years for Eastern Saxony. After a very harsh winter, which lasted into early May, there were more cold winds and a frost as late as 7 July. A severe drought and water shortage followed, ponds dried up, meadows and crops were scorched. The climatic abnormalities in turn caused local famines, outbreaks of disease and cattle plague. The East Elbian Slavs immediately exploited the sudden dislocation of their Saxon enemies in order to defect. Their own economy may have been less vulnerable to this particular combination of mishaps or perhaps they were spared. In June also the Danish pirates raided the Lower Elbe with calamitous consequences for the counts of Stade, Thietmar's maternal uncles.[37] The next year, the Quedlinburg annalist commented, was even worse, with a pestilence emptying whole villages, a more widespread famine and in its wake Slav incursions.[38] It is quite possible that Adelheid's entry to the canonical life at this time (October 995) could be seen and was intended to be seen as a propitiatory offering, a sacrifice in a Christian form. If her future had been decided at birth, it is odd that her vows were so long delayed. It must be recalled that her sister Sophia, who was nurtured at Gandersheim, had taken the veil there some years earlier, most probably in 987 when she had reached the canonical minimum age of twelve.[39] Mathilda of Quedlinburg and Hathui of Heeslingen had been no older—Mathilda of Quedlinburg was in her twelfth year—when they were not only blessed in but also made abbesses. Adelheid, who was already or very nearly eighteen, in the annalist's words, vowed herself to Quedlinburg's patron saints, St Dionysius and St Servatius, 'pro patria'. Her presence was meant to ensure better times, continuity, stability and peace. We must beware of being too sceptical about the ideas behind her conversion, although the Quedlinburg author had obvious reasons for dwelling on them. Writing about Theophanu's daughters, Thietmar used a more conventional but distantly related image. He saw their entry into religion as the empress's tithe offering to God.[40]

All these are nuances and inferences, rarely free from ambiguities. If we wish to answer the question how the Ottonians built up the representation of their kingship as something God-given, sacrosanct and awe-demanding, we must turn to the great churches and *palatia* they caused to be built of stone and mortar, especially in Saxony. By the end of the tenth century they commanded an imposing array of edifices to display the celestial drama of their royalty to assemblies of princes, lesser vassals and the crowd. Even Henry I did not only raise fortifications against Magyar raids. The evidence for building activities, new structures and decorations from literary sources, diplomata and papal privileges is for once backed by archaeology and surviving remains.[41] It is not possible to follow the evolution of the royal ritual, the festival coronations, processions and banquets in detail. We do not know, for instance, how Otto I kept Easter at Quedlinburg in 941 without diminishing anything of the *decus maiestatis regiae*, though well aware of a plot against his life.[42] He almost certainly wore his crown. The study of the tenth-century Ottonians' itinerary has shown, however, a certain fixity of habits and preference for keeping the great feasts at the same places in Saxony, Lotharingia and Francia wherever they happened to be. When they were in Saxony the Liudolfing rulers, beginning with Henry I, usually wanted to celebrate Easter at Quedlinburg. Palm Sunday was often spent at Magdeburg and probably also the feast of St Maurice (22 September), Otto I's patron saint. Their Christmas courts were less important but Pöhlde and Dornburg may have accommodated them at that season.[43]

This formality was a new development and became part of the kings' legitimation. The later Ottonians were anxious to spend especially the first Palm Sunday of their reigns at Magdeburg and their first Easter at Quedlinburg, where they were near the tombs of Otto I, Henry I and Mathilda. It was like a sacral family reunion. When Henry the Wrangler attempted to wrest the kingship from his cousin, the infant Otto III, in 984, he duly visited Magdeburg on Palm Sunday and then went to Quedlinburg for Easter. There his followers in the Saxon nobility called him king and *laudes* were sung to him. Two years later Otto III kept Easter at Quedlinburg, where four dukes, including Henry, now served him at his banquet after the procession from the abbey church on the hill.[44] The succession crisis was clearly over. To reassure the Saxon lords and make it appear that there was no break, Henry II too spent his first Palm Sunday (1003) at Magdeburg and then came to Quedlinburg for Easter 'more avorum atavorumque priorum regum'.[45]

The massive foundations and buildings of Otto I and his mother Mathilda were decisive in forming the new habits of representation. At Magdeburg he raised the monastic church which then became the cathedral. Pope John XIII in his bull of 967 described it as 'mire magnitudinis ecclesia' and Otto also filled it with imported relics, marble columns and other treasures.[46] It is ironical that he enjoyed the full splendours of his work only once, at his last visit on Palm Sunday 973. Quedlinburg, the Easter centre, was built up especially by Henry I's widow who, in the words of the annalist, wanted it to be a 'regnum gentibus'.[47] Massive agrarian resources, labour as well as tribute from Sclavania, were concentrated in and round these sacral buildings with their royal tombs. Crown wearings and festival coronations were elaborate rituals which demanded as a rule two churches and a great hall. In creating the imposing setting for these occasions and the large assemblies which attended them in their *palatia* and new bishoprics, the Ottonians also created their own masterful and transcendent conception of their kingship.

Genealogical table:
The Liudolfing Posterity, 850–c. 1025

In building up a genealogical table of Liudolfing posterity over six generations, beginning with the ninth-century Count Liudolf and his long-lived wife, Oda, the founders of Gandersheim, I adopted a lay-out similar to that of Karl Ferdinand Werner in his 'Die Nachkommen Karls des Grossen bis um das Jahr 1000 (1.–8. Generation)' which appeared in the fourth volume of *Karl der Grosse* (Düsseldorf, 1967) with the title *Das Nachleben*. My purpose, however, differed from his. It was to study and compare the survivorship of women and men in an identifiable group, in particular that of wives as against husbands and sisters as against brothers. My debt to Karl Ferdinand Werner's table and notes is great and obvious. For the early Liudolfings Sabine Krüger's *Studien zur Sächsischen Grafschaftsverfassung im 9. Jahrhundert*, Studien und Vorarbeiten, 19, proved invaluable. There remain, however, a number of unavoidable gaps. The posterity of Duke Brun, who fell in 880, cannot be reconstructed and that of Otto I's aunt, Oda, by her second marriage to the Frankish Count Gerhard, which has been elucidated recently by E. Hlawitschka, *Die Anfänge des Hauses Habsburg-Lothringen*, is still not wholly firm. I have not been able to consult Hlawitschka's predecessor on this topic, H. Renn, *Das erste Luxemburger Grafenhaus (963–1136)* (Bonn, 1941) and have not tried to take his tree (*Anfänge*, pp. 138, 146) beyond my fourth generation where vital dates are scarce enough. There remain other blanks. The dates of some wives' deaths are not known or at least I have not been able to discover them in the literature available to me.

   The marriages of Otto I's sisters in West Francia profoundly shaped the nobility of that kingdom. Ottonian names like Gerberga, Hathui, Brun, Otto and Liudolf are scattered among the counts of later tenth-century France, their wives and the episcopate. They also entered the nomenclature of the Carolingian house. Even so, we have not yet succeeded in explaining and grasping the network of the Ottonians' western consanguinity in full. One hundred and fifty persons make up our genealogy, 82 of them men, 68 women. Once again it is probable that there were women, including wives, who have escaped notice. Count Gilbert of Roucy, for instance, appears without a wife on Werner's table, yet he certainly had one. He died in his forties and it was very unusual indeed for important lay nobles in prominent positions not to marry. Such oddities attracted notice, as can be shown from the anecdotes that gathered round the misogyny of the Conradine Count Conrad, one of

Otto I's allies in that family, who died in 948 (Ekkehart IV, *Casus sancti Galli*, c. 50). The later Ottonians' family strategy, the rare marriages of their daughters, diminished the resort of their kinship. It ceased to expand, or rather to reinforce itself. The solitude of sacral kingship had its drawbacks.

I have given a few references. For the early Liudolfings, the writings of one of their own, Agius, are essential. They were devoted to the life of his sister, Hathumoda, the first abbess of Gandersheim (*SS* IV, pp. 165 ff.)

Notes to the Genealogical Table

1 Agius, c. 2.

2 Hlawitschka, *Anfänge*, pp. 58 ff.

3 Above, pp. 54 and nn. 42, 43.

4 F. Lot, *Hugues Capet*, pp. 417 ff.

5 cf. Werner, p. 479.

6 Mentioned 965, see Werner, p. 478.

7 According to Werner, VIII 92.

8 DH II. 79 and *RI* II, 4, no. 1574.

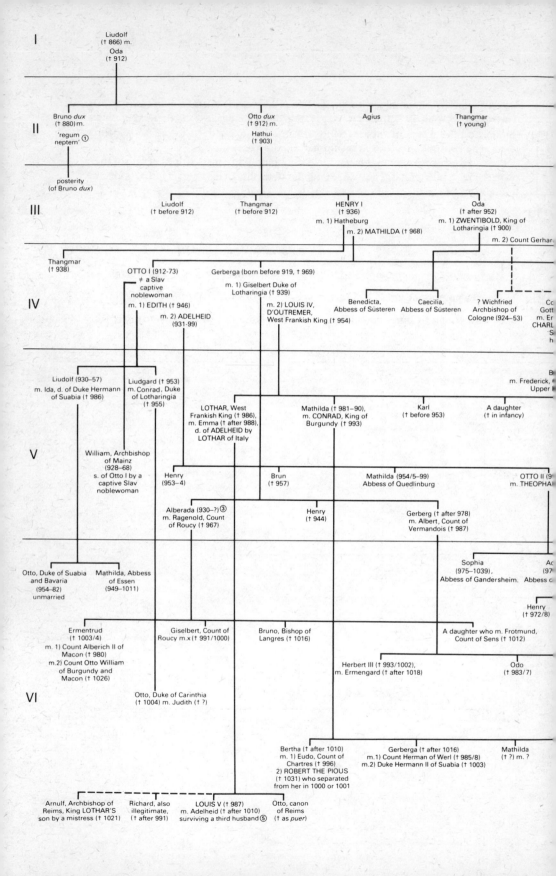

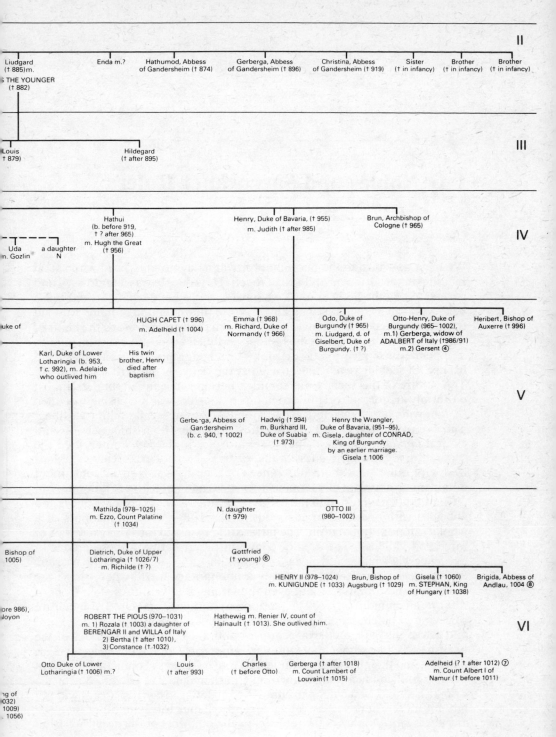

I

II

Liudgard
(† 885) m.
S THE YOUNGER
(† 882)

Enda m.?

Hathumod, Abbess
of Gandersheim († 874)

Gerberga, Abbess
of Gandersheim († 896)

Christina, Abbess
of Gandersheim († 919)

Sister
(† in infancy)

Brother
(† in infancy)

Brother
(† in infancy)

III

Louis
(† 879)

Hildegard
(† after 895)

IV

Uda
m. Gozlin

a daughter
N

Hathui
(b. before 919,
† ? after 965)
m. Hugh the Great
(† 956)

Henry, Duke of Bavaria, († 955)
m. Judith († after 985)

Brun, Archbishop of
Cologne († 965)

V

uke of

HUGH CAPET († 996)
m. Adelheid († 1004)

Emma († 968)
m. Richard, Duke of
Normandy († 966)

Odo, Duke of
Burgundy († 965)
m. Liudgard, d. of
Giselbert, Duke of
Burgundy. († ?)

Otto-Henry, Duke of
Burgundy (965– 1002),
m.1) Gerberga, widow of
ADALBERT of Italy (†986/91)
m.2) Gersent ④

Heribert, Bishop of
Auxerre († 996)

Karl, Duke of Lower
Lotharingia (b. 953,
† c. 992), m. Adelaide
who outlived him

His twin
brother, Henry
died after
baptism

Gerberga, Abbess of
Gandersheim
(b. c. 940, † 1002)

Hadwig († 994)
m. Burkhard III,
Duke of Suabia
(† 973)

Henry the Wrangler,
Duke of Bavaria, (951–95),
m. Gisela, daughter of CONRAD,
King of Burgundy
by an earlier marriage.
Gisela † 1006

VI

Bishop of
1005)

Mathilda (978–1025)
m. Ezzo, Count Palatine
(† 1034)

N. daughter
(† 979)

OTTO III
(980–1002)

Dietrich, Duke of Upper
Lotharingia († 1026/7)
m. Richilde († ?)

Gottfried
(† young) ⑥

HENRY II (978–1024)
m. KUNIGUNDE († 1033)

Brun, Bishop of
Augsburg († 1029)

Gisela († 1060)
m. STEPHAN, King
of Hungary († 1038)

Brigida, Abbess of
Andlau, 1004 ⑧

ore 986),
loyon

ROBERT THE PIOUS (970–1031)
m. 1) Rozala († 1003 a daughter of
BERENGAR II and WILLA of Italy
2) Bertha († after 1010),
3) Constance (†.1032)

Hathewig m. Renier IV, count of
Hainault († 1013). She outlived him.

Otto Duke of Lower
Lotharingia († 1006) m.?

Louis
(† after 993)

Charles
(† before Otto)

Gerberga († after 1018)
m. Count Lambert of
Louvain († 1015)

Adelheid (? † after 1012) ⑦
m. Count Albert I of
Namur († before 1011)

ng of
032)
1009)
. 1056)

9
Lay Nobles and Sacrosanct Rulers

We must now turn to the question of how the lay nobility lived with sacral kingship in the Ottonian and Salian *Reich*. How deeply was it impressed and permeated by the body of ideas we have surveyed and what part did these beliefs play in its relations with kings? Were they common ground? Beyond this lies the deeper question, whether we can really penetrate to the heart of this lay aristocracy of which the bishops and their synods, the sacramentaries and penitentials give so stark a view—a teeming pool of lawlessness and licence, of seeking revenge even against the deity, as one writer lamented.[1] The culture of this society was complex because its elite, despite its almost uniformly aristocratic origins and bonds of kinship, was increasingly divided by following either the clerical and monastic or the secular military calling. The rise of the Ottonian bishops' cities, with their flourishing schools and clerical *familiae*, and the monastic renaissance in the *Reich* intensified the separation and distinctiveness of the 'orders'. No modern society is organized with quite such sharp differences of identity between its constituent dominant groups. Not all German lay princes and nobles were illiterate, but power in the main rested in the hands of bishops and, less often, abbots and abbesses with one kind of consciousness and margraves and counts of a wholly different orientation. The latter still possessed the larger reserves of force and violence. The area of communication between these modes of existence was smaller and means of communicating ideas across the barriers of experience were fewer than in a contemporary world where there are violent clashes of interest, but even the strangest subcultures stem from or refer to a common source. The paradox of antiquity and late Latin culture surviving in patches among barbarian peoples was thus dragged deep into and across the early medieval centuries until the cultural revolutions of the twelfth. On the whole the Ottonian emperors, and their successors as patrons, and their bishops did far less to integrate these conflicting norms of outlook and conduct than at any rate Charlemagne had tried to do for the Frankish elite. The need for an educated and lettered lay aristocracy was felt but not met.[2] There was as yet no agreed syllabus for them other than the *conversio morum*, that is the rebirth in religion. Most of the great subsisted on a regime of vicarious piety. They remained what they were and endowed or patronized monastic communities to pray for their redemption. These paradoxes also haunted the operation and acceptance of sacral kingship. Some of them must now be looked at.

Let us begin with Conrad II. Of the rulers who came to the East Frankish and incipient German kingship between 973 and 1056, he had to cross by far the largest gulf between his embattled past as a half-disinherited prince and the duties of the *vicarius Christi* which awaited him after his election in 1025. Exaltation was justified by humiliation and it is not surprising to find this theme to the fore in Wipo's account of Conrad's sacring. The hard times he had known became the subject of the archbishop of Mainz's imputed sermon. That the new king wept as he listened and that he promised to forgive his former enemies now when he might be avenged on them was a good omen. It served Wipo as proof that he had truly been elected by God and that the magic of his consecration would work and make a new man out of him.[3] The earthly Conrad was not quite so forgiving nor could he afford to be. The Salian houselands were not overlarge and any king who wished to increase his demesne within those stem-regions where it was scarce could only do so at the expense of their aristocracies, exploiting their feuds, their imprecise inheritance customs or his own role as judge. In Wipo's biography, the Conrad whose charismatic inheritance on his mother's side was perpetual conflict with kings and dukes and the Conrad chosen by God did not fall apart. The qualities of *virtus* and *probitas* joined his past to his new character but there were strains.[4]

There were also incongruities. In between crown-wearings and the reception of kings as the blessed of the Lord, the Ottonians and their successors, and for that matter Edgar of Wessex, had to live at close quarters with their aristocratic following and could not afford to be so unapproachable as the illuminations of donating and enthroned rulers with their celestial company and homaging provinces suggest. The ritual which periodically set them apart from their *primores*, their princes, margraves and counts, was not like the court ceremonial of a Byzantine emperor, continuous and all-embracing. And even Byzantine emperors, as Hans-Georg Beck has shown, had their *hetaireia*, their circle of cronies with whom they consorted informally. These men often held no court rank.[5]

Western kings were anointed and their nobles were not but they shared with them the cult of their own ancestry and, through their house monasteries and clerical following the leading aristocratic clans too wanted to be exalted. Saxon margraves had chaplains, they sometimes even had visions like their kings.[6] They possessed from of old a sacrality and charisma of their own. The nobles' burials in their proprietary monasteries, which often formed part of their dwellings, corresponded to the great royal mausolea like Quedlinburg, Speyer and commemorative foundations like Memleben and Nordhausen. Had this not been so it would be quite impossible to explain the horror and indignation which struck Henry IV's friends and enemies alike when they heard of the peasant mob which in 1074 broke and defiled the royal tombs and relics in the chapel of the Harzburg.

Aristocratic ambition and even opposition could use the idiom of ritual which properly belonged to the *vicarius Christi* alone. The greatest princes might invade their royal lord's sacral sphere. The best known example is that of Hermann Billung whom Otto I had left in charge of Saxony, a *procuratio* for the whole stemland, when he went on his third Italian expedition in 966. Sometime after 968 Hermann held an assembly in Magdeburg and had himself led to the new cathedral by Archbishop Adalbert with all the bells ringing, candles lit and a clerical procession. Then he dined in the emperor's place, surrounded by bishops just as after a crown wearing. Only a rival, Thietmar of Merseburg's maternal grandfather, Count Henry (of Stade), protested and was ordered off to see the emperor at Rome.[7] It is characteristic that in the end not Hermann Billung but Archbishop Adalbert was fined, although in 973 Hermann also gave Otto exceptionally rich gifts as if to make belated amends.[8] The first archbishop of Magdeburg had offended the *unctus Domini* by bestowing a ritual which imitated the coming of Christ on someone other than Otto, thus suggesting that the emperor was not uniquely set apart. This is how his wrath became understandable to the author of the Magdeburg Annals.[9]

The incident left a deep impression behind in Saxony. For, when in 1135 Lothar of Süpplingenburg ordered that Duke Boleslas of Poland should be given a liturgical reception in Magdeburg, the Saxon Annalist and the Magdeburg Annals both reported it with indignation. They recalled that Archbishop Adalbert had barely been able to placate Otto I after exalting Hermann Billung in this way. It seemed wrong that a Slav stranger should enjoy honours which were begrudged to the first Billung duke, who is styled 'defensor ecclesiarum' by the annalist.[10] One hundred and sixty-five years lay between the two solemnities. It would be mistaken to belittle the importance of a king's ritual entry and the impression it made on those who took part or watched.

Ceremony was the vehicle of a language of intent, of right enjoyed and of right challenged. During the interregnum of 1002 an assembly of Saxon nobles met at Werla in mid-April and gave their promises of favour to Duke Henry of Bavaria, the future Henry II. In doing so they disappointed the candidate from their own ranks, Margrave Ekkehard of Meissen, who had nursed hopes of the kingship and found considerable support. Towards the evening he and his followers seized the dinner table and the meal which had been prepared in the *palatium* for Sophia of Gandersheim and Adelheid of Quedlinburg. Here he feasted with his backers, notably Duke Bernhard Billung and Bishop Arnulf of Halberstadt, and so announced that he would not quit the contest for the succession. It was not merely an act of boorish discourtesy but a deliberate assault on the sacrosanctity, dignity and honour of the surviving Ottonians. Next day Bishop Bernward of Hildesheim received Ekkehard with regal panoply in his city but on 30 April a group of his enemies, the young counts of Northeim and Katlenburg, killed him in the royal residence at Pöhlde where he had taken quarters for the night.[11] The insult he had done to Otto II's daughters was, as we have seen, one good reason for the murder.

When risings failed and nobles were forced to surrender and face retribution, their acts of submission were not formless but followed a certain rite. We read of footfalls but above all there was contrition and penitence for having sinned against the king, their lord, in his character as Christ's vicar.[12] So Thietmar of Merseburg's grandfather Liuthar, as we saw, raised a house for canons at Walbeck to purge his treasonable offence. Most of the greater Saxon comital families sooner or later endowed monasteries or nunneries but Thietmar's *motif* for this relatively early domestic foundation should not be dismissed lightly. His cousin, Henry of Schweinfurt, who rose unsuccessfully against Henry II in 1003, surrendered to the king in the manner and garb of a penitent.[13] He kept his life and his patrimony thanks to the intervention of powerful advocates, Archbishop Tagino of Magdeburg, Henry's friend, and Duke Bernhard, but he had to accept detention at the king's pleasure. The archbishop's fortress, Giebichenstein, became his prison and here he recited the Psalter and did many other good works.[14] In defeat, important men like Henry and even more eminent ones like Otto I's brother, his son Liudolf, Duke Conrad of Lotharingia and later Henry the Wrangler lost less face by giving themselves up as repentant sinners 'to God and the king' from whom they had strayed.[15] Sacral kingship could not prevent risings but it could help to restore a measure of harmony afterwards and make reconciliation, even on very unfavourable terms, easier for the losers. Conversely it enabled an enraged king not to lose face in turn when he failed to or did not want to exact the full revenge which harsh custom, his own threats and reputation for terror demanded. It opened a route of escape also from the bitter struggles which were fought out in his own entourage over the fate of vanquished rebels. It offered a higher and more objective kind of constraint to which all sides could bow.

The great, the lay aristocracy, thus were not sceptics and scoffers of the cult of kingship. They had their own good reasons not to be but they could dissent. Some of their discontents could follow the paths of the episcopal *admonitio regis*.[16] Conversely the bishops themselves, despite their orders, still felt with and for their lay kinsmen. Thietmar has faithfully recorded for us his conflicting emotions when his own kin fell foul of the king. Close though he was to Henry II, he could speak very ill of him. In 1014 his cousin Werner died after abducting an heiress who stood under the king's special *mund* (protection). Had he survived his wounds, Henry would not have been very gentle with him and now he ordered some of Werner's lands to be adjudged to his rival and enemy, Margrave Bernhard of the Northern March. Thietmar had not approved of his cousin's escapade but he was deeply indignant about his treatment. Werner was brought to the house of an imperial reeve who, 'villicus iniquitatis' (Luke, 16.8), betrayed his sick guest into the emperor's power; and of the unjust judgment he wrote: 'The people muttered and said as loudly as they dared that the anointed of the lord was sinning.'[17] Yet the bishop of Merseburg was not consistent, perhaps because the very substance of divinity in kings could not be consistent. His kinsman, Henry of Schweinfurt, margrave of the Bavarian Nordgau, had taken up arms against Henry II over a broken promise. He had been led to expect the

duchy of Bavaria as his reward for supporting the Liudolfing's struggle for
the kingship. Thietmar conceals neither the strength of his cousin's case nor
the groundswell of lay opinion supporting his conduct, but he disapproved of
it all the same. As all lordship was of God, he wrote in a famous passage, he
who rose against such lordship offended the divine majesty. He counselled
patience and waiting for better days.[18] Later he returned to the theme in a
mood of controversy against those who would stand no nonsense from their
lords. It is evident from his pages that kingship was a subject of intensive
debate.[19]

Dissent could take many forms. Against Ruotger's and Liudprand's
panegyric of the four-year-old Brun saving the Lower Rhine from further
Viking visitations by his mere presence stands the sentiment of a contemporary clerk in the diocese of Utrecht, who wrote a life of Bishop Radbod
(died 917), Balderich's predecessor. He endowed his subject with the gift of
prophecy, a frequent device of early medieval biographers with a message to
their own times, and he had Radbod declare that the *principes* of Germany
would not enjoy their new *imperium* for very long. He meant the Ottonians.[20] Liudprand, Widukind, Hrotsvitha and Ruotger all saw in Henry I
the man whom God had elevated and wanted to rule. Duke Arnulf of
Bavaria, his rival, who was raised to a breakaway kingship in 919, is dismissed, by Liudprand especially, as one who at first resisted the *divina
ordinatio*.[21] There is, however, the leaf of a chronicle, a fragment acciden-
tally preserved in a Martianus Capella manuscript which once belonged to St
Emmeram's, Regensburg, where Arnulf is clothed in all the epithets befitting
a ruler by divine grace.[22] The author of the *Fragmentum* only echoed the
proud *intitulatio* of Arnulf's charter of 908, which proclaimed a regal kind of
lordship over the Bavarians and the adjoining lands 'divina ordinante pro-
videntia'. It was God's doing that Arnulf's adversary, Henry I, had been
driven back at his first coming, the invasion of 921, by the inhabitants of a
single manor. It was clearly a war miracle in Arnulf's favour. The Luitpolding duke could be presented as the descendant of emperors and kings and,
what is more, as the deliverer of the *populus christianus*, that flexible entity
which could mean the whole of Christendom or the inhabitants of only one
region, from the sword of the pagans.[23] Yet the mainstream of the historical
tradition has flung aside and almost buried this panegyric. It is a measure of
the success of the Ottonians and early Salians in the *Reich*, north of the Alps,
that history was almost wholly written for the victors. In Italy and beyond the
frontiers of their empire they did much less well. With the rise of aristocratic
house history during the second half of the eleventh century, the *res gestae* of
Christo-centric emperors and their bishops ceased to monopolize historical
writing and thinking.[24] In this new genre, the charisma of aristocratic
families and their heroic, legendary pasts began to compete with the *virtus* of
kings. The Hohenstaufen later sought to reverse this trend but their success
was modest. Princely self-consciousness now commanded a historical and
literary culture of its own.

The minority of Henry IV seems to lie between this development and the
much less articulate opposition of the lay aristocracy of the Ottonian and

early Salian period. From the very beginning Henry IV did not fit and failed to grow into his appointed role as *vicarius Christi*. Soiled by the experiences of his minority, he dispensed with the restraints which it imposed upon him. At least his enemies later were able to destroy this ideal dimension of his kingship, which by tradition belonged to it. It is customary to blame Gregory VII for this and, of course, he helped. But some of the work of destruction had already begun during the king's minority and for this the lay and ecclesiastical princes were solely responsible. Lampert of Hersfeld, himself no friend of Henry IV's blamed them for the insults they heaped upon the boy king and the violence which shattered the solemnity and state of his Easter, Whitsun and Christmas courts. In the first place the abduction of the twelve-year-old from Kaiserswerth in 1062 roused his alarm because it impaired the *regia maiestas*.[25] Christmas at Goslar in the same year was disturbed by an angry clash between Bishop Hezilo of Hildesheim and Abbot Widerad of Fulda about seating arrangements and precedence. At the Whitsun court of 1063, which was also held at Goslar, the same protagonists fought out their quarrel once more but this time with armed forces. Hezilo had enlisted Count Ekbert of Brunswick, Henry IV's kinsman, and the abbot of Fulda brought his vassals. There were plenty of casualties and the king's attempts to stop the bloodshed were ignored.[26] All this happened in the minster of St Simon and Jude, specially built by Henry III as a church for crown-wearing. Coming of age did not save Henry from similar indignities. In 1071 the monks of Stavelot crashed the heavy shrine of their patron saint, St Remacles, on the king's dinner table at Liège in order to reclaim the monastery of Malmédy, which Henry had given to his relentless *magister*, Archbishop Anno of Cologne, in 1065.[27] Tumults and even bloodshed had occasionally marred royal courts and feasts before this time, but kings were very sensitive about such incidents and punished those responsible for them severely.[28] Henry IV's experiences during the years of his helplessness and youth prompt the conclusion that the sacrality of his kingship was imperilled from the very beginning. He never recovered it. We must now turn to the question, what led up to this manifest crisis, even before the orchestrated voices of reform and reformers drowned all others?'

10
The Vicarius Christi and Justice

History was the province of clerks and monks and they manipulated it to preach the right lessons. Yet it is obvious that the imposing ritual edifice of sacral kingship had cracks and suffered from at times unbearable strains throughout the Ottonian century and long before the crisis of Henry IV's minority. To experience the uneasy side-by-side of royal sacrosanctity and the kings' year-in, year-out dealings with the lay aristocracy, we must return once more to the pages of Thietmar's chronicle-memoir. Let us recall the story of Bishop Hildiward of Halberstadt, to whom Otto I gave the staff in 968 with the words, 'Take here the wergild for your father', one of the conspirators of 941 whom he had ordered to be killed.[1] Let us recall also the story of Margrave Gero's namesake and nephew, the imperial chaplain and archbishop-elect of Cologne, whom Otto for a time refused to invest because he was at odds with his brother, Margrave Thietmar of Serimunt. Whatever the latter had done to rouse the emperor's much-famed anger almost certainly reflected his and his family's discontent when nearly all the lands of his uncle, the great margrave and Otto's friend, went to Gernrode, his monastic foundation, presided over by his daughter-in-law Hathui.[2] These stories cannot be ignored and they suggest a conflict of roles.

They also conjure up quite another set of values and conventions underlying the actions of kings, nobles and sometimes even bishops. These conventions had, as we shall see, rituals of their own. One such must be mentioned here and now because it belonged to the very inauguration of Otto I's kingship. In Widukind's famous account of his coronation at Aachen on 7 August 936, we read that first of all the dukes, leading counts and greater vassals gave him their hands (that is, they became his men), swore him fealty and placed him on a royal seat which stood in the atrium in front of the west door of Charlemagne's basilica, and so 'they made him king after their fashion' (*more suo*).[3] All this happened before the archbishops of Mainz, Cologne and Trier received Otto in the church to invest, anoint and crown him. It was this throne and not the one in the upper storey of the minster which, according to Wipo, counted as the public throne *par excellence*, the *archisolium regni* going back to former kings and especially Charlemagne. A ruler had to be seen occupying it to be truly king and both Henry II and Conrad II hurried to Aachen as soon as they could to take possession of it, and the Lotharingians seem to have insisted on acclaiming them there. The kingship was rooted in custom and this could never be wholly submerged or elbowed aside by its increasing clericalization.

In the ninth century, we noted in an earlier chapter, the Liudolfings had been the neighbours and *cognati* of the Saxon nobility which they now ruled as kings. These relationships entailed mutual expectations of inheritance and this did not change when they became regal and lavished new *honores*, lands, slaves and treasure on their foremost followers. They could not help, therefore, being a party to the unending feuds and inheritance disputes of their great men, let alone those within their own kin which usually channelled the rivalries of the *proceres*. These feuds were not only fought out in the field or by depredations on men and lands. They were also conducted before the king himself as judge and at his court. There were ways of ruining an enemy by royal judgment, accusations of infidelity, trumped up appeals ending in a judicial duel. Mention has already been made of Thietmar of Merseburg's cousin, Werner of Walbeck, some of whose lands Henry II wished to see adjudged to his rival after his death in 1014.[4] Werner's troubles had begun earlier. In 1009 he nearly lost his *beneficium*, the Northern March, and the king's grace at the prompting of another enemy, Count Dedi (a Wettin). On this occasion he was saved by a sudden illness and counsels of delay, but sometimes these judicial intrigues succeeded.[5] The destruction in 979 of another kinsman of Margrave Gero, Count Gero of Alsleben, by his enemies, especially Archbishop Adalbert of Magdeburg and Margrave Dietrich of the Northern March, was an engineered plot even more than Count Dedi's efforts against Werner of Walbeck. Thietmar wanted his readers to know how deeply the emperor, Otto II, was implicated in this, to him, shocking episode. For once, moreover, the bishop's view is reinforced by another source. Count Gero's fall became a *cause célèbre* and was widely reported by the chroniclers: how he had to fight his accuser Waldo on an island in the Elbe, failed in the duel and was beheaded by Otto II's and the princes' judgment at Magdeburg, although Waldo too died of his wounds. Wolfhere, the biographer of Bishop Godehard of Hildesheim, writing in the mid-eleventh century, mentioned that the *vox populi* thought Gero innocent. It was to him one of the emperor's sins, explaining perhaps his early death at Rome in 983. Thietmar went much further. For he tells us that the count's body and clothes were found entire three years after his burial at Alsleben, where he had founded a nunnery shortly before his appalling end when the accusation and future trial may already have loured on the horizon. The miracle thus challenged and defied the outcome of the ordeal. It was the true as against a false manifestation of divine justice.[6]

With the advent of Henry II, the sacral representation of kingship and its mode of appearance imitating the Saviour were consciously enhanced. For economic reasons he stayed far more often in bishops' cities than his predecessors had done, so that his festival coronations and crown- wearings showed him to more people. Henry, moreover, added Whitsun to the great feasts which were solemnly kept with the full royal ritual. Thirteen of his Whitsun courts are known, while those of the Ottos have only rarely come down to us.⁷ Yet these developments must be seen in the light of Henry's long and hard struggle for the succession. They were perhaps even meant to banish the memory of the wheeling and dealing which accompanied it. Kings were chosen by collectivities, by groups of nobles, but also each great man, duke, count or bishop, chose his king for himself.⁸ This created a face-to-face relationship between the ruler and his *primores* in the various stem-regions. Loyalty was a gift that called for returns.

Henry first met the Saxons at Merseburg on 25 July 1002 in royal *ornatus* and was asked by their spokesman, Duke Bernhard Billung, what he would do for them.⁹ The king's response was at heart cautious. He promised what he could and what he had to, and there was just a hint that the Saxons were still the people especially close to the kingship. At any rate his audience was gratified and the duke then gave him, in the name of all, possession of the *cura regni*, the governance of the *Reich*, by handing him the Holy Lance. Henry, of course, had brought it to Merseburg and it rarely went out of the keeping of his itinerant court chapel. The ceremony was, we must note, mainly secular. The bishops merely watched and the *laudes*, here songs of praise and thanksgiving, were sung by all.¹⁰ A coronation and enthronement may have followed but the whole act recalls the lay princes' king-making *more suo* in the atrium of the Aachen minster in 936.¹¹ It was an unusual ritual in order to give the Saxons their due share in the elevation of the new king. They too can be said to have raised him *more suo*, to echo Widukind's words.

The Merseburg court of July 1002 was in many ways symptomatic. The Saxon great and their military followings honoured Henry as king but there had to be both general and specific promises. Thanks to Thietmar, we can follow these hard face-to-face relationships between the emperor and individual Saxon princes, not least of all the Billungs, for much of his reign. Henry, as has been shown, had to confront a new kind of opposition in Saxony. There was now no rival Liudolfing to collect his enemies about him: this role fell for a few years to Boleslas Chrobry of Poland.¹² The war against him was to some extent an inner-Saxon conflict. Henry therefore had to exploit the feuds of the East Saxon lords, especially their endemic internecine struggles for the great *honores* of the frontier, the countships and margraviates on which their future depended. His real and his ideal powers could not but clash. Let us follow one episode. After the murder of Margrave Ekkehard of Meissen during the troubles of the interregnum in Saxony, his son Hermann and his brother Gunzelin became enemies, each striving to gain possession of the fortress to secure the succession to the margraviate. Behind Gunzelin, however, stood Boleslas of Poland, who wanted Meissen for himself having already overrun the East Elbian tribute-paying regions of the huge march. This was a concession Henry II refused to make at Merseburg but he was reluctantly persuaded to give the key fortress and the remainder of the honour to Gunzelin, Boleslas's friend and probably brother-in-law.¹³ His opportunity to rid himself of a margrave he distrusted came in 1009 when the uneasy peace of the region was broken by open war between Gunzelin and his two nephews, Hermann and the younger Ekkehard. It was a typical uncle-nephew feud which both sides, however, waged with exceptional ferocity attacking, stripping and burning one another's fortresses.[14] The king hurried to Merseburg to sit in judgment but he had scores of his own to settle with Gunzelin and so he placed the whole blame on him. The margrave had in the past slighted him and the opportunity for revenge was as welcome as it was unexpected. Among other things, Henry complained that he was far too intimate with Boleslas and there were men ready to challenge Gunzelin to a judicial duel as a traitor, a *reus maiestatis*. Thietmar here allows us to hear the din and the sulphurous wrangles of a real trial with its long *lamentationes* (plaints) and rebuttals. Gunzelin and his friends stood their ground. Henry then sought the counsel of his princes, as he was bound to do, and they told him after long and secret discussions: 'We know that he [the accused] stands before you not without a good answer.' But they also knew their king and what he wanted and hoped that God and political prudence would make him show clemency. Gunzelin escaped with his life but had to surrender into the custody of Bishop Arnulf of Halberstadt. His imprisonment lasted for eight years and he lost his march, which not long afterwards was given to his nephew Hermann. Once again we observe the sinister uses of judicial duels and the way the king is shown standing within and not beyond the perimeter of revenge. It was the princes who spoke up for mercy, the virtue demanded from a true vicar of Christ.

The Ottos, Henry II and still less the Salians thus could not be the unquestioned representatives of a higher and more than earthly justice in the eyes of their great nobles. Christo-centric ideas of kingship only shaped the edges of the relations between these men and their royal overlords. These beliefs sat fitfully upon them and theirs was a splintered universe which the divine penetrated in more than one form, some dark and archaic, some stamped by the homiletics of their episcopal teachers. The Old-Testamentary *aequitas*, which the bishops enjoined on kings with such urgency in the texts of the coronation *ordines,* was not so easily translated into the everyday business of 'giving men their law', rewarding and punishing, in short, governing.[15] Nor were the bishops themselves disinterested. It was not the exaltation of kingship as such by anointing and *laudes* and its visual representation so near to God that alienated individual nobles or whole kins from their emperors but the partiality and favour shown to bishops over disputed lands, royal rights, forests and especially—as we saw—proprietary monasteries. Sacrality suffered because it was exploited by those who could be seen to do most in conferring it on kings, the bishops and their clerical throngs. Thietmar of Merseburg himself was not above redrafting a diploma in the name of Otto II in order to defeat the claims of the Ekkehardine margraves of Meissen on a large stretch of forest between the Saale and the Mulde. Not surprisingly, the brothers Hermann and the younger Ekkehard, when they left the emperor's *curia* at Magdeburg in 1017 after losing their case, were heard to mutter: 'What we have done in this matter so far was done not out of spite but because we believed that right was on our side. Now we might as well give it up', that is to say, use other means in order to have justice. They began building huge game traps and launched a series of raids on the bishop's villages in the neighbour-hood.[16]

The ritual and sacral role of the Ottonian emperors thus came into conflict with their day-to-day stint of ruling, especially in such sensitive areas as disputed inheritances, succession to high office on the frontier and family feuds. At this point we must enlarge our horizons and turn first of all to the peoples of the Eurasian steppes, the contemporaries of the late-Carolingian Franks and Saxons. It is possible that the ninth-century Chazars and after them the Magyars developed a dual kingship to hold together their extensive empires in southern Russia, one ruler being sacred, remote and invisible, the other active and leading expeditions (though his colleague might accompany them).[17] The divine ruler was held responsible for cosmic accidents and failure in war. Divine kings who had few other tasks than cultic ones and were not expected or even allowed to govern are well enough known in a good number of African societies. They too could become the victims of princely rebellions, as E. E. Evans-Pritchard showed in his Frazer Lecture on the nilotic Shilluk. When calamities struck home, like crop failures, human and cattle disease or defeat in war, the kings were blamed. The real causes of the risings which followed lay in the deep-seated regional particu-larisms dividing the Shilluk; hence 'the kingship embodies a contradiction between dogma and social facts'.[18] The point we must note here is that the divine ruler and the cult of his heroic ancestor stood for what unity could be achieved. It is reinforced by Max Gluckmann's study, 'The Frailty in Authority', based on African societies which did expect their kings to govern and rejected them not only for disasters beyond their control but also for those that sprang from the misuse of power and errors of judgment. In these kingdoms, as he described them, there was no integrated economic framework to hold different interests and dispersed populations together. Communications were poor. Against such odds, divine kingship and the struggle for the possession of it held together empires acquired by conquest. 'All sections struggle for the kingship and that unifies them.'[19] It is important also that in these societies royal princes were the born leaders of rebellion, often enough prodded by their followers to chance their arm. Gluckmann rightly thought that the existence of towns and a more differentiated economy distinguished the medieval state from the Zulus he had been observing. He might have added the church and, in the tenth century, the powerful influence of Byzantium and the memories of classical Rome. Yet one or two lessons about the place of sacral kingship in the Ottonian *Reich* and in early medieval kingdoms in general can perhaps be learned from these models.

The Ottonian empire functioned and functioned well with a modest array of institutions. Royal lordship sat unequally on the *regna* and *patriae* over which the Liudolfings gained ascendancy and a measure of power in the course of a few decades. They held these gains, their *imperium*, with rather less apparatus of governance than the Carolingians had developed and used.

There were now no *missi dominici* north of the Alps and very little that could be called legislation or administrative instructions.[20] Royal chaplains were sometimes sent on missions outside the court, not only to represent the king at a synod or to introduce a newly appointed bishop to his see but also on secular business.[21] Henry II despatched his Bavarian chaplain, Helmiger, into Carinthia to organize the seizure of a pass for his Italian campaign of 1004.[22] He also sent his *nuncii* to compel the advocates of the see of Worms and the abbey of Lorsch to correct wrongs committed by their respective *familiae*.[23] Such missions from the court may have occurred more often than we can now know but they were *ad hoc* rather than regular. The diplomata which the Ottonians granted to churches and laymen could impose profound changes on individuals, local communites and their neighbours, but at the most they applied general rules to particular cases.[24] The privileges and immunities of one monastery were frequently granted to others. Sometimes this was done systematically but even in the imperial church there was no uniformity. Ecclesiastical franchises developed fitfully and each larger immunity nursed its own customs. Yet what diplomata lacked as substitutes for legislation they characteristically made up for by their sacral aura. Their solemn *intitulatio*, the divine grace formula and the *arenga* which employed the language of sermon and liturgy disseminated something of the theology of kingship to the local world of the grantee. Diplomata might be recited verbatim and then expounded in church, like a sermon. They helped to ward off the 'iniquity of judges' against which priests prayed.[25]

In a society which possessed few means of delegating power safely and which had not mastered the art of keeping a central source of authority in constant communication with local assemblies presided over by counts, margraves and dukes, cohesion and continuity were at risk. There is some widely dispersed evidence of the Ottonians sending orders and messages to their counts and of men bringing news of upheavals and troubles to a distant court.[26] We do not know the density and frequency of this traffic but large numbers of messengers must have been employed. We have two famous letters of Otto I addressed to the Saxon great, one preserved by Widukind, the other, ordering the election and reception of Archbishop Adalbert in 968, which the emperor wanted to be kept at Magdeburg for ever.[27] By far the most important and reliable means of communication was the royal *iter*.

Itineracy was the lot of kings, long absence the great evil. Thietmar exclaimed that he could not record all the comings and goings of Otto III through his bishoprics and *comitatus* as if he felt he really ought to.[28] The contemporary biographer of Henry II, Bishop Adalbold of Utrecht, formerly his chaplain, explained his master's decision to go to Upper Lotharingia in 1003 thus: 'For he knew that the land which the king does not visit most often abounds in the outcries and woes of the poor.' As if to confirm this, the author of the *Life of Bishop Adalbero II of Metz* (984–1005), who wrote in 1015, rebuked the third Otto because 'he passed nearly all his time at Rome and therefore the kingdoms and regions [*patriae*] of his empire were so laid waste that even princes, bishops and the leading men could scarcely live in safety.'[29] Kings spent at least half their time on the roads. To read the

Quedlinburg Annals, the reign of Henry II was one long procession, often punctuated by campaigns, but it was essentially a sacral procession from holy day to holy day, from one church dedication to another, most of them followed by assemblies which the leading men in each region attended and where the emperor did justice, presided over synods, received envoys and deliberated on peace and war. Henry's real itinerary was more complex than the annalist would have his readers believe, but these solemnities with their festival coronations, crown-wearings and _laudes_ defined it and formed its peaks. The liturgical spectacle preceded the judgments and decision-making about rewards, favours and penalties, with their inevitable backlash of disappointed expectations. It announced the all-importance of the king's coming and his office as the force of cohesion.

The journeys of the Ottonians were planned well ahead and the _palatia_ and bishoprics to be stayed in received, as a rule, good notice. It is no accident that we know more about the royal _iter_ and its organization than about almost any other institution of the early medieval _Reich_, court chapel and chancery excepted. The kings' itineraries were determined by the necessities of the moment but their range of action by the means of support available on the way, the possession of _palatia_, fiscs and patrimony, the _servitia_ of bishops and, less often, of royal abbots. Certain areas, like much of Bavaria, Carinthia and the northernmost fringes of Saxony, remained outside and beyond their reach or were visited only, if at all, during campaigns beyond the frontiers, be it because they were underdeveloped and sparsely populated or because they contained no royal centres to stay in. Their _proceres_ had to come and attend court assemblies held in places which lay on the royal route and the kings granted away lands in these regions of which they knew very little.[30] Upper Lotharingia, likewise, was rarely visited and the Ottonians travelled through it mainly for their occasional meetings with the West Frankish kings at Ivois on the Chiers. In the tenth century the number of royal stays in Saxony, especially East Saxony, the homeland of the Liudolfings, compared with those in the other duchies of the _Reich_ (excluding Italy), was roughly 18 to 1. Under Henry II there was a shift. Bavaria and Suabia saw much more of him than they did of the Ottos and Henry I but the number of Saxon stays still predominated in the proportion of 10 to 1.[31] The prominence of Saxony meant that the Saxon aristocracy from about 945 onwards shared the splendours of many great occasions with their native kings. Embassies from Byzantium, Cordoba, Ifriquiya perhaps, Kiev, Bulgaria, Hungary and Italy arrived in Saxon _palatia_ to bear their messages and present their much-coveted exotic gifts.[32] This did not happen every year but suitors and those seeking to obtain favours and grants had to travel north more often than south to make their requests.

Nonetheless, the Ottonian _Reich_ was far less clearly dominated by Saxons than the Carolingian had once been by Franks. It was in the tenth century a conglomerate of _regna_, and we do not know whether men north of the Alps and east of the Rhine already felt it to be a _regnum Teutonicorum_. The Liudolfing rulers, by their marriages, inheritances, confiscations and new connections, held these _regna_ together within their larger _regnum_ and collected the fealties of their princes, counts and vassals about them. The divine matter of their kingship and its imagery gave an objective and super-personal quality to these fragile bonds. In this way sacrality—and this was true not only of the Ottonian *Reich*—was a substitute for inadequate or failing institutions. It could not, as such, preserve order and peace. On the contrary, it almost engendered, as we saw, certain kinds of conflict. But as long as opposition to the Ottonian king gathered round the *stirps regia* or affinity—the king's brother, son, son-in-law or cousins—conflict itself ensured a measure of unity and continuity. If it was still possible for the *regna*, Bavaria, Suabia and Lotharingia, to go their own way in 919 and again in 938–9, this danger dwindled and segmentation was halted. The dismemberment of the Carolingian *Reich* went no further in the Lotharingian and East Frankish portion of it. Otto I knew what he was doing when he demanded in 953 that his son Liudolf must hand over the instigators of the rising, the 'seducers' as Ruotger, the biographer of Brun of Cologne, called them. That he summoned the young Otto II to Rome in 967 and kept him near his person to the end of his days had, as has been shown, more than one reason.

The sacrosanctity of kings must be treated by historians as a diversified, growing and changing phenomenon, not as an inert body of ideas. It has already been noted that the late-Carolingian theology of kingship was reinterpreted in the entourage of the Ottonians. They came to practise its rites, which manifested their sacrality, more often and more methodically. The Saxon emperors did not invent, as was once thought, festival coronations. They inherited them like so much else from the Carolingians.[33] The adaptations, the new and firmer accents, the more conspicuous display, all these expressed, however, two predicaments of their regime. One, the indivisibility of kingship, has already been discussed. The whole Liudolfing *agnatio* and the royal wives shared charismatic qualities and possessed, as the *Lives* of Queen Mathilda prove, unusual spiritual gifts, but certain attributes belonged to the *senior*, the king, alone. The sacral sphere enveloping the individual Liudolfing ruler, beginning with his unction and constantly reaffirmed by crown-wearings, festival coronations and other liturgical honours paid to him, thus helped to set him off against his excluded kin. There was a special significance in Otto I's Easter-keeping on 18 April 941, when he abated nothing in his royal style and appearance before the nobles and so defied his brother and would-be assassins. Liudolf's fears about his future in 953, when Otto's second wife Adelheid began to bear him sons, were justified because, though designated, sworn to and shown to the peoples of the *Reich* as their future king, he had not been anointed and crowned.

The second predicament was nothing other than the growth and development of the imperial church, the *Reichskirche*, itself. It is perhaps too readily regarded as the conscious creation in every way of the Ottonian emperors. By the turn of the millennium some of the bishops had indeed become or were fast becoming 'terrae principes', to use Thietmar of Merseburg's words, while their royal lords advanced further and deeper into the inner economy of the church's life, summoning synods, directing them, decreeing on the obits and memorials of bishops and forcing reform on reluctant imperial abbeys. The sacrality of kingship justified, explained and set the stage for this interpenetration of functions and responsibilities. Its enemies, even in the tenth century, had sometimes called it confusion.[34] Yet the very forces which from the second quarter of the eleventh century onwards were to question and challenge the status of kings, and of prelates who served them too well, owed their own rise more to the successes than the failures of the so-called Ottonian system, to the four generations of hard-headed crowned migrants whose *regalis potestas* had to be hallowed because it was so desperately needed.

No ruler in the tenth century enjoyed much security and we have seen that even after his triumphs in 955 Otto I's situation was at times very precarious.[35] Yet compared with most of their crowned contemporaries the Ottonians and early Salians did not do so badly. Between 919 and 1056 seven kings ruled in the *Reich*. The plot to kill Otto I in 941 had no sequel and, although Ruotger in the *Vita Brunonis* has him complain that the enemies who misled his son also wanted to kill him (the father) with 'sacrilegious daring', there is no other evidence for this.[36] In 1047–8 Count Thietmar Billung was alleged to have plotted an ambush against Henry III when he came as far north as Bremen at the invitation of Archbishop Adalbert. Thietmar's resentments and feuds against the emperors went back to Henry II's time and once again inheritance, the possession of a monastery, had been at stake. He chose to fight a duel against one of his own men who came forward as his accuser. Later Henry III overcame another and more serious conspiracy agains his life (1055).[37]

During the same period in England we find thirteen kings ruling Wessex and the *regna* forced to accept their *imperium*. Of these, two, Edmund and Edward the Martyr, were murdered. No Liudolfing prince, moreover, ever suffered a fate as horrible as that of Alfred the Aetheling, who was blinded and tortured in 1036. In his charter for the new minster at Winchester (966), Edgar called himself vicar of Christ but he also warned his successor never to force an outsider as abbot on the Benedictine monks lest God should damn and deprive them of rule and life. His father Eadmund had been killed at a drunken feast in honour of St Augustine. Was there less of the *regalis disciplina* which shielded a king on such occasions? It was the cult of Edward the Martyr rather than the precedent of Edgar's consecration in 973, perhaps to imitate the baptism of Christ, that cast the more potent spell over Aethelred II's reign.[38] But let us note also that the government of England was more sophisticated and uniform than that of the Ottonian *Reich*. By means of their coinage, especially the frequent and regular new issues of currency, the Anglo-Saxon kings had harder and more tangible ways of making themselves known to their subjects.[39] The use of the written vernacular, moreover, furnished them with a marginally better educated lay nobility so that Carolingian accomplishments in government, especially legislation and surveys, were more thoroughly absorbed in Alfridian and tenth-century Wessex than they had been in ninth-century and Ottonian Saxony.[40] Only the organization of the eastern marches on conquered Slav soil, with their burgwards, flow of tribute and rotating garrisons in key fortresses, can be compared to such measures as the creation of the Mercian shires or the burghal hidage. Yet the astonishing uniformity and fiscalism of later Anglo-Saxon government only proves once more that in the middle ages greater stability and security did not necessarily stem from advanced institutions and administrative virtuosity.

Lastly Byzantium. Of the fourteen emperors covering the same span of time, 919–1056, two were murdered, two deposed and one deposed and blinded. In the all-pervasive, professional and technically excelling ritual of the Byzantine court, it was possible to express an imperial theology of great refinement without much concern for the person embodying it at any one time. It was different in the streets of the capital where the names of the last two Macedonian princesses, Zoe and Theodora, could be conjured with. Only the Capetian contemporaries of Henry II and of the early Salian emperors seem to have been no less secure than their towering eastern neighbours. Despite their diminished territorial reach, they quietly began to build up that indwelling sacrality of which neither the papacy nor the theological enlightenment of the twelfth century were later able to deprive them.

If this rough and ready comparison seems reassuring on the side of the western emperors it does not prove that, regardless of strains, the belief in the innate *virtus* and sacrosanctity of rulers was more deep-seated in the *Reich* than in most other kingdoms of Europe. Sacral kingship in the middle ages is far too elusive a phenomenon for such a diagnosis and nowhere did it wear the same aspect or fulfil exactly the same functions. The strains in Germany were also becoming more serious and the confrontations between the early Salians and individual nobles as well as whole groups of them were now controlled by a sense of alienation. The manifold and close cognatic connections between the Ottonians and the Saxon aristocracy receded into the past. More frequent intermarriages between the leading Saxon families and their peers in other regions of the *Reich* or outside its frontiers created new solidarities, competing with those fostered through the royal *iter* and episcopal appointments. The Salian emperors in turn sought to apply more uniform rules and procedures in asserting their rights over lands and high offices lacking direct heirs. During Henry III's reign, moods and attitudes towards the emperor changed markedly and the boy king Henry IV inherited from his father a reputation for injustice and want of *timor Dei* long before he acquired it in his own right.[41] The crisis of kingship was already smouldering before it fused in the humiliations and losses of Henry's minority and exploded in the Saxon revolt of 1073—and therefore also before Gregory VII's thirst for *justitia* astonished and upset his German enemies and allies alike.

Plate I: Processional Cross from the Treasury of the Minster at Essen, showing the children of Otto I's son Liudolf, Abbess Mathilda of Essen and her brother, Duke Otto of Suabia and Bavaria. The date must be between 973, when Mathilda entered on her charge, and 980, when her brother left for Italy where he died. The abbess appears to receive the cross from Otto but it may well have been a joint gift (See *supra*, pp. 50 and 53 and *Das erste Jahrtausand*, Tafelband, no. 376.)

HOC AVGVSTE LIBRO:

TIBI COR DS INDVAT OTTO

QVEM DE LIVTHARIO · TE

SVSCEPISSE · MEMENTO ·

Plates II and III: The Liuthar Gospels in the treasury of the Aachen Minster (fol. 15 v/16r), about the year 1000. Otto III is seen enthroned in a mandorla usually occupied by Christ (cf. plate IV) and crowned by the hand of God. Two princes with banners on their lances bow to him and below are two warriors and two clerical attendants. The throne is sustained by the figure of the earth. On the right the artist of the manuscript approaches, the monk Liuthar of Reichenau. The inscription reads: 'May God clothe your heart, Otto Augustus, with this book. Remember that you received it from Liuthar.' (298 by 215 mm. See Schramm and Mütherich, p. 154, no. 103, and K. Hoffman, *Taufsymbolik* pp. 14 ff.)

Plate IV: Henry II crowned by Christ. He is supported by two saint bishops, St Udalrich of Augsburg and St Emmeran of Regensburg. Angels hand him lance and sword. The manuscript, a sacramentary, was created at Regensburg between 1002 and 1014 and given by the king to his episcopal foundation, Bamberg. It is now in the Bavarian State Library at Munich (Clm. 4456, fol. 11r). (298 by 241 mm. See G. Swarzenski, *Die Regensburger Buchmalerei*, p. 64 f. and pl. VIII, no 19, and also Schramm and Mütherich, p. 157, no. 111.)

Epilogue

We have studied kingship in the light of one of its functions—to resolve or cope with conflict. It would be mistaken to think that the tensions surveyed here exhaust the topic and that what has been said about the Saxon nobles' feuds and risings in the tenth century applied to all other manifestations of unrest and discontent with Ottonian rule as well. In 958 Otto I and his brother Brun banished and dispossessed the nephews of Duke Giselbert of Lotharingia, who had himself perished in the waters of the Rhine at Andernach in 939. The struggles of the Reginars of Hainault and Louvain to regain their inheritances and positions in Lower Lotharingia were not inhibited or guided by the family feuds of the Ottonian house. They sought and found royal support from the West Frankish Carolingian kings if they sought it at all. Likewise a Frankish malcontent, who had been embroiled with the bishop of Como at the siege of Comacina in 964, conspired with King Adalbert of Italy, the son of Berengar II, and was banished in 966. He had to forswear the northern kingdom and, although he broke his oath and returned to Germany in the same year, he was unable to find sympathizers.[1] It is at least noteworthy that these Lotharingian and Rhine-Frankish adversaries of Otto I sought links with other rulers, the West-Frankish claimants of the middle kingdom and the most obvious rival of the Saxon emperor in the Italian kingdom. On the whole they preferred not to risk resistance, revenge or offensive operations supported only by their own resources and local friends. It is almost possible to say therefore that purely aristocratic risings and conspiracies against the East Frankish kings begin only in the eleventh century. Under the Ottos, after Otto I's early, desperately hard-fought but decisive struggles, they became and remained isolated and relatively rare.

Only seventy years separate the death of Otto III from the secular explosion of the Saxon rising against the Salian king, Henry IV, in 1073, less than fifty if we regard Henry II as the last Saxon emperor. Yet the malaise which began to poison the relationships between an important and growing section of the Saxon higher nobility and the *Reich* cannot be put down solely to Henry's dubious dealings with a handful of Saxon bishops and lay lords.

There were more deep-seated anomalies in the make-up of the Ottonian empire. Saxon nobles could intermarry with their Frankish, Bavarian, Suabian and Lotharingian peers but, even during the Liudolfings' most aggressive and acquisitive decades in the tenth century, they could not aspire to the role which the companions of Pippin and Charlemagne had once played in their empire. The great Austrasian aristocratic clans, the neighbours of the Carolingians, had spread themselves in all the areas which fell under their domination. They not only married into but also displaced at least part of the nobility in the conquered lands, in Italy, it can be said, the largest part. The estates, honours and connections so gained were rewards but they also gave Frankish lordship a footing among what Einhard and other courtiers of Charlemagne and Louis the Pious still liked to call *gentes subactae*, the subject peoples. Conversely Alemans, Bavarians, north Spanish, some Lombard and some Saxon families were drawn into the circles of the leading Frankish clans and shared some of their advantages. These alliances, which sometimes even preceded the military onslaughts of the Carolingian kings, ensured that interests friendly to the Franks welcomed and helped to maintain the new order. They tempered the rigours of conquest.

The creation of a nobility with lands and positions in many parts of the Frankish Empire was thus an indispensable part of Carolingian political strategy. Its existence gave substance to the idea of the Franks as a dominant people, even if the ruling strata at Charlemagne's and Louis the Pious's courts were increasingly heterogeneous and badly in need of new ideas to make their cooperation more lasting and effective. Even failure and disintegration in the late ninth century did not wholly undermine the belief that the Franks, in other words, their nobility, were a chosen people. Regino of Prüm, the historian and moralist of their internecine struggles, did not question the *virtus* of the Frankish princes as such. Did not all the 'new' dynasties in Italy, Provence, Burgundy and Aquitaine, like himself, belong to this group? Only *virtus* alone was not enough.

The tenth-century Saxon writers, more especially Widukind, the author of the older *Life of Queen Mathilda*, later also Thietmar and the Quedlinburg Annalist, received the idea of a ruling people from the Carolingian past. Saxony was now, as Widukind proudly wrote, the mistress of many peoples and this included other German stems.[2] The whole East Frankish kingdom could be called a *regnum Saxonum* in the *Hildesheim Annals* when the writer recorded Otto I's return from Italy in 965.[3] The idea of a *Reichsvolk*, of being a dominant people associated with the larger rule of kings from their own midst, was the only secular political programme which the Franks bequeathed to the Saxons, but from the very beginning it did not work because it could not be fitted into the circumstances which enabled Otto I to win his early battles and conquer new ground for his own house. Just as the Liudolfings could not divide the kingship any more, so they could not implant their Saxon nobles massively and systematically in the southern duchies nor could Saxon nobles monopolize all the best places in the royal entourage. At times, and very critical times, the king had to rely on other men and stems, for instance in the suppression of the rising of 941 when it was, as we saw, by Frankish advice that he took his toll of blood. Widukind's intention when mentioning these influences may have been to shift the blame for the death of Saxon lords away from Otto, who had to possess the virtue of *clementia*, especially in his dealings with his brother Henry, the ringleader of the 941 plot.[4] Yet these incidents, quite early in Otto's reign, also show why the tenth-century Saxon historians could not turn the Saxon nobles into a *Reichsvolk*, a ruling people, very easily. They were unable to make the idea sound altogether convincing either to themselves or their audience. Sometimes Widukind presented the Liudolfings' accession as a partnership between the Saxons and the Franks so that the 'populus Francorum atque Saxonum' became the principal agents and decision-makers.[5] The Franci here may have included the leading men of the south and of the west as well as the Conradine and Salian families of Rhenish Francia, Hessia and the Main Valley.

Partnership between the leading families in the duchies rather than Saxon domination, then, lay embedded in the very foundation of the Saxon *Reich*. Otto I could not carry his Saxon nobles with him all the way in the process of his own family's aggrandizement and these nobles could share the ascendancy of their kings only up to a point. This was one of the anomalies which ran counter to current and inherited assumptions. It was reinforcd by another, the problem of deployment. Here the leading East Saxon families and their warlike followings had to come to terms with a paradox. Their native country in the tenth century became the wealthy centre of a far-flung empire while remaining what it had always been, an exposed frontier province. The enemy was never more than a few miles away and the East Saxon nobles were really pinned down at their posts. Very few of them took part in the battle at the Lech against the Magyars in 955. They could not be spared from the pressing Slav wars. Conversely the Bavarians and Suabians did not think of the Saxon frontiers as their business. Their annals were silent about the catastrophic rising of the northwestern Slavonic tribes in 983 or they treated this shattering blow with laconic, almost shoulder-shrugging indifference. 'There was', as the year-books of Niederaltaich recorded, 'trouble [*seditio*] between the Slavs and the Saxons.' The Slavs, the writer added, 'destroyed churches, monasteries and many fortresses'.[6]

The impossibility, and hence the Ottonians' failure in finding a consistent role for their Saxon nobles was fraught with grave consequences for the *Reich* they left behind them. Saxon stem-consciousness was fostered but it had of necessity to become particularistic. With the advent of the Salians, royal rule lost the last remaining traces of its familial and domestic character in Saxony which had counted for so much in the tenth century. The Salians did not lack all kinship in the Saxon nobility, thanks to an earlier marriage of Conrad II's empress, Gisela, with Bruno of Brunswick and of her half-sister Mathilda with Count Esico of Ballenstedt, but the intimacy and closeness of Otto I's time were now remote, albeit cherished, memories. The Saxon revolt against Henry IV—continued over so many years, resumed under Henry V and still not a dead echo even in 1180 and 1181 when Frederick Barbarossa marched into Saxony with his hosts to execute the sentence felled against Henry the Lion—was the consequence of this defect in the Ottonians' legacy. For the history of Germany it mattered, if anything, still more than the avatars of Gregorianism. Their coincidence was fortuitous although it meant that violence, the collisions between Henry IV and his Saxon opponents grouped round Rudolf of Rheinfelden, now achieved a global theme which it had not possessed before. The wars fought between the *fideles Sancti Petri* against the Salian king and his supporters were fought almost as wars of religion. To succumb or to suffer in them was to experience sanctifying martyrdom.

We have sought to explain how in the tenth century Ottonian kingship gave focus and profile to aristocratic rivalries and feuds. They were, from 938 onwards, drawn increasingly into the feuds within the royal kin. As has also been shown, in the eleventh century this changed. Conrad, Henry IV's son, in 1093, and the young Henry V in 1104, joined risings and discontents which had for many years already fed upon their own aristocratic and, in Italy, also urban substance. The Salian cadets, even the hard and astute Henry, thus became the playthings of conflict, not its centres and motor nerves. For the rise of the estate of princes as the new and decisive political class in German society this was perhaps already a symptom and certainly a portent.

Appendix: MS. John Rylands, 88

There is a further, unexpected, piece of circumstantial evidence to show that what happened in 942 was not out of keeping with Otto I's known ways of settling with his enemies and that the Walbeck counts suffered permanent loss for their share in the conspiracy. The John Rylands Library in Manchester possesses an eleventh-century Gospel Book (MS. John Rylands, 88) from the canons' house at Walbeck, Liuthar's foundation. Its fine script and especially the three surviving drawings of the Evangelists are well known to art-historians but, besides the sacred text, or because of it, we find a number of diverse later entries.[1] M. R. James in his catalogue has described them and on folio 7r he noted a list of lands belonging to the chapter in a number of villages, beginning with Scapendal, Nyendorp and followed by others, of which he cited a fair selection. To a reader of Thietmar's *Chronicon*, some of the place names must have an instantly familiar ring. Here we find Gross-Rottmersleben, Nord-Germersleben, obviously Walbeck, and also Tundersleben, which we know, albeit not from the bishop's history but from the *Chronica Episcoporum Ecclesia Merseburgensis*, to have belonged to the family.[2] A look at the manuscript itself shows that James's description is inadequate. We are dealing not simply with a list of estates but with a survey, recording the number of *mansi* held in various villages and what they paid in kind and in money. Some of the possessions were grouped into bailiwicks of which the global expected income was calculated and a sum total for the entire mass of holdings appears at the end. James dated the hand of this well-written and coherent statement of dues and revenues, covering just over three quarto leaves, as perhaps early fourteenth century. It could be taken back to the thirteenth and seems to be one of the earliest of the miscellaneous entries in the Gospel Book. The text should be of considerable interest to agrarian historians.

The survey remained unknown to Meibom and the eighteenth-century editors of his *Walbeckische Chronike* but it began to interest local scholars after the dissolution of the canons' house in 1810. Count Liuthar's foundation had an unbroken history of over 850 years, surviving the Reformation only to fall victim, like so many others, to the policies of the Napoleonic regime in Westfalia. Its lands and treasures were dispersed and the Gospel Book seems at first to have come into the possession of a civil servant, a Herr von Werder, in Magdeburg. In 1835 the survey of estates and renders was edited for the journal of the *Thüringisch-Sächsische Verein* by Behrends, the parson of Nord-Germersleben, chiefly for its topographical interest.[3] How the Gospel Book migrated from Magdeburg into the notorious collection of Guillaume Libri cannot be traced here. It was sold in England in 1859 and acquired for the Crawford Library in 1893.[4] Helmut Beumann, in an early article discussing the clashes between the canons of Walbeck and the nearby Cistercian monastery, Marienthal, founded before 1146, was aware of the Gospel Book in Manchester and used Behrends's edition of the survey but he did not know that it had been taken from the John Rylands Library treasure.[5]

Now it is startling to find that most of the family lands mentioned in Thietmar's *Chronicon*, the *Merseburg Episcopal History* and a notice in the *Life of Bishop Meinwerk of Paderborn* occur also in the survey of the Walbeck canons' lands in the thirteenth century, except for the two which Otto I is supposed to have given Count Liuthar after his failed rebellion.[6] Yet it is all the more surprising not to find any trace of them in the survey if we remember the circumstances of the foundation. To have offended the king was seen as having offended God: the very act of atonement had to express this belief.[7] To make amends Liuthar gave, or had to give, the tenth part of his inheritance to endow his collegiate church. Noble families in Ottonian Saxony and elsewhere often set up their religious houses at one of their principal residences and the lands assigned to them ran alongside those which remained under the immdiate lordship of the founders. They did not at once form wholly separate estates and in the tenth and earlier eleventh centuries the lay lords as advocates expected to remain the unfettered masters of their monasteries. In addition, these domestic sanctuaries with their ancestral tombs served to maintain some cohesion and continuity in fluctuating families and to safeguard a portion of their lands against the erosive effects of partitions. It is strange, therefore, that Liuthar or one of his successors should not have given some part of their Santersleben and Gutenswegen lands to Walbeck, especially if they held them because of a recent gift of the king's. Royal grants to lay nobles sometimes helped them to endow monasteries, although this gave the king a stake in the foundation. From what Thietmar tells us it is clear that Walbeck was very much an *Eigenkirche* down to his own days. He himself had been a canon there and inherited half its lands when his mother died. The two estates lay close to places where the canons can be found to be holding *mansi* at the time of the survey.[8] All this suggests that in 942 the two *predia* had been lost rather than gained.

Walbeck must have enlarged its possessions from the lands of the founders' heirs over the decades, as succeeding counts made their peace with God and perhaps especially in the eleventh century when the family's identity was blurred and merged with others as a result of too many daughters. If it is thought that the canons themselves sold off their estates at Santersleben and

Gutenswegen in the course of time, this would mean that they kept something from all the other known founders' possessions except these. It is true
that the bishop of Merseburg in 1233 sold the vill of Tundersleben, which his
church owed to the gift of its greatest pastor and his kin. Yet Tundersleben
lay a long way from Merseburg and the memory of Count Henry's (Thietmar's brother) and his own donation was not lost after the alienation.[9]

There are, however, three other estates mentioned by Thietmar in the
Chronicon as his or his family's, which cannot be traced in the Walbeck
survey. Two of these need not detain us for very long. His *curtis* with the Slav
name 'Malacin'—in German it was called Eisdorf—lay in the *pagus* Chutizi,
the Merseburg country (near Lützen) and it was his because it belonged to
the temporalities of his see.[10] In the north the *curtis* Heeslingen in the
diocese of Bremen can have come to him only after the death of his mother,
Kunigunde, in 997.[11] The distance between these lands and the Walbeck
centres of gravity on the Aller and in the northern tracts of the Nordthüringau was considerable. The counts of Stade, his maternal kin, were advocates
of the nunnery of Heeslingen and formidable *co-heredes* to have. On the
other hand, Wolmirstedt, near the mouth of the Ohre, presents more serious
difficulties. Thietmar called the fortress 'urbs nostra' and his cousin
Werner's wife, Liudgard, lay there mortally ill in 1012 when the bishop
hurried to her deathbed.[12] Werner had already lost his *beneficium* in 1009 so
that Wolmirstedt must have been held in proprietary tenure. We do not
know what lands he had to sacrifice in 1013 to regain the king's grace nor
what was lost after Werner's death in 1014. He died having abducted an
heiress, which exposed him once again to Henry II's retribution. Wolmirstedt had a church dedicated to St Pancras, the patron saint of the Walbeck
family and to him also, after the Virgin, they had dedicated their collegiate
foundation. The canons, therefore, may have held the church in Wolmirstedt for a time, although it did not belong to them later. In the eleventh
century the fortress fades out of sight to re-emerge as a possession of Albrecht
the Bear, the Ascanian margrave of the Northern March (1134–70). One of
his *ministeriales* can be found settled there in 1159. Wolmirstedt became
important again when a later margrave, Albrecht II, built a new castle there
in 1208. From now on it was the main stronghold and administrative centre
of this corner of the Ascanian principality. The rights over the church were
granted to a Cistercian nunnery in 1228.[13]

We can only speculate how the Ascanians came by Wolmirstedt. Albrecht
the Bear's biographer, O. v. Heinemann, thought that some of the former
Walbeck lands fell to him when he was awarded the disputed inheritance of
Count Bernhard of Plötzkau in 1152. Bernhard had fallen on the Second
Crusade and he was the last male of his line. His grandfather had married the
grand-daughter and heiress of Thietmar of Merseburg's brother, Frederick,
the burgrave of Magdeburg. Here it must be stressed that the Saxon Annalist
is our main source for the later history and the marriages of the family, and his
sweeping assertions about the descent of the inheritance cannot be tested
fully against other evidence.[14] In any case, Wolmirstedt did not—and this
was also Heinemann's view—fall to Albrecht by this route but it came to him

as part of the march with which the Emperor Lothar of Süpplingenburg invested him in 1134. More recently it has been suggested that Albrecht occupied the site about the year 1129 in his struggle to gain the succession to the margraviate. Now if Wolmirstedt was in the twelfth century regarded as an appurtenance of the march, this clashes with Thietmar's description of the place as 'urbs nostra' ('our family's fortress') and the St Pancras *patrocinium* of its church. Yet it seems that the constitutional status of the stronghold was already in dispute and fought over in the chronicler's own time. For as he himself tells us, Count Dedi, allied by marriage to the old rivals, neighbours and enemies of the Walbeck counts, caused Wolmirstedt to be sacked and burnt down, most probably during the interregnum after Otto III's death and shortly before that of Margrave Liuthar in 1003.[15] It was a blow struck at his heirs and their prospects to possess the march. Violence and sharp practice inevitably had their place in the descent of lands, given the fluidity of partible inheritances and undocumented grants. We must not be surprised to find that the canons of Walbeck had no rights in Wolmirstedt later.

It must finally be asked whether what can be known about the subsequent history of Gutenswegen and Santersleben, the two places named by Thietmar, is compatible with the view that Count Liuthar's estates there passed out of his and his family's possession in 942. Here we must pause and first of all note that his phrase, 'cum magna pecunia et predio in Sonterslevo et in Vodenesvege iacenti' ('land lying in Santersleben and Gutenswegen'), suggests that these estates did not consist of the two vills in their entirety. There were other landlords besides the Walbeck family in 941–2 and later. This makes it difficult to identify twelfth-century holdings with early ones. The historian of medieval East Saxony must not expect evidence like Domesday Book, its satellites and the Exchequer surveys. The most that can be attempted is to note the families and churches who subsequently had estates in these two places and to ask whether they could have inherited them ultimately from the last of Count Liuthar's descendants. Let us begin with Gutenswegen. Here we find that already in 937, in his first solemn diploma for St Maurice, Magdeburg, Otto I appears to grant what he had in Gutenswegen to his new foundation.[16] It figures in a long list of vills attached to and serving the great royal *curtis* in Magdeburg, which formed the core of the monastery's and later archbishopric's imposing landed fortune. In 973 Otto II confirmed his father's gift and the list of vills is repeated in his diploma.[17] Later confirmations were couched in more general terms and did not recite the string of placenames of the earliest grant. Had Otto I bestowed an estate in Gutenswegen on Liuthar of Walbeck in 942, he would have had to take it away from Magdeburg again. It seems unlikely. Later, in Thietmar's own lifetime, we find another noble family established there, besides the lands of St Maurice. The Saxon Annalist mentioned that the father of Archbishop Gero of Magdeburg (1012–23) was a certain Dedi of Gutenswegen.[18] This is a twelfth- and not a tenth-century appellation but Gero's religious foundation in the city, the collegiate church of St Sebastian where he chose to be buried, had lordship over Gutenswegen throughout the middle ages.[19] It is worth noting in passing that Gero's other foundation, the canonry and later Premonstratensian house of Unser Lieben Frauen, possessed a sizable estate and revenues at Gutenswegen in the sixteenth century, although the spurious foundation charter under the year 1015 did not mention the vill among the endowments.[20]

We can thus be fairly certain that the 'land lying in Vodenesvege' (Thietmar, II, 21) ceased to be a Walbeck possession in 941. A *ministerialis* of the counts of Hillersleben can be found there in the early thirteenth century. This family had counted for much in the Nordthüringau until 1154. Part of their ancestry can be traced back to the early eleventh century, the family of Archbishop Walthard of Magdeburg, and perhaps to a certain Milo who killed his enemy Brun in his (Brun's) own house. From the way Thietmar of Merseburg wrote about these happenings we can be fairly sure that Milo was no kinsman of his, nor was the archbishop.[21]

The later history of Santersleben is more difficult. It would not be so if we could be sure that sixty *Hufen* in 'Sandersleben' which Henry IV granted to the see of Speyer early in 1086, lay in the Magdeburg district.[22] Unfortunately, however, the diploma setting out Henry's gift, an original, omitted the name of the *pagus* and that of the count in whose jurisdiction the lands lay, leaving the spaces meant for them blank. A place called 'Scenderslebe' (Sandersleben), situated not in the Nordthüringau but in the Saxon Schwabengau, now Anhalt, occurs in a diploma of Henry III's, dated 2 July 1046, and here the Salians evidently had come by much land.[23] The editor of Henry IV's diplomata and other scholars have left open the question whether Santersleben in the Magdeburg region or in Anhalt was meant. It is worth recalling that Henry had recently won (albeit unreliable) allies in Saxony and had camped for some time near Magdeburg where he was received with royal honours, something which had not happened for many years. He and his entourage therefore could have known what lands were available for grant. The resumption of the practice of endowing churches closely connected with the Salian house in Eastern Saxony may have been premature. In the summer of 1086 the emperor had to resume military operations against his Saxon opponents and shortly afterwards they returned to the counterattack in the Main valley.

Sandersleben in Anhalt is not the only placename to confound us. By 1221 Santersleben in the Magdeburg region had become two localities, 'Gross-' and 'Klein Santersleben'.[24] Antiquaries and historians have assigned the estates mentioned by Thietmar under the year 942 to the one and the other. Gross Santersleben had a church dedicated to St Stephan and was thus probably an early, that is ninth-century, parish in the see of Halberstadt.[25] Here we must look for the core of settlement. In the twelfth century the village appears as the meeting place of a comital gemot, at first presided over by the counts of Hillersleben. Here, on 14 July 1167, the prelates, nobles and *ministeriales* of the church of Cologne received the solemnly sworn assurances of a group of Saxon princes and Magdeburg vassals that they would act together and lend their aid in warring against Henry the Lion.[26] It is noteworthy that Alt-Haldensleben was one of the most fought over of the duke's strongholds during these struggles. We hear of Santersleben again as the seat of a comital *placitum* in 1189, when Count Adolf of Schaumburg renewed the sale of some lands at Salbke before Count Otto of Falkenstein who had succeeded those of Hillersleben.[27] However, much the most important evidence about the tenure of land in the vill is to be found in a diploma of the Emperor Lothar of Süpplingenburg for the monastery of Königslutter, dated 1 August 1135.[28] Königslutter had been founded by Margrave Bernhard of the Northern March, Werner of Walbeck's enemy and successor in 1009 (or his like-named son), who can be traced in office and possession until 1044.[29] Originally Lutter was a house for canonesses and it should be added to the long list of these establishments in the diocese of Halberstadt, but nothing is heard of it before 1135, the year of its eclipse. For the canonesses at Lutter had, like so many others in the twelfth century, outlived their usefulness to their patrons and were 'by the advice of prudent and good men removed elsewhere because on account of their frivolity the property and religion of their church had dwindled and decayed'. Reform here, as elsewhere, meant the introduction of Benedictine monks who were to be quit of secular services. Next the diploma turned to the house's endowment and conferred freedom from services on everything which the canonesses had possessed at their first foundation and which by the emperor's own grant had now become the monks' property. Lothar was anxious to stress that the former Haldensleben lands were now his and part of his paternal inheritance. The devolution of these estates was perhaps, as in many such cases, far from simple and there may have been other claimants to the inheritance of the former margraves of the Northern March. Lothar's diploma listed the Königslutter holdings. They were substantial and at Santersleben amounted to no less than twenty-one *mansi.*

It would seem, then, that the Haldensleben comital family, the long-standing enemies of the Walbeckers, had possessed a sizable estate at Santersleben which the Süpplingenburgers inherited, partly as lords and advocates of Lutter and, as we shall see, in part directly. It is tempting to conclude, although it cannot be proved, that Otto I conferred the lands at Santersleben, which he had exacted from Liuthar of Walbeck as the price of his restitution, upon Count and later Margrave Dietrich, either at once or perhaps after the great rising of 953–4 when Dietrich, unlike others, had remained conspicuously loyal. This can be no more than a conjecture, but Otto I quite often granted forfeited and confiscated lands to others so that the burden of defending them against the aggrieved former holders or their heirs should not fall on him alone, but be borne largely by the beneficiaries. Here lay further fuel for the enmity between the all too closely neighbouring families of the Walbeckers and the Haldensleben counts. Let it be remembered that Liuthar, the conspirator of 941, is not known to have regained more than Otto I's bare grace. He remained outside the emperor's circle of friends and closer adherents in Saxony, as far as we know.

If Lothar of Süpplingenburg's heirs, the Welfs, had succeeded to his kingship, as seemed likely in 1137, Königslutter might have become their permanent mausoleum, a great sanctuary hallowed by royal burials. Here

Lothar himself, his wife Richenza and his son-in-law, Henry the Proud, were laid to rest. At first the Welfs remained firmly in control, as may be seen from Henry the Lion's charters.[30] It can be shown, moreover, that not all the Haldensleben holdings in Santersleben had accrued to the monastery. Some must have remained in Lothar's and the Welfs' possession to be granted out as fiefs to their vassals. Thus six *mansi* were held of William of Lüneburg, Henry the Lion's third son (died 1213) by Count Siegfried II of Blankenburg. Our source of information is a contemporary list of Siegfried's fiefs. The manner in which this document mentions more than once that a Count Poppo (of Blankenburg) was his grandfather, hints at the origin of the enfeoffment.[31] Poppo had been a prominent vassal of Henry the Lion's, who appears as a witness on some of the duke's earliest charters, beginning in 1143.[32] He had served Henry the Proud and rose to comital rank as Lothar's man. Once again we are led back to the Süpplingenburg inheritance. In 1215 also Otto of Lüneburg, William's son, gave the land on which the church stood, the *jus patronatus* and eight and a half *mansi* to the Templars, who established a commandery at Santersleben. The eight and a half *mansi* had been held of Otto by another vassal, who requested that this gift should be made.[33] Altogether then we can account for thirty-five and a half *mansi* of Welfic and Königslutter possessions in Santersleben, as well as the *jus patronatus*.

Not only their family monastery but even the seat from which they took their name had come to the Süpplingenburgs through their Haldensleben inheritance, that is to say the marriage of Lothar's father Gebhard, who fell in battle against Henry IV in 1075, with Hadwig of Formbach, herself the daughter of Gertrude of Haldensleben.[34] The lottery of survival determined that he, rather than the Billungs or the Bavarian Formbach family, should eventually possess the fortune of the erstwhile Saxon margravial clan, although Gertrude lived until 1116. Now as both Lutter and the Süpplingenburg lay quite close to the centres of the former Walbeck counts, an older generation of historians and genealogists believed that the Süpplingenburgs themselves were descended from the Walbeckers and so could have inherited part of their fortune.[35] It is possible to show that this was not so, even though the later history of Thietmar's family is blurred and very difficult to follow once the great memorialist had fallen silent. At the time of his death in 1018, there were already two distinct branches of his family, the descendants of Count Siegfried (died 991) and those of Margrave Liuthar (died 1003). Of Siegfried's sons, Thietmar's brothers, we know only the posterity of Frederick, thanks to one of the detailed genealogical asides in the Saxon Annalist's work.[36] Frederick rose to the burgraviate of Magdeburg, evidently after 1018 since there is no mention of his advancement in the *Chronicon*. His earlier career had been more modest: he can be found commanding Thietmar's *satellites* and helping his cousin Werner in his dangerous exploits, the abduction of his first wife Liudgard in 998 and the slaying of Count Dedi in 1009.[37] A woman, the Marchioness Irmgard of Plötzkau, was the last representative of Frederick's line. We know of some of her landed possessions and they did not include the two places here under review.[38] Whether Count Henry, Frederick's elder brother and Count Siegfried's successor, had any descendants, is not known. He can be found officiating as count up to 1014. His wife died while Thietmar was provost of the canons of Walbeck (1002–9). He buried her in the church and reproached himself bitterly for moving the tomb of an earlier provost to do so.[39] Henry could have married again. We do not know when he died. Possibly his inheritance came to his brother Frederick, the burgrave. Thietmar mentioned no sister in his *Chronicon* but the Saxon Annalist, in his genealogical excursus on the Walbeck counts, gave him one named Oda. He confused generations and was almost certainly mistaken.[40]

The posterity of Margrave Liuthar and their fortunes are shrouded in even greater obscurity. It does not appear that Werner of Walbeck left a family behind him. The early death of his wife Liudgard (1012), the daughter of Ekkehard of Meissen, may have driven him to his last and fateful escapade, the abduction of the Beichlingen heiress suggesting that there was as yet no offspring. He had however two brothers, one called Berthold, the name reflecting the Schweinfurt connection, the other called Dietrich. Dietrich was a clerk and belonged to the Magdeburg cathedral community. He served Archbishops Tagino and Walthard as chaplain and was taken into the royal chapel after Henry II had rejected his election as archbishop of Magdeburg to succeed Walthard.[41] This was often a consolation prize for disappointed candidates since the king might promote them later from the *capella* if they had served him well and a suitable vacancy arose. However, it does not appear that Dietrich was one of the fortunate ones.

The circumstances of Werner's death and his disfavour meant that his other brother, Berthold, a layman, had few chances to hold on to a comital position in Eastern Saxony. After a formal reconciliation and settlement with his principal adversary, Margrave Bernhard (of Haldensleben) early in 1017 in which Dietrich, the imperial chaplain shared, Berthold exiled himself to the Lower Rhine.[42] He was soon embroiled in the vicious feuds between Count Balderich and the avengers of Count Wichmann III, whom Balderich and his wife Adela had caused to be slain in autumn 1016. Berthold seized and held a fortress, Monreberg, but later surrendered it to Henry II who ordered it to be destroyed. Behind the partisans of the tempestuous couple stood Archbishop Heribert of Cologne (999–1021), who offered shelter to men who had lost the emperor's goodwill. It has already been mentioned that the Walbeck counts, especially Margrave Liuthar, had interests in Cologne and perhaps his wife Godila, Berthold's mother, had brought them a Rhenish inheritance. We do not know whom Berthold married, how long he lived and whether he left any sons and daughters behind. His only sister was an abbess.

Some historians have assumed that there were other brothers not mentioned by Thietmar in his *Chronicon*, while ignoring Dietrich the chaplain.[43] It seems improbable, but a Count Liuthar officiating in parts of the Nordthüringau and the neighbouring Derlingau appears in diplomata of Henry III's and Henry IV's between 1049 and 1063.[44] Once at least he is found in an area where Werner of Walbeck had formerly been in charge but where his enemy, Margrave Bernhard of the Northern March, held office as recently as 1044.[45] Years later, in 1068 and again in 1083, a Count Siegfried can be traced on roughly similar ground in the Nordthüringau. In 1068 a large fief, once held of the king by Count Liuthar, was granted by Henry IV to the brother of the grasping and pushing Bishop Burchard II of Halberstadt.[46] In 1083 the anti-king, Hermann of Salm, gave Burchard an estate which had escheated to him thanks to the heirlessness of a certain Dietrich—which is, as we have seen, again a Walbeck name.[47] Among the places mentioned in both diplomata there were several in which the canons of Walbeck held land, according to their thirteenth-century survey in MS. John Rylands Library, 88.[48] Yet before we rush to conclusions we must note that in 1068 the lord of the lands was the king and that in 1083 Count Siegfried was obviously not Dietrich's heir.

There has indeed been no want of speculation about the identity of these two counts, Liuthar and Siegfried. In the first place it is not at all clear whether they were father and son. If Siegfried was Liuthar's son, it is noteworthy that Liuthar's large fief passed him by and was turned into *proprietas* for the Suabian family of Burchard of Halberstadt and this when he was probably no longer a minor. Liuthar has been assigned to the house of Stade, the Süpplingenburgs, the Ascanians and the Walbeckers, assuming that one of Thietmar's cousins had descendants after all who achieved some measure of restoration or that his brother Henry enjoyed posterity.[49] There is no clear evidence. For Count Siegfried, a 1087 charter for the monks of Ilsenburg in the name of Bishop Burchard appears to offer us just that, for among the witnesses it cited a 'Siffredus comes de Wallebike'. Yet the document is an ill-contrived forgery of very much later date in the Ilsenburg cartulary and above all its witness list will not pass muster.[50] It leaves us, however, with the haunting question where the forger could have found a 'Count Siegfried of Walbeck'. Whoever the count of the 1068 and 1083 diplomata was, he cannot have been a person of the first consequence for he is not to be found among the *dramatis personae* of the Saxon rising in either Lampert of Hersfeld's *Annals* or Brun's *Book of the Saxon War*.

That the Süpplingenburgers were not related to the Walbeck family can perhaps best be shown with the help of a story in Thietmar. It is his account of his uncle's doings during the succession crisis of 1002. Liuthar of Walbeck may well have been the first Saxon lord who promised to help Henry win over his Saxon peers to the cause of the Bavarian Liudolfing's kingship. When he secretly went to see Henry at Bamberg in March he did not travel alone but brought with him his maternal uncle, Ricbert.[51] Ricbert had a grievance, for Otto III had removed him from his countship in the Harzgau and appointed a vassal of Bishop Arnulf of Halberstadt in his place, a man named Liudger. In later Ottonian Saxony countships were by no means always heritable or securely held by their incumbents. Margrave Liuthar had good reasons for wishing to have Henry as his king rather than Ekkehard of Meissen. All the same and very characteristically, he did not offer his services for nothing. The price included among other things the restoration of Ricbert to his comital office. A bargain must have been struck for we meet

Ricpert, also called Ippo, as count in the Harzgau in 1003 and 1009. He must have been reappointed quite soon for, when the Saxon princes met Henry and swore to him at Merseburg on 25 July, only Liudger, Ricbert's rival, hung back and refused to do homage.[52]

His estrangement was not lasting. From 1021 onwards and probably earlier, a Count Liudger officiated in the Harzgau and the Nordthüringau and there can be little doubt that he was the man who had clashed with Margrave Liuthar and his kinsman Ricbert in 1002.[53] By this time Margrave Liuthar's sons had lost the emperor's goodwill. Count Liudger can be followed into the reign of Conrad II and he was in part of the localities of his *comitatus* succeeded by Lothar of Süpplingenburg's grandfather and father.[54] Lothar himself is often called Liudger in narrative sources and occasionally also in Halberstadt charters and it is tempting to regard the Harzgau count as his ancestor.[55] If we do, then what we observe here are the workings of *inimicitia*, enmity, and the quicksands of royal favour, rather than close kinship and succession bonds between the families of Walbeck and Lothar's forbears. They both shared, it is true, affinity with the nobles of Querfurt but where the Süpplingenburgs, as they were to be called later, invaded the sphere of lordship once possessed by Werner of Walbeck, it was as opponents and better favoured rivals that they came to the fore.

Even now we have not quite reached the end of our road. No one dealing with Santersleben's medieval tenants can altogether ignore Hermann of Lerbeck, the late fourteenth-century Dominican to whom we owe a history of the bishops of Minden, printed by Leibnitz in his *Scriptores Rerum Brunswicarum* and a *Chronicle of the Counts of Schaumburg*.[56] Hermann of Lerbeck thought that the counts had originally come from Santersleben and had been in office there before they built the Schaumburg and moved to Holsatia. Meibom the Elder and the editors of his *Walbeckische Chronike* used this tradition to assert that a Schaumburg ancestor, an 'Adolf of Santersleben', was a grandson of Margrave Werner of Walbeck. It was thought that Conrad II, at a diet in Minden which he never held, had raised Adolf to the rank of an imperial count.[57] Behrends, the antiquary and editor of the Walbeck survey, gave some countenance to this construction, although here 'Adolf of Santersleben' became a grandson of the conspirator of 941, Count Liuthar.[58] To be brief, whatever fiefs and advowsons the counts of Schaumburg later held in Santersleben and in nearby Schakensleben, the story of their descent from the Walbeckers is a wishful fantasy hazarded by Meibom and, more cautiously, by his eighteenth-century editors. It should be firmly rejected.[59]

In conclusion, then, the evidence concerning Santersleben is not as clear and unequivocal as that concerning Gutenswegen. We must, however, note the very considerable holdings of Königslutter and the Welfs in the village and the strong probability that it had come to them from the Haldensleben family, the rivals of the counts of Walbeck. We cannot exclude the possibility that the Salians themselves were landlords in Santersleben and in other areas where the counts of Walbeck had once possessed estates. *Besitzge-schichte* is treacherous ground. Given a lay society which seldom recorded its inheritance arrangements, it is dangerous to reconstruct the movements of land too rigorously. Surveying the fragments of evidence, however, it still remains significant that in the thirteenth century the collegiate church of Walbeck, the foundation of Count Liuthar, had no lands in either Santersleben or Gutenswegen. Once more it seems the estates there had been lost rather than gained after the conspiracy of 941.

Bibliography

Sources

Manuscripts

Herzog August Bibliothek, Wolfenbüttel, MS. 17. 14 Aug. 2—the still partly unpublished *Miracula Sancti Wigberhti*.
Paris, Bibliothèque Nationale MS. Lat. 11851—the *Annalista Saxo*.
Brussels, Bibliothèque Royale MS. 7503–18—the Corvey version of Thietmar of Merseburg's *Chronicon*.
MS. John Rylands Library, 88—the Walbeck Gospels.

Adalboldi Vita Heinrici II. Imperatoris, ed. G. Waitz, *MGH*, *SS* IV (Hanover, 1841).
Adam of Bremen, *Gesta Hammaburgensis Ecclesiae Pontificum*, 3rd edn, B. Schmeidler, *SRG* (Hanover and Leipzig, 1917).
Agius, *Vita et Obitus Hathumodae*, ed. G. H. Pertz, *MGH*, *SS* IV (Hanover, 1841).
Alpert, *De Diversitate Temporum*, ed. G. H. Pertz, *MGH*, *SS* IV.
Altfridi Vita S. Liudgeri, ed. G. H. Pertz, *MGH*, *SS* II (Hanover, 1829).
Annales Altahenses Maiores, ed. E. L. B. Oefele, *SRG* (Hanover, 1891).
Annales S. Disibodi, ed. G. Waitz, *MGH*, *SS* XVII (Hanover, 1861).
Annales Corbeienses in *Monumenta Corbeiensia*, Bibliotheca Rerum Germanicarum I, ed. P. Jaffé (Berlin, 1864).
Annales Einsidlenses, ed. G. H. Pertz, *MGH*, *SS* III (Hanover, 1839).
Annales Fuldenses, ed. F. Kurze, *SRG* (Hanover, 1891).
Annales Hildesheimenses, ed. G. Waitz, *SRG* (Hanover, 1878 and reprinted 1947).
Annales Laureshamenses and *Annales Laurissenses Minores*, ed. G. H. Pertz, *MGH*, *SS* I (Hanover, 1826).
Annales Magdeburgenses, ed. G. H. Pertz, *MGH*, *SS* XVI (Hanover, 1869).
Annales Necrologici Fuldenses, ed. G. Waitz, *MGH*, *SS* XIII (Hanover, 1881).
Annales Palidenses, *MGH*, *SS* XVI.
Annales Pegavienses, *MGH*, *SS* XVI.
Annales Quedlinburgenses, ed. G. H. Pertz, *MGH*, *SS* III.
Annales Regni Francorum, ed. F. Kurze, *SRG* (Hanover, 1895 and reprinted 1950).
Annales Sangallenses Maiores, ed. I. von Arx, *MGH*, *SS* I.
Annales Stederburgenses, ed. G. H. Pertz, *MGH*, *SS* XVI.

Annalista Saxo, ed. G. Waitz, *MGH*, *SS* vi (Hanover, 1844).
Anselmi Gesta Episcoporum Leodensium, ed. R. Köpke, *MGH*, *SS* vii (Hanover, 1846)
Arnold of St. Emmeram, *De Miraculis Beati Emmerammi*, ed. G. Waitz, *MGH*, *SS* iv.

P. W. Behrends, 'Güterverzeichnis des ehemaligen Collegiatsstifts zu Walbeck aus dem dreizehnten Jahrhundert', *Neue Mittheilungen aus dem Gebiet historisch-antiquarischer Forschungen, Thüringisch Sächsischer Verein* 2 (1835), pp. 38–61.
Berthold of Reichenau, *Annales*, ed. G. H. Pertz, *MGH*, *SS* v (Hanover, 1844).
Die Briefe des Abtes Bern von Reichenau, ed. F.-J. Schmale, *Veröffentlichungen der Kommission für Geschichtliche Landeskunde in Baden-Württemberg* Reihe A, Quellen, 6 (Stuttgart, 1961).
Die Briefsammlung Gerberts von Reims, ed. F. Weigle, *MGH*, *Die Briefe der Deutschen Kaiserzeit* ii (Berlin, Zürich, Dublin, 1966).
Brunos Buch vom Sachsenkrieg, ed. H.-E. Lohmann, *MGH*, *Kritische Studientexte* 2 (Leipzig, 1937) and also in *Quellen zur Geschichte Heinrichs IV.*, ed. F.-J. Schmale, *Ausgewählte Quellen* xii (Darmstadt, 1963).
Brun of Querfurt, *Vita S. Adalberti*, ed. G. H. Pertz, *MGH*, *SS* iv.
Brun of Querfurt, Letter to King Henry II, 1008, in W. Giesebrecht, *Geschichte der deutschen Kaiserzeit* ii, 5th edn (Leipzig, 1885), pp. 702–5.

Iohannes Canaparius, *Vita S. Adalberti Episçopi*, ed. G. H. Pertz, *MGH*, *SS* iv.
Capitularia Regum Francorum, 2 vols, ed. A. Boretius and V. Krause, *MGH*, *Legum Sectio II* (Hanover, 1883–97).
Codex diplomaticus Anhaltinus i and ii, ed. O. v. Heinemann (Dessau, 1867–75).
Constantine, Abbot of St Symphorion, *Vita Adalberonis II. Mettensis Epsicopi*, ed. G. H. Pertz, *MGH*, *SS* iv.
Constitutiones et Acta Publica Imperatorum et Regum i, ed. L. Weiland, *MGH*, *Legum Sectio IV* (Hanover, 1893).
Chronicon Eberspergense, ed. W. Arndt, *MGH*, *SS* xx (Hanover, 1868).
Chronica Episcoporum Ecclesiae Merseburgensis, ed. R. Wilmans, *MGH*, *SS* x (Hanover, 1852).
Cronecken der Sassen (Mainz, 1492).
Cronica Ducum de Brunswick, ed. L. Weiland, *MGH*, *Deutsche Chroniken* ii (Hanover, 1877).

E. Dümmler, 'Das alte Merseburger Todtenbuch', *Neue Mittheilungen aus dem Gebiet historisch-antiquarischer Forschungen* 11(1867).

Einhard, *Vita Karoli Magni*, 6th edn O. Holder-Egger, *SRG* (Hanover, Leipzig, 1911, reprinted 1947).
Ekkeharti (IV.) *Casus sancti Galli*, ed. G. Meyer von Knonau, *Mittheilungen zur Vaterländischen Geschichte*, NF. 5, 6 (St Gallen, 1877).

Les Annales de Flodoard, ed. P. Lauer, *Collection de Textes pour servir à l'Étude et à l'Enseignement de l'Histoire* (Paris, 1905).
Fragmentum de Arnulfo duce, ed. P. Jaffé, *MGH*, *SS* xvii.
Fundatio Monasterii Schildecensis, ed. O. Holder-Egger, *MGH*, *SS* xv, ii (Hanover, 1888).
Fundatio Oratorii S. Mariae ad Crucem iuxta Hervordiam, ed. O. Holder-Egger, *MGH*, *SS* xv, ii (Hanover, 1888).

Gerhardi Vita S. Oudalrici Episcopi Augustani, ed. G. Waitz, *MGH*, *SS* IV.
Gesta Episcoporum Cameracensium, ed. L. C. Bethmann, *MGH*, *SS* VII.
Gesta Episcoporum Halberstadensium, ed. L. Weiland, *MGH*, *SS* XXIII (Hanover, 1874).
Gesta Archiepiscoporum Magdeburgensium, ed. W. Schum, *MGH*, *SS* XIV (Hanover, 1883).
Gesta Episcoporum Virdunensium Continuatio, ed. G. Waitz, *MGH*, *SS* IV.
'Das Güterverzeichnis und das Lehnregister des Grafen Siegfried II. von Blankenburg aus den Jahren 1209–1227', *Zeitschrift des Harz-Vereins für Geschichte und Alterthumskunde* 3 (1869).

G. Hahn, *Historia Martisburgica, darinnen Chronica Ditmari, Bischofs zu Marssburg* . . . (Leipzig, 1606).
Helgaud, *Epitoma Vitae Regis Rotberti Pii*, ed. R.-H. Bautier and G. Labory, *Sources d'Histoire Médiévale* 1 (Paris, 1965).
Hermanni de Lerbeke Chronicon Comitum Schauenburgensium, in H. Meibom Jr., *Rerum Germanicarum Tomi III* (Helmstädt, 1688) I.
Hermanni de Lerbeke Chronicon Episcoporum Mindensium, ed. G. G. Leibnitz, *Scriptores Rerum Brunswicarum* (Hanover, 1707–11) II.
Hrotsvithae Opera, ed. P. Winterfeld, *SRG* (Berlin, Zürich, 1965).

John of St Arnulf, *Vita Iohannis Abbatis Gorziensis*, ed. G. H. Pertz, *MGH*, *SS* IV.

Lamperti Monachi Hersfeldensis Opera, ed. O. Holder-Egger, *SRG* (Hanover, Leipzig, 1894).
K. Langosch, *Waltharius. Ruodlieb. Märchenepen*, 3rd edn *WBG* (Darmstadt, 1967).
Leges Saxonum et Lex Thuringorum, ed. C. v. Schwerin, *MGH*, *Fontes Iuris Germanici Antiqui* (Hanover, Leipzig, 1918).
Die Werke Liudprands von Cremona, 3rd edn J. Becker, *SRG* (Hanover, Leipzig, 1915).
Das Leben der Liutbirg, ed. O. Menzel, *MGH*, *Kritische Studientexte* 3 (Leipzig, 1937).

Magdeburger Schöppenchronik, ed. K. Janicke, *Die Chroniken der deutschen Städte* 7 (Leipzig, 1869).
Regesta Archiepiscopatus Magdeburgensis, ed. G. A. von Mülverstedt, 3 vols (Magdeburg, 1876-81).
Heinrich Meiboms des älteren Walbeckische Chronike, ed. C. F. Dingelstädt and C. Abeln (Helmstädt, 1749).
MGH, *Diplomata Regum Germaniae ex stirpe Karolinorum* III, *Arnolfi Diplomata*, ed. P. Kehr (Berlin, 1955).
MGH, *Diplomata Regum Germaniae ex stirpe Karolinorum* IV, *Zwentiboldi et Ludowici infantis Diplomata*, ed. T. Schieffer (Berlin, 1960).
MGH, *Diplomatum Regum et Imperatorum Germaniae Tomus I. Conradi I. Heinrici I. et Ottonis I. Diplomata*, ed. T. Sickel (Hanover, 1879–84).
MGH, *Diplomatum Regum et Imperatorum Germaniae Tomi II. pars prior. Ottonis II. Diplomata* (Hanover, 1888).

MGH, Diplomatum Regum et Imperatorum Germaniae Tomi II. pars posterior. Ottonis III. Diplomata, ed. T. Sickel (Hanover, 1893).

MGH, Diplomatum Regum et Imperatorum Germaniae Tomus III. Heinrici II. et Arduini Diplomata, ed. H. Bresslau (Hanover, 1900–3).

MGH, Diplomatum Regum et Imperatorum Germaniae Tomus IV. Conradi II Diplomata, ed. H. Bresslau (Hanover and Leipzig, 1909).

MGH, Diplomatum Regum et Imperatorum Germaniae Tomus V. Heinrici III. Diplomata, ed. H. Bresslau and P. Kehr (Berlin, 1931).

MGH, Epistolae Selectae, I, S. Bonifacii et Lulii Epistolae, 2nd edn M. Tangl (Berlin, 1955).

MGH, Epistolae Karolini Aevi, II, ed. E. Dümmler (Berlin, 1895).

MGH, Legum Sectio III. Concilia, II, i, ed. A. Werminhoff (Hanover and Leipzig, 1906).

Monumenta Moguntina, Bibliotheca Rerum Germanicarum, III, ed. P. Jaffé (Berlin, 1866).

Monumenta Novaliciensia vetustiora, ed. C. Cipolla, FSI (Rome, 1901).

Necrologium Monasterii S. Michaelis, ed. A. C. Wedekind (Brunswick, 1833).

Die Lebensbeschreibung der Kaiserin Adelheid von Abt Odilo von Cluny, ed. H. Paulhart, *MIÖG*, Ergbd. xx, 2 (1962).

Johannes Pomarius, *Chronica der Sachsen und Nidersachsen* (Wittenbergk, 1588).

F. W. Oediger, *Die Regesten der Erzbischöfe von Köln im Mittelalter* I, *313–1099*, *Publikationen der Gesellschaft für Rheinische Geschichtskunde* XXI (Bonn, 1954–61).

Origines Guelficae, ed. C. L. Scheidius (Hanover, 1753).

Poeta Saxo, ed. P. Winterfeld, *MGH, Poetarum Latinorum Medii Aevi Tomus IV, i*. (Berlin, 1909).

Regesta Historiae Westfaliae, accedit Codex Diplomaticus, ed. H. A. Erhard, 2 vols (1847–51).

Regesta Historiae Westfaliae, Additamenta, ed. R. Wilmans (Münster, 1877).

Regesta Historiae Westfaliae, Westfälisches Urkundenbuch, Supplement, ed. W. Diekamp (Münster, 1885).

Regesta Imperii: see Abbreviations, p. ix.

Regino of Prüm, *Libri Duo de Synodalibus Causis et Disciplinis Ecclesiasticis*, ed. F. G. A. Wasserschleben (Leipzig, 1840).

Reginonis Abbatis Prumiensis Chronicon cum Continuatione Treverensi, ed. F. Kurze, *SRG* (Hanover, 1890).

J. Reviron, *Jonas d'Orléans et son "De Institutione Regia"*, *Etude et Texte Critique* (Paris, 1930).

Richer, Histoire de France (888–995), ed. R. Latouche, *Les Classiques de l'Histoire de France au Moyen Age* (Paris, 1930–7), 2 vols.

Ruotgeri Vita Brunonis Archiepiscopi Coloniensis, ed. I. Ott, *SRG*, NS x (Weimar, 1951).

Sachsenspiegel Landrecht, 2nd edn K. A. Eckhardt, *MGH, Fontes Iuris Germanici*, NS I, i (Göttingen, 1955).

Sigebert of Gembloux, *Chronica*, ed. D. L. C. Bethmann, *MGH, SS* VI.

Sigebert of Gembloux, *Vita Deoderici Episcopi Mettensis*, ed. G. H. Pertz, *MGH, SS* IV.

Die Tegernseer Briefsammlung (Froumund), ed. K. Strecker, *MGH*, *Epistolae Selectae* III (Berlin, 1925, reprinted 1964).
Thietmari Merseburgensis Episcopi Chronicon, ed. R. Holtzmann, *SRG*, NS IX (Berlin, 1955).
Die Dresdner Handschrift der Chronik des Bischofs Thietmar von Merseburg, preface by L. Schmidt (Dresden, 1905).
Die Chronik des Thietmar von Merseburg, translated (into German) by M. Laurent, 2nd edn J. Strebitzki, revised by W. Wattenbach, *Die Geschichtschreiber der deutschen Vorzeit*, 2nd edn. (Leipzig, 1892).
Thietmar von Merseburg Chronik, Neu übertragen von W. Trillmich, *Ausgewählte Quellen* IX *WBG* (Darmstadt, 1957).
J. F. Ursinus, *Dithmar Bischofs von Merseburg Chronik aus der lateinischen in die deutsche Sprache übersetzt* (Dresden, 1790).
Translatio S. Alexandri, ed. B. Krusch, *Nachrichten von der Gesellschaft der Wissenschaften zu Göttingen Philol.-Histor. Klasse* (1933), pp. 405–36.
Triumphus Sancti Remacli de Malmundariensi Coenobio, ed. W. Wattenbach, *MGH*, *SS* XI (Hanover, 1854).

Die Urkunden Heinrichs des Löwen Herzogs von Sachsen und Bayern, ed. K. Jordan, *MGH* (Weimar, 1949).
Urkundenbuch des Hochstifts Halberstadt und seiner Bischöfe 1, ed. G. Schmidt, *Publicationen aus den Königlich Preussischen Staatsarchiven* 17 (1883).
Urkundenbuch des Hochstifts Hildesheim und seiner Bischöfe 1, ed. K. Janicke, *Publicationen aus den Königlich Preussischen Staatsarchiven* 56 (Leipzig, 1896).
Urkundenbuch des Klosters Ilsenburg I, ed. E. Jacobs, *Geschichtsquellen der Provinz Sachsen* 6, 1 (Halle, 1875).
Lüneburger Urkundenbuch, ed. W. v. Hodenberg, VII Abt., *Archiv des Klosters S. Michaelis zu Lüneburg* (Celle, Hanover, 1861).
Urkundenbuch des Erzstifts Magdeburg I (937–1192), ed. F. Israel and W. Möllenberg, *Geschichtsquellen der Provinz Sachsen und des Freistaates Anhalt, Neue Reihe* 18 (Magdeburg, 1937).
Urkundenbuch des Klosters Unser Lieben Frauen zu Magdeburg, ed. G. Hertel, *Geschichtsquellen der Provinz Sachsen* 10 (Halle, 1878).
Urkundenbuch der Klöster der Grafschaft Mansfeld, ed. M. Krühne, *Geschichtsquellen der Provinz Sachsen* 20 (Halle, 1888).
Urkundenbuch des Hochstifts Merseburg I, ed. P. Kehr, *Geschichtsquellen der Provinz Sachsen* 36 (Halle, 1899).
Urkundenbuch des Klosters Stötterlingenburg, ed. C. v. Schmidt-Phiseldeck, *Geschichtsquellen der Provinz Sachsen* 4 (1874).

Vita Bernwardi Episcopi Hildesheimensis, ed. G. H. Pertz, *MGH*, *SS* IV.
Vita Burchardi Episcopi Wormatiensis, ed. G. H. Pertz, *MGH*, *SS* IV.
Vita Erhardi Episcopi Bavarici, ed. W. Levison, *MGH*, *Scriptores Rerum Merowingicarum* VI (Hanover, Leipzig, 1913).
Vita Mathildis Reginae antiquior, ed. R. Köpke, *MGH*, *SS* X.
Vita Mathildis Reginae (posterior), ed. G. H. Pertz, *MGH*, *SS* IV.
Vita Meinwerci Episcopi Patherbrunnensis, ed. F. Tenckhoff, *SRG* (Hanover, 1921).
Vita Radbodi Episcopi Traiectensis, ed. O. Holder-Egger, *MGH*, *SS* XV, i.
C. Vogel and R. Elze, *Le Pontifical Romano-Germanique du Dixième Siècle, Studi e Testi*, 226 (Città del Vaticano, 1963).

Widukindi Monachi Corbeiensis Rerum Gestarum Saxonicarum libri tres, 5th edn H.-E. Lohmann and P. Hirsch, *SRG* (Hanover, 1935).

P. Wigand, *Traditiones Corbeienses* (Leipzig, 1843).
Willelmi Malmesbiriensis De Gestis Regum Anglorum, ed. W. Stubbs, 2 vols, *Rolls Series* (London, 1887–9).
Wiponis Opera, 3rd edn H. Bresslau, *SRG* (Hanover and Leipzig, 1915).
Wolfherii Vita Godehardi Episcopi (Hildenesheimensis) prior,
  Wolfherii Vita Godehardi Episcopi posterior, ed. G. H. Pertz, *MGH, SS* xi.

H. Zimmermann, *Papstregesten 911–1024*: see Abbreviations, p. ix.

Secondary Works

To the titles cited in the notes I have added a few others of general interest for the themes here raised.

H. A. Anton, *Fürstenspiegel und Herrscherethos in der Karolingerzeit, Bonner Historische Forschungen* 32 (Bonn, 1968).

E. Bachmann, *Das Kloster Heeslingen-Zeeven. Verfassungs- and Wirtschaftsgeschichte* (Stade, 1966).
W. Baetke, 'Yngvi und die Ynglinger', *SB. der Sächsischen Akademie der Wissenschaften, Philol.-Histor. Klasse* (Berlin, 1964).
H. Bannasch, *Das Bistum Paderborn unter den Bischöfen Rethar und Meinwerk (938–1036)*, (Paderborn, 1972).
H.-G. Beck, 'Byzantinisches Gefolgschaftswesen', *SB. der Bayerischen Akademie der Wissenschaften, Philol.-Histor. Klasse* (1965) and in his *Ideen und Realitaeten in Byzanz, Gesammelte Aufsaetz*, Variorum Reprints (London, 1972).
F. Becker, *Das Königtum der Thronfolger im Deutschen Reich des Mittelalters, Quellen und Studien zur Verfassungsgeschichte des Deutschen Reiches in Mittelalter und Neuzeit* v, 3 (Weimar, 1913).
P. W. Behrends, *Neuhaldenslebische Kreis-Chronik*, 2 vols (Neuhaldensleben, 1824–6).
H. Beumann, 'Der Streit der Stifte Marienthal und Walbeck um den Lappwald', *Studien und Mitteilungen zur Geschichte des Benediktiner-Ordens* 53 (1935).
'Zur Frühgeschichte des Klosters Hillersleben', *Sachsen und Anhalt* 14 (1938).
Widukind von Korvei (Weimar, 1950).
'Die Historiographie des Mittelalters als Quelle für die Ideengeschichte des Königtums', *HZ* 180 (1955) and in his *Ideengeschichtliche Studien zu Einhard und anderen Geschichtsschreiben des Früheren Mittelalters*, *WBG* (Darmstadt, 1962).
'Das Kaisertum Ottos des Grossen. Ein Rückblick nach tausend Jahren', *HZ* 195 (1962) and in *Wissenschaft vom Mittelalter*.
'Grab und Thron Karls des Grossen zu Aachen', *Karl de Grose, IV, Das Nachleben*, ed. W. Braunfels and P. E. Schramm (Düsseldorf, 1967).
'Die sakrale Legitimierung des Herrschers im Denken der ottonischen Zeit', in *Königswahl und Thronfolge in Ottonisch-Frühdeutscher Zeit*, *Wege der Forschung* CLXXVIII, *WBG* (Darmstadt, 1971).
Wissenschaft vom Mittelalter Ausgewählte Aufsätze (Cologne, Vienna, 1972).
B. Bischoff, 'Das Thema des Poeta Saxo', *Speculum Historiale Johannes Spörl . . . dargebracht*, ed. C. Bauer, L. Boehm, M. Müller (Freiburg, München, 1965).
H. Bloch, 'Montecassino, Byzantium and the West in the Earlier Middle Ages', Dumbarton Oaks Papers 3 (1946).

P. Bloch, *Der Darmstädter Hitda Codex* (Berlin, 1968).

P. Bloch and H. Schnitzler, *Die Ottonische Kölner Malschule* (Düsseldorf, 1967).

1000 Jahre Borghorst, ed, W. Kohl (Münster, 1968).

L. Bornscheuer, *Miseriae Regum*, *Arbeiten zur Frühmittelalterforschung* 4, ed. K. Hauck (Berlin, 1968).

C. A. Bouman, *Sacring and Crowning* (Gronigen, Djakarta, 1957).

A. Brackmann, 'Die politische Bedeutung der Mauritius-Verehrung im frühen Mittelalter' in his *Gesammelte Aufsätze* (Weimar, 1941).

H. Bresslau, *Jahrbücher des Deutschen Reichs unter Konrad II.*, 2 vols (Leipzig, 1879–84, reprinted Berlin, 1967).

K. Brunner, 'Die fränkischen Fürstentitel im neunten und zehnten Jahrhundert' in *Intitulatio* II, ed. H. Wolfram, *MIÖG*, *Ergbd.* XXIV (1973).

C. Brühl, 'Fränkischer Königsbrauch und das Problem der "Festkrönungen" ', *HZ* 194 (1962).

Fodrum, Gistum, Servitium Regis, *Kölner Historische Abhandlungen* 14/I–II (Cologne, Graz, 1968).

Dia Anfänge der Deutschen Geschichte, *SB. der Wissenschaftlichen Gesellschaft an der Johann Wolfgang Goethe-Universität Frankfurt/Main* 10 (1972), no. 5.

W. Brüske, *Untersuchungen zur Geschichte des Lutizenbundes*, *Mitteldeutsche Forschungen* 3 (Munster, Cologne, 1955).

A. Büsing, *Mathilde, Gemahlin Heinrichs I.* (Halle, 1910).

T. Buddensieg, 'Beiträge zur ottonischen Kunst in Niedersachsen', *Miscellanea pro Arte*, *Herrmann Schnitzler zur Vollendung des 60. Lebensjahres*, ed. P. Bloch and J. Hoster (Düsseldorf, 1965).

A. R. Burn, ' "Hic Breve Vivitur": A Study of the Expectation of Life in the Roman Empire', *P & P* 4 (1953).

J. Campbell, 'Observations on English Government from the tenth to the twelfth century', *TRHS* 25 (1975).

P. Classen, 'Karl der Grosse und die Thronfolge im Frankenreich', *Festschrift für Hermann Heimpel* (Göttingen, 1972) III.

D. Claude, *Geschichte des Erzbistums Magdeburg bis in das 12. Jahrhundert*, *Mitteldeutsche Forschungen* 67/I–II (Cologne, Vienna, 1972–5).

'Die Pfalz Dahlum', *Festschrift für Helmut Beumann*, ed. K.-U. Jäschke and R. Wenskus (Sigmaringen, 1977).

E. R. Coleman, 'L'infanticide dans le haut Moyen Age', *AESC* 29 (1974).

K. Czegledy, 'Das sakrale Königtum bei den Steppenvölkern', *Numen* XIII (1965).

J. Deér, 'Das Kaiserbild im Kreuz', *Schweizer Beiträge zur Allgemeinen Geschichte* 13 (1965).

Heidnisches und Chrisliches in der altungarischen Monarchie, *WBG* reprint (Darmstadt, 1969).

R. Deshman, ' "Christus rex et magi reges", Kingship and Christology in Ottonian and Anglo-Saxon Art', *Frühmittelalterliche Studien* 10, ed. K. Hauck (Berlin, New York, 1976).

Deutsche Königspfalzen, Beiträge zu ihrer historischen und archäologischen Erforschung, 2 vols, *Veröffentlichungen des Max-Planck-Instituts für Geschichte* 11/1–2 (Göttingen, 1963–5).

J. Devisse, *Hincmar Archevêque de Reims 845–882*, 2 vols (Geneva, 1976).

J. Diestelmann, 'Zur Klosterreform des 12. Jahrhunderts in Niedersachsen', *Jahrbuch für Niedersächsische Kirchengeschichte* 53 (1955).

I. Dietrich, 'Die Konradiner im fränkisch-sächsischen Grenzraum von Thüringen und Hessen', *Hessisches Jahrbuch für Landesgeschichte* 3 (1953).

G. Droege, 'Fränkische Siedlung in Westfalen', *Frühmittelalterliche Studien* 4, ed. K. Hauck (Berlin 1970).

E. Dümmler, *Geschichte des Ostfränkischen Reiches*, 3 vols, *WBG* reprint (Darmstadt, 1960).

Early Medieval Kingship, ed. P. H. Sawyer and I. N. Wood (School of History, University of Leeds, 1977).

K. A. Eckhardt, 'Domina Sophia constructrix et procuratrix sanctimonialium Aeskinewag', *Archiv für Diplomatik* 3 (1957).

Das erste Jahrtausend Kultur und Kunst im Werdenden Abendland an Rhein und Ruhr, ed. V. H. Elbern, 3 vols (Düsseldorf, 1962–4).

S. Epperlein, 'Sachsen im frühen Mittelalter', *Jahrbuch für Wirtschaftsgeschichte*, part I (Berlin, 1966).

'Herrschaft und Volk im karolingischen Imperium', *Forschungen zur mittelalterlichen Geschichte* 14 (Berlin, 1969).

M. Erbe, *Studien zur Entwicklung des Niederkirchenwesens in Ostsachsen vom 8. bis zum 12. Jahrhundert, Studien zur Germania Sacra 9, Veröffentlichungen des Max-Planck-Instituts für Geschichte* 26 (Göttingen, 1969).

G. Erdmann, *Forschungen zur Politischen Ideenwelt des Frühmittelalters*, ed. F. Baethgen (Berlin, 1951).

Ottonische Studien, ed. and introduced by H. Beumann, *WBG* (Darmstadt, 1968).

C. Erickson and K. Casey, 'Women in the Middle Ages. A Working Bibliography', *Medieval Studies* XXXVII (1975).

E. E. Evans-Pritchard, 'The Divine Kingship of the Shilluk of the Nilotic Sudan' (Frazer Lecture, 1948), in his *Essays in Social Anthropology* (London, 1962).

D. E. C. Eversley, 'The Validity of Family and Group Statistics as Indicators of Secular Population Trends', in F. Bechhofer (ed.), *Population Growth and the Brain Drain* (Edinburgh, 1969).

H. E. Feine, *Kirchliche Rechtsgeschichte Die Katholische Kirche*, 4th edn. (Cologne, Graz, 1964).

La Femme, Recueil de la Société Jean Bodin pour l'Histoire Comparative des Institutions XII (1962).

L. Fenske, *Adelsopposition und Kirchliche Reformbewegung im Östlichen Sachsen, Veröffentlichungen des Max-Planck-Instituts für Geschichte* 47 (1977).

H. Fichtenau, *Arenga, Spätantike und Mittelalter im Spiegel von Urkundenformeln, MIÖG, Ergbd.* XVIII (1957).

N. Fickermann, 'Eine hagiographische Fälschung ottonischer Zeit aus Gernrode', *Corona Quernea, Festgabe Karl Strecker, Schriften der MGH* 6 (Stuttgart, 1941).

J. Fleckenstein, 'Königshof und Bischofsschule unter Otto dem Grossen', *AKG* 38 (1956).

'Rex Canonicus, Über Entstehung und Bedeutung des mittelalterlichen Königskanonikates', *Festschrift Percy Ernst Schramm*, ed. P. Classen and P. Scheibert (Wiesbaden, 1964) I.

Die Hofkapelle der deutschen Könige II: *Die Hofkapelle im Rahmen der Ottonisch-Salischen Reichskirche, Schriften der MGH* 16/II (Stuttgart, 1966).

'Otto der Grosse in seinem Jahrhundert', *Frühmittelalterliche Studien* 9, ed. K. Hauck (Berlin, New York, 1975).

H.-J. Freytag, *Die Herrschaft der Billunger in Sachsen, Studien und Vorarbeiten* 20 (Göttingen, 1951).

W. H. Fritze, 'Probleme der abodritischen Stammes- und Reichsverfassung und ihrer Entwicklung vom Stammesstaat zum Herrschaftsstaat', in *Siedlung und*

Verfassung der Slawen zwischen Elbe, Saale und Oder, ed. H. Ludat (Giessen, 1960). .

H. Fuhrmann, *Einfluss und Verbeitung der pseudoisidorischen Fälschungen*, Schriften der MGH 24, I–III (Stuttgart, 1972–4).

I. Gampl, *Adelige Damenstifte, Untersuchungen zur Entstehung adeliger Damenstifter in Österreich unter besonderer Berücksichtigung der alten Kanonissenstifte Deutschlands und Lothringens, Wiener Rechtsgeschichtliche Arbeiten* V (Vienna, Munich, 1960).

F. L. Ganshof, *Feudalism*, translated P. Grierson (London, New York, Toronto, 1952).

L. Génicot, 'La noblesse dans la société médiévale. A propos des dernières études relatives aux terres d'Empire', *Le Moyen Age* 71 (1965).

W. von Giesebrecht, *Geschichte der deutschen Kaiserzeit*, 5th edn., I and II (Leipzig, 1881–5).

J. B. Gillingham, *The Kingdom of Germany in the High Middle Ages (900–1200)*, Historical Association (London, 1971).

M. Gluckman, *Politics, Law and Ritual in Tribal Society* (Oxford, 1965).
Custom and Conflict in Africa (Oxford, 1973).

H. Goetting, 'Die Exemptionsprivilegien Papst Johannes' XII. für Gernrode und Bibra', *MIÖG, Ergbd.* 14 (1939).
Das Reichsunmittelbare Kanonissenstift Gandersheim, Germania Sacra, N. F. 7, *Das Bistum Hildesheim* (Berlin, New York, 1973), 2 vols.
'Die beiden ältesten Halberstädter Bischofsurkunden von 965 und ihre Siegel', *Grundwissenschaften und Geschichte. Festschrift für Peter Acht, Münchener Historische Studien, Abt. Geschichtliche Hilfswissenschaften* (Kallmünz, 1976).

F. Grauss, *Volk, Herrscher und Heiliger im Reich der Merowinger* (Prague, 1965).

P. Grimm, *Die Vor- und Frühgeschichtlichen Burgwälle der Bezirke Halle und Magdeburg, Deutsche Akademie der Wissenschaften zu Berlin, Schriften der Sektion für Vor- und Frühgeschichte* 6 (Berlin, 1958).

H. Grundmann, 'Die Frauen und die Literatur im Mittelalter', *AKG* 26 (1936).

S. Haider, *Die Wahlversprechungen der Römisch-Deutschen Könige bis zum Ende des zwölften Jahrhunderts* (Vienna, 1968).

K. Hallinger, *Gorze—Kluny, Studia Anselmiana* XXII–XXIII (Rome, 1950–1).

M.-L. Harksen, *Die Kunstdenkmale des Kreises Haldensleben* (Leipzig, 1961).

A. Hauck, *Kirchengeschichte Deutschlands* II and III, 3rd and 4th edn. (Leipzig, 1906, 1912).

K. Hauck, 'Geblütscheiligkeit', *Liber Floridus, Mittellateinische Studien P. Lehmann gewidmet*, ed. B. Bischoff and S. Brechter (St Ottilien, 1950).
'Die geschichtliche Bedeutung der germanischen Auffassung von Königtum und Adel', *Rapports III Moyen Age, XI Congrès International des Sciences Historiques*, Stockholm, 21–8 August 1960 (Uppsala, 1960).
'Haus- und sippengebundene Literatur mittelalterlicher Adelsgeschlechter, von Adelssatiren des 11. und 12. Jahrhunderts her erläutert', *Geschichtsdenken und Geschichtsbild im Mittelalter*, ed. W. Lammers, *Wege der Forschung* XXI *WBG* (Darmstadt, 1961). English translation by T. Reuter, *The Medieval Nobility, Europe in the Middle Ages; Selected Studies* 14, general editor R. Vaughan (Amsterdam, New York, Oxford, 1979).
'Erzbischof Adalbert von Magdeburg als Geschichtsschreiber', *Festschrift für Walter Schlesinger* II, ed. H. Beumann, *Mitteldeutsche Forschungen* 74, II (Cologne, Vienna, 1974).

J. Heineken, *Die Anfänge der sächsischen Frauenklöster* (Göttingen, 1909).

O. von Heinemann, *Albrecht der Bär* (Darmstadt, 1864).

K. Heinemeyer, 'Adel Kirche und Königtum an der oberen Weser im 9. und 10. Jahrhundert', *Historische Forschungen für Walter Schlesinger*, ed. H. Beumann (Cologne, Vienna, 1974).

M. Hellmann, 'Die Synode von Hohenaltheim (916)', *Die Entstehung des Deutschen Reiches (Deutschland um 900)*, prefaced by H. Kämpf, *Wege der Forschung* I, *WBG* (Darmstadt, 1956).

L. Henry, 'Démographie de la Noblesse Britannique', *Population* 20, 4 (1965).

D. Herlihy, *Medieval and Rennnaissance Pistoia: The Social History of an Italian Town, 1200–1430* (New Haven and London, 1967).

'Land, Family and Women in Continental Europe, 701–1200', *Traditio* XVII (1961).

W. Hessler, *Mitteldeutsche Gaue des Frühen und Hohen Mittelalters*, *Abhandlungen der Sächsischen Akademie der Wissenschaften zu Leipzig, Philol.-Histor. Klasse* 49, 2 (Berlin, 1957).

N. Heutger, *Das Stift Möllenbeck an der Weser* (Hildesheim, 1962).

W. Hillebrand, *Besitz- und Standesverhältnisse des Osnabrücker Adels bis 1300*, *Studien und Vorarbeiten* (Göttingen, 1961).

H. Hirsch, *Die Klosterimmunität seit dem Investiturstreit* (Weimar, 1913 and repr. *WBG* Darmstadt, 1967).

E. Hlawitschka, *Lothringien und das Reich an der Schwelle der deutschen Geschichte*, *Schriften der MGH* 21 (Stuttgart, 1968).

Die Anfänge des Hauses Habsburg-Lothringen, Genealogische Untersuchungen zur Geschichte Lothringens und des Reiches im 9. 10. und 11. Jahrhundert (Saarbrücken, 1969).

Zum Werden der Unteilbarkeit des mittelalterlichen Deutschen Reiches, *Jahrbuch der Universität Düsseldorf* (1969/70), erweiterter Nachdruck.

O. Höfler, 'Der Sakralcharakter des germanischen Königtums', *Das Königtum Seine geistigen und rechtlichen Grundlagen*, *Vorträge und Forschungen* III (reprinted *WBG* Darmstadt, 1963).

A. K. Hömberg, *Westfalen und das Sächsische Herzogtum*, *Schriften der Historischen Kommission Westfalens* 5 (Münster, 1963).

'Grafensippen? Kritische Bemerkungen zu Ruth Schölkopf, *Die Sächsischen Grafen (919–1024)*', *Osnabrücker Mitteilungen, Mitteilungen des Vereins für Geschichte und Landeskunde in Osnabrück* (Historischer Verein) 68 (1959).

K. Hörger, 'Die reichsrechtliche Stellung der Fürstäbtissinen', *AUF* IX (1926).

H, Hoffman, 'Zur Geschichte Ottos des Grossen', *DA* 28 (1972).

K. Hoffman, *Taufsymbolik im mittelalterlichen Herrscherbild*, *Bonner Beiträge zur Kunstwissenschaft* 9 (Düsseldorf, 1968).

'Das Herrscherbild im "Evangeliar Ottos III" (Clm 4453)', *Frühmittelalterliche Studien* 7, ed. K. Hauck (Berlin, New York, 1973).

A. Hofmeister, 'Puer, Iuvenis, Senex. Zum Verständnis der mittelalterlichen Altersbezeichnungen', *Papsttum und Kaisertum Forschungen zur politischen Geschichte und Geisteskultur des Mittelalters Paul Kehr ... dargebracht*, ed. A. Brackmann (Munich, 1926).

'Studien zu Theophano,' *Festschrift Edmund E. Stengel* (Münster-Cologne, 1952).

T. H. Hollingsworth, *The Demography of the British Peerage*, supplement to *Population Studies* XVIII, 2 (1964).

'A Demographic Study of the British Ducal Families', in *Population in History, Essays in Historical Demography*, ed. D. V. Glass and D. E. C. Eversley (London, 1965).

Historical Demography (London, 1969).

R. Holtzmann, *Geschichte der Sächsischen Kaiserzeit (900–1024)*, 3rd edn. (Munich, 1955).
Aufsätze zur Deutschen Geschichte im Mittelelberaum, ed. A. Timm, *WBG* (Darmstadt, 1962).
W. Holtzmann, 'Wettinische Urkundenstudien', *Festschrift Robert Holtzmann*, *Historische Studien* 238 (1933).
K. Honselmann, 'Reliquientranslationen nach Sachsen', *Das Erste Jahrtausend*, *Textband* I, ed. V. H. Elbern (Düsseldorf, 1962).
'Alte Corveyer Mönchslisten.—Der Corveyer Konvent unter Abt Folkmar', *Ostwestfälisch-Weserländische Forschungen zur Geschichtlichen Landeskunde*, ed. H. Stoob (Münster, 1970).
H. Hoogeweg, *Verzeichnis der Stifter und Klöster Niedersachsens* (Hanover and Leipzig, 1908).
R. Hucke, *Die Grafen von Stade* (Stade, 1956).
N. Huyghebaert, 'Les femmes laiques dans la vie réligieuse des XIe et XIIe siècles dans la province écclésiastique de Reims', *I laici nella "Societas Christiana" dei secoli XI e XII*, *Publicazioni dell' Universita Cattolica del Sacro Cuore*, *Miscellanea del centro di studi medioevali* 5 (Milan, 1968).

F. Irsigler, '*Divites* und *pauperes* in der *Vita Meinwerci*', *VSWG* 57 (1970).

H. Jakobs, *Die Hirsauer, Kölner Historische Studien* 4, ed. T. Schieffer (Cologne, Graz, 1961).
M. R. James, *A Descriptive Catalogue of the Latin Manuscripts in the John Rylands Library* (Manchester and London, 1921).
H. Jantzen, *Ottonische Kunst* (Munich, 1947).
K.-U. Jäschke, 'Studien zu Quellen und Geschichte des Osnabrücker Zehntstreits unter Heinrich IV.', *Archiv für Diplomatik* 9/10 (1963–4), 11/12 (1965–6).
Die älteste Halberstädter Bischofschronik, *Mitteldeutsche Forschungen* 62/1 (Cologne, Vienna, 1970).
Burgenbau und Landesverteidigung um 900, *Vorträge und Forschungen Sonderband 16*, edited by the Konstanzer Arbeitskreis für mittelalterliche Geschichte (Sigmaringen, 1975).
E. John, *Orbis Britanniae and other Studies* (Leicester, 1966).
K. Jordan, 'Sachsen und das Deutsche Königtum im Hohen Mittelalter', *HZ* 210 (1970).
'Der Harzraum in der Geschichte der deutschen Kaiserzeit', *Festschrift für Helmut Beumann*, ed. K.-U. Jäschke and R. Wenskus (Sigmaringen, 1977).

R. Kahsnitz, 'The Gospel Book of Abbess Svanhild of Essen in the John Rylands Library', *BJRL* 53 (1970–1).
H. Keller, 'Das Kaisertum Ottos des Grossen im Verständnis seiner Zeit', *DA* 20 (1964).
Kloster Einsiedeln im Ottonischen Schwaben, Forschungen zur Oberrheinischen Landesgeschichte XIII (Freiburg, 1964).
F. Kern, *Gottesgnadentum und Widerstandsrecht im früheren Mittelalter*, 2nd edn. R. Buchner (Münster, Cologne, 1954). English translation with an introduction by S. B. Chrimes under the title, *Kingship and Law in the Middle Ages* (Oxford, 1948).
W. Kienast, 'Germanische Treue und "Königsheil" ', *HZ* 227 (1978).
H.-W. Klewitz, 'Die Festkrönungen der deutschen Könige,' *ZRG* LIX, *Kanon. Abt.* XXVIII (1939) and separately, *WBG* (Darmstadt, 1966).
'Königtum, Hofkapelle und Domkapitel im 10. und 11. Jahrhundert', *Archiv für Urkundenforschung* XVI (1939) and separately, *WBG* (Darmstadt, 1960).

R. Köpke and E. Dümmler, *Kaiser Otto der Grosse, Jahrbücher der Deutschen Geschichte* (Leipzig, 1876).

R. Kötzschke, *Deutsche und Slaven im Mitteldeutschen Osten, Ausgewählte Aufsätze*, ed. W. Schlesinger, *WBG* (Darmstadt, 1961).

O.-H. Kost, *Das östliche Niedersachsen im Investiturstreit, Studien zu Brunos Buch vom Sachsenkrieg, Studien zur Kirchengeschichte Niedersachsens* 13 (Göttingen, 1962).

H. Krause, 'Königtum und Rechtsordnung in der Zeit der sächsischen und salischen Herrscher', *ZRG, GA* LXXXII (1965).

K. A. Kroeschell, 'Zur Geschichte des Reichsklosters Hilwartshausen und des Reichsguts an der oberen Weser', *Niedersächsisches Jahrbuch für Landesgeschichte* 29 (1957).

S. Krüger, *Studien zur Sächsischen Grafschaftsverfassung im 9. Jahrhundert, Studien und Vorarbeiten* 19 (Göttingen, 1950).

H.-W. Krumwiede, *Das Stift Fischbeck an der Weser, Untersuchungen zu seiner Frühgeschichte, 955–1158* (Göttingen, 1955).

Kunst und Kultur im Weserraum 800–1600 I, *Beiträge zu Geschichte und Kunst*, Austellung des Landes Nordrhein-Westfalen (Corvey, 1966).

Kunst und Kultur im Weserraum 800–1600, 2 Katalog, 3rd edn (Münster, 1967).

Kunst und Kultur im Weserraum 800–1600, 3 *Forschungsband = Ostwestfälisch-Weserländische Forschungen zur geschichtlichen Landeskunde*, ed. H. Stoob, *Veröffentlichungen des Provinzialinstituts für Westfälische Landes- und Volkskunde* I, 15 (Münster, 1970).

H.-P. Lachmann, *Untersuchungen zur Verfassungsgeschichte des Burgwaldes im Mittelalter, Schriften des Hessischen Landesamtes für geschichtliche Landeskunde* 31 (Marburg, 1967).

K.-H. Lange, *Der Herrschaftsbereich der Grafen von Northeim 950 bis 1144, Studien und Vorarbeiten* 24 (Göttingen, 1969).

A. Lasch und C. Borchling, *Mittelniederdeutsches Handwörterbuch* I (Neumünster, 1956).

M. Last, 'Zur Einrichtung geistlicher Konvente in Sachsen während des frühen Mittelalters', *Frühmittelalterliche Studien* 4, ed. K. Hauck (Berlin, 1970).

'Burgen des 11. und frühen 12. Jahrhunderts in Niedersachsen', in *Die Burgen im Deutschen Sprachraum Ihre rechts- und verfassungsgeschichtliche Bedeutung* I, ed. H. Patze, *Vorträge und Forschungen* XIX (Sigmaringen, 1976).

P. Lauer, *Le Régne de Louis IV d'Outre-Mer, BEHE* 127 (Paris, 1900).

W. Levison, *Das Werden der Ursula-Legende* (Cologne, 1928), reprinted from *Bonner Jahrbücher* 132 (1927).

'Zur Geschichte der Kanonissenstifter', *Westdeutsche Zeitschrift XXVII*, 1908 and reprinted in *Aus Rheinischer und Fränkischer Frühzeit, Ausgewählte Aufsätze von Wilhelm Levison* (Düsseldorf, 1948).

C. Lévi-Strauss, *The Elementary Structures of Kinship*, translated by J. H. Bell, J. R. von Sturmer and R. Needham (London, 1969).

C. Lévy et L. Henry, 'Ducs et pairs sous l'Ancien Régime. Charactéristiques d'une caste', *Population* 15, 5 (1960).

K. Leyser, 'The Battle at the Lech, 955. A Study in Tenth-Century Warfare', *History* L (1965).

'Henry I and the Beginnings of the Saxon Empire', *EHR* LXXXIII (1968).

'The German Aristocracy from the Ninth to the early Twelfth Century: A Historical and Cultural Sketch', *P & P* 41 (1968).

'Debate, Maternal Kin in Early Medieval Germany', *P & P* 49 (1970).

'The Tenth Century in Byzantine-Western Relationships', in D. Baker (ed.) *Relations between East and West in the Middle Ages* (Edinburgh, 1973).

M. Lintzel, *Ausgewählte Schriften*, 2 vols (Berlin, 1961).

H. Lippelt, *Thietmar von Merseburg Reichsbischof und Chronist, Mitteldeutsche Forschungen* 72 (Cologne, Vienna, 1973).

P. C. Lloyd, 'The Political Structure of African Kingdoms: An Exploratory Model', in *Political Systems and the Distribution of Power*, ed. M. Banton, *ASA Monographs* 2 (London, 1965).

'Conflict Theory and Yoruba Kingdoms', in *History and Social Anthropology*, ed. I. M. Lewis, *ASA Monographs* 7 (London, 1968).

U. Lobbedey, 'Zur archäologischen Erforschung westfälischer Frauenklöster des 9. Jahrhunderts', *Frühmittelalterliche Studien* 4 ed. K. Hauck (Berlin, 1970).

E. M. Loeb, 'Die Institution des sakralen Königtums', *Paideuma* x (1964).

F. Lot, *Les Derniers Carolingiens Lothaire Louis V.–Charles de Lorraine 954–991, BEHE* 87 (Paris, 1891).

F. Lotter, *Die Vita Brunonis des Ruotger Ihre historiographische und ideengeschichtliche Stellung, Bonner Historische Forschungen* 9 (Bonn, 1958).

H. Ludat, *An Elbe und Oder um das Jahr 1000* (Cologne, Vienna, 1971).

S. Lüpke, *Die Markgrafen der Sächsischen Ostmarken in der Zeit von Gero bis zum Beginn des Investiturstreites, 940–1075* (Halle, 1937).

H. Maurer, *Konstanz als ottonischer Bischofssitz, Studien zur Germania Sacra* 12, *Veröffentlichungen des Max-Planck-Instituts für Geschichte* 39 (Göttingen, 1973).

T. Mayer, *Fürsten und Staat* (Weimar, 1950).

H. Mitteis, *Der Staat des Hohen Mittelalters*, 4th edn (Weimar, 1953) and translated by H. Orton, *The State in the Middle Ages, North-Holland Medieval Translations* I (Amsterdam, Oxford, New York, 1975).

E. Müller-Mertens, *Regnum Teutonicum* (Vienna, Cologne, Graz, 1970).

'Der Stellingaaufstand seine Träger und die Frage der politischen Macht', *Zeitschrift für Geschichtswissenschaft* xx (1972).

F. Mütherich, 'Ottonian Art: Changing Aspects', in *Romanesque and Gothic Art, Studies in Western Art, Acts of the Twentieth International Congress of the History of Art* I (Princeton, 1963).

H. Naumann, 'Rätsel des letzten Aufstandes gegen Otto I. ((953–954)', *AKG* 46 (1964) and in *Otto der Grosse*, ed. H. Zimmermann, *Wege der Forschung* ccccl, *WBG* (Darmstadt, 1976).

J. L. Nelson, 'Royal Saints and Early Medieval Kingship', in *Sanctity and Secularity, Studies in Church History* 10, ed. D. Baker (Oxford, 1973).

'Inauguration Rituals', in *Early Medieval Kingship*, ed. P. H. Sawyer and I. N. Wood (Leeds, 1977).

E. Nickel, 'Magdeburg in karolingisch-ottonischer Zeit', *Vor- und Frühformen der europäischen Stadt im Mittelalter* I, ed. H. Jankuhn, W. Schlesinger, H. Steuer, *Abhandlungen der Akademie der Wissenschaften in Göttingen, Philol.-Histor. Klasse*, 3rd series 83 (Göttingen, 1973).

P. W. Oediger, 'Adelas Kampf um Elten (996–1002)', *Annalen des Historischen Vereins für den Niederrhein* 155/6 (1954).

H. Patze, *Die Entstehung der Landesherrschaft in Thüringen* I, *Mitteldeutsche Forschungen* 22 (Cologne, Graz, 1962).

'Adel und Stifterchronik. Frühformen territorialer Geschichtsschreibung im hochmittelalterlichen Reich', *Blätter für deutsche Landesgeschichte* 100 (1964), 101 (1965).

(ed.), *Geschichte Niedersachsens*, 1 *Grundlagen und frühes Mittelalter, Veröffentlichungen der Historischen Kommission für Niedersachsen und Bremen* xxxvi (Hildesheim, 1977).

H. Patze and W. Schlesinger, *Geschichte Thüringens* ii, 1, *Mitteldeutsche Forschungen* 48/II, 1 (Cologne, Vienna, 1974).

P. Perst, 'Die Kaisertochter Sophie Äbtissin von Gandersheim und Essen (975–1039)', *Braunschweigisches Jahrbuch* 38 (1957).

'Zur Reihenfolge der Kinder Ottos II. und der Theophanu', *DA* 14 (1958).

H. C. Peyer, 'Das Reisekönigtum des Mittelalters', *VSWG* 51 (1964).

W. Podehl, *Burg und Herrschaft in der Mark Brandenburg, Mitteldeutsche Forschungen* 76 (Cologne, Vienna, 1975).

Population in History, ed. D. V. Glass and D. E. C. Eversley (London, 1965).

O. Posse, *Die Markgrafen von Meissen und das Haus Wettin bis zu Konrad dem Grossen* (Leipzig, 1881).

Die Siegel der deutschen Kaiser und Könige von 751–1806, 4 vols (Dresden, 1909–13).

F. Prinz, *Frühes Mönchtum im Frankenreich* (Munich, Vienna, 1965).

G. Rathgen, 'Untersuchungen über eigenkirchliche Elemente der Kloster- und Stiftsvogtei . . .', *ZRG, Kanon. Abt.* xvii, 48 (1928).

La regalita sacra (Leyden, 1959).

K. Reindel, *Die bayerischen Luitpoldinger 893–989, Quellen und Erörterungen zur bayerischen Geschichte*, NF xi (Munich, 1953).

T. Reuter (ed. and transl.), *The Medieval Nobility: Studies on the Ruling Classes of France and Germany from the Sixth to the Twelfth Century, Europe in the Middle Ages Selected Studies* 14, general editor R. Vaughan (Amsterdam, New York, Oxford, 1979).

H. Richtering, 'Stifte und Klöster im Weserraum bis in das 16. Jahrhundert', *Ostwestfälisch-Weserländische Forschungen zur geschichtlichen Landeskunde*, ed. H. Stoob (Münster, 1970).

H. J. Rieckenberg, 'Königsstrasse und Königsgut in Liudolfingischer und Frühsalischer Zeit (919–1056), *AUF* xvii (1941) and separately *WBG* (Darmstadt, 1965).

J. C. Russell, *Population in Europe 500–1500, The Fontana Economic History of Europe* i, 1, ed. C. M. Cipolla (London, Glasgow, 1973).

K.H. Schäfer, *Die Kanonissenstifter im deutschen Mittelalter, Kirchenrechtliche Abhandlungen* 43, 44 (Stuttgart, 1907).

T. Schieffer, 'Heinrich II. und Konrad II.' *DA* 8 (1951) and separately with an epilogue, *WBG* (Darmstadt, 1969).

Die Lothringische Kanzlei um 900 (Cologne, Graz, 1958). Also in *DA* 14 (1958).

(ed.), *Europa im Wandel von der Antike zum Mittelalter, Handbuch der Europäischen Geschichte*, ed. T. Schieder, I (Stuttgart, 1976).

K. Schiller and A. Lütken, *Mittelniederdeutsches Wörterbuch* i (Bremen, 1875).

W. Schlesinger, *Die Entstehung der Landesherrschaft* (Dresden, 1941) and reprinted with a new preface, *WBG* (Darmstadt, 1964).

(with H. Beumann), 'Urkundenstudien zur deutschen Ostpolitik unter Otto III.', in W. Schlesinger, *Mitteldeutsche Beiträge zur deutschen Verfassungsgeschichte des Mittelalters* (Göttingen, 1961).

Kirchengeschichte Sachsens im Mittelalter, *Mitteldeutsche Forschungen* 27/I and 27/II, 2 vols (Cologne, Graz, 1962).

'Die Anfänge der deutschen Königswahl', in *Die Entstehung des Deutschen Reiches*, prefaced by H. Kämpf, *Wege der Forschung* I, *WBG* (Darmstadt, 1956) and with additional notes in W. Schlesinger, *Beiträge zur deutschen Verfassungsgeschichte des Mittelalters* I (Göttingen, 1963).

'Die Grundlegung der deutschen Einheit im frühen Mittelalter', in *op. cit.*

'Die Auflösung des Karlsreiches', *Karl der Grosse Lebenswerk und Nachleben* I, *Persönlichkeit und Geschichte*, ed. H. Beumann (Düsseldorf, 1965).

'Zur Geschichte der Magdeburger Königspfalz', *Blätter für deutsche Landesgeschichte* 104 (1968).

'Erbfolge und Wahl bei der Königserhebung Heinrichs II. 1002', *Festschrift für Hermann Heimpel* III (Göttingen, 1972).

K. Schmid, 'Zur Problematik von Familie, Sippe und Geschlecht, Haus und Dynastie beim mittelalterlichen Adel', *Zeitschrift für die Geschichte des Oberrheins* 105 (1957).

'Über die Struktur des Adels im früheren Mittelalter', *Jahrbuch für fränkische Landesforschung* 19 (1959) and translated by T. Reuter, *The Medieval Nobility* (Amsterdam, New York, Oxford, 1979).

'Neue Quellen zum Verständnis des Adels im 10. Jahrhundert', *Zeitschrift für die Geschichte des Oberrheins* 108 (1960).

'Die Thronfolge Ottos des Grossen', *ZRG*, *GA* 81 (1964) and in E. Hlawitschka (ed.), *Königswahl und Thronfolge in Ottonisch-Frühdeutscher Zeit*, *Wege der Forschung* CLXXVIII *WBG* (Darmstadt, 1971).

'Die Nachfahren Widukinds', *DA* 20 (1964).

R. Schmidt, 'Königsumritt und Huldigung in Ottonisch-Salischer Zeit', *Vorträge und Forschungen* VI (Constance, Stuttgart, 1961).

'Zur Geschichte des fränkischen Königsthrons', *Frühmittelalterliche Studien* 2, ed. K. Hauck (Berlin, 1968).

L. Schmitz-Kallenberg, *Monasticon Westfaliae* (Münster, 1909).

R. Schneider, 'Die Königserhebung Heinrichs II. im Jahre 1002', *DA* 28 (1972).

R. Schölkopf, *Die Sächsischen Grafen (919–1024)*, *Studien und Vorarbeiten*, 22 (Göttingen, 1957).

P. E. Schramm, *Die Deutschen Kaiser und Könige in Bildern ihre Zeit* I, *751–1152*, *Text* (Leipzig, 1928) and *Tafeln*.

Herrschaftszeichen und Staatssymbolik, *Schriften der MGH* 13/I–III (Stuttgart, 1954–6).

Kaiser Rom und Renovatio, 2nd edn (Darmstadt, 1957).

Kaiser, Könige und Päpste III, IV, 1 and 2 (Stuttgart, 1969–71).

and F. Mütherich, *Denkmale der deutschen Könige und Kaiser* (Munich, 1962).

R. Schröder, E. v. Künssberg, *Lehrbuch der deutschen Rechtsgeschichte*, 7th edn (Leipzig, 1932).

J. Schultze, 'Proprietas und Hereditas östlich Elbe und Oder', *Blätter für deutsche Landesgeschichte* 104 (1968).

H. Schulze, *Das Erb- und Familienrecht der deutschen Dynastien des Mittelalters* (Halle, 1871).

H. K. Schulze, *Adelsherrschaft und Landesherrschaft*, *Mitteldeutsche Forschungen* 29 (Cologne, Graz, 1963).

(with R. Specht and G. Vorbrodt), *Das Stift Gernrode*, *Mitteldeutsche Forschungen* 38 (Cologne, Graz, 1965).

Die Grafschaftsverfassung der Karolingerzeit in den Gebieten östlich des Rheins, *Schriften zur Verfassungsgeschichte* 19 (Berlin, 1973).

B. Schwineköper, 'Die Anfänge Magdeburgs', *Studien zu den Anfängen des Europäischen Städtewesens, Vorträge und Forschungen* IV (Lindau, Constance), 1958).
Handbuch der Historischen Stätten Deutschlands 11, Provinz Sachsen Anhalt (Stuttgart, 1975).
Königtum und Städte bis zum Ende des Investiturstreits, Vorträge und Forschungen, Sonderband 11 (Sigmaringen, 1977).
J. Semmler, 'Corvey und Herford in der benediktinischen Reformbewegung des 9. Jahrhunderts', *Frühmittelalterliche Studien* 4, ed. K. Hauck (Berlin, 1970).
W. Smidt, *Deutsches Königtum und Deutscher Staat des Hochmittelalters während und unter dem Einfluss der Italienischen Heerfahrten* (Wiesbaden, 1964).
M. Spindler (ed.), *Handbuch der bayerischen Geschichte,* I, *Das alte Bayern Das Stammesherzogtum bis zum Ausgang des 12. Jahrhunderts* (Munich, 1968).
H. Sproemberg, 'Die lothringische Politik Ottos des Grossen', in his *Beiträge zur Belgisch-Niederländischen Geschichte* (Berlin, 1959).
H.-D. Starke, *Die Pfalzgrafen von Sachsen bis zur Entstehung des jüngeren Reichfürstenstands*, Kiel dissertation (Kiel, 1953).
'Die Pfalzgrafen von Sommerschenburg (1088–1179)', *Jahrbuch für die Geschichte Mittel- und Ostdeutschlands* IV (1955).
'Die Pfalzgrafen von Sachsen bis zum Jahre 1088', *Braunschweigisches Jahrbuch* 36 (1955).
F. Steinbach, 'Die Ezzonen', *Das Erste Jahrtausend, Textband II*, ed. H. Elbern (Düsseldorf, 1964).
E. Steindorff, *Jahrbücher des Deutschen Reichs unter Heinrich III.*, 2 vols (Leipzig, 1874–81).
W. Störmer, *Früher Adel Studien zur politischen Führungsschicht im Fränkisch-Deutschen Reich vom 8. bis 11. Jahrhundert*, 2 vols, *Monographien zur Geschichte des Mittelalters* 6, I, II, ed. K. Bosl (Stuttgart, 1973).

G. Taddey, *Das Kloster Heiningen von der Gründung bis zur Aufhebung, Studien zur Germania Sacra* 4, *Veröffentlichungen des Max-Planck-Instituts für Geschichte* 14 (1966).
G. Tellenbach, 'Die Unteilbarkeit des Reiches. Ein Beitrag zur Entstehungsgeschichte Deutschlands und Frankreichs', in *Die Entstehung des Deutschen Reiches*, prefaced by H. Kämpf, *Wege der Forschung* I, *WBG* (Darmstadt, 1956).
'Otto der Grosse', in *Die Grossen Deutschen* I, ed. H. Heimpel, T. Heuss, B. Reifenberg (Berlin, 1956).
A. Timm, *Studien zur Siedlungs- und Agrargeschichte Mitteldeutschlands* (Cologne, Graz, 1956).

K. Uhlirz, *Jahrbücher des Deutschen Reiches unter Otto II. und Otto III., Erster Band: Otto II. 973–983* (Leipzig, 1902).
M. Uhlirz, 'Studien über Theophano', *DA* 9 (1951).
Jahrbücher des Deutschen Reiches unter Otto II. und Otto III., Zweiter Band: Otto III. 983–1002 (Berlin, 1954).
W. Ullmann, 'Der Souveränitätsgedanke in den Krönungsordines', in *Festschrift P. E. Schramm*, I, ed. P. Classen and P. Scheibert (Wiesbaden, 1964).
The Carolingian Renaissance and the Idea of Kingship (London, 1969).

T. Vogelsang, *Die Frau als Herrscherin im hohen Mittelalter* (Göttingen, Frankfurt, Berlin, 1954).
H. W. Vogt, *Das Herzogtum Lothars von Süpplingenburg. Quellen und Darstellungen zur Geschichte Niedersachsens* 57 (Hildesheim, 1959).

G. Waitz, 'Die ersten sächsischen Pfalzgrafen', *Forschungen zur deutschen Geschichte* XIV (1874).
Deutsche Verfassungsgeschichte V and VI, *Die Deutsche Reichsverfassung von der Mitte des neunten bis zur Mitte des zwölften Jahrhunderts*, 2nd edn by K. Zeumer and G. Seeliger (Berlin, 1893 and 1896).
Jahrbücher des Deutschen Reichs unter König Heinrich I., 4th edn WBG (Darmstadt, 1963).

J. M. Wallace-Hadrill, *Early Germanic Kingship in England and on the Continent* (Oxford, 1971).

W. Wattenbach and R. Holtzmann, *Deutschlands Geschichtsquellen im Mittelalter Deutsche Kaiserzeit* I, 1, 3rd edn, I, 2, 3, 4, 2nd edn (Tübingen, 1948).

W. Wattenbach, R. Holtzmann and F.-J. Schmale, *Deutschlands Geschichtsquellen im Mittelalter, Dritter Teil*, WBG (Darmstadt, 1971) with supplements to the above.

W. Wattenbach, F.-J. Schmale, *Deutschlands Geschichtsquellen im Mittelalter. Vom Tode Kaiser Heinrichs V. bis zum Ende des Interregnum* I, WBG (Darmstadt, 1976).

R. Wenskus, *Studien zur Historisch-Politischen Gedankenwelt Bruns von Querfurt*, *Mitteldeutsche Forschungen* 5 (Münster, Cologne, 1956).
'Das südliche Niedersachsen im frühen Mittelalter', *Festschrift für Hermann Heimpel* III (Göttingen, 1972).
Sächsischer Stammesadel und fränkischer Reichsadel, Abhandlungen der Akademie der Wissenschaften in Göttingen, Philol.-Histor. Klasse, 3rd series, 93 (Göttingen, 1976).

G. Wentz and B. Schwineköper, *Das Erzbistum Magdeburg* I, 1 *Das Domstift St Moritz in Magdeburg, Germania Sacra*, ed. by the Max-Planck-Institut für Geschichte (Berlin, New York, 1972).

Werdendes Abendland an Rhein und Ruhr, ed. V. H. Elbern, Catalogue of the exhibition in Villa Hügel (Essen, 1956).

K. F. Werner, 'Die Nachkommen Karls des Grossen bis um das Jahr 1000 (1.–8. Generation)', in *Karl der Grosse, Lebenswerk und Nachleben, IV, Das Nachleben*, ed. W. Braunfels and P. E. Schramm (Düsseldorf, 1967).
'Heeresorganisation und Kriegführung im Deutschen Königreich des 10. und 11. Jahrhunderts', *Ordinamenti Militari in Occidente nell' alto Medioevo Settimane di studio del Centro italiano di studi sull'alto medioevo* XV (Spoleto, 1968).

Helge bei der Wieden, *Schaumburgische Genealogie, Schaumburger Studien* 14 (Bückeburg, 1966).

F. P. Wimmer, *Kaiserin Adelheid Gemahlin Ottos I. des Grossen in ihrem Leben und Wirken von 931–973*, 2nd edn. (Regensburg, 1897).

G. Wolf, 'Über die Hintergründe der Erhebung Liudolfs von Schwaben', *ZRG, GA* 80 (1963) and *Otto der Grosse*, ed. H. Zimmermann, *Wege der Forschung* CCCCL, WBG (Darmstadt, 1976).

H. Wolfram, 'Methodische Fragen zur Kritik am "sakralen" Königtum germanischer Stämme', *Festschrift Otto Höfler* II (Vienna, 1968).

C. P. Wormald, 'The Uses of Literacy in Anglo-Saxon England and its Neighbours', *TRHS*, 5th series 27 (1977).

F. Wormald, 'Late Anglo-Saxon Art: Some Questions and Suggestions', *Romanesque and Gothic Art, Studies in Western Art* I (Princeton, 1963).

T. L. Zotz, *Der Breisgau und das alemannische Herzogtum, Vorträge und Forschungen, Sonderband* 15 (Sigmaringen, 1974).

Notes

Introduction

1 DDO I. 14, 15, 16.
2 *MGH*, *Capitularia Regum Francorum* I, p. 123. In general see B. Schwineköper, *Königtum und Städte bis zum Ende des Investiturstreits*, *Vorträge und Forschungen Sonderband 11*. Herausgegeben vom Konstanzer Arbeitskreis für mittelalterliche Geschichte (Sigmaringen, 1977), pp. 55 ff. and nn. 210 and 211 for further recent literature. cf. below, p. 90 nn. 41, 43.
3 e.g. *Traditiones Corbeienses*, 244, ed. P. Wigand (Leipzig, 1843), p. 49. For an exchange see *MGH*, *Diplomata Regum Germaniae ex stirpe Karolinorum, III, Arnolfi Diplomata*, ed. P. Kehr (Berlin, 1955) no. 28 of 10 June 888.
4 *Annales Fuldenses*, 872, ed. F. Kurze, *SRG* (Hanover, 1891), p. 75 f.
5 *Annalium Fuldensium Continuatio Ratisbonensis* in *Annales Fuldenses*, p. 109.
6 *ibid.*, p. 115.
7 *Annales Fuldenses*, p. 42.
8 *Poeta Saxo* v, lines 651 ff. ed. P. Winterfeld, *MGH*, *Poetae Latini* IV, i (Berlin, 1909), p. 70 f. and see B. Bischoff, 'Das Thema des Poeta Saxo' in *Speculum Historiale Johannes Spörl . . . dargebracht*, ed. C. Bau r, L. Boehm, M. Müller (Munich, 1965), pp. 198–203.
9 *Poeta Saxo* iv, lines 93–138. The authenticity and sources of the Poet's story and the question whether there ever was a formal peace settlement have remained contentious issues. See M. Lintzel, 'Der Sachsenfriede Karls des Grossen' in his *Ausgewählte Schriften* (Berlin, 1961) I, pp. 175–98 and K.–U. Jäschke, *Die Älteste Halberstädter Bischofschronik, Mitteldeutsche Forschungen* 62/I (Cologne, Vienna, 1970), pp. 94–101.
10 *Poeta Saxo* iv, lines 131–2, p. 49.
11 *Poeta Saxo* v, lines 123–48, p. 58 f. and lines 415–24, p. 65 on Arnolf. For the theme of gratitude see v, lines 21 ff., p. 56.

Otto I and his Saxon Enemies

Chapter 1
1 *AQ*, 1021, *SS* III, p. 86.

2   DO III., 403 of 12 May 1001. On the Ottonian itineraries see below, p. 90 and H.
    J. Rieckenberg, 'Königsstrasse und Königsgut in Liudolfingischer und
    Frühsalischer Zeit (919–1056)', *AUF* XVII (1941), pp. 42 ff. and repr. *Wissen-*
    schaftliche Buchgesellschaft Darmstadt, 1965). C. Brühl, *Fodrum, Gistum,*
    Servitium Regis, Kölner Historische Abhandlungen 14/1 (Köln, Graz, 1968),
    pp. 116 ff. For Otto III's many and long stays in Aachen see J. Fleckenstein, *Die*
    Hofkapelle der deutschen Könige, II *Die Hofkapelle im Rahmen der*
    Ottonisch-Salischen Reichskirche, Schriften der MGH 16/ii (Stuttgart, 1966),
    pp. 140–51.
3   K. Leyser, 'Henry I and the beginnings of the Saxon Empire', *EHR* LXXXIII
    (1968), p. 14 for these *beneficia.* The evidence for 'castle guard' is mainly in
    Thietmar of Merseburg's *Chronicon* iv. 38 (Arneburg), vi. 59 (Lebusa), v. 36,
    vi. 55, 79, vii. 53 (Meissen), ed. R. Holtzmann, *SRG*, NS IX (Berlin, 1955), pp.
    175 ff., 260, 342, 368, 464.
4   See Adalbert's *Continuatio Reginonis,* 953, in *Reginonis Chronicon,* ed. F.
    Kurze, *SRG* (Hanover, 1890), p. 166 and Widukind of Corvey, *Rerum gestarum*
    saxonicarum libri tres iii. 14, 5th edn by H.-E. Lohmann and P. Hirsch, *SRG*
    (Hanover, 1935), p. 111 and R. Köpke and E. Dümmler, *Kaiser Otto der*
    Grosse, Jahrbücher der Deutschen Geschichte (Leipzig, 1876), pp. 211 ff.
5   Widukind, i. 38, p. 55. The *civilia discordia* set off against *bella externa* do not
    necessarily allude to Henry I's early Suabian and Bavarian campaigns (i. 27, p.
    39 ff.) since Widukind elsewhere regarded Franks and Lotharingians as
    enemies of the Saxons like Danes and Slavs (cf. ii. 20, p. 84). Sometimes he
    spoke of *bella intestina* and meant both inner-Saxon clashes as well as struggles
    within the *Reich* at large.
6   *Ruotgeri Vita Brunonis Archiepiscopi Coloniensis,* c. 3, ed. I. Ott, *SRG*, NS x
    (Weimar, 1951), p. 4 and cf. also c. 2 *ibid*: 'represso etiam intestine cladis
    periculo.' Historians, however, did not consider that Henry met with any
    opposition in Saxony, e.g. W. Schlesinger, *Die Entstehung der Landesherrschaft*
    (repr. Darmstadt, 1964), p. 190 and already G. Waitz, *Jahrbücher des Deut-*
    schen Reiches unter König Heinrich I, 3rd edn (Leipzig, 1885 and repr. Darm-
    stadt, 1963), p. 109.
7   DO II. 100 of 25 April 975. Two years later Otto II stayed in Lingen, sanctioning
    grants of the bishop to one of his vassals and converting his *beneficia* into
    proprietas (DO II. 169). On Liudolf who served in Otto I's chapel and as his
    chancellor before his promotion to the see of Osnabrück (967) see Flecken-
    stein, *Hofkapelle*, p. 32 f. K. Schmid, 'Die Nachfahren Widukinds', *DA* 20
    (1964), pp. 13 ff., 25 ff., 37 and R. Wenskus, *Sächsischer Stammesadel und*
    fränkischer Reichsadel, Abhandlungen der Akademie der Wissenschaften in
    Göttingen Philolog.-Histor. Klasse, 3rd series, no. 93 (Göttingen, 1976), pp.
    108 ff., 228 ff.
8   Cf. what the *Chronica Episcoporum Merseburgensium* had to say about the
    parents of Bishop Thietmar (*SS* x, p. 173): 'Erat utique uterque parens pollens
    pia gloria in seculo, dives in praedio.'
9   *Annales Fuldenses,* 880, ed. F. Kurze, *SRG* (Hanover, 1891), p. 94, Dümmler,
    Geschichte des Ostfränkischen Reiches (Leipzig, 1888 and repr. Darmstadt,
    1960) III, pp. 135 ff.
10 The point is well made by R. Schölkopf, *Die Sächsischen Grafen* (919–1024),
    Studien und Vorarbeiten zum Historischen Atlas Niedersachsens 22 (Göttingen,
    1957), p. 107.
11 Widukind, i. 16, p. 26.
12 DO I. 50 and DO I. 306. The Count Liudolf of the Hasegau (Westfalia) whom

we meet in DO i. 91 of 947 was the father of Otto I's chancellor Liudolf, later bishop of Osnabrück. cf. above, p. 10.

13 Widukind, ii. 4, p. 70 f.

14 *Vita Bernwardi Episcopi Hildesheimensis*, c. 38, *SS* iv, p. 775 and *Vita Meinwerci Episcopi Patherbrunnensis*, c. 7, ed. F. Tenckhoff, *SRG* (Hanover, 1921), p. 13 f.

15 Wenskus, *op. cit.*, p. 393.

16 Widukind, iii. 60 (p. 136): 'Bonis promissionibus ab imperatore erectus'.

17 Near Goslar. See Thietmar, iv. 3, p. 134 and n. 10.

18 Thietmar, ii. 31, p. 76 f. It has long been thought that the bishop was Wichmann the Elder's son but in the *Annalista Saxo* (*SS* vi, pp. 615), a passage not taken from Thietmar, he is merely called a *cognatus* of Duke Hermann.

19 Thietmar, i. 5, p. 8 f. On Merseburg and the Ottonians see W. Schlesinger, 'Merseburg' in *Deutsche Königspfalzen, Veröffentlichungen des Max-Planck-Instituts für Geschichte* 11/1 (Göttingen, 1963) I, pp. 173 ff.

20 On Mathilda's *hereditas* see W. Hillebrand, *Besitz- und Standesverhältnisse des Osnabrücker Adels bis 1300, Studien und Vorarbeiten* 23 (Göttingen, 1961), pp. 26–9 but based on a mistaken genealogy. A. K. Hömberg, *Westfalen und das Sächsische Herzogtum* (Münster, 1963), pp. 14 ff. and Wenskus, *op. cit.*, pp. 115 ff., who suggested that the marriage gave Henry above all preponderance in Eastern Saxony. Given that Mathilda had three sisters and at least one brother, Archbishop Robert of Trier (931–56), all entitled to inherit, this is unlikely even if the Immedings, her kindred, had as much land there as the author argues.

21 Thietmar, i. 6, p. 10.

22 It is impossible to establish all Hatheburg's connections. We do not know who her first husband had been. According to Thietmar (i. 5, p. 8) she had a sister but he did not mention her name. If she married who was her husband? On the family of Margrave Gero see K. Schmid, 'Neue Quellen zum Verständnis des Adels im 10. Jahrhundert', *Zeitschrift für die Geschichte des Oberrheins* 108 (1960), pp. 211 ff.

23 *Continuatio Reginonis*, 939, p. 161.

24 Widukind, ii. 9, 11, pp. 73 and 76. Thietmar, ii. 2 (p. 40) who saw the rift as 'discordia inter concives consociosque'.

25 Thietmar, i. 16, p. 22. The context suggests that *regnum* here meant Saxony. cf. the parallel example, ii. 40 (p. 88), where it stood for Bavaria.

26 H. Lippelt, *Thietmar von Merseburg Reichsbischof und Chronist, Mitteldeutsche Forschungen* 72 (Cologne, Vienna, 1973), p. 148 and M. Lintzel, *Ausgewählte Schriften* (Berlin, 1961) II, p. 105.

27 Widukind, ii. 3, p. 68 f. and Leyser, 'Henry I', p. 12.

28 Widukind, i. 36, p. 52 and cf. the incident on Otto I's first campaign in 936 (above, p. 11). Count Wichmann the Elder withdrew from the host.

29 Widukind, ii. 11, p. 77 and Thietmar, ii. 2, p. 40. On Thangmar see below, p. 87 and also Leyser, 'The German Aristocracy from the Ninth to the Twelfth Century', *P & P* 41 (1968), p. 41.

30 K. F. Werner, 'Die Nachkommen Karls des Grossen bis um das Jahr 1000', *Karl der Grosse*, IV. *Das Nachleben*, ed. W. Braunfels and P. E. Schramm (Düsseldorf, 1967), p. 445 and the genealogical table on Drogo and Hugh.

31 On Charles the Bald's sons see Werner, *op. cit.*, p. 453, nn. 36, 37 and E. Dümmler, *Geschichte des Ostfränkischen Reiches* II, pp. 320 ff., 356–9.

32 Thietmar, ii. 23, p. 66.

33 *Vita Mathildis Reginae (posterior)*, c. 11, *SS* iv, p. 291, line 12. On the settlement and Mathilda's opposition to it see K. Schmid, 'Neue Quellen', p. 201 and in

Königswahl und Thronfolge in Ottonisch-Frühdeutscher Zeit, ed. E. Hlawitschka (Darmstadt, 1971), pp. 411–14.

34   Widukind, ii. 2, p. 67.

35   On Louis the German's settlement see Dümmler, *op. cit.* ii, p. 119 f. and W. Schlesinger, 'Die Anfänge der deutschen Königswahl' in his *Beiträge zur deutschen Verfassungsgeschichte des Mittelalters* (Göttingen, 1963) I, p. 141 f. For Arnolf see Regino of Prüm, *Chronicon*, 895, p. 143, T. Schieffer, *Die Lothringische Kanzlei um 900* (Cologne, Graz, 1958), p. 10 f. and E. Hlawitschka, *Lotharingien und das Reich an der Schwelle der deutschen Geschichte*, Schriften der MGH 21 (Stuttgart, 1968), pp. 132, 209–11.

36   K. Schmid, 'Die Thronfolge Ottos des Grossen' in *Königswahl und Thronfolge in Ottonisch-Frühdeutscher Zeit*, ed. E. Hlawitschka (Darmstadt, 1971), pp. 478–90, 501–5, 507, originally published in *ZRG, GA* 81 (1964), pp. 80 ff. The version published in 1971 will be cited here.

37   This is not to say that the East Frankish kingdom was immune against breaking up in 919 and 938–9. The Bavarian and Lotharingian *regna* were at risk, had Otto I not emerged as victor.

38   G. Tellenbach, 'Die Unteilbarkeit des Reiches' in *Die Entstehung des Deutschen Reiches*, ed. H. Kämpf (Darmstadt, 1956), pp. 110 ff. Hlawitschka, *Lotharingien*, pp. 214–19, especially p. 219: 'einen geistigen Erkenntnisvorgang bei den führenden Grossen'. See also Hlawitschka, 'Zum Werden der Unteilbarkeit des mittelalterlichen Deutschen Reiches', *Jahrbuch der Universität Düsseldorf*, 1969/70, erweiterter Nachdruck.

39   So especially W. Schlesinger, 'Die Grundlegung der deutschen Einheit im frühen Mittelalter', *Beiträge* I, pp. 261–85 and 'Die Auflösung des Karlsreiches', *Karl der Grosse* I, ed. H. Beumann (Düsseldorf, 1965), p. 854 (for the passage translated here). His view is questioned by Hlawitschka, *Lotharingien*, pp. 210, 219.

40   Regino, *Chronicon*, 888, p. 129.

41   Tellenbach, *op cit.,* Hlawitschka, *op. cit.*

42   Liudprand, *Antapodosis* iv. 18, *Die Werke Liudprands von Cremona*, 3rd edn by J. Becker, *SRG* (Hanover and Leipzig, 1915), p. 114 and *Vita Mathildis*, c. 9, *SS* iv, p. 289, R. Holtzmann, *Geschichte der Sächsischen Kaiserzeit* (Munich, 1943), p. 106 and W. Ohnsorge, *Das Zweikaiserproblem im früheren Mittelalter* (Hildesheim, 1947), p. 49.

43   The tenacious survival of the idea of shared rule in Ottonian historiography, as cultivated in monasteries close to the Saxon kings, has been overlooked by the historians who have sought to elucidate the rise of indivisibility.

44   Hrotsvitha, *gesta Ottonis,* lines 25–32, *Hrotvithae Opera* iii, 1, ed. P. Winterfeld, *SRG* (repr. Berlin, Zürich, 1965), p. 205.

45   Widukind, ii. 15, p. 79.

46   ii. 36, p. 95.

47   Leyser, *The Tenth Century in Byzantine-Western Relationships* in *Relations between East and West in the Middle Ages*, ed. D. Baker (Edinburgh, 1973), p. 35.

48   *Vita Godehardi . . prior*, c. 1, *SS* xi, p. 170. Here, however, Bavaria, often referred to as a *regnum*, is called *provincia* and this usage was not unknown in the tenth century. Gerhard, *Vita S. Oudalrici*, c. 28, *SS* iv, p. 417: 'cum exercitu ambarum provinciarum' (Bavaria and Suabia).

49   Ruotger, c. 39, p. 41, though Ruotger did not omit to call Otto Brun's *senior*, his lord, as well as *germanus*, his brother.

50   ii. 15, p. 79: 'ne rei fraternae discordiae invenirentur' and earlier about Meginzo, the *miles* who killed Thangmar: 'fraternae fautor discordiae'.

51 Hrotsvitha, *gesta Ottonis*, lines 177–8 (p. 209): 'At cum quisque sui peteret solamina domni,/Hinc gravior dominis discordia nascitur ipsis.' Ruotger, c. 18, p. 17, Liudprand, *Antapodosis* iv. 18, p. 114, *Continuatio Reginonis*, 937, p. 160: 'Graves et intestinae discordiae inter Heinricum fratrem regis et Eberhardum ducem Francorum nascuntur ob exortas inter vassallos eorum inimicicias.'

52 Widukind, ii. 18, 19, p. 83 f.

53 See above, p. 13 f.

54 On Bruning's feuds with Eberhard see Widukind, ii. 6, p. 71 f. and 10, p. 73. On Henry's see *Continuatio Reginonis*, 937, p. 160. On Brunicho's forfeitures see DO I. 96 of 948. Otto characteristically exchanged this and much other forfeited estate with Hersfeld. On former fiefs of Bruning and his son Amalung, ninth-century Billung names, see DO I. 197 of 958. Among the Thuringian estates given to Hersfeld in 948 one lay in a vill called Amalungesdorpf.

55 iii. 16, p. 112.

56 For the fortresses see Widukind, ii. 29, p. 91. The royal grants sponsored by Henry in 940 were DO I. 31 for a Lotharingian donee and DO I. 32, a Bavarian one.

57 e.g. in 977 a Dedi raided Zeitz evidently as an accomplice of Henry the Wrangler, Henry's son (Thietmar, iii. 18, p. 120). If he was related to the man who betrayed Henry's fortresses in 939, as I believe he was, he now stood with the Bavarian Liudolfings as did Count Wilhelm (of Weimar) in 984, whose ancestor had also been handed over to Duke Henry in 953 to be exiled in Bavaria. On the other hand a Brunig and his vassals (Thietmar, iv. 2, p. 134), certainly a descendant of Henry's ally in 937, stood by the infant Otto III in 984. For the family of Thietmar of Merseburg see below pp. 34 ff. Also on Otto III's side in 984 were again Dedi and Ekkehard who had supported the Wrangler in 976–7. Count Ekbert who followed Liudolf against his uncle in 953 helped the younger Henry in 977 (see next note). Nobles, we may conclude, were prepared to rise behind any disaffected member of the royal family. Alliances shifted and changed, often quite rapidly.

58 For the excommunications see *MGH*, *Leges* iii, p. 485. For Count Ekbert's capture and exile see Thietmar, iii. 7, p. 104 and *Annales Hildesheimenses*, 978, ed. G. Waitz, *SRG* (Hanover, 1878 and repr. 1947), p. 23.

59 On Gerberga see below, pp. 54, 55.

60 The grant, DO I. 114, converted fief into *proprietas* for the lives of the grantee and his wife.

61 Otto II's short stay is attested by DO II. 79 of 24 May. For Gisela's prolonged and enforced residence we must rely on Thietmar, iv. 7, p. 138: 'ubi ductrix Gisla longo tristis sedebat abcessu'. W. Schlesinger, *Kirchengeschichte Sachsens im Mittelalter, Mitteldeutsche Forschungen* 27/1 (Cologne, Graz, 1962) I, p. 33 but with no sources.

62 Thietmar, iv. 7, p. 138. Walbeck, the royal *curtis* in the Schwabengau, must not be confused with Walbeck on the Aller, the seat of Thietmar's own family.

63 Brühl, *Fodrum*, p. 128.

64 Hrotsvitha, *gesta Ottonis*, lines 455–66, p. 217. K. Schmid, 'Thronfolge', p. 463.

65 H. Keller, *Kloster Einsiedeln im Ottonischen Schwaben, Forschungen zur Oberrheinischen Landesgeschichte* XIII (Freiburg, 1964), p. 41.

66 DO I. 134, shortly before the Italian expedition. Gero, however, remained loyal to Otto I and later fought for him against Liudolf outside Regensburg (Widukind, iii. 37, p. 121.). On Serimunt and the three marches, see W. Hessler, *Mitteldeutsche Gaue des frühen und hohen Mittelalters, Abhandlungen der Sächsischen Akademie der Wissenschaften zu Leipzig, Philologisch-historische Klasse* 49,2 (Berlin, 1957), p. 32 f.

67   Widukind, iii. 9, p. 109 and cf. ii. 15, p. 79, Thietmar, ii. 5, p. 44, *Continuatio Reginonis*, 952, p. 165.
68   cf. n. 64 above.
69   iii. 10, p. 110: 'Heinricus autem sciens adolescentem maternis destitutum suffragiis, contemptui eum coepit habere.'
70   *Continuatio Reginonis*, 953 (p. 166) did not mention Suabians but that Liudolf as duke of Suabia had them in his following is obvious and can be inferred from the *Vita S. Oudalrici*, c. 10, *SS* iv, p. 398 f.
71   *Vita Brunonis*, c. 19, p. 18. Adalbert's description of Liudolf's following (n. 70) should be compared with what we know about Otto I's at the battle by the Lech in 955. See Widukind, iii. 44, p. 124 f. and Leyser, *History* l (1965), p. 16.
72   For all this see Widukind, iii. 19, 23–5, pp. 114–16. cf. also Thietmar's shorter account based on Widukind (ii. 6, pp. 44 ff.) and Freytag, *Billunger*, pp. 70–2.
73   Widukind, iii. 29, p. 117.
74   iii. 50, p. 129 f.
75   It was Liudolf's, Duke Conrad's and their allies' aim, according to Ruotger: 'ut maximis intra regnum urbibus et his opulentissimis, quocumque ingenio potirentur' (*Vita Brunonis*, c. 19, p. 18).
76   Widukind, iii. 50, p. 130 and W. Brüske, *Untersuchungen zur Geschichte des Lutizenbundes, Mitteldeutsche Forschungen* 3 (Münster, Cologne, 1955), pp. 23–9.
77   As Widukind makes clear, iii. 64, 68, pp. 139, 143. In general see below, pp. 29, 36 ff.
78   Widukind, iii. 60, p. 136. His brother Ekbert was reconciled to Otto I through the good offices of Archbishop Brun of Cologne but he re-emerged as an enemy of Otto II's in 977–8 (see above p. 18) if not before. On Hathui and Siegfried, see below, pp. 52, 55 f.
79   Widukind, iii. 66, p. 141.
80   *ibid*. Brüske, *op. cit.*, p. 30 f. and H. Ludat, *An Elbe und Oder um das Jahr 1000* (Cologne, Vienna, 1971), pp. 34, 132 ff.
81   Widukind, iii. 54, p. 134: 'At Gero cum amicis Ruanis'. His friends, the Rani (of Rügen), saved the Ottonian host in an extremely dangerous situation just before the battle at the Recknitz in 955. Yet the permanent war against the Obotrite group of peoples was Hermann Billung's assignment.
82   Widukind, iii. 69, pp. 143–5 and cf. 50, p. 129.
83   DO i. 200. cf. the sack of an important fortress by Wichmann and his Slav allies in April 955, described by Widukind, iii. 52, p. 131.

Chapter 2
1   DO i. 60 of 944, DO i. 152 of 952, Do i. 198 of 958 and DO i. 223 of 961.
2   DO i. 329.
3   DO i. 363 and DO ii. 19 of 968 and see D. Claude, *Geschichte des Erzbistums Magdeburg bis in das 12. Jahrhundert*, i. *Mitteldeutsche Forschungen* 67/i (Cologne, Vienna, 1972), pp. 11, 48, 50, 97, 267.
4   *RI* ii, 5, no. 314. For the text of the privilege see C. L. Scheidius, *Origines Guelficae* (Hanover, 1753) iv, p. 556 f.
5   H. Goetting, 'Die Exemptionsprivilegien Papst Johannes xii. für Gernrode und Bibra', *MIÖG, Ergbd* 14 (1939), pp. 71 ff. and Claude, *op. cit.*, p. 97. For Gero's *traditio* see *CDA* i, no. 36.
6   DDO i. 232, 281, 303.

7 cf. DO I. 165 of 953 and DO I. 329 of 966: 'ipse vero [Billing] econtra quitquid coniunx sua hereditarii iuris habere videbatur, nobis donavit.' Schölkopf, *Die Sächsischen Grafen*, p. 159 concluded from this that husbands could dispose freely of their wives' inheritances. The cancellation of the exchange argues for the opposite; that they could not do so. See below pp. 59, 65 f.
8 It comes from a diploma of Henry II's of 2 November, 1010 (DH II. 224).
9 *Annales Corbeienses*, 968, *Monumenta Corbeiensia*, ed. P. Jaffé, *Bibliotheca Rerum Germanicarum* I (Berlin, 1864), p. 36. Wenskus, p. 239, without mention of the papal privilege.
10 Thietmar, ii. 24, p. 68. Otto yielded after a threatening vision.
11 DO I. 311.
12 DO II. 28. On Margrave Thietmar see R. Kötzschke, 'Die Anfänge der Markgrafschaft Meissen' in the collection of his papers *Deutsche und Slaven im Mitteldeutschen Osten*, ed. W. Schlesinger (Darmstadt, 1961), p. 106 f. and nn. 28, 29, R. Holtzmann, *Aufsätze zur Deutschen Geschichte im Mittelelberaum*, ed. A. Timm (Darmstadt, 1962), p. 127 f. Schölkopf, pp. 45–7, not without errors.
13 See below, pp. 66, 69.
14 Thietmar, ii. 29, p. 74. The chronicler's own father, Siegfried, took part in this escapade. See below p. 43. Ludat, *An Elbe und Oder*, p. 41 and n. 313. On Hodo's defeat see also Brun of Querfurt's *Vita S. Adalberti*, c. 10, *SS* IV, p. 598.
15 Thietmar, ii. 28, p. 74 and below, p. 94.
16 So M. Lintzel, 'Die Kaiserpolitik Ottos des Grossen', *Ausgewählte Schriften* (Berlin, 1961) II, pp. 192–4, 199 and W. Smidt, *Deutsches Königtum und Deutscher Staat des Hochmittelalters während und unter dem Einfluss der Italienischen Heerfahrten* (Wiesbaden, 1964), pp. 48–51.
17 DO I. 355 preserved only in Widukind, iii. 70, pp. 146–8. He reshaped the text.
18 Widukind, i. 34, p. 48, line 10, a passage borrowed from Livy.
19 For the rumours of a rising see Widukind, iii. 75, p. 152. For the false report of Otto's death see DO I. 421 of 17 September 972, a falsification based on a genuine precept, For this see K. U. Jäschke, 'Studien zu Quellen und Geschichte des Osnabrücker Zehntstreits unter Heinrich IV', *Archiv für Diplomatik*, 9/10 (1963–4), p. 256. Jäschke does not discuss the main features of the *narratio*. The falsifier must have possessed a source for the circumstantial and very probable story he tells. See also Smidt, *op. cit.*, pp. 50, 104–7.
20 e.g. iii. 46, p. 126.
21 The letter is in *Monumenta Moguntina*, ed. P. Jaffé, *Bibliotheca Rerum Germanicarum* III (Berlin, 1866), pp. 347–50: 'omnis ordo omnisque cognatio detestatur. Non est regi locus regendi' (p. 348). For literature and comments see *RI* II, 5, no. 249.
22 Widukind, iii. 57, p. 135 f., *Continuatio Reginonis*, 956, 957, p. 169.
23 Widukind, iii. 58, p. 136: 'de caetero, qui adhuc ordinavit imperium suum, rectori omnium Deo fideliter commisit.' On Henry I's 'house order' of 929 see K. Schmid, 'Thronfolge', pp. 439 ff. He was then 50 years old. Liudolf was 27 when he died, Duke Henry of Bavaria only about 35. Otto I had reached his 48th year when he lost his son by Edith.
24 *Vita Mathildis ant.* cc. 13, 14 (*SS* X, p. 580) and *Vita Mathildis (post.)*, c. 21 (*SS* IV, p. 297) and also *Vita Brunonis*, c. 41, p. 44: 'Imperatoris . . . reditum frater eius nocte dieque sollicitus expectavit.' On the foundation of Nordhausen see below, p. 67.
25 UB Halberstadt, I, no. 34 of 965. For an amended edition see H. Goetting, 'Die beiden ältesten Halberstädter Bischofsurkunden von 965 und ihre Siegel' in

Grundwissenschaften und Geschichte. Festschrift für Peter Acht, Münchener Historische Studien, Abt. Geschichtliche Hilfswissenschaften (Kallmünz, 1976), p. 59: 'Si quo autem, quod absit, regni discidio vel sterilitate terre vinum denegaretur, pondus IIII marcarum argenti representaretur.' The charter is in the Lower Saxon State Archive in Wolfenbüttel. I am much indebted to Professor Goetting for giving me a facsimile and an offprint of his article.

26 Goetting, pp. 58–72.
27 *ibid.*, p. 65. The other suspect elements are the anachronistic sum of four marks and th mention of Bishop Alfred (? for Altfried) of Hildesheim among those present at the transaction, but that there should have been a clause stipulating some alternative to the two cartloads of wine is not unreasonable. The bad harvests which could also disrupt the supply must not be overlooked.
28 *Continuatio Reginonis*, p. 156: 'ne in eligendo post se rege discidium regni fieret'.
29 Thietmar, ii. 28, p. 74. R. Hucke, *Die Grafen von Stade* (Stade, 1956), p. 13 can only prove distant kinship by marriage between the Ottonians and Count Henry whose first wife Judith was a cousin of Liudolf's wife Ida. If there was consanguinity between Otto I and the count it must go back to the ninth century. For Bishop Berengar of Cambrai see the *Gesta Episcoporum Cameracensium* i. 80, *SS* VII, p. 431. Flodoard described him as a relative of Bishop Bovo of Chalons (*Les Annales de Flodoard*, ed. P. Lauer, p. 143). For another Saxon Berengar, 'primi Ottonis imperatoris consanguineus', see *Gesta Episcoporum Virdunensium Continuatio*, c. 2, *SS* IV, p. 45.
30 A large number of them were his kinsmen too. cf. n. 29 and A. Hauck, *Kirchengeschichte Deutschlands* (3rd edn, Leipzig, 1906) III, p. 31.
31 See below, p. 52, Ludat, pp. 82 ff., F. Steinbach, 'Die Ezzonen', *Das Erste Jahrtausend*, Textband II, ed. V. H. Elbern (Düsseldorf, 1964), pp. 857 ff. The marriage raised the family of Mathilda's husband, the Rhenish Count Palatine Ezzo, to a commanding position in the Frankish Rhineland during the first half of the eleventh century and taught it to think and act regally. Ezzo's daughter Richeza became queen of Poland. She married Miesco II, the son of Boleslas Chrobry. All his other daughters, and he had six more, were made abbesses, thus imitating the Ottonian example. Five of them bore Ottonian names: Adelheid, Mathilda, Sophia, Theophanu and Ida. On Ezzo's enmity with Henry II see Ludat, *loc. cit.*
32 Widukind, ii. 28, p. 91. For the elder Ansfried's place in Mathilda's family see Thietmar, v. 31, p. 169. If the chronicler is right, he must have been her brother.
33 Widukind. ii. 11, p. 75.
34 *ibid.*
35 *Nekrologium Monasterii S. Michaelis*, ed. A. C. Wedekind (Brunswick, 1833) under the date 10 July. For the charter see *Lüneburger Urkundenbuch*, ed. W. v. Hodenberg, VII Abt. *Archiv des Klosters St. Michaelis zu Lüneburg* (Celle, Hanover, 1861), no. 8.
36 M. Gluckman, *Politics, Law and Ritual in Tribal Society* (Oxford, 1965), p. 109 f., 123–68, 279–86 and, critical, P. C. Lloyd, 'The Political structure of African Kingdoms: An Exploratory Model' in M. Banton (ed.) *Political Systems and the Distribution of Power*, ASA Monographs 2 (London, 1968), pp. 63 ff. and 'Conflict Theory and Yoruba Kingdoms' in I. M. Lewis (ed.), *History and Social Anthropology*, ASA Monographs 7 (London, 1968), pp. 25 ff. with a brief survey of theories. The discussion is flawed by a terminological jungle. I have not incorporated Lloyd's own conflict model which isolates the political and institutional apparatus as sources of conflict. He has in fact only loosened a stone or two in the wall of the prevailing equilibrium theories.

37 Widukind, iii. 68, p. 143: 'Milites Wichmanni variis poenis afflixit' (Hermann Billung in 966 or 967).
38 iii. 18, p. 113 and Ruotger, cc. 18, 19, pp. 16–19. H. Naumann, 'Rätsel des letzten Aufstandes gegen Otto I. (953–954)', *AKG* 46 (1964), pp. 133 ff. has wholly failed to see this point.
39 But the same could have been said against Brun's alliances in Lotharingia, especially his understanding with Count Reginar III of Hainault, the nephew of the former Duke Giselbert, who was of course an enemy of Duke Conrad. See Leyser, *History* L (1965), p. 9 f.
40 *Annales Regni Francorum*, 771, ed. F. Kurze, *SRG* (Hanover, 1895 and repr. 1950), pp. 32, 33.
41 *Einhardi Vita Karoli Magni*, c. 2, ed. O. Holder-Egger, *SRG* (Hanover and Leipzig, 1911, repr. 1947), p. 4 f.
42 DO I. 423 for Bishop Pilgrim of Passau: 'interventus nepotis nostri karissimi ducis Heinrici'. On Duke Henry's early years see K. Reindel in M. Spindler, *Handbuch der bayerischen Geschichte* I (Munich, 1968), pp. 221 ff. In 984 Archbishop Adalbero of Reims or rather Gerbert accused him of having plotted also against Otto I's life. See *Die Briefsammlung Gerberts von Reims*, ed. F. Weigle, *MGH, Die Briefe der Deutschen Kaiserzeit* II (Berlin, Zürich, Dublin, 1966), no. 27.
43 See above n. 17.
44 F. Becker, *Das Königtum der Thronfolger im Deutschen Reich des Mittelalters, Quellen und Studien zur Verfassungsgeschichte des Deutschen Reiches in Mittelalter und Neuzeit* V.3 (Weimar, 1913), pp. 3–13.
45 *Ekkeharti (IV) Casus sancti Galli*, c. 146, ed. G. Meyer von Knonau, *Mittheilungen zur Vaterländischen Geschichte* 5, 6 (St Gallen, 1877), p. 449.
46 Thietmar, iv. 49, p. 188. On this conspiracy see P. E. Schramm, *Kaiser Rom und Renovatio*, 2nd edn (repr. Darmstadt, 1957), p. 183 f.
47 On this see below, p. 95 f. Henry's brother was reputed to have been his lifelong enemy and the emperor banished him in 1024.
48 For their risings in 1018 (Thietmar Billung) and 1020 (Duke Bernhard II) see H. Bannasch, *Das Bistum Paderborn unter den Bischöfen Rethar und Meinwerk (983–1036)* (Paderborn, 1972), pp. 179 f., 182 ff. where the sources are given.
49 Below, pp. 100 ff.

Chapter 3
1 The chief sources for what follows are Widukind, ii. 30, pp. 91–3, *Continuatio Reginonis*, 941, p. 162, *AQ*, 941, *SS* III, p. 56, Thietmar, ii. 21, p. 62, Hrotsvitha, *gesta Ottonis*, lines 316–71, Köpke-Dümmler, *Otto der Grosse*, pp. 115–18, *RI* II, 1, nos. 94a, 94b, R. Holtzmann, *Geschichte der Sächsischen Kaiserzeit* (Munich, 1943), p. 130 f. and Leyser, 'Henry I and the beginnings of the Saxon Empire', *EHR* LXXXVIII (1968), pp. 13–15.
2 Above, p. 18.
3 Above, p. 14.
4 K. F. Werner, 'Heeresorganisation und Kriegführung im Deutschen Königreich des 10. und 11. Jahrhunderts', *Ordinamenti Militari in Occidente nell' Alto Medioevo, Settimane di studio del Centro italiano di studi sull'alto medioevo* XV (Spoleto, 1968), p. 828 speaks of a Slav *Leibgarde* under the Ottos but without citing the evidence. The best I have found is the *miles* Zolunta who adopted the German name Henry and served near Otto II's person. He was placed by the emperor on one of the two Greek ships which he took into his service for the

Calabrian expedition that ended so disastrously at Cape Colonne in July 982
(Thietmar, iii. 21, 22, 23, pp. 124–8). In general Slav auxiliary forces played a
very important part in Ottonian warfare.

5   K. Schmid, 'Neue Quellen zum Verständnis des Adels im 10. Jahrhundert', pp.
211–23 and Wenskus, *op. cit.* pp. 388, 392 f.

6   The Quedlinburg Annals record his birth in 923 (*SS* iii, p. 52).

7   On Hildiward's schooling see Thietmar, iv. 18, p. 152.

8   ii. 20, p. 62: 'ad hoc presignatum'. In Thietmar the reigning bishop's utterances
on the succession are presented as prophecies which affirm and strengthen the
successor's election. They had the function of suggesting that the electors,
fallible men though they were, had really fulfilled God's will and found the
divinely ordained person.

9   *AS*, 968 (*SS* vi, p. 621): 'ab Herimanno . . . duce . . . constitutus'. It meant
leading the bishop-elect to an episcopal throne. cf. Thietmar, v. 41, p. 268.

10   Not Rome, as Thietmar wrote in error. See *RI* ii, 1, no. 473a.

11   Thietmar, ii. 21, p. 62: 'per manus suscepit eundem curamque ei baculo com-
mittens pastoralem: "Accipe", infit, "precium patris tui"'.' 'per manus suscepit'
meant that Hildiward now became Otto's man. See Fleckenstein, *Hofkapelle* ii,
p. 177.

12   For another example see below, p. 85 and Otto III's lighthearted verse on the
elevation of his chancellor Heribert to the see of Cologne in P. E. Schramm,
Kaiser Könige und Päpste III (Stuttgart, 1969), p. 300.

13   Two of Thietmar's great-grandfathers fought and fell at Lenzen. See Waitz,
Heinrich I., p. 130. On Dietrich see Schölkopf, *Grafen*, p. 94. Already *sub anno*
955 Widukind (iii. 45, p. 126) described him as *preses*, a word he often used for
'margrave'. Dietrich led an expedition against the Slavs, perhaps as Gero's
deputy, and was defeated.

14   Thietmar, ii. 21, p. 62: 'Avum autem meum nomine Liutharium, eiusdem
consilii participem, libenter perdere voluit; sed sibi familiarium devictus con-
silio principum, captum misit *tunc* Bawariam ad comitem Bertoldum,
comprehensis *sibi* omnibus suimet rebus ac *late* distributis, usque in annum
integrum; tuncque gratiam regis et sua omnia cum magna pecunia et predio in
Sonterslevo et in Vodenesvege iacenti acquisivit.' The correction and additions
in Thietmar's own hand are in italics. For a facsimile edition of his own MS. of
the *Chronicon* see *Die Dresdner Handschrift der Chronik des Bischofs Thietmar
von Merseburg*, prefaced by L. Schmidt (Dresden, 1905). For this passage see
fol. 23b.

15   *Die Chronik des Thietmar von Merseburg, Die Geschichtschreiber der deutschen
Vorzeit*, 3rd edn (Leipzig, 1892), p. 41 and *Thietmar von Merseburg Chronik*,
neu übertragen und erläutert von W. Trillmich, *Ausgewählte Quellen zur Deutschen Geschichte des Mittelalters* ix (Darmstadt, 1957), pp. 56, 57.

16   *Historia Martisburgica, darinnen Chronica Ditmari, Bischofs zu Marssburg . . .
Alles zum Theil erst verdeutschet . . . durch Georgium Hahn* (Leipzig, 1606), p.
28 and J. F. Ursinus, *Dithmar Bischofs zu Merseburg, Chronik . . . aus der
lateinischen in die deutsche Sprache übersetzt* (Dresden, 1790), p. 78.

17   *Heinrich Meiboms des älteren Walbeckische Chronike*, ed. F. Dingelstädt and C.
Abeln (Helmstädt, 1749), p. 12. Dümmler, *Kaiser Otto der Grosse*, p. 117,
Schölkopf, pp. 74, 82. She thought at the same time that Liuthar received a
compensation in money. This misreads both Thietmar and the later medieval,
vernacular versions of the incident. For these see below, p. 39.

18   *AS*, 952, *SS* vi, p. 608 followed by an anecdote of Otto's unrelenting severity.

19   cf. above, p. 9, n. 1 and the *Mainz Ordo*: 'Accipe virgam virtutis atque

aequitatis, qua intellegas mulcere pios et terrere reprobos', here cited from the edition in P. E. Schramm, *Kaiser, Könige und Päpste* III (Stuttgart, 1969), p. 100.

20 Liudprand, *Antapodosis* iv. 15, p. 113.

21 Ruotger, c. 18, p. 17: 'Si paulo iratior est seductoribus tuis, cito mitescet', but Liudolf knew his father too well to be satisfied with this.

22 Richer, *Histoire de France* ii. 29, ed. R. Latouche, *Les Classiques de l'Histoire de France au Moyen Age* (Paris, 1930) I, p. 170.

23 Below, p. 94.

24 ii. 6, p. 44. Thietmar evidently thought the demand unwise and disapproved of it. Lippelt, *op. cit.*, p. 154 overlooked the critical note.

25 Bruno, *Vita S. Adalberti*, c. 9, *SS* IV, p. 598.

26 Beumann, *Widukind von Korvei* (Weimar, 1950), pp. 113–21, 141 and Einhard, *Vita Karoli*, c. 7, p. 10: 'ac perpetua tam in adversis quam in prosperis mentis constantia'.

27 iii. 16, p. 112: 'Preterea rex severiorem animum gerens ex recenti iniuria.' I cannot therefore concur with Beumann's view (*loc. cit.*) about the role of *clementia* in Widukind's portrait of Otto I, nor with G. Tellenbach who thought Otto I endowed with this quality more than most other rulers. See his 'Otto der Grosse' in *Die Grossen Deutschen* I, ed. H. Heimpel, T. Heuss, B. Reifenberg (Berlin, 1956), p. 36.

28 Beumann, *op. cit.*, pp. 115–17 does not ignore these.

29 ii. 11, p. 77. For the expression 'regiae discipline terror' see ii. 36, p. 96.

30 ii. 31, p. 92.

31 In his epilogue on Otto I (ii. 45, p. 94) he exhorted the faithful to pray to God for the emperor's soul 'ut flagicia servi peccatoris innumera, quae in tot sibi subditis rebus precaveri nequiverant, clementer ignoscat'.

32 cf. above, p. 35 and n. 18 and also the *Annales Palidenses, SS* XVI, p. 63.

33 DDO I. 59, 60, 61 (a confiscated *beneficium*), 107, 115, 135, 155, 166, 171, 189, 194, 195, 197 (*beneficia*), 200, 201, 204, 207, 217, 219, 226, 236, 316, 320, 321, 331, 332, 333, the last three being grants of lands and of a nunnery forfeited by two brothers, Eberhard and Conrad, on the grounds of illegitimacy; but the importance of the properties and the brothers' names suggest another curtailment of Conradine possessions.

34 DDO I. 155, 166, 189, 201, 236 and see H. Keller, *Kloster Einsiedeln im Ottonischen Schwaben, Forschungen zur Oberrheinischen Landesgeschichte* XIII (Freiburg, 1964), pp. 99 ff and T. L. Zotz, *Der Breisgau und das alemannische Herzogtum, Vorträge und Forschungen, Sonderband* 15 (Sigmaringen, 1974), pp. 26–43. Adelheid was the grand-daughter of Duke Burchard I of Suabia († 926) and the daughter of King Rudolf II of Burgundy († 937). By marrying her and favouring her kin, Otto I also overlooked and hemmed in his son Liudolf's position in the duchy, perhaps another reason for the rift between them.

35 DO I. 107 of 949: 'pro cuiusdam viri commissu Adam'. He may have been occupying former Carolingian royal demesne as the Liudolfings had done themselves in the ninth century. See Keller, *op. cit.*, p. 99, Zotz, p. 27.

36 DO I. 217 of 960 and cf. no. 219.

37 DO I. 189 of 6 January 958 at Pöhlde and DO I. 201 of 14 April, 959 at Walbeck.

38 DDO I. 320, 321 of 966: 'latrocinia et malefacta'. For Wulfhard see above, p. 22, n. 83. For Ernst see DO I. 204 and Widukind, iii. 23, p. 118. Other diplomata mention *infidelitas* and rebellion as the reasons for expropriation and forfeiture (DO I. 115 of 949, DO I. 195 of 958).

39 Widukind, iii. 15, p. 112 and iii. 18, p. 114: 'fautores insidiarum expostulat.'
40 *loc. cit.*
41 Some vassals of Bishop Henry of Augsburg (973–82) held their *beneficia* in
    defiance of their lord on the strength of the services they had rendered to Otto I
    on expeditions. See Gerhard's *Vita S. Oudalrici*, c. 28, *SS* iv, p. 416. See also
    Thietmar, v. 33, p. 258 for Count Berthold I of the Nordgau standing with Otto
    II against his lord, Duke Henry II of Bavaria. For the famous episode of the two
    Suabian counts who refused to stand by Duke Ernst against the emperor see
    Wipo, *Gesta Chuonradi Imperatoris*, c. 20, ed. H. Bresslau *SRG* (Hanover,
    Leipzig, 1915), p. 40. In general H. Mitteis, *The State in the Middle Ages*,
    translated by H. F. Orton (Amsterdam, Oxford, 1975) pp. 136 ff. and F. L.
    Ganshof, *Feudalism*, translated by P. Grierson (London, New York, Toronto,
    1952), pp. 145 ff.
42 Flodoard, *Annales*, 956, p. 142.
43 Widukind, iii. 57, p. 135: 'Liudolfus autem . . . cum fidem vult servare amicis'
    suggests that they were to be compensated for losses suffered in Saxony and
    Francia. Hrotsvitha, *gesta Ottonis*, line 1169, p. 226.
44 MS. Bibl. Royale, Brussels, 7503–7518, fol. 218r. On this recension of Thiet-
    mar's text see R. Holtzmann's introduction to his edition, pp. xxxvii ff. and the
    observations of K.-U. Jäschke, *Die Älteste Halberstädter Bischofschronik, Mit-
    teldeutsche Forschungen* 62/i (Cologne, Vienna, 1970), pp. 9 ff.
45 Thietmar (Corvey version), p. 63: 'et usque in annum integrum exiliavit.'
    Exiliare can mean 'To be sent into exile' and 'to live in exile'.
46 Paris, Bibl. Nat MS. Lat. 11851, fol. 58r (*SS* vi, p. 604): 'duci bertoldo in
    Bavvaria mittitur usque in annum integrum, tuncque regis gratiam et sua omnia
    cum magna pecunia et predio . . . adquisivit.' The punctuation suggests that the
    annalist too understood Liuthar's exile to have been a fixed penalty. For the
    question of his identity and in general see Wattenbach-Schmale, *Deutschlands
    Geschichtsquellen im Mittelalter. Vom Tode Kaiser Heinrichs V. bis zum Ende
    des Interregnum* i (Darmstadt, 1976), pp. 14–18 as against Jäschke, *op. cit.*, p. 36 f.
47 *Annales Magdeburgenses*, 968, c. 32, *SS* xvi, p. 148 f.
48 ed. K. Janicke, *Die Chroniken der deutschen Städte* 7 (Leipzig, 1869), p. 59:
    'und wolde greven Lutharium ok hebben dodet laten. do beden de vorsten vor
    on. des nam om de keiser al sin gut und sande on gevangen to Beieren. ein jar
    was he gevangen. dar na wart om des keisers hulde dedinget, also dat he grot gelt
    gaf und losede mit sik dat vorwerk to Santersleven und dat to Godeswegen und
    he stichtede gode, to beteringe vor dat he an dem keiser gebroken hadde, dat
    closter to Walbeke . .' To arrive at the first translation *mit* stands for *da met* =
    (modern) *damit* and a comma must be placed after *sik*. I am indebted to
    Professor P. Ganz on this point.
49 Cronecken der Sassen, 969 (Mainz, 1492): 'unde gaff grot gelt dar he sick mit
    losede. Und dat vorwarke to Sentersleve moste in beteringh holden unde
    stichten dat closter to Walpecke'. For 'in beteringh holden' (High German: 'in
    Besserung halten') see K. Schiller and A. Lütken, *Mittelniederdeutsches Wör-
    terbuch* i (Bremen, 1875), pp. 300 ff. and A. Lasch and C. Borchling, *Mittel-
    niederdeutsches Handwörterbuch* i (Neumünster, 1956), col. 258, also R.
    Schröder, E. v. Künssberg, *Lehrbuch der deutschen Rechtsgeschichte*, 7th edn
    (Berlin, Leipzig, 1932), pp. 793, 795. Literally, 'to maintain in a good condi-
    tion', but *beteringh* also means a) amends, penalty, b) surplus. The passage is
    corrupt but seems to indicate an impaired tenure of the land with part or the
    whole of the yield going elsewhere.
50 The earlier editions were listed by Holtzmann in his own, p. xxxix.

51 Johannes Pomarius, *Chronica der Sachsen und Nidersachsen* (Wittenbergk, 1588), p. 146 and Meibom, *op. cit.*, p. 12.
52 Thietmar, p. xxxi.
53 vi. 50, p. 336 and v. 9, p. 230.
54 vi. 90, p. 382: 'comprehensis omnibus suimet rebus' and cf. ii. 21: 'comprehensis sibi omnibus suimet rebus'.
55 p. 382: 'gratiam et incolatum cum predio suimet et auro comparavit.'
56 vi. 81, p. 372.
57 vi. 86, p. 376 f.
58 vi. 65, p. 354: 'Harnaburg et Frasam ac Pretim urbes cum curte una, quae Eseconis fuit comitis, suae acquisivit aecclesiae.'
59 ii. 21, p. 63 (the Corvey version): 'Quam multa predia huius noxa perdidit.'
60 iv. 17, p. 150 f.
61 vi. 86, p. 376 and see pp. ix, xiv, xviii and Schölkopf, p. 76.
62 vi. 40, p. 322.
63 Thietmar mentioned his own and other family possessions in i. 13, vi. 39 (Rottmersleben), iv. 38 (Nord-Germersleben), vi. 49, 84 (Wolmirstedt), viii. 15 (Heeslingen), Walbeck, *passim*.
64 For more evidence and the later history of these estates, see Appendix.

Chapter 4
1 DO i. 306.
2 Thietmar, ii. 29, p. 74.
3 iv. 18, p. 152.
4 Above, p. 25 and n. 12.
5 In the eleventh-century *Gesta Episcoporum Virdunensium, Continuatio*, c. 3 (*SS* iv, p. 46) Wicfried is described as coming from Bavaria. Yet he belonged to the clerical entourage of Archbishop Brun of Cologne to whom he owed his promotion to Verdun in 959–60. If he was related to Brun's predecessor, Archbishop Wicfried († 953), himself the son of Otto I's aunt Oda (below, p. 53), it would explain why Otto II mediated to arrange the match. Godila was his kin. It might also explain Liuthar's interest in Cologne. He and his sons acquired claims, connections and perhaps possessions in Lower Lotharingia through this marriage. See E. Hlawitschka, *Die Anfänge des Hauses Habsburg-Lothringen* (Saarbrücken, 1969), pp. 97, 101. The Bavarian descent of Bishop Wicfried was probably on his mother's side.
6 See *Handbuch der bayerischen Geschichte* I, p. 223.
7 Thietmar, iv. 2, p. 132 f.
8 Ludat, p. 24 and W. H. Fritze, 'Probleme der abodritischen Stammes und Reichsverfassung und ihrer Entwicklung vom Stammesstaat zum Herrschaftsstaat' in *Siedlung und Verfassung der Slawen zwischen Elbe, Saale und Oder*, ed. H. Ludat (Giessen, 1960), p. 159 f.
9 *AQ*, 985, *SS* iv, p. 67: 'humilis habitu, humilis et actu', he did homage to the infant Otto III and became his *miles*. This must be contrasted with the annalist's account of his reinstatement: 'eum . . . deinde non tantum inter amicos, sed etiam inter amicissimos, uti ius propinquitatis exigebat . . . venerantur', *i.e.* Adelheid, Theophanu and Mathilda.
10 The date of Liuthar's advancement is disputed. Schölkopf (p. 75 f.) argued for his early succession. Ludat, *An Elbe und Oder* (p. 26), thought there was a long vacancy but the situation on the frontier remained much too critical for that.
11 iii. 17, p. 118 but see also Adam of Bremen, *Gesta Hammaburgensis Ecclesiae Pontificum* ii. 42, Schol. 27, 28, ed. B. Schmeidler, *SRG* (Hanover and Leipzig,

1917), p. 102. According to Adam, Schol. 31 (p. 104) and the Saxon Annalist, 983 and 998 (*SS* VI, pp. 631, 642) Dietrich was deposed.
12 iv. 16, p. 150.
13 Thietmar, v. 3, p. 222 and see Appendix, below p. 121 f.
14 iii. 9, p. 106 and below, p. 99.
15 On Bernhard see viii. 10, p. 504. The enemy who wept when Werner died of his injuries in 1014 was the Wettin Dietrich. Werner had killed his father, and his mother, Thietburga, was a daughter of Margrave Dietrich of the Northern March (vii. 7, p. 406). The king too was sorry, Thietmar wrote.
16 *AS*, 977, *SS* VI, p. 627.
17 Further examples are: Mathilda, the daughter of Hermann Billung, married Count Baldwin III of Flanders in 961; Count Wichmann of Hamalant on the Lower Rhine, a daughter of Count Arnulf of Flanders. The Slav marriages of Saxon noble families are discussed in Ludat, *An Elbe und Oder*.
18 Wenskus, pp. 473 ff.
19 *MGH, Capitularia Regum Francorum* II, p. 207, c. 4 and p. 235 f. cc. 39 (39a).
20 On the question when can we begin to speak of Germany as a political entity, a self-conscious political society, see W. Schlesinger, 'Die Grundlegung der deutschen Einheit im frühen Mittelalter' in his *Beiträge zur deutschen Verfassungsgeschichte des Mittelalters* (Göttingen, 1963) I, pp. 245 ff., E. Müller-Mertens, *Regnum Teutonicum* (Vienna, Cologne, Graz, 1970), C. Brühl, *Die Anfänge der Deutschen Geschichte, Sitzungsberichte der Wissenschaftlichen Gesellschaft . . . Frankfurt* 10 (1972), no. 5 and a poignant survey by J. B. Gillingham, *The Kingdom of Germany in the High Middle Ages* (900–1200), Historical Association (London, 1971).
21 Holtzmann's Thietmar edn. p. viii and Hucke, pp. 11–14.
22 See below p. 95.
23 *Brunos Buch vom Sachsenkrieg,* c. 30, ed. H.-E. Lohmann *MGH Kritische Studientexte* 2 (Leipzig, 1937), p. 33 or ed. F.-J. Schmale, *Quellen zur Geschichte Kaiser Heinrichs IV., Ausgewählte Quellen* (Darmstadt, 1963), p. 232.
24 iii. 44, 52, 59, 70 (pp. 123, 131, 136, 148) and more generally the anxieties expressed in i. 34 (p. 48): 'donec dilatatae [the res Saxonum] ipsa sua iam magnitudine laborant.'

The Women of the Saxon Aristocracy

Chapter 5
1 Although Sigebert of Gembloux described Widukind's work as a life of Otto I, making it appear as if he also wrote a Saxon history down to the year 973. See his *Chronica*, 973, *SS* VI, p. 351. cf. also p. ix of the P. Hirsch and H.-E. Lohmann edition of the *Res Gestae Saxonicae*.
2 Thietmar, iv. 40–42, pp. 176–80.
3 See below, p. 94 and Thietmar, v. 7, p. 228.
4 *AS* (*SS* VI, p. 619) but using almost certainly a lost section of the Quedlinburg Annals. Mathilda was veiled and made abbess even before she reached the age of twelve, probably because Otto and Adelheid wanted to see her settled before their impending departure for another Roman expedition.
5 That Mathilda's *velatio* served as a precedent for Sophia's in 987 has perhaps been overlooked. Yet the settlement of the first clash between Archbishop Willigis of Mainz and Bishop Osdag of Hildesheim suggests that the protocol of 966 was remembered. Willigis took part only in Sophia's *velatio*, those of other girls being reserved for the bishop of Hildesheim acting alone as diocesan.

6   *Die Lebensbeschreibung der Kaiserin Adelheid von Abt Odilo*, c. 10, ed. H. Paulhart, *MIÖG, Ergbd* xx, 2 (1962), p. 37 and *RI* ii, 3, no. 1213b. For the Synod of Dortmund see Thietmar, vi. 18, p. 294 f. and *RI* ii, 4, no. 1597 a. See also T. Vogelsang, *Die Frau als Herrscherin im hohen Mittelalter* (Göttingen, 1954), p. 29.

7   As did Godila, Margrave Liuthar's widow, in 1003 securing the margraviate for her son Werner (cf. above, p. 41, n. 57). It is noteworthy that Werner was not a minor in 1003. He must have been over twenty. Another example is Swanehild, the widow of the murdered Margrave Ekkehard, trying to secure Meissen together with her sons in 1002 (Thietmar, v. 8, p. 230).

8   On the Essen treasures connected with Abbess Mathilda (973–1011), Liudolf's daughter and those made for Abbess Theophanu (a grand-daughter of Otto II's) see H. V. Elbern, *Das Erste Jahrtausend, Tafelband* (Düsseldorf, 1962), nos. 376, 378, 382, 383, 384, 385 and see plate I. For the Borghorst Cross (1025–50), *ibid* nos. 392, 393 and below, p. 71. On the Svenhilda Gospels (MS. John Rylands Lat. no. 110) with a picture of the patronesses, see R. Kahsnitz, 'The Gospel Book of Abbess Svanhild in the John Rylands Library', *BJRL* 53 (1970–71), pp. 123 ff. On the Quedlinburg Gospels see *Kunst und Kultur im Weserraum* 2 (3rd edn, Münster, 1967), no. 162. It was probably created at Corvey and perhaps given to Quedlinburg by Otto I, though this must remain a conjecture. On the Hitda Gospels made for Abbess Hitda of Meschede see P. Bloch, *Der Darmstädter Hitda Codex* (Berlin, 1968), p. 73 and pl. 3 and P. Bloch and H. Schnitzler, *Die Ottonische Kölner Malschule* (Düsseldorf, 1967), p. 52 f. and p. 64.

9   C. Levi-Strauss, *The Elementary Structures of Kinship* (London, 1969), pp. 103–6 links undifferentiated descent especially with the transmission of rights to land. On the family structure of the Frankish and post-Frankish aristocracy with a discussion of the work of K. Schmid see Leyser, *P & P* 41 (1968), pp. 32 ff.

10   As can be seen from K. F. Werner, 'Die Nachkommen Karls des Grossen' in *Karl der Grosse, IV, Das Nachleben*, ed. W. Braunfels and P. E. Schramm (Düsseldorf, 1967), pp. 416 ff.

11   *Lex Saxonum*, cc. xv, xx, xxvi and xlii, xlv, *Leges Saxonum et Lex Thuringorum*, ed. C. v. Schwerin, *MGH, Fontes Iuris Germanici Antiqui* (Hanover and Leipzig, 1918).

12   Self-awareness, *Selbstverständnis*, has had more than its fair share in recent studies of the early medieval German nobility.

13   T. H. Hollingsworth, 'A Demographic Study of the British Ducal Families', *Population in History*, ed. D. V. Glass and D. E. C. Eversley (London, 1965), pp. 354–78 and C. Levy and L. Henry, 'Ducs et pairs sous l'Ancien Régime. Caractéristiques démographiques d'une caste', *Population* 15, 5 (1960), pp. 807–27.

14   'The Demography of the British Peerage', *Population Studies* xviii, 2 (supplement).

15   On the problems of studying sub-groups and closed populations see D. E. C. Eversley, 'The Validity of Family and Group Statistics as Indicators of Secular Population Trends' in F. Bechhoser (ed.), *Population Growth and the Brain Drain* (Edinburgh, 1969), and T. H. Hollingsworth, *Historical Demography* (London, 1969), pp. 199 ff.

16   e.g. the brother of Bishop Liudolf of Osnabrück (967–78), Count Gottschalk (cf. above, p. 10), *Westfälisches UB, Supplement*, ed. W. Diekamp (Münster, 1885), no. 470.

17   Thietmar, iv. 39, p. 176. The last year in which Otto II could have persuaded his

kinsman, Bishop Wigfried of Verdun, to agree to the marriage was 980, before he departed to Italy. We possess a diploma of his, confirming the bishop's gifts to St Vanne (DO II, 218 of 3 June 980 at Margut, Ardennes) proving that he met him. Werner must have been born in 981 at the latest because in 998 he was old enough to abduct his bride-to-be, Liudgard, from Quedlinburg (Thietmar, iv, 41).

18 Thietmar, vii. 3, p. 400.

19 iv. 60, p. 200. On Mathilda's birth see O. Perst, 'Zur Reihenfolge der Kinder Ottos II. und der Theophanu', *DA* 14 (1958), pp. 230–36 as against A. Hofmeister, 'Studien zu Theophano', *Festschrift Edmund E. Stengel* (Münster, Cologne, 1952), pp. 225–32. According to F. Steinbach, 'Die Ezzonen' (*Das erste Jahrtausend* ii, p. 858), Theophanu was still alive when they married and did not object to the alliance. As she died in 991 the bride would then have been even younger. More likely the wedding took place after her death when Otto III, still not of age, was unable to control his house.

20 *Vita Karoli Magni*, c. 19, p. 24. For the deaths of his infant children see K. F. Werner, 'Die Nachkommen' in *op. cit.*, p. 444, no. 10 and the family tree.

21 Krüger, p. 67.

22 Thietmar, i. 7, p. 10 and Widukind, i. 21, p. 30. Their names were Thangmar and Liudolf. For the story in the *Annalista Saxo sub anno* 907 cf. below, p. 68.

23 For Otto I's sons by Adelheid see Widukind, iii. 12 and nn. 7, 8 (p. 110 f.). For Otto II's unnamed daughter see DO II. 229 of 8 October 980 and K. Uhlirz, *Jahrbücher . . . Otto II*, p. 111. Most likely she was born in 979. For a discussion and further literature on Otto II's offspring see O. Perst, 'Zur Reihenfolge der Kinder Ottos II. und der Theophanu'.

24 Conrad II lost two daughters. See Wipo's *Gesta Chuonradi*, c. 32, p. 51 and DC II. 233 of 25 October 1036. Henry III in 1055 lost his second son, Conrad, born in 1052. See E. Steindorff, *Jahrbücher des deutschen Reiches unter Heinrich III.* (Leipzig, 1881) II, pp. 219, 317. Henry IV lost a newborn son in 1071. See Lampert of Hersfeld, *Annales*, p. 131 and *Annales Altahenses Maiores*, p. 84. Henry V had an illegitimate daughter.

25 See Krüger, *op. cit.*, p. 67. For Oda's age see the *Vita Bernwardi Episcopi*, c. 12, *SS* IV, p. 763 and esp. Hrosvitha of Gandersheim's *primordia coenobii Gandeshemensis*, line 575. Duke Otto, Oda's son, died in 912, eight days after the birth of his grandson Otto, the future emperor. Dümmler, *Kaiser Otto der Grosse*, p. 7. For Christina see Hrotsvitha, *loc. cit.* and the Bernward *vita, loc. cit.*

26 Widukind, i. 16, p. 27 and see A. Hofmeister, 'Puer, Iuvenis, Senex, Zum Verständnis der Mittelalterlichen Altersbezeichnungen' in *Papsttum und Kaisertum*, ed. A. Brackmann (Munich, 1926), pp. 287–316 and esp. p. 316.

27 *Reginonis Chronicon*, 897 (p. 145) and 900 (p. 148). For Count Gerhard's death after a stormy career see H. Hlawitschka, *Lotharingien und das Reich*, p. 191 f. and n. 21. Oda was alive in 952 when she made over some land in Deventer to her nephew, Otto I. See DO I. 159. For her family by Count Gerhard see Hlawitschka, *Die Anfänge*. pp. 58–61. To judge by DO I. 181 of 956 she may have been dead by then. See genealogical table.

28 On Mathilda's death on 14 March 968 see Dümmler, *Otto der Grosse*, p. 440 n. 1.

29 On Louis IV's death see Flodoard, p. 138 and P. Lauer, *Le Règne de Louis IV d'Outremer* (Paris, 1900), p. 231. For the date of Gerberga's death (969) see F. Lot, *Les derniers Carolingiens* (Paris, 1891), p. 62.

30 *Sigeberti Chronicon*, 965, *SS* VI, p. 351. She died on a 10 May but the year is not

known for certain. See Lot, *op. cit.*, p. 48 n. 3. She did however outlive her husband.

31 Lothar died in 950. See the *Chronicon Novaliciense* v. 3, 4, *FSI Monumenta Novaliciensia vetustiora* II, ed. C. Cipolla (Rome, 1901), pp. 240 ff. and Flodoard, *Annales*, p. 128; Adelheid in 999. See *Epitaphium*, c. 21, p. 44.

32 Henry died in 955 (Dümmler, *Otto der Grosse*, p. 267, n. 5). On the date of the Duchess Judith's death see K. Reindel, *Die Bayerischen Luitpoldinger*, no. 131.

33 Otto II *ob*. 7 December 983. (*RI* II, 2, no. 919 e with all the sources.) Mathilda died on 8 February 999 according to the *Annales Necrologici Fuldenses*, *SS* XIII, p. 208 and *RI* II, no. 1302d. Whether both were born in 955 is not quite clear (cf. Hofmeister, 'Studien', p. 227, n. 5) but there was only a year between them.

34 Theophanu, *ob*. 15 June, 991 (*RI* II, 3, no. 1035b). Ida 'regalis domina' died in 986 (*AQ*, p. 67).

35 He died on 31 October. See *RI* II, 2, no. 884a. For Mathilda, abbess of Essen see *AQ*, p. 80. For both see plate I.

36 For Duke Burkhard's death on 17 November 973, see *Annales Sangällenses Maiores*, *SS* I, p. 80 and H. Keller, *Kloster Einsiedeln*, p. 162. Hadwig died in 994 (*Annales Einsiedlenses*, *SS* III, p. 144). The age relationships set out in the text are established as follows: Henry was born in 951 (*AQ*, p. 58). By this time Hadwig had already been the prospective bride of Romanus II the son of Constantine Porphyrogenitus. (*RI* II, 1, no. 174a). Her mother Judith married in 938. Hadwig's husband, Duke Burkhard II of Suabia, on the other hand, must have been born before 926, the year his father, Duke Burkhard I was killed in Italy (Waitz, *Heinrich I*, p. 84). For Henry the Wrangler's and Hadwig's sister Gerberga, abbess of Gandersheim, see below, p. 55 n. 47.

37 DO III. 146.

38 For their careers and ages at death see Hofmeister, *op. cit.*, pp. 225–37.

39 See the genealogical table, p. 00.

40 In Roman law of late antiquity the marriageable age for girls was twelve. At the age of twelve also noble girls might enter the canonical life and be veiled as the alternative to earthly marriage.

41 Liudprand, *Antapodosis* iv. 31, p. 126.

42 For the date of the marriage see K. Schmid, 'Die Thronfolge Ottos des Grossen' in *Königswahl und Thronfolge*, pp. 440 and 453 f and n. 137.

43 K. F. Werner, 'Nachkommen', p. 464, no. 18.

44 Before Henry I married her in 909 she lived under the tutelage of her paternal grandmother, the abbess of Herford and her biographers suggest that she was still or had only just ceased to be 'of tender age'. See the *Vita Mathildis . . . antiquior*, cc. 2, 3 (*SS* x, p. 576) and *Vita Mathildis*, cc. 2, 3 (*SS* IV, p. 285). See also A. Büsing, *Mathilda, Gemahlin Heinrichs I*. (Halle, 1910), p. 29 f.

45 She was born in 931, for in Odilo of Cluny's *Epitaphium domine Adelheide auguste*, c. 1 (ed. H. Paulhart), p. 29 she is said to have been sixteen when she married Lothar.

46 For Otto II's and Theophanu's children see the literature cited above, n. 19.

47 Gerberga was born possibly before 940 and entered Gandersheim as a child. She succeeded the Abbess Wendilgard in 949 although she does not appear to have been consecrated before 956. For details and sources, see Goetting, *Gandersheim*, p. 293 f.

48 Thietmar, iv. 16, p. 150 and *AQ*, 991.

49 She outlived her son, Count Siegfried, by eight months. On Count Liuthar's death see above, p. 41.

50 Thietmar, vii. 19, p. 420.

51   *Annales necrologici Fuldenses*, p. 204 and *RI*, ii. 2, no. 802a.
52   See the genealogical table in Freytag, *Herrschaft der Billunger* where, however, the second husband of Mathilda is erroneously given as Godfrey, duke of Lower Lotharingia instead of Count Godfrey of Verdun.
53   *AQ*, p. 82 and Thietmar, vii. 3, p. 400.
54   That he was still under age when his father died in 944 is clear from his accusations against his uncle Hermann Billung. See above, p. 21.
55   See DC ii. 19 for Kemnade of 8 February 1025. No very good reason has been adduced by Bannasch, *Das Bistum Paderborn*, p. 48 or Freytag, p. 48 and Dümmler, *Otto der Grosse*, p. 580 for regarding Friderun and the Countess Imma as daughters of the elder Wichmann. That the abbess, Friderun, was named after his wife, Queen Mathilda's sister, would be as congruous in the second as in the first generation of a descent group. Friderun and Imma were described as foundresses of Kemnade in Henry II's and Conrad II's diplomata for the house (DH ii.87 of 1004, DH ii. 362 of 1017 and the DC ii. 19) but in the *Annalista Saxo*, 967 and 970 (pp. 621, 624) it was Otto I who endowed the nunnery with half of Wichmann's lands. The discrepancy is resolved if the two daughters of the rebel were not yet of age when he died and were later enabled to confirm the foundation by granting the lands for their part and as their *hereditas*. Hermann Billung's foundation, St Michael, Lüneburg received the other half of Wichmann the Younger's lands from Otto I. (*AS, loc. cit.*).
56   957–63 are the likeliest years. According to Widukind, iii. 59, 60, 64, Count Wichmann visited his home and wife secretly from exile in France sometime in 957 and he lived peacefully, in the king's grace, on his wife's patrimony between 958 and 963. We do not know who she was.
57   For Rothgard see the *Vita Bernwardi*, c. 42 (*SS* iv, p. 776 f.) and the charter of 1003 edited by Waitz. (See below, p. 60 n. 91.) For Bishop Folcmar see Schölkopf, p. 117 and Fleckenstein, *Hofkapelle*, p. 68 f.
58   Thietmar, i. 19, p. 24 f.
59   DO i. 174 and see below, n. 61.
60   DO i. 395.
61   For Helmburg's daughters and endowments see below pp. 60, 65 and the charter published by G. Waitz, 'Die ersten sächsischen Pfalzgrafen', *Forschungen zur deutschen Geschichte* xiv (1874), pp. 26–8. For Aeddila's family see DO i. 206 of 960 and DO ii. 6 of 963 and below pp. 60, 65, 69. The problem of Helmburg's and Aeddila's family links has been discussed by H.-W. Krumwide, *Das Stift Fischbeck an der Weser, Untersuchungen zur Frühgeschichte*, 955–1158 (Göttingen, 1955) and Wenskus, p. 305 f.
62   *Fundatio Monasterii Schildecensis*, *SS* xv, ii, pp. 1045 ff. and see Schölkopf, pp. 154–6, Bannasch, pp. 43–6.
63   e.g. A. R. Burn,' "Hic Breve Vivitur": A Study of the Expectation of Life in the Roman Empire', *P & P* 4 (1953), pp. 2–31. D. Herlihy, *Medieval and Renaissance Pistoia* (New Haven and London, 1967), pp. 89–91. J. C. Russell, 'Population in Europe 500–1500' in *The Fontana Economic History of Europe* 1, ed. C. M. Cipolla (London and Glasgow, 1977), pp. 42–5, and the archaeological studies cited by Hollingsworth, *Historical Demography*, pp. 289–92. See also H. Fuhrmann, *Deutsche Geschichte im hohen Mittelalter* (Göttingen, 1978) p. 22.
64   E. R. Coleman, 'L'infanticide dans le haut Moyen Age', *AESC* 29 (1974), pp. 315–35. The authoress assumed that the sex ratio at birth was already slightly in favour of men.
65   See the comparative tables in L. Henry, 'Démographie de la Noblesse Britannique', *Population* 20, no. 4 (1965), p. 703 and in C. Lévy and L. Henry, 'Ducs et

Pairs', p. 826. The authors (p. 825) held that the situation was seemingly less favourable for women than for men in their group though there could have been an element of chance in the sampling. For the European ruling families see S. Peller, 'Births and Deaths among Europe's Ruling Families', in Glass and Eversley, *op. cit.*, pp. 86–100 and esp. pp. 91–9.

66 Hollingsworth in Glass and Eversley, p. 362.

67 *op. cit.*, p. 358 f.

68 That he was the son of Count Ekbert is disputed by A. K. Hömberg, *Westfalen und das Sächsische Herzogtum*, p. 104, n. 58 and Wenskus, p. 242, n. 2138a. To say that he was a descendant of Count Wichmann the Younger (*ibid.*) instead, remains a conjecture.

69 Adam of Bremen, *Gesta* ii, 80, p. 138.

70 E. Steindorff, *Jahrbücher des Deutschen Reiches unter Heinrich III*. (Leipzig, 1881) ii, pp. 16, 40 f.

71 Chief source for the events of 1009 and the important inheritance arrangements of 1017 is Thietmar, vi. 49, p. 336 and vi. 50, p. 460. The later murder is reported in the *Annales Hildesheimenses*, 1034, ed. G. Waitz, *SRG* (Hanover, 1878 and repr. 1947), p. 39. For the later devolution see O. Posse, *Die Markgrafen von Meissen und das Haus Wettin bis zu Konrad dem Grossen* (Leipzig, 1881), pp. 21 ff. and the genealogical table, p. 304.

72 The chief source is Thietmar, iv. 19 (p. 154) and iv. 23–5 (pp. 158–62). The others are given in *RI* ii, 3, no. 1114a (*regestum* inaccurate) and see also Hucke, p. 15 f.

73 Thietmar, vi. 7, 8 (p. 282), vii. 47 (p. 456).

74 E. Dümmler, 'Das alte Merseburger Totenbuch' (*Necrologium Merseburgense*), *Neue Mitteilungen aus dem Gebiet historisch-antiquarischer Forschungen* 11 (1867) under the dates 28 June, 16, 26, 30 July, 3, 20 August, 1, 5, 7 September. The *Necrologium*'s close connection with Thietmar's *Chronicon* is made very clear by some of these entries. *Necrologium Monasterii S. Michaelis*, ed. A. C. Wedekind (Brunswick, 1833) under the dates 13, 16, 17, 26 June, 12, 14 July, 10 August (battle at the Lech), 10, 22 September and 27 October. The campaigning season from June to September is very neatly defined by this type of entry.

75 *Annales necrologici Fuldenses*, *SS* xiii, p. 205. Thietmar, iii. 20, p. 124. The sources for the battle and the casualties are collected in K. Uhlirz, *Jahrbücher des Deutschen Reiches unter Otto II and Otto III* (Leipzig, 1902) i, pp. 254 ff. and esp. p. 256, n. 2.

76 Thietmar, iii. 8, p. 106. Many others succumbed to disease.

77 Thietmar, ii. 25, p. 68 f. However, the Duchess Judith of Bavaria, the wife of Duke Henry I, pilgrimaged to Jerusalem during her long widowhood. See the eleventh-century *Vita Erhardi episcopi Bavarici auctore Paulo*, ed. W. Levison, *MGH, Scriptores rerum Merowingicarum* vi (Hanover, Leipzig, 1913), p. 19.

78 *Lex Saxonum*, cc. xli, xliv.

79 *Das Leben der Liutbirg*, c. 1, ed. O. Menzel, *MGH, Kritische Studientexte* 3 (Leipzig, 1937), p. 10. That a Count Bernhard was the brother or the nephew of the *dux* Hessi has been suggested by Krüger, pp. 84 ff. esp. p. 89 but is disputed by Wenskus, pp. 181 and 195. The problem of inheritance is here made more difficult by the early and close Frankish connections of the Hessi clan.

80 Thietmar, vii, 50, p. 460, a famous passage which has attracted much comment.

81 *Sachsenspiegel Landrecht*, i 17 §1, ed. (2nd) K. A. Eckhardt, *MGH, Fontes Iuris Germanici N.S.* i, i (Göttingen, 1955), p. 82. H. Schulze, *Das Erb und Familienrecht der deutschen Dynastien des Mittelalters* (Halle, 1871) is still useful.

82   *Sachsenspiegel Landrecht*, 1 5 § 2, p. 77. The clause deals with the daughter living at home who on her mother's death could have all her furnishings and jewellery (*rade*) without having to divide it with the daughter who had already been endowed with such goods and set up, *i.e.* married. Yet if there was any landed inheritance (*erve*) it had to be shared between the sisters.

83   *op. cit.*, 1 5 §3.

84   1 31 §1, 2, p. 96.

85   1 17 §1, p. 82.

86   e.g. DO I. 40 of June 7, 941, a grant converting *beneficia* held by Margrave Gero into *proprietas* for his son Siegfried. Otto was here clearly rewarding the loyalty and services of his margrave after the recent plots. See also DO I. 69 of 11 June, 945.

87   For examples see the *Vita Meinwerci*, c. li (p. 43): 'annuente matre sua, herede iustissima', the grant of a *nobilis homo* and cf. also cc. lxxiv, lxxxii, lxxxv (pp. 49, 51 f.).

88   *Regesta Historiae Westfaliae*, ed. H. A. Erhard (Münster, 1847–51), *Codex Diplomaticus*, nos. xcv, xcvi and the *Vita Meinwerci*, c. xlix, p. 41 f. See also Bannasch, pp. 260–63.

89   cf. above p. 13.

90   DO I. 206.

91   'Quod bene ita poterant, quia unusquisque illarum hereditarium jus ab aliis possidebat.' From the charter of 1003 (cf. above, p. 56, n. 61). Two of the daughters, however, raised claims later. In general see K. A. Kroeschell, 'Zur Geschichte des Reichklosters Hilwartshausen und des Reichguts an der oberen Weser', *Niedersächsisches Jahrbuch für Landesgeschichte* 29 (1957), pp. 1–23 and K. Heinemeyer, 'Adel Kirche und Königtum an der oberen Weser im 9. und 10. Jahrhundert', *Historische Forschungen für Walter Schlesinger*, ed. H. Beumann (Cologne, Vienna, 1974), pp. 111–49.

92   Some of the *notitiae* have survived as such, many more were embodied in the *Vita Meinwerci*. For *traditiones* by nuns see *Vita*, cc. xli–xlviii, by noble and free lay women, cc. cvii–cxxvi. Of about 100 *traditiones* recorded by Meinwerk's biographer, 28 were made by women. In general see F. Irsigler, '*Divites* und *pauperes* in der *Vita Meinwerci*', VSWG 57 (1970), pp. 449–99. Meinwerk also purchased land outright from noblewomen (c. cxxix).

93   *Vita*, c. cxli, p. 72.

94   See below, p. 66 and *Regesta Historiae Westfaliae, Additamenta* ed. R. Wilmans (Münster, 1877), no. 117, ii, p. 103.

95   Thietmar, vi. 76, p. 366. For Walthard's family see Schölkopf, pp. 139–41.

96   *Gesta Episcoporum Halberstadensium*, SS xxiii, p. 85. On the complex genesis of the *Gesta* see Jäschke, *op. cit.* and Wattenbach-Schmale, p. 395 f. Jäschke unfortunately does not discuss this passage or assign it a place in the development of the text. For another example of a bishop's sister living at his court see the *Vita Burchardi Episcopi*, c. 12, SS iv, p. 837.

97   Thietmar, iv. 17, p. 152.

98   F. W. Oediger, 'Adelas Kampf um Elten (996–1002)', *Annalen des Historischen Vereins für den Niederrhein* 155/156 (1954), pp. 67–86.

99   Thietmar, vii. 4, p. 402. In a diploma for Fulda, preserved with interpolations in the twelfth-century *Codex Eberhardi*, the Emperor Otto II assented to the grant made by a *matrona* Wendilgirt, 'quae sub regali et imperiali patrocinio nostro semper esse videbatur.'

100 Wipo, *Gesta Chuonradi*, c. 3, p. 23.

Chapter 6

1 J. Heineken, *Die Anfänge der sächsischen Frauenklöster* (diss., Göttingen, 1909), K. H. Schäfer, *Die Kanonissenstifter im deutschen Mittelalter, Kirchenrechtliche Abhandlungen*, 43 & 44 (Stuttgart, 1907), G. Rathgen, 'Untersuchungen über eigenkirchliche Elemente der Kloster- und Stiftsvogtei vornehmlich nach thüringischen Urkunden bis zum Beginn des XIII. Jahrhunderts', *ZRG, Kanon. Abt.* xvii, 48 (1928), pp. 1 ff., K. Hörger, 'Die reichsrechtliche Stellung der Fürstäbtissinen', *AUF* ix (1926), pp. 195–270 and T. Mayer, *Fürsten und Staat* (Weimar, 1950), pp. 36–8, 224–6.

2 The sources for this count are A. Hauck, *Kirchengeschichte Deutschlands*, 3rd and 4th edn. iii (Leipzig, 1906), pp. 1011 ff., H. Hoogeweg, *Verzeichnis der Stifter und Klöster Niedersachsens* (Hanover and Leipzig, 1908) and L. Schmitz-Kallenberg, *Monasticon Westfaliae* (Münster, 1909). See also H. Richtering, 'Stifte und Klöster im Weserraum bis in das 16. Jahrhundert', *Ostwestfälisch-Weserländische Forschungen zur geschichtlichen Landeskunde*, ed. H. Stoob (Münster, 1970), pp. 376–412. A few slightly later foundations of the same *genre* should be added to the total, e.g. Überwasser in Münster (before 1041) and Wimmelburg (diocese of Halberstadt, before 1038). The very existence of some houses for women going back to the Ottonian period can only be inferred from their transformation by the twelfth-century reformers, e.g. Schöningen and Lutter. See below, pp. 65, 118. A. Hauck's lists must be used with caution and suffer from errors and omissions.

3 They were Quedlinburg, Frohse, a foundation of Margrave Gero's at first for men and then converted into one for women, subject to Gernrode (cf. DO i. 130 of 950 and DO ii. 4 of 961), Gernrode, Hadmersleben, Drübeck, Alsleben, Kalbe, Gerbstedt, St. Maria Münzenberg Quedlinburg, Vitzenburg, St. Andreas Walbeck (in the Schwabengau), Stötterlingenburg, Hillersleben and probably Schöningen.

4 St Mary in the upper part of Gandersheim largely founded by the Abbess Gerberga (DO ii. 35 of 973), Heiningen, Steterburg, Ringelheim.

5 Fischbeck, Kemnade, Walsrode, Widegenburg, St Maria in Minden (after 1022).

6 There was however one nunnery, dedicated to St Lawrence, in the city of Magdeburg itself. See Thietmar, i. 12, p. 16 and n. 10. Bremen had Bassum (before 865) and Heeslingen (by 973).

7 Thietmar, iii. 18, p. 120 (Kalbe); iv. 52, p. 190 f. (Hillersleben) and H. Beumann, 'Zur Frühgeschichte des Klosters Hillersleben', *Sachsen und Anhalt* 14 (1938), pp. 82 ff. See also Schulze, *Adelsherrschaft*, p. 30 f.

8 See the horrible tale in the *Vita Liudgeri*, c. 6 (*SS* ii, p. 406) where the female child of a Frisian noblewoman already on the Christian side of the frontiers of belief was to be killed by the servants of her mother-in-law. However, most of the examples from literary and canonistic sources cited by Coleman, *op. cit.*, pp. 326–7 do not specifically point to the killing of baby girls.

9 See the remarkable article by Sonia Hawkes and C. Wells, 'Crime and Punishment in an Anglo-Saxon Cemetery', *Antiquity* xlix (1975), pp. 118–22. For the savage penalties inflicted on offending women and adulterous men in pagan Old Saxony see the admonishing letter of St Boniface to King Aethelbald of Mercia (746–7) in *MGH, Epistolae Selectae* i (Berlin, 1955), no. 73, p. 150.

10 e.g. Regino of Prüm, *Libri Duo de Synodalibus Causis et Disciplinis Ecclesiasticis*, ed. F. G. A. Wasserschleben (Leipzig, 1840), especially Book ii of the early tenth century.

11 Kaufungen was founded by the Empress Kunigunde (1017), Eschwege by

Sophia, Otto II's daughter, perhaps between 997 and 1002. See K. A. Eckhardt, 'Domina Sophia constructrix et procuratrix sanctimonialium Aeskinewag', *Archiv für Diplomatik* 3 (1957), pp. 29–78. On Wetter see H.-P. Lachmann, *Untersuchungen zur Verfassungsgeschichte des Burgwaldes im Mittelalter, Schriften des Hessischen Landesamtes* 31 (Marburg, 1967), pp. 60–7.

12   The majority of the houses we have discussed here did not follow the Benedictine rule in the tenth and early eleventh centuries but a form of the Aachen rule, the *Institutio sanctimonalium* of 816, itself modelled on the *Institutio canonicorum* of the same year. The obligations of the *sanctimoniales* were set out succinctly in Otto I's diploma for Hilwartshausen (DO I. 206 of 960): 'Canonice vivere, claustra tenere rectamque regulam virginum servare.' Already in Carolingian texts the followers of this less rigorous rule had sometimes been called *canonicae*, 'canonesses', but only from the late twelfth century onwards did this designation gain ground fast. See Schäfer, *op. cit.*, p. 119 and W. Levison, 'Zur Geschichte der Kanonissenstifter' in *Aus Rheinischer und Fränkischer Frühzeit, Ausgewählte Aufsätze von Wilhelm Levison* (Düsseldorf, 1948), pp. 489–511. More recently scholars have again disagreed about the early observances of foundations for women. Against J. Semmler, 'Corvey und Herford in der benediktinischen Reformbewegung des 9. Jahrhunderts' in *Frühmittelalterliche Studien* 4, ed. K. Hauck (Berlin, 1970), pp. 289–319, H. Goetting, *Das Reichsunmittelbare Kanonissenstift Gandersheim, GermaniaSacra*, NF7, *Das Bistum Hildesheim* I (Berlin, New York, 1973), pp. 146–8 is more sceptical about the Benedictine orientation of Gandersheim in the ninth century and certain that it had become a house for 'canonesses' in the spirit of the Aachen rule by the middle of the tenth. What matters here is that whatever kind of religious community the women entered, they could not marry. When occasionally one of them left to do so, even if it was 'propter salutem patriae', it caused much scandal. See Thietmar, iv. 57, p. 196. At the same time it was not unusual to have noble girls nurtured and brought up in such houses who were not intended to take the veil.

13   *UB Halberstadt* I, no. 150 of 1121. The change had already taken place during the pontificate of Bishop Burchard II (1050–88). Wimmelburg was first mentioned in the Hildesheim Annals *sub anno* 1038.

14   *UB Halberstadt* I, nos. 149, 151, two charters of Bishop Rainer of 1120 and 1121. Schöningen was converted into a house for Augustinian canons whose common life was set against the *inutilis conversatio* of the expelled nuns. From no. 151 it is clear that the lands of the decayed house of Kalbe, the foundation of a Countess Oda, were applied to the new community at Schöningen. On Kalbe see R. Holtzmann, 'Das Laurentius-Kloster zu Calbe', *Sachsen und Anhalt* 6 (1930), pp. 177–206, reprinted in *Aufsätze*, pp. 163–92. For Hillersleben see *UB Halberstadt*, no. 118. See also above, p. 64, n. 7 and L. Fenske, *Adelsopposition und Kirchliche Reformbewegung im Östlichen Sachsen, Veröffentlichungen des Max-Planck-Instituts für Geschichte* 47 (Göttingen, 1977), pp. 228 ff. Benedictine monks replaced *sanctimoniales* as early as 1022 when the house was revived by Archbishop Gero of Magdeburg and his sister Ennihilde. The expulsion of the nuns from Vitzenburg by Wiprecht of Groitsch in 1110, backed by the authority of Bishop Otto of Bamberg, is vividly described in the *Annales Pegavenses*, SS XVI, p. 250 and see H. Jakobs, *Die Hirsauer* (Cologne, Graz, 1961), p. 65. For Walsrode and Oldenstadt see Hauck, pp. 1030, 1025. This list of conversions is by no means complete.

15   *Annales Stederburgenses*, 1142, SS XVI, p. 204. The bishops of Hildesheim had administered the foundation for some time before. For Heiningen see G.

Taddey, *Das Kloster Heiningen von der Gründung bis zur Aufhebung, Studien zur Germania Sacra*, 4 (Göttingen, 1966), pp. 28 ff. For Heeslingen see E. Bachmann, *Das Kloster Heeslingen-Zeven Verfassungs- und Wirtschaftsgeschichte* (Stade, 1966), pp. 27 ff.

16   e.g. Herzebrock (diocese of Osnabrück) founded by a widow, Waldburg and her daughter Duda, Metelen (diocese of Münster) founded by Friduwi, 'religiosa femina' (*DA* 59 of 889) and Möllenbeck (diocese of Minden) founded by a noblewoman, Hiltipurg and the priest Folchart (*DA* 147 of 896).

17   See DH I. 20 of 929. She founded a house for canons at Pöhlde. The remaining two *civitates* were Duderstadt and Grone.

18   To square the claims of Duke Hermann and other Billungs Otto gave half of Wichmann's *hereditas* to St Michael, Lüneburg. See *AS*, 967 (p. 621) and 970 (p. 624). For the endowment of Kemnade see DH..II, 87 of 1004 where the whole mass of lands appeared as the two women's gift. cf. above p. 56, n. 55.

19   See DH II. 261 of 1013 granting protection and the right to elect the abbess under the supervision of the bishop of Hildesheim. In a list of Hildesheim charters made after a fire in 1013, Heiningen was described as an *abbaciuncula*. See *UB Hildesheim*, no. 60, p. 54.

20   For most of what can be known about Vitzenburg and its founders we depend on the diploma of Otto III of 991 (DO III. 68). For the twelfth-century history of the house see Fenske, *op. cit.*, pp. 270–2.

21   See DH II. 126 of 1007. The list of Hildesheim charters (see n. 19) referred to Steterburg as 'Pauperrima abbaciuncula'. There is an account of the foundation in the late twelfth-century *Annales Stederburgenses, SS* XVI, pp. 199–201.

22   The story can be pieced together from Otto III's diploma of 9 February 989 (DO III. 52) and *cf.* also DO II. 86 of 974 and the *spurium*, DO I. 450. Schölkopf, p. 156 f. is misleading, H. J. Warnecke, 'Studien zur frühen Geschichte von Borghorst' in *1000 Jahre Borghorst*, ed. W. Kohl (Münster, 1968) unsubstantiated. The Borghorst *Necrologium*, with many entries relating to the tenth and early eleventh centuries, requires a critical edition. It is MS. VII, 1322 in the State Archive at Münster.

23   Schildesche, Fischbeck, Hilwartshausen, Borghorst, Kalbe, Vitzenburg, Steterburg, Heiningen, Oedingen.

24   *SS* XV, ii, p.1053 f., a foundation narrative of the first half of the twelfth century and see Bannasch, pp. 48 ff, 164, 211. Godesti evidently founded St Mary *ad crucem* in part to protect her inheritance against the pressures of her own kin, notably her brother Count Thietmar.

25   For St Andreas see Otto III's diploma of 993 (DO III.81) and *AS*, 992, *SS* VI, p. 638. For the Münzenberg see *AQ*, 986 (*SS* III, p. 67) 'sub religione regulae sancti Benedicti'. For St Mary, Gandersheim see Henry II's diploma of 1014 (DH II.323) where it was described as poor and also Goetting, *Hildesheim*, II, pp. 102–5.

26   For Hadmersleben see DO II. 2 of 961, Oldenstadt DH II. 107 of 1006. Stötterlingenburg was founded by Bishop Hildiward of Halberstadt. See *AQ*, *SS* III, p. 73. The annalist gave a precise date, 21 July 995 for the foundation. See also *Urkundenbuch des Klosters Stötterlingenburg*, ed. C. v. Schmidt-Phizeldeck, *Geschichtsquellen der Provinz Sachsen* 4 (1874), no. 1 of 1106–9.

27   cf. below, pp. 87 f., 93.

28   *Vita Mathildis reginae*, c. 22, *SS* IV, p. 297 f. Henry and Gerberga were born at Nordhausen. A tradition that Mathilda suffered exceptionally during her confinements appears perhaps in Thietmar, i. 9 (p. 14): 'doloremque partus tantae stirpis dulcedine superavit.'

29   *Fundatio Monasterii Schildecensis*, c. 2, *SS* xv, ii, p. 1045 of the later twelfth century.
30   For Gerbstedt see *AS*, 985, p. 633. It was endowed by Margrave Ricdag of Meissen. His sister, the co-foundress, became abbess. A large group of people had proprietary interests in Drübeck, including Margrave Dietrich of the Northern March and Margrave Wigger of the March of Zeitz. See DO ii. 225 of 980. For Wigger see Schölkopf, pp. 61–4. For Geeske see DO i. 158 of 952 and Bannasch, pp. 52 ff. on the family which founded it, the Haolde.
31   *AS*, 907, p. 592.
32   DO ii. 6 of 20 July.
33   DO iii. 235 of 18 December at Nijmegen.
34   DH ii. 87 of 2 November 1004. It is worth quoting the passage: 'Ad hec statuimus, ut in prefatae abbatisse suaeque sororis comitisse potestate predictum monasterium et abbacia nostro persistat concessu diebus vite eorum, post obitum vero utrarumque earum ad nostrum publicum eadem abba[ci]a ius perpetuum pertineat.' The phrase 'nostro concessu' is especially revealing. It must be remembered (*cf. supra* p. 56 n. 55) that Count Wichmann the Younger's *hereditas* had been forfeited to Otto I so that his daughters, as I believe the two women were, enjoyed a life interest only by royal grace.
35   DO i. 190 of 12 January.
36   DH ii. 44 of 22 March 1003. See *RI* ii, 4, no. 1537 and *cf*. DO ii.190 of 979, 20 May. This and a papal privilege (*RI* ii, 5, no. 572) were granted shortly before Count Gero's ruin by the judicial duel forced upon him by his enemies (see above, p. 45). For the interest of the Stade family see *AS*, 979, p. 627 and Hucke, pp. 149–52.
37   For Drübeck see above pp. 37, 68, n. 30. For Vreden see *AQ*, 1014 (p. 82) and *sub anno* 1024 (p. 90). Here Conrad II stayed on his way to Dortmund and Minden to be met by Adelheid and Sophia, the surviving Ottonians. On Vreden's history and church see U. Lobbedy, 'Zur archäologischen Erforschung westfälischer Frauenklöster', *Frühmittelalterliche Studien* 4, pp. 326–30. For the grant of Schildesche to Paderborn see DH ii. 403 of 20 March 1019, and *Vita Meinwerci*, c. 165, p. 87.
38   The struggle for the possession of Heeslingen can be followed with the help of Thietmar, iv. 42, p. 90 who had land there (cf. above, p. 41), Adam of Bremen, ii. 13, p. 70 and especially by comparing DO iii. 24b for Archbishop Adaldag (17 March 986) with the draft, DO iii. 24a. See also Bachmann, pp. 17 ff. and Hucke, pp. 152–5). Heeslingen was henceforth counted among the monasteries belonging to the endowment of the see and serving the archbishops.
39   For Metelen see the diploma of Arnolf, DA 59, 16 August, for Hilwartshausen DO i. 206 of 960 and DO ii. 6 of 963.
40   DO iii. 52 of 989. This *traditio in ius imperatoris* was explained, 'lest envious persons should seize anything thereof', i.e. the endowments.
41   Helmarshausen was granted to Paderborn in 1017 (*Vita Meinwerci*, c. 144 and DH ii. 371), Arneburg to Magdeburg in 1006 (DH ii 111), i.e. all the lands once belonging to the abbey which had evidently not survived the Slav wars of Otto III's reign. For Reepsholt see Adam of Bremen, ii.13, p. 70 and DO ii. 302 of 983.
42   The royal diploma of protection and immunity for Nienburg (DH ii. 43 of 1003) included a new clause about the king's *commendatio* of the abbot-elect.
43   To the literature cited p. 63 n. 1, H. Hirsch, *Die Klosterimmunität seit dem Investiturstreit* (Weimar, 1913 and repr., Darmstadt, 1967) should be added.
44   DO iii. 363 of 18 May 1000.

45 See above, p. 31.
46 This does not mean that there were none in the early twelfth century. See Leyser, 'The German Aristocracy', *P & P* 41 (1968), p. 51.
47 e.g. to Gernrode through its founder and to Quedlinburg through grants made to Mathilda. See DO I. 65 of 945, DO I. 134 of 951 (discussed above, p. 20 and n. 66), DO III. 7 of 985 and DO III.131 of 993 where Potsdam 'in the province of the Hevelli' was given to Mathilda of Quedlinburg.
48 DO II.35.
49 DO II.190 of 20 May 979: 'triginta quatuor et eo amplius sanctimoniales . . . ex dei nuto numero et meritis praeaugmentandas.' The discussion of numbers in Schäfer, *Kanonissenstifter* (pp. 128–35) is based on very much later evidence.
50 *CDA* II, 1212–1300, p. 338, no. 467, a letter to Pope Gregory X and H. K. Schulze, R. Specht and G. W. Vorbrodt, *Das Stift Gernrode, Mitteldeutsche Forschungen* 38 (Cologne, Graz, 1965), p. 33 f. where the canonesses' claim is simply accepted.
51 *Urkundenbuch der Klöster der Grafschaft Mansfeld*, ed. M. Krühne, *Geschichtsquellen der Provinz Sachsen* 20 (Halle, 1888), no. 8. The text of the document is mutilated but there can be little doubt that the Benedictine rule was introduced. So much seems clear from a fourteenth-century notice on the dorse and Pope Innocent II's unimpeachable privilege for Gerbstedt, dated 1137 (printed *op. cit.*, no. 7) which prescribed that the abbess must be elected by common consent or 'sororum pars consilii sanioris secundum dei timorem et beati Benedicti regulam.' W. Holtzmann, 'Wettinische Urkundenstudien', *Festschrift Robert Holtzmann, Historische Studien* 238 (1933), pp. 167–90 has shown that what purported to be a charter of Margrave Conrad was an important later twelfth-century record of Gerbstedt's troubled history during the wars between the Salian emperors and their Saxon opponents.
52 C. Honselmann, 'Alte Corveyer Mönchslisten—Der Corveyer Konvent unter Abt Folkmar', *Ostwestfälisch-Weserländische Forschungen*, p. 73.
53 Herford, however, suffered serious damage from a Magyar raid in 924 or 926.
54 *Das Erste Jahrtausend, Tafelband*, nos. 392, 393.
55 For an edition and critical introduction to the *Life*, see N. Fickermann, 'Eine hagiographische Fälschung ottonischer Zeit aus Gernrode' in *Corona Quernea, Festgabe Karl Strecker* (Stuttgart, 1941), pp. 159–98. Fickermann's witty and trenchant exposure of Nadda's methods did not quite do justice to the martial and aristocratic setting he wanted to create for the saint and martyr. On Gernrode's church see Vorbrodt in *Das Stift Gernrode* and L. Grodecki, *L'Architecture Ottonienne* (Paris, 1958). On the significance of the Old Saxon Psalter in Gernrode see H. Grundmann, 'Die Frauen und die Literatur im Mittelalter', *AKG* 26 (1936), pp. 129 ff.
56 *Vita Mathildis antiquior*, cc. 13, 14, *SS* x, p. 580 and the later *Vita*, c. 21, *SS* IV, p. 297, Thietmar, i. 21 (p. 26), ii. 44 (p. 92).
57 *Vita . . . antiquior*, c. 15 (p. 581): 'Quin etiam computarium, in quo erant nomina procerum scripta defunctorum, in manum ipsius dans, animam illi commendavit Heinrici nec non et suam, sed et omnium quorum ipsa memoriam recolebat fidelium.' cf. the later *Vita*, c. 26.
58 Thietmar, ii. 45 (p. 94) and above, p. 36 n. 31.
59 ii. 40, p. 88 f.
60 vi. 86, p. 376 and c. 85 *ibid.* for Liudgard. Lippelt, *Thietmar*, p. 129 f. Her example served Thietmar to add a homily on the usefulness of good works *pro memoria*, even if the person for whom they were performed was not allowed to benefit, i.e. had to suffer punishment in after life.

61   *Ruodlieb* xvii, lines 85–7 in K. Langosch, *Waltharius, Ruodlieb, Märchenepen* (3rd edn, Darmstadt, 1967), p. 210.

Sacral Kingship

1   For a valuable discussion of these problems see J. Nelson, 'Royal Saints and Early Medieval Kingship' in *Sanctity and Secularity, Studies in Church History* 10, ed. D. Baker (Oxford, 1973), pp. 39–44. I cannot however agree with Dr Nelson's distinctions, expressed thus: 'Sacrality constitutes an ascribed, not an achieved status', (p. 42) and 'Nothing has to be proved or disproved: sacrality goes with the job, is carried in the blood.' Sanctity was surely also 'ascribed' and, as Dr Nelson herself points out, needed not only the sanction of authority which usually came later, but also popular support. Conversely a royal charisma could be tested and rejected just as much as the cult of a saint might decline.
2   On Otto III's Gospel Book see K. Hoffmann, *Taufsymbolik im Mittelalterlichen Herrscherbild, Bonner Beiträge zur Kunstwissenschaft* 9 (Düsseldorf, 1968), pp. 14–47 and here plates II and III. For the painting of Henry II in the Gospel Book he gave to Montecassino (MS. Vat. Ottob. lat. 74) see *op. cit.*, pp. 70–81 and J. Déer, 'Das Kaiserbild im Kreuz', *Schweizer Beiträge zur Allgemeinen Geschichte* 13 (1955), pp. 48–110 and esp. pp. 69 ff. and H. Bloch, 'Montecassino, Byzantium and the West in the Earlier Middle Ages', *Dumbarton Oaks Papers* 3 (1946), pp. 177–87. For both, see P. E. Schramm and F. Mütherich, *Denkmale der deutschen Könige und Kaiser* (Munich, 1962), nos. 103 and 141.

Chapter 7
1   Thietmar, ii. 9 p. 48.
2   *Annales Laureshamenses*, 793, *SS* i, p. 35.
3   According to Arnold of St Emmeram's *De Miraculis Beati Emmerammi*, c. 17 (*SS* iv, p. 554), Bishop Michael of Regensburg was present, struck down and mutilated but if we accept Thietmar, ii. 27 (p. 72) this happened in an earlier encounter.
4   C. Vogel and R. Elze, *Le Pontifical Romano-Germanique du Dixième Siècle, Studi e Testi*, 226, i, pp. 257, 258.
5   Thietmar, ii. 10 p. 48. For another example of a king, Robert the Pious, praying for the sins of all his people see Helgaud's *Epitoma Vitae Regis Roberti*, c. 7, ed. R. H. Bautier and G. Labory, *Sources d'Histoire Médiévale* 1 (Paris, 1965), p. 68.
6   J. Fleckenstein, 'Rex Canonicus, Über Entstehung und Bedeutung des mittelalterlichen Königskanonikates' in *Festschrift Percy Ernst Schramm*, ed. P. Classen and P. Scheibert (Wiesbaden, 1964) i, pp. 57–71. J. M. Wallace-Hadrill, *Early Germanic Kingship in England and on the Continent* (Oxford, 1971), K. Hauck, 'Geblütsheiligkeit' in *Liber Floridus, Mittellateinische Studien P. Lehmann . . . gewidmet*, ed. B. Bischoff and S. Brechter (St Ottilien, 1950), pp. 187–240. For more general literature on sacral kingship, see the bibliography.
7   J. Reviron, *Jonas d'Orleans et son 'De Institutione Regia' Étude et Texte Critique* (Paris, 1930), c. 7, p. 155: 'Nemo regum a progenitoribus regnum sibi administrari, sed a Deo veraciter atque humiliter credere debet dari.' In general see H. A. Anton, *Fürstenspiegel und Herrscherethos in der Karolingerzeit, Bonner Historische Forschungen* 32 (Bonn, 1968) and Wallace-Hadrill, *op. cit.* pp. 135 ff. On Hincmar, J. Devisse, *Hincmar Archevêque de Reims 845–882* (Geneva, 1976) ii, pp. 671–723.

8 W. Ullmann, *The Carolingian Renaissance and the Idea of Kingship* (London, 1969), pp. 111 ff. and his 'Der Souveränitätsgedanke in den Krönungsordines' in *Festschrift P. E. Schramm* I, pp. 79 ff.

9 *MGH, Capitularia Regum Francorum* II, no. 252, p. 212, the A and B prologues.

10 C. Erdmann, *Forschungen zur Politischen Ideenwelt des Frühmittelalters* (Berlin, 1951), pp. 52 ff. esp. pp. 59, 63 and p. 89 for the *sta et retine* formula paraphrased above.

11 Schramm-Mütherich, *Denkmale*, no. 103 and Hoffmann, *Taufsymbolik*, pp. 14 ff. The inscription reads: 'Hoc Auguste libro tibi cor Deus induat Otto Quem de Liuthario te suscepisse memento.' See plates II and III.

12 *Vita Bernwardi*, c. 27, *SS* IV, p. 771: 'ante omnia, ne quid nimium pertinaciter intentet', giving a clear insight into Otto III's youthful over-eagerness. The text of Brun's letter to Henry II is in W. Giesebrecht, *Geschichte der deutschen Kaiserzeit*, 5th edn (Leipzig, 1885) II, pp. 702–5. R. Wenskus, *Studien zur Historisch-Politischen Gedankenwelt Bruns von Querfurt, Mitteldeutsche Forschungen* 5 (Münster, Cologne, 1956), pp. 126 ff. Wipo, *Gesta Chuonradi*, c. 3 pp. 21–3.

13 *Brunos Buch vom Sachsenkrieg*, cc. 48, 49 ed. H.-E. Lohmann, *Kritische Studientexte MGH* (Leipzig, 1937), pp. 46–8.

14 D.-H. Kost, *Das östliche Niedersachsen im Investiturstreit Studien zu Brunos Buch vom Sachsenkrieg* (Göttingen, 1962), pp. 43–63. On the *familiaritas regis* as a divine gift see also the important passage in a letter of Abbot Bern of Reichenau to Archbishop Gero of Magdeburg (1012–23): 'Oportet autem, ut talentum regiae familiaritatis in miseria et afflictione positis pie ac misericorditer per intercessionis auxilium subveniendo Domino, a quo illud percepistis, reportetis cum lucro.' *Die Briefe des Abtes Bern von Reichenau*, ed. F.-J. Schmale, *Veröffentlichungen der Kommission für Geschichtliche Landeskunde in Baden-Württemberg*, Reihe A, Quellen 6 (Stuttgart, 1961), no. 3, p. 21 f.

15 For Henry III's penances after his victory over the Hungarians at the Raab in 1044 see E. Steindorff, *Jahrbücher des Deutschen Reiches unter Heinrich III* (Leipzig, 1874) i, p. 209 f. and Abbot Bern's letter no. 24 (*op. cit.*, p. 54).

16 Thietmar, i. 26, p. 34. Cathwulf's letter to Charlemagne in *MGH, Epistolae Karolini Aevi* II, p. 503 and Ullmann, *Carolingian Renaissance*, p. 49 f.

17 *Vita Mathildis, praefatio, SS* IV, p. 284.

18 'sanctae ecclesiae districtus auriga', literally 'charioteer', Giesebrecht, II, p. 702.

19 *Die Tegernseer Briefsammlung*, ed. K. Strecker *MGH, Epistolae Selectae* (Berlin, 1925, repr. 1964), nos. 125, 126 and cf. the address, no. 124.

20 H. Jantzen, *Ottonische Kunst* (Munich, 1947), p. 103 and see plate IV.

21 *Gesta Episcoporum Leodensium* ii, c. 66, *SS* VII, p. 229 f.

22 Fleckenstein, 'Rex Canonicus'.

23 *MGH, Epistolae Karolini Aevi* II, p. 51, Alcuin writing to King Aethelred of Northumbria, 793, is sometimes cited as evidence for the belief in an indwelling royal magic. e.g. W. Schlesinger, 'Die Anfänge der deutschen Königswahl' in his *Beiträge zur deutschen Verfassungsgeschichte des Mittelalters* (Göttingen, 1963) I, p. 157, n. 87 and Hauck, 'Geblütsheiligkeit', p. 227.

24 Schlesinger, *loc. cit.* and K. Hauck, 'Die Germanische Auffassung von Königtum und Adel', *Rapports* III, *XIe Congrès International des Sciences Historiques* (Stockholm, 1960), pp. 96–120, esp. pp. 109, 114.

25 Widukind, i. 25, p. 38. Einhard, *Vita Karoli*, c. 2, p. 4. H. Beumann, 'Die sakrale Legitimierung des Herrschers im Denken der Ottonischen Zeit' in *Königswahl und Thronfolge*, pp. 148–98 and esp. p. 194. K. Hauck, 'Haus- und sippengebundene Literatur mittelalterlicher Adelsgeschlechter' in *Geschichts-*

denken und Geschichtsbild im Mittelalter, ed. W. Lammers (Darmstadt, 1961), pp. 165–99.

26   Widukind, i. 39, p. 57 f., iii. 49, p. 128 f. and Hauck, 'Geblütsheiligkeit', pp. 230 ff.

27   Beumann, 'Die Historiographie des Mittelalters als Quelle für die Ideengeschichte des Königtums' in his *Ideengeschichtliche Studien zu Einhard und anderen Geschichtsschreiben des früheren Mittelalters* (Darmstadt, 1962), p. 72 f. wrestles with this problem. Also in Beumann, *Wissenschaft vom Mittelalter* (Cologne, Vienna, 1972), pp. 201 ff.

28   Hauck, 'Geblütsheiligkeit', pp. 189 ff. and 'Germanische Auffassung', p. 107, O. Höfler, 'Der Sakralcharakter des germanischen Königtums', *Das Königtum, Vorträge und Forschungen* III (Lindau, Konstanz, 1963), pp. 88–91.

29   F. Grauss, *Volk, Herrscher und Heiliger im Reich der Merowinger* (Prague, 1965), pp. 313–20 and W. Baetke, 'Yngvi und die Ynglinger', *SB. der sächsischen Akademie der Wissenschaften, Philologisch-Historische Klasse* (Berlin, 1964).

30   Beumann, 'Die Historiographie des Mittelalters', p. 43 and *Wissenschaft vom Mittelalter*, p. 204 f.

31   *op. cit.*, p. 40 (*Wissenschaft*, p. 205): 'die Institution [i.e. kingship] . . . deren geschichtliche Effektivität ganz wesentlich von den Vorstellungen abhing, die die Zeitgenossen davon hatten.'

32   F. Kern, *Gottesgnadentum und Widerstandsrecht im früheren Mittelalter*, ed. R. Buchner (Münster, Cologne, 1954). As the translation by S. B. Chrimes, *Kingship and Law* (Oxford, 1948) omits most of the notes and appendices in the German original, the latter must be cited here.

33   e.g., p. 149 n. 320 and p. 161 n. 348.

34   pp. 98, 198, 205 f.

Chapter 8

1   *Annales Altahenses Maiores*, ed. E. L. B. Oefele, *SRG* (Hanover, 1891), p. 85.

2   *Annales*, 1076, p. 261 f. and *cf. Brunos Buch vom Sachsenkrieg*, c. 84, p. 80: 'Vos etiam fautores iniquitatis' must refer to Otto and other partisans of Henry IV in Saxony.

3   Bruno, c. 131, p. 123.

4   *Bertholdi Annales, SS* v, p. 287.

5   Widukind, ii. 36, p. 97: 'oculi rutilantes et in modum fulguris cita repercussione splendorem quendam emittentes', and cf. Ekkehart, *Casus sancti Galli*, cc. 131, 146 on Otto I's ever vigilant, leonine look. Ed. G. Meyer von Knonau, *Mitteilungen zur Vaterländischen Geschichte* 15, 16 (St Gallen, 1877), pp. 421, 449. Einhard had said of Charlemagne that he had very large and lively eyes (*Vita Karoli*, c. 22). The *Poeta Saxo*, writing c. 890 turned this into 'late fulgentes oculi'. See *Poeta Saxo* v. line 339, ed. P. Winterfeld, *MGH, Poetae* IV, i (Berlin, 1899), p. 63. Widukind went further still to create a near-magic gaze for Otto. On his probable use of the *Poeta Saxo* see M. Lintzel's article in *Neues Archiv* 49 (1930), pp. 183–8 and *Ausgewählte Schriften* (Berlin, 1961) II, pp. 312–15.

6   For the participants at Mainz see Erhard, *Regesta Historiae Westfaliae. Urkundenbuch*, no. 34, p. 29 f., at Tribur, *Capitularia* II, p. 210 f. On Hohenaltheim see M. Hellmann, 'Die Synode von Hohenaltheim (916)' in *Die Entstehung des Deutschen Reiches*, ed. H. Kämpf (Darmstadt, 1956), pp. 289–312, Ullmann, *Carolingian Renaissance*, pp. 128 ff. and H. Fuhrmann, *Einfluss und Verbreitung der pseudoisidorischen Fälschungen* II, p. 313 and n. 47, *Schriften der MGH* XXIV, 2 (Stuttgart, 1973).

7 On the *Miracula sancti Wigberhti* see C. Erdmann, *Ottonische Studien*, p. 84 and pp. 131 ff. and also Leyser, 'Henry I', *EHR* LXXXIII (1968), p. 27 f.
8 Hrotsvitha, *gesta Ottonis*, lines 237–43, 251–5.
9 *Antapodosis*, iv. 24–6, pp. 117–22.
10 Widukind, ii. 25 (p. 87), ii. 11 (p.75).
11 iii. 33, p. 120: 'Deo regique sese iungentes'.
12 Thietmar, ii. 26, 27, pp. 70–2 but cf. the more menacing vision reported in c. 24 and above, p. 24, n. 10.
13 i. 39, p. 59 and ii. 36, p. 96 (about Otto I): 'preter regiae disciplinae terrorem semper iocundus'.
14 *Vita Mathildis antiquior*, c. 11, *SS* x, p. 579: 'nisi tantum secularibus vestium floresceret ornamentis', against Widukind (iii. 74, p. 151): 'tamen nihil de honore regio minuebat.' Beumann, *Widukind*, p. 256 f. For a different interpretation see L. Bornscheuer, *Miseriae Regum* (Berlin, 1968), p. 71.
15 P. Classen, 'Karl der Grosse und die Thronfolge im Frankenreich', *Festschrift für Hermann Heimpel* (Göttingen, 1972) III, pp. 129–31.
16 *Capitularia Regum Francorum* I, no. 45, c. 18, p. 120 f. For the death of Pippin the Hunchback see *Annales Laurissenses Minores*, *SS* I, p. 121.
17 *RI* II, 1, no. 239b. That Conrad retained a powerful mounted following is clear from Widukind's account of his share in the victory over the Magyars at the Lech. See Leyser, 'The Battle at the Lech', *History* L(1965), pp. 15, 18 f., 23.
18 For Liudolf and Archbishop Brun of Cologne see Ruotger, c. 36, p. 37. For his participation in the war against the Obotrites in autumn 955 see the *Annales Sangallenses Maiores*, *SS* I, p. 79. For his *amici* and the Italian venture of 956 see above, p. 26.
19 Widukind, iii. 18, p. 114: 'Rex autem non inveniens, quomodo meritas poenas filio inferret, fautores insidiarum expostulat.'
20 Beumann, *Widukind*, p. 119.
21 Ruotger, c. 4, p. 5. For the date of the *Vita Brunonis* see I. Ott's introduction to her edition, p. x.
22 *Antapodosis*, iv. 15, p. 113.
23 Widukind, ii. 11, pp. 74–7 and Hrotsvitha, *gesta Ottonis*, lines 180–6 (p. 209), suppressing however Thangmar's share in Henry's capture and his death in the Eresburg altogether.
24 Widukind (p. 77): 'pro laude eius [i.e. Thangmar] pauca locutus'. cf. iii. 75, p. 153 about Otto I: 'Populus autem pro eius laude et gratiarum actione multa locutus', and see Beumann, *Widukind*, p. 175 f. Otto's speech was, however, I would submit, more than a formality.
25 A distinction should perhaps be drawn between *mêlées* where great men might be killed or wounded by humbler ones though even that could have serious repercussions (see above, p. 28, n. 34) and individual encounters. See William of Malmesbury's story of the mercenary knight who threw down William Rufus outside Mont-St-Michel in 1091 and was then startled to discover that he had nearly killed the king. *Gesta Regum* iv. 309, ed. W. Stubbs, Rolls Series (London, 1889) II, p. 364.
26 *Necrologium Merseburgense*, p. 238 under 28 July.
27 Thietmar, ii. 2, p. 40: 'quem rex postea crudeli morte vindicaverat.' Meginzo probably rejoined his lord, Henry, now fighting against Otto and was killed by the king's men. Thietmar's statement did not just rest on a misunderstanding of Widukind's text (ii.17, p. 83): 'Sed et Maincia . . . eo die cecidit' as Holtzmann (n. 10, p. 41) and following him Trillmich (n. 19, p. 37) annotated.

28 F. Prinz, *Frühes Mönchtum im Frankenreich* (Munich, Vienna, 1965), pp. 493–6.
29 A. Brackmann, 'Die Politische Bedeutung der Mauritiusverehrung im Frühen Mittelalter', *Gesammelte Aufsätze* (Weimar, 1941), pp. 211–41 and esp. Beumann, 'Das Kaisertum Ottos des Grossen. Ein Rückblick nach tausend Jahren', *HZ* 195 (1962), pp. 553–61 and *Wissenschaft vom Mittelalter*, pp. 435–43. For the dedication of a round church to St Maurice by Bishop Conrad of Constance (934–75) to proclaim his closeness and loyalty to the Ottonians, see H. Maurer, *Konstanz als ottonischer Bischofssitz, Studien zur Germania Sacra* 12 (Göttingen, 1973), p. 54.
30 For the holy lance of the Piasts see the passage in the *Gallus Anonymus* cited in *RI* ii, no. 1349d and P. E. Schramm, *Herrschaftszeichen und Staatssymbolik, Schriften der MGH* 13/ii (Stuttgart, 1955) ii, p. 517 f. For the Hungarian lance see M. Uhlirz, *Jahrbücher des Deutschen Reiches . . . Otto III* (Berlin, 1954), pp. 503 ff.
31 *Gesta Regum* ii. 135 (i, p. 150 f.) and Leyser, 'The Tenth Century in Byzantine-Western Relationships', p. 42 and nn. 78, 79.
32 *Antapodosis*, iv. 25, p. 119.
33 W. Levison, *Das Werden der Ursula-Legende* (Cologne, 1928), pp. 68–78.
34 *Annales Hildesheimenses*, 986, ed. G. Waitz, *SRG* (Hanover, 1878 and repr. 1947), p. 24 and *AQ, SS* iii, p. 67.
35 *Annales Hildesheimenses*, 992, p. 25. Otto campaigned also in 991 when Miesco joined the Saxon host once more.
36 For their composition and date see R. Holtzmann, 'Die Quedlinburger Annalen', *Sachsen und Anhalt* 1(1925), pp. 64–125 and esp. p. 114 and *Aufsätze* (Darmstadt, 1962), pp. 243 ff.
37 *AQ*, 994, *SS* iii, p. 72 and above, p. 57 f.
38 *ibid.* '995. Saxonibus peior annus priore exoritur'.
39 Sophia was placed in Gandersheim, four years old, in September 979 (DO ii. 201) and it was clearly intended that she should remain there and embrace the canonical life as the text of the diploma shows: 'sacrae scripturae literas ut ibi ediscat vitamque et conversationem dignam sanctimonialium deo ibi servientium imitetur.' It would appear from the Quedlinburg Annalist's panegyric about Adelheid's *velatio* that her career had not been mapped out so clearly even though she almost certainly dwelt at Quedlinburg under her aunt's tutelage already for some time before 995 (see *AQ*, 999, p. 76). Sophia was veiled by Archbishop Willigis of Mainz and Bishop Osdag of Hildesheim (985–9) on 18 October (*Vita Bernwardi*, c. 13, *SS* iv, p. 764) but the year is disputed. Goetting, *Gandersheim* (p. 296) preferred 987 because Sophia had then reached the age of twelve. M. Uhlirz (*RI* ii, 3, no. 1017e) argued for 989 and so did O. Perst, 'Die Kaisertochter Sophie Äbtissin von Gandersheim und Essen (975–1039), *Braunschweigisches Jahrbuch* 38 (1957), pp. 5 ff. although on quite different grounds. Perst himself showed convincingly that Sophia was born in 975, the oldest of Otto II's and Theophanu's children (see above, p. 52, n. 19) and not in 978 as Uhlirz maintained. As she was destined for Gandersheim, custom, e.g. the example of Mathilda of Quedlinburg, prescribed this solemn act in the presence of her mother and brother, at the age of twelve. Perst opted for 989 (Otto III's itinerary excludes 988) because of the king's gifts to Gandersheim and to Sophia in 990 (DDO iii. 66, 67). A close reading of DO iii. 66 however does not support the view that the market, mint and toll then granted to the nunnery were a 'dowry' like e.g. DO i. 184 of 956 (for Mathilda) and DO iii. 177 of 995, 'pro Adelheida nostra sorore dilecta'. An ample 'dowry' moreover had

already been made on Sophia's behalf by her father, Otto II, in 979, i.e. DO II. 201. The grant of sixty *mansus* of land to her in 990 (DO III. 67 of 10 August) I would connect with her being now of age.

40 iv. 10, p. 142: 'De fructu vero ventris sui decimas Deo obtulit filias suas.'

41 For a survey of some of the most important East Saxon *palatia* of the Ottonians, their antecedents, the literary, topographical and archaeological evidence for their make-up and history, see the two capital volumes, *Deutsche Königspfalzen, Veröffentlichungen des Max-Planck-Instituts für Geschichte* 11/1–2 (Göttingen, 1963–65). On Henry I's buildings see the articles by W. Schlesinger, 'Merseburg' (*op. cit.* I, pp. 158 ff.) and A. Gauert, 'Zur Struktur und Topographie der Königspfalzen' (II, pp. 1 ff.) On Otto I's unique *palatium* at Magdeburg with its apses and spiral staircases, much influenced by Byzantine models, see E. Nickel, 'Magdeburg in karolingisch-ottonischer Zeit', in *Vor- und Frühformen der enropäischen Stadt im Mittelalter* I, ed. H. Jankuhn, W. Schlesinger, H. Steuer, *Abhandlungen der Akademie der Wissenschaften in Göttingen, Philol.-Histor. Klasse* 3rd series, no. 83 (Göttingen, 1973), pp. 294–331, esp. pp. 321 ff.

42 H.-W. Klewitz, 'Die Festkrönungen der deutschen Könige', *ZRG, Kanon. Abt.* XXVIII (1939), p. 81 and separately (Darmstadt, 1966), p. 38.

43 Klewitz, *op. cit.*, pp. 79 ff. and pp. 36 ff. (repr.) Rieckenberg, 'Königstrasse', *AUF*, pp. 42 ff. Fleckenstein, *Hofkapelle* II, pp. 136 ff, Brühl, *Fodrum*, pp. 125 ff. and W. Schlesinger, 'Zur Geschichte der Magdeburger Königspfalz', *Blätter für deutsche Landesgeschichte* 104 (1968), pp. 1–31.

44 Thietmar, iv. 2, p. 132 and iv. 9, p. 140.

45 *AQ*, 1003, *SS* III, p. 78. Very soon he changed the locations of his Easter courts, drastically and deliberately. See the literature cited in n. 43.

46 F. Israel and W. Möllenberg, *Urkundenbuch des Erzstifts Magdeburg* I (Magdeburg, 1937), p. 73, no. 52 and Thietmar, ii. 17, p. 58 for the marble and relics. See also Schlesinger, *op. cit.*

47 *AQ*, 936.

Chapter 9

1 From the *Miracula Sancti Wigberhti*, MS. 76. 14 Aug. 2, fol. 39 v, Herzog August Bibliothek, Wolfenbüttel: 'Adhuc etiam presumptorem quasi contra divinitatem ultiones illaturum sibi iniuriarum machinantem, ultima est vindicta consecuta.' This was written about a persistent invader of an important estate belonging to the abbey of Hersfeld. Only the beginning of this miracle, illustrating the saint's power, was edited by Waitz, *SS* IV, p. 216. See Leyser, 'Henry I', *EHR* LXXXIII (1968), p. 27 f.

2 See Wipo's exhortation to Henry III in the *Tetralogus*, lines 190–202, *Die Werke Wipos*, p. 81 f. and the lament in the mid-eleventh century *Chronicon Eberspergense*, *SS* XX, p. 14.

3 *Gesta Chuonradi*, c. 3, p. 23.

4 c. 2, p. 15: 'Quae Adelheida [Conrad's mother] soror erat comitum Gerhardi et Adalbertis qui semper cum regibus et ducibus confligentes', but the weight of opinion, according to Wipo, favoured Conrad's election in 1024 'propter virtutem et probitatem illius'.

5 H. G. Beck, 'Byzantinisches Gefolgschaftswesen', *Sitzungsberichte der Bayerischen Akademie der Wissenschaften, Philologisch-Historische Klasse* (1965).

6 For a margrave's chaplain see Thietmar, vii. 26, p. 430. For a clerk of Margrave Gero II, see *ibid*. vi. 96, p. 388. For a vision see iii. 17, p. 118. For miracles and

pilgrimages to the tombs of Count Henry II of Stade and his wife see *AS*, 1016, *SS* vi, p. 670.

7   Thietmar, ii. 28, p. 74.
8   *Annales Altahenses Maiores*, 973, p. 11. It could represent a part of the tribute collected during Otto's absence but also a voluntary fine.
9   *Annales Magdeburgenses*, 972, *SS* xvi, p. 152 of the twelfth century but with earlier components.
10   *AS*, 1135, *SS* vi, p. 769 f. and also *Annales Magdeburgenses*, p. 180. The two notices stand very close to one another.
11   Thietmar, v. 4–7, pp. 224–8. For a recent discussion of Ekkehard's candidature and murder see R. Schneider, 'Die Königserhebung Heinrichs II. im Jahre 1002', *DA* 28 (1972), pp. 81–7.
12   A systematic study of the forms of submission after risings does not exist to the best of my knowledge. For footfalls see below n. 15.
13   Thietmar, vi. 2, p. 276: 'Heinricus vero . . . more et habitu penitentis regi se tradidit.'
14   *loc. cit.* His literacy is noteworthy but by no means the only instance.
15   On Duke Henry I's submission see Hrotsvitha, *gesta Ottonis*, lines 336–70, p. 214 f. He appeared in simple dress without princely ornament and in the poem prostrated himself before the altar rather than his brother who forgave him in honour of the day and imitating Christ who came to save a world that deserved to perish. For Liudolf's submission see Widukind, iii. 40, p. 122: 'patri nudatis plantis prosternitur, intima tactus poenitentia, oratione flebili.' On Conrad see Ruotger, *Vita Brunonis*, c. 35, p. 36: 'cilicio membra domans'. Henry the Wrangler's penitence, contrition and self-humiliation clothes his homage to the child-king, Otto III in AQ 985, *SS* iii, p. 66 f. and cf. Thietmar, iv. 20, p. 154. On surrender 'to God and the king', see above, p. 85. Pardoning imprisoned rebels was also turned into a religious act, e.g. Thietmar, vi. 13, p. 290.
16   cf. above, p. 78 f.
17   Thietmar, vii. 4–8, pp. 402–6, esp. c. 8: 'omnes populi mussant et christum Domini peccare occulte clamant.'
18   v. 32, p. 256.
19   vi. 48, p. 334.
20   *Vita Radbodi Episcopi Traiectensis*, c. 6, *SS* xv, p. 568. The author addressed himself to Bishop Balderich but his sympathies were West Frankish.
21   *Antapodosis*, ii. 22, 23, p. 48 f.
22   The codex is in Munich (Clm. 14729), *Fragmentum de Arnulfo duce*, *SS* xvii, p. 570 and Reindel, *Luitpoldinger*, nos. 48, 56.
23   On Duke Arnulf's quasi-regal style see K. Brunner, 'Die fränkischen Fürstentitel im neunten und zehnten Jahrhundert', H. Wolfram, *Intitulatio* ii, *MIÖG*, Ergbd. xxiv (1973), p. 243 f.
24   H. Patze, 'Adel und Stifterchronik. Frühformen territorialer Geschichtsschreibung', *Blätter für deutsche Landesgeschichte* 100 (1964), pp. 8–81, 101 (1965), pp. 67–128.
25   Lampert, *Annales*, 1062, *Lamperti Monachi Hersefeldensis Opera*, ed. O. Holder-Egger, *SRG* (Hanover and Leipzig, 1894), p. 80.
26   Lampert, pp. 81–4.
27   *Triumphus Sancti Remacli de Malmundariensi coenobio*, c. 9, *SS* xi, p. 453 and see F. W. Oediger, *Die Regesten der Erzbischöfe von Köln*, i. 313–1099, *Publikationen der Gesellschaft für Rheinische Geschichtskunde* xxi (Bonn, 1954–61), no. 995 with references to the other sources and literature.
28   The coronation of Kunigunde and the consecration of Sophia as abbess of

Gandersheim by Archbishop Willigis of Mainz at Paderborn on 10 August 1002 were marred by a severe clash between Henry II's Bavarian *milites* and the inhabitants (Thietmar, v. 19, pp. 243 ff.) Duke Bernhard Billung restored order: 'Post haec autem castigati sunt omnes, quicumque inveniri poterant tanti scleris auctores' (p. 245). cf. also the earlier incident at the end of the Merseburg *curia* of 24–8 July (see below, p. 100) where Duke Boleslas's and Henry of Schweinfurt's men came armed in breach of a rule and were attacked (v. 18, pp. 24 ff.). Both incidents illustrate the insecure beginnings of a new king's reign.

Chapter 10

1 Above, p. 33.
2 Above, p. 25.
3 Widukind, ii. 1, p. 64 and see H. Beumann, 'Grab und Thron Karls des Grossen zu Aachen', *Karl des Grosse*, IV *Das Nachleben* (Düsseldorf, 1967), pp. 9–38, esp. pp. 27–9 and in *Wissenschaft*, pp. 347 ff. Important also is R. Schmidt, 'Zur Geschichte des fränkischen Königsthrons', *Frühmittelalterliche Studien*, 2 ed. K. Hauck (Berlin, 1968), pp. 45–57, and see J. Nelson, 'Inauguration Rituals', in *Early Medieval Kingship*, ed. P. H. Sawyer and I. N. Wood (Leeds, 1977), p. 54.
4 Above, p. 95.
5 Thietmar, vi. 48, p. 334.
6 Thietmar, iii. 9, 10, p. 106 f. The numerous other sources are listed in K. Uhlirz, *Jahrbücher . . . Otto II*, p. 124 but the passage in Wolfhere's *Vita Godehardi posterior*, c. 5, *SS* XI, p. 199 is omitted and overlooked also in *RI*, II, 2, no. 787b. Less than two months lay between Otto II's diploma for Alsleben (see above, p. 69 n. 36) and the count's execution on August 11.
7 Rieckenberg, 'Königsstrasse', p. 91 and Brühl, *Fodrum*, p. 129 and n. 60.
8 This is well illustrated by Thietmar, iv. 52, p. 90. At Frohse, in March 1002, Margrave Liuthar persuaded his Saxon fellow princes, including Archbishop Giselher of Magdeburg 'se nullum sibi dominum vel regem communiter vel singulariter electuros' before their next meeting at Werla in April.
9 Thietmar, v. 15–18, pp. 236–41 and esp. pp. 239 ff. The election of Henry II and the Saxons' part in it have recently evoked an astonishingly rich literature: R. Schmidt, 'Königsumritt und Huldigung in ottonisch-salischer Zeit', *Vorträge und Forschungen* VI (1961), pp. 118–25, S. Haider, *Die Wahlversprechungen der Römisch-Deutschen Könige bis zum Ende des zwölften Jahrhunderts* (Vienna, 1968), pp. 22–5, R. Schneider, *op. cit.* above, p. 94, n. 11 and W. Schlesinger, 'Erbfolge und Wahl bei der Königserhebung Heinrichs II. 1002', *Festschrift für Hermann Heimpel* III, pp. 1–36.
10 Thietmar, v. 17, pp. 239 ff. and cf. Wipo, *Gesta Chuonradi*, c. 3 (p. 20): 'Ibant gaudentes, clerici psallebant, laici canebant, utrique suo modo', after Conrad's election at Kamba in 1024.
11 Both coronation and enthronement were mentioned by Adalbold as the penultimate acts in a chain of quasi-elective and constitutive ceremonies in his *Vita Heinrici Imperatoris*, c. 10, *SS* IV, p. 686.
12 Henry II's brother Brun was a clerk and canon of Hildesheim but this did not prevent him from joining Margrave Henry of Schweinfurt's rising and fleeing to Hungary when it failed. Reconciled, he became Henry's chancellor and bishop of Augsburg in 1006 but even so a danger to the emperor.
13 Thietmar, v. 9, 10, 18, pp. 230–2, 241. On the much disputed alignments in the conflicts for the succession to Meissen and Ekkehard's march see W.

Schlesinger and H. Beumann, 'Urkundenstudien zur Deutschen Ostpolitik unter Otto III', in W. Schlesinger, *Mitteldeutsche Beiträge zur deutschen Verfassungsgeschichte* (Göttingen, 1961), pp. 385, 388 f. and H. Ludat, *An Elbe und Oder*, pp. 27–9, 78–81. I cannot, however, follow Ludat's combination who would have it that Ekkehard's son Hermann in 1002 agreed with his uncle Gunzelin's and Boleslas's plans (pp. 29, 79 and nn. 209, 462, where Hermann is described as 'standing on Boleslas's side'). This is wholly belied by Thietmar, v. 9, p. 230. Hermann and his father's leading vassals had to quit Meissen after a murderous assault on them. The gates were then opened to the Polish duke.

14 Thietmar, vi. 53, 54, pp. 340 ff. Posse, *Markgrafen*, pp. 68–70. Ludat, p. 30 and n. 225 but without attaching much importance to the family feud and how Henry II used it.

15 *Aequitas* in the Mainz Pontifical was especially enjoined in the *formulae* which accompanied the delivery of the sword, rod and sceptre, the *insignia* of judgment and coercive regal power. See Vogel-Elze, *Le Pontifical Romano-Germanique* I, pp. 255–7.

16 Thietmar, viii. 20–2, pp. 516 ff. The interpolated diploma is DO II. 90 of 974. See W. Schlesinger, *Kirchengeschichte Sachsens* I, p. 82 and Lippelt, pp. 94, 106–8, 113 f.

17 On this see the suggestive article by K. Czeglédy, 'Das sakrale Königtum bei den Steppenvölkern', *Numen* XIII (1966), pp. 14–26. The sources are mainly Arabic ethnography of the tenth century. See also J. Déer, *Heidnisches und Christliches in der altungarischen Monarchie* (Darmstadt, 1969, a reprint with a postscript of the 1934 original), pp. 66 ff.

18 E. E. Evans-Pritchard, 'The Divine Kingship of the Shilluk of the Nilotic Sudan' in his *Essays in Social Anthropology* (London, 1962), pp. 66–86. The quotation is from p. 85.

19 M. Gluckmann, *Custom and Conflict in Africa* (Oxford, 1973), pp. 27–53 and here p. 45.

20 G. Waitz, *Die Deutsche Reichsverfassung von der Mitte des neunten bis zur Mitte des zwölften Jahrhunderts* VI (2nd edn. Berlin, 1896), pp. 448–53 and H. Krause, 'Königtum und Rechtsordnung in der Zeit der sächsischen und salischen Herrscher', *ZRG, GA* LXXXII (1965), pp. 1–98.

21 Fleckenstein, *Hofkapelle* II, pp. 32, 102 f.

22 Adabold, *Vita Heinrici II*, c. 34, *SS* IV, p. 691.

23 DH II. 501 of 2 December 1023.

24 Krause, *op. cit.* pp. 19 ff.

25 H. Fichtenau, *Arenga*, *MIÖG, Ergbd.* XVIII (1957), pp. 19, 39 f., 84. Thietmar, iii.1 (p. 98) reports the recitation of a diploma, granting the Magdeburg clerks the right to elect their archbishop, in the cathedral (DO II. 207 of 979) and hence also the *Gesta Archiepiscoporum Magdeburgensium*, c. 12, *SS* XIV, p. 385. The emperor was present, however. The *preceptum* was given to Magdeburg together with a book containing illuminations of Otto and Theophanu on gold which Archbishop Adalbert held up after his sermon. For imperial confirmations of older privileges as a shield 'contra iniquitates iudicum', see Sigebert of Gembloux, *Vita Deoderici Episcopi Mettensis*, c. 11, *SS* IV, p. 469. The former grants are called *leges*, the confirmation an *edictum*.

26 It is not possible to assemble a large number of instances here but a high proportion of the evidence bears on the relations of bishoprics and abbeys with the travelling court, *e.g.* the Tegernsee letters cited above p. 79 f., n. 19.

27 Widukind, iii. 70 (p. 146 f.) of 18 January 968, mentioned above, p. 25 and DO I. 366, also of 968.

28 Thietmar, iv. 47, p. 186 and *cf.* Wipo. *Gesta Chuonradi*, c. 6, p. 27 f.
29 *Vita Heinrici II*, c. 19, *SS* iv, p. 688 and *Constantini Vita Adalberonis II*, c. 25, *SS* iv p. 667.
30 e.g. DO iii. 128 of 993 and DO iii. 355 of 1000, both grants of lands in Carinthia. In the latter case the donee, Margrave Adalbero, could choose the lands himself.
31 cf. the tables in Rieckenberg, 'Königsstrasse', pp. 68, 89 and p. 90, n. 2 and Brühl, *Fodrum*, pp. 117, 128.
32 In 945, 950, 952, possibly 956, 973 and 991. See e.g. the *Annales Altahenses Maiores*, 945 (p. 8), 973 (p. 11). *AQ*, 991, *SS* iii, p. 68. Widukind's notice of the embassies from Byzantium, Cordoba and Rome in 956 (iii. 56, p. 135) suggests that they came also to Saxony.
33 C. Brühl, 'Fränkischer Krönungsbrauch und das Problem der "Fest-krönungen" ', *HZ* 194 (1962), pp. 265–326.
34 See the letter of Archbishop William of Mainz to Pope Agapitus II in autumn 955. P. Jaffé, *Monumenta Moguntina*, pp. 347–50. For the tenth-century conflict over the tasks of bishops see F. Lotter, *Die Vita Brunonis des Ruotger, Bonner Historische Forschungen* 9 (Bonn, 1958), pp. 115 ff.
35 Above, pp. 23 ff.
36 c. 20, p. 20.
37 On Thietmar Billung's plot and the later conspiracy against Henry III see Steindorff, *Jahrbücher . . . Heinrich III* ii, pp. 16, 40 and 317–19.
38 On the charter see F. Wormald, 'Late Anglo-Saxon Art: Some Questions and Suggestions', *Romanesque and Gothic Art, Studies in Western Art* i (Princeton, 1963), pp. 23–6. E. John, *Orbis Britanniae and Other Studies* (Leicester, 1966), pp. 271–5. On the meaning of the coronation see p. 288. See also J. Nelson, 'Inauguration Rituals', pp. 63–70.
39 J. Campbell, 'Observations on English Government from the Tenth to the Twelfth Century', *TRHS* 25 (1975), pp. 39–54.
40 So much can be said notwithstanding the cautionary observations in C. P. Wormald's penetrating article 'The Uses of Literacy in Anglo-Saxon England and its Neighbours', *TRHS* 27 (1977), pp. 95–114.
41 Lampert, *Annales*, 1057, p. 71.

Epilogue

1 *Continuatio Reginonis*, pp. 175, 177.
2 Widukind, i. 34, p. 48.
3 *Annales Hildesheimenses*, p. 22.
4 See *supra*, p. 36.
5 Widukind, i. 16, p. 26, i. 26, p. 39, ii. 1, p. 63, iii. 63, p. 137.
6 *Annales Altahenses Maiores*, 983, p. 15.

Appendix

1 M. R. James, *A Descriptive Catalogue of the Latin Manuscripts in the John Rylands Library* (Manchester and London, 1921) i, p. 159 f. For a discussion of the drawings see T. Buddensieg, 'Beiträge zur Ottonischen Kunst in Nieder-sachsen' in *Miscellanea Pro Arte, Hermann Schnitzler zur Vollendung des 60. Lebensjahres*, ed. P. Bloch and J. Hoster (Düsseldorf, 1965), pp. 68–76.
2 *Chronica episcoporum ecclesiae Merseburgensis*, c. 4, *MGH, SS* x, p. 175 f.

178 *Rule and Conflict in an Early Medieval Society*

3   P. W. Behrends, 'Güterverzeichniss des ehemaligen Collegiatsstifts zu Walbeck aus dem dreizehnten Jahrhundert,' *Neue Mittheilungen aus dem Gebiet historisch-antiquarischer Forschungen*, *Thüringisch Sächsischer Verein* II (1835), pp. 38–61. Henceforth cited: *Güterverzeichnis*.

4   Catalogue of the . . . collection of . . . manuscripts formed by *M. G. Libri* (London, 1859), No. 358.

5   H. Beumann, 'Der Streit der Stifte Marienthal und Walbeck um den Lappwald', *Studien und Mitteilungen zur Geschichte des Benediktiner-Ordens* 53 (1935), pp. 376–400.

6   *Vita Meinwerci*, c. 52, p. 43 and cf. *Güterverzeichnis*, p. 46. Nordgermersleben (Thietmar, iv. 38) cf. *Güterverzeichnis*, p. 45, Rottmersleben (Thietmar, i. 13, vi. 39, vi. 47), cf. *op. cit.* p. 45 f., Tundersleben (above, n. 2), *ibid.*, Walbeck, p. 48.

7   See above, p. 95.

8   Walbeck held two *mansi* in Schakensleben (*Güterverzeichnis*, p. 45) which lay near Klein-Santersleben but was divided from it by the River Olve. The distance to Gross-Santersleben was over two kilometres.

9   *Urkundenbuch des Hochstifts Merseburg* I, ed. P. Kehr, *Geschichtsquellen der Provinz Sachsen* 36 (Halle, 1899), nos. 51, 52, 214, 215, pp. 49, 170 ff. In 1148 the canons of Walbeck exchanged some lands with the monks of Hillersleben (above, p. 65) 'pro commoditate et situ'. What they gave lay well away from the core of their holdings. See *UB. Halberstadt* I, no. 207.

10 Thietmar, vi. 42, p. 326 and viii. 7, p. 500. W. Schlesinger, *Kirchengeschichte Sachsens im Mittelalter, Mitteldeutsche Forschungen* 27/I (Cologne, Graz, 1962) I, pp. 60, 252, 320.

11 Thietmar, viii. 15, p. 512.

12 vi. 49, p. 336 and vi. 84, p. 374.

13 H. K. Schulze, *Adelsherrschaft und Landesherrschaft, Mitteldeutsche Forschungen* 29 (Cologne, Graz, 1963), pp. 53 f., 190. M. Erbe, *Studien zur Entwicklung des Niederkirchenwesens in Ostsachsen vom 8. bis zum 12. Jahrhundert, Studien zur Germania Sacra* 9, Veröffentlichungen des Max-Planck-Instituts für Geschichte, 26 (Göttingen, 1969), p. 78.

14 O. von Heinemann, *Albrecht der Bär* (Darmstadt, 1864), p. 173 f. and see *AS, SS* VI, p. 688 *sub anno* 1049.

15 Thietmar, vi. 49, p. 334 f. Schulze, *op. cit.*, pp. 53 f., 190 f. and W. Podehl, *Burg und Herrschaft in der Mark Brandenburg, Mitteldeutsche Forschungen* 76 (Cologne, Vienna, 1975), pp. 31, 41 f.

16 DO I. 29 of September 937: 'Uuuatanesveg'.

17 DO II. 29 of 4 June 973: 'Uuodenesuueg'.

18 *AS*, 1023, *SS* VI, p. 876.

19 G. Wentz and B. Schwineköper, *Das Erzbistum Magdeburg, Germania Sacra* (Berlin, New York, 1972) I, 2, p. 603.

20 *Urkundenbuch des Klosters Unser Lieben Frauen zu Magdeburg*, ed. G. Hertel, *Geschichtsquellen der Provinz Sachsen* 10 (Halle, 1878), p. 381.

21 Schulze, *op. cit.*, p. 40, L. Fenske, *Adelsopposition und Kirchliche Reformbewegung im Östlichen Sachsen*, pp. 222 ff. Thietmar vii. 6, p. 404. It was not at all improbable that a murderous deed should mark the emergence of a family and stand at the head of its ancestral history.

22 DH IV. 383 of 12 January 1086. In general see P. Grimm, *Die Vor- und Frühgeschichtlichen Burgwälle der Bezirke Halle und Magdeburg, Deutsche Akademie der Wissenschaften zu Berlin, Schriften der Sektion für Vor- und Frühgeschichte* 6 (Berlin, 1958), no. 827 and M.-L. Harksen, *Die Kunstdenkmale des Kreises Haldensleben* (Leipzig, 1961), pp. 302 f., 437 f. Harksen held

that Thietmar referred to 'Gross Santersleben' for certain. See below nn. 24, 25.

23 DH III. 157 of 2 July 1046 granting what he had inherited from a certain Irmgard in three places including Santersleben.

24 G. A. v. Mülverstedt, *Regesta Archiepiscopatus Magdeburgensis* (Magdeburg, 1881) II, p. 292 f., no. 640.

25 Erbe, *op. cit.*, p. 146.

26 *Urkundenbuch des Erzstifts Magdeburg* I (937–1192), ed. F. Israël and W. Möllenberg (Magdeburg, 1937), no. 324, p. 423.

27 *UB. Unser Lieben Frauen*, p. 58, no. 65 and Schulze, p. 43.

28 DL III. 74. This text has not been cited by either Grimm or Harksen (cf. n. 22).

29 *Cronica Ducum de Brunswick*, c. 11, ed. L. Weiland, *MGH, Deutsche Chroniken* II, p. 581.

30 *MGH, Die Urkunden Heinrichs des Löwen*, ed. K. Jordan (Weimar, 1949), nos. 10, 20 but in 1192 Henry VI granted the *curtis* and the abbey at Lutter to the see of Magdeburg. See *RI* IV, 3, no. 221.

31 'Das Güterverzeichnis und das Lehnregister des Grafen Siegfried II. von Blankenburg aus den Jahren 1209–1227', *Zeitschrift des Harz-Vereins für Geschichte und Alterthumskunde* 3 (1869), pp. 71–94. See p. 92: 'Haec sunt bona, quae comes Sigfridus, cuius avus est comes Poppo, habet a Duce Wilhelmo de Luneburg', and p. 94: 'sex mansos in Santersleve'.

32 *Die Urkunden Heinrichs des Löwen,* nos. 4, 5, 6, 7, 10. For his earlier history see Fenske, pp. 172–9 and H. W. Vogt, *Das Herzogtum Lothar's von Süpplingenburg, Quellen und Darstellungen zur Geschichte Niedersachsens* 57 (Hildesheim, 1959), p. 35 f. He rose as Lothar's vassal.

33 *Origines Guelficae*, ed. C. L. Scheidius (Hanover, 1753) IV, p. 97.

34 Vogt, *op. cit.*, p. 141 and genealogical table.

35 Cited by H.-D. Starke, *Die Pfalzgrafen von Sachsen bis zur Entstehung des jüngeren Reichsfürstenstandes* (diss., Kiel, 1953), pp. 71 ff. and esp. p. 75. I should like to thank Professor H. E. Mayer of the University of Kiel for making the text of the relevant section of Starke's thesis available to me. For a summary, see H.-D. Starke, 'Die Pfalzgrafen von Sommerschenburg (1088–1179)', *Jahrbuch für die Geschichte Mittel- und Ostdeutschlands* IV (1955), pp. 23 ff.

36 *AS*, 1049, *SS* VI, p. 688.

37 Thietmar, i. 13, p. 18, iv. 41, p. 178, vi. 49, p. 336.

38 Starke, *Die Pfalzgrafen von Sachsen*, pp. 78–83.

39 vi. 45, p. 330.

40 *AS*, p. 688.

41 Thietmar, vi. 38, p. 321, vi. 67, p. 356, vi. 74, p. 362, vi. 81, p. 370. Fleckenstein, *Hofkapelle* II, pp. 177, 182 where, however, Dietrich is called a nephew of the bishop of Merseburg. He was his cousin.

42 On Berthold see Thietmar, vii. 50, p. 460, vii. 53, p. 464, viii. 17, p. 514. He is however not mentioned by Alpert in his *De diversitate temporum*, the most detailed account of the feud between Wichmann and Balderich.

43 So Starke, in his thesis, pp. 69, 71.

44 DDH III. 229 of 1049, 264 of 1051, 267 of 1051, 280 of 1052, 366 of 1056, DH IV. 108 of 1063.

45 The place was Rodensleben in the Nordthüringau. cf. DH II. 110 of 1006: 'in comitatu Uuerinzonis marchionis', DH III. 125 of 1044: 'predium Rodonesleba . . . in pago Nordturingun et in comitatu Berenhardi marchionis' and DH III. 264 of 1051: 'Rodenesleba . . . in pago Nortduringun et in comitatu

Liutherii comitis'. Liuthar therefore can only have succeeded to this countship after 1044. Bernhard the *marchio* had sons and one of them, William, followed him in the tenure of the Northern March.

46 DH ɪᴠ. 207 of 5 August.
47 D. Herm. 2 of 13 April.
48 The places mentioned in Henry IV's diploma of 1068, also found in the Walbeck survey, are Bregenstedt (Güterverzeichnis, p. 46), Lemsell (*op. cit.*, p. 47), Stempel (*ibid.*). In Herman's diploma we find Oschersleben (*Güterverzeichnis*, p. 43), Peseckendorf (p. 41 f.)
49 Starke, pp. 73–82 surveyed these ascriptions without committing himself. Vogt, pp. 136–42 leaned towards the view that Count Liuthar was a 'Süpplingenbur-ger'. See below n. 54. He failed to consider the later Count Siegfried.
50 *Urkundenbuch des . . . Klosters Ilsenburg* ɪ, ed. E. Jacobs, *Geschichtsquellen der Provinz Sachsen* 6, i (Halle, 1875), pp. 8 ff. no. 7. Fenske, p. 128, n. 155 and K. Hallinger, *Gorze-Kluny, Studia Anselmiana* xxɪɪ-xxɪɪɪ (Rome, 1950–1) ɪ, pp. 638–49.
51 Thietmar, v. 3, p. 222 f.
52 v. 18, p. 241: 'Luidgero solo remanente'. For Ricbert as count in the Harzgau see DDH ɪɪ. 46 of 15 April 1003 and 205 of 3 September 1009.
53 DH ɪɪ. 260 of 1013, a twelfth-century text based on an original and a list of estates in which Count Liudger appears; DDH ɪɪ. 449 of 1021, 452 and 480 of 1022.
54 DC ɪɪ. 164 of 23 March 1031: 'in pago Hardagouue in comitatu Liutgeri comitis'. Lothar's grandfather was a Count Bernhard who must not be confused with the margrave of the Northern March. In the remaining (easterly) parts of Count Liudger's *comitatus* the Count Liuthar mentioned above (n. 44) officiated, albeit after an interval of eighteen years. Vogt was therefore inclined to regard him as a Süpplingenburger, perhaps Count Bernhard's brother.
55 e.g. *Annales Corbeienses*, 1112, 1114, *Chronographus Corbeiensis*, 1114, in *Monumenta Corbeiensia*, ed. P. Jaffé, *Bibliotheca Rerum Germanicarum* ɪ (Berlin, 1864), p. 42 f., *Annales Hildesheimenses*, 1110, 1115, 1120, 1121, 1125. *SRG* (Hanover, 1947, repr.), pp. 61, 63, 65, 66. *Annales S. Disibodi*, 1075, 1106, *SS* xvɪɪ, pp. 7, 19. *UB. Halberstadt* ɪ, no. 136.
56 *Hermanni de Lerbeke Chronicon Episcoporum Mindensium* in *op. cit.* (Hanover, 1707–11) ɪɪ, p. 177 and *Hermanni de Lerbeke . . . Chronicon Comitum Schauenburgensium* in H. Meibom junior, *Rerum Germanicarum Tomi III* (Helmstädt, 1688) ɪ, p. 497.
57 *Heinrich Meiboms des älteren Walbeckische Chronike*, p. 82 f. See H. Bresslau's cautionary footnote in his *Jahrbücher des Deutschen Reiches unter Konrad II* ɪ, p. 305, n. 3.
58 P. W. Behrends, *Neuhaldenslebische Kreis-Chronik* (Neuhaldensleben, 1824–1826) ɪɪ, p. 325.
59 G. Schmidt, *Die alte Grafschaft Schaumburg, Studien und Vorarbeiten* 5 (Göttingen, 1928), p. 14 f.

Index

Aachen, 9, 16, 80, 99, 100; ivory situla at, 80; Gospel Book at, 77, 78, plates II, III; Otto I's coronation (936), 98

Abu al Quasim, emir of Sicily, 58

Adalbero II, bishop of Metz (984–1005), his *Life*, 103

Adalbero, Saxon count palatine, 60

Adalbert, king of Italy, 26, 109

Adalbert of St Maximin, royal chaplain, continuator of Regino of Prüm, first archbishop of Magdeburg, 13, 17, 26, 27, 35, 40, 45, 84, 99, 103; offends Otto I. 94

Adalbert, archbishop of Hamburg-Bremen (1043–72), 106

Adalbold, bishop of Utrecht (1010–26), biographer of Henry II, 103

Adaldag, archbishop of Hamburg-Bremen (937–88), 69

Adela, countess, mother of Bishop Meinwerk of Paderborn, 60, 62, 66, 120

Adelheid, daughter of Otto II, abbess of Quedlinburg, 12, 47, 54, 69, 89, 94

Adelheid, empress, 20, 30, 37, 44, 46, 49, 50, 52, 53, 55, 72, 105

Aeddila, chief foundress of Hilwartshausen, 56, 60, 65

Aethelred II, king, 106

African societies, 102

Agapitus II, pope (946–55), 25

Agius, *Life of Hathumoda*, first abbess of Gandersheim, 124

Alberada, daughter of Giselbert, duke of Lotharingia and Gerberga, sister of Otto I, 54, 55

Albrecht the Bear, margrave of Northern March (d. 1170), 115

Albrecht II, margrave of Brandenburg (d. 1220), 115

Alcuin, on royal charisma, 80

Alemans *see* Suabians

Alfred the Aetheling, 106

Alsace, 37

Alsleben, nunnery, 69, 71, 99

Ammianus Marcellinus, on Burgundian kings, 80

Amulrada, mother of Archbishop Walthard of Magdeburg, 61

Amulrada, sister of Archbishop Walthard of Magdeburg, mother of Pope Clement II, 61

Andernach, battle (939), 28, 53, 54, 109

Anno, archbishop of Cologne (1056–75), 97

anointing of kings, 26, 78, 80, 81, 85, 93, 98, 101, 105

Anselm of Liège, historian of the see, 80

Ansfried, 28

Aquilea, march of, 20

arengae, 81, 103

Aribo, archbishop of Mainz (1021–31), 79

Arn, bishop of Würzburg (855–92), 5

Arnolf of Carinthia, East Frankish king and emperor (887–99), 2, 3, 4, 6, 15, 53, 78

Arnulf, bishop of Halberstadt (996–1023), 94, 101, 121

Arnulf, bishop of Metz (d. 640), 6

Arnulf, duke of Bavaria (d. 937), 96

Arpads, Hungarian royal family, 88

Ascanians, 121

Asselburg, 44

Athelstan, king of Wessex, 53; relics sent to by Duke Hugh the Great, 88

Augsburg, 36, 65, 77

Austrasian noble families as Carolingian ruling class, 110

Azela, nun at Elten, Bishop Meinwerk's sister, 60

Babenbergs, East Frankish noble family: Count Poppo, 3; Count Henry, 5

Bacco, conspirator in 941, 33
Baetke, W., 81
Balderich, bishop of Utrecht (918–75), 14, 86
Balderich, count, 120
Baldwin III, count of Flanders (d. 962), 55
Bamberg, 45, 121; sacramentary given by Henry II to 80, plate IV
Bardowick, 2
Bavaria, duchy, 23, 28, 37, 39, 43, 44, 83, 96 104, 105
Bavarians, 110, 112
Beck, H.-G., 93
Behrends, P. W., antiquary and editor, 114, 122
Belecke, fortress in Westfalia, 14, 17, 28
Benedictine rule, 65, 66, 71
Berengar II, king of Italy (d. 966), 20, 26, 86, 109
Berengar, bishop of Cambrai (956–62), Otto I's kinsman, 27
Bernhard, bishop of Halberstadt (923–68), 33; charter (965), 26–7; vision, 61
Bernhard, nephew of Louis the Pious, blinded (818), 86
Bernhard, *Legatus* at battle of Lenzen (929), 34
Bernhard, margrave of Northern March, 40, 56, 95, 120, 121; and succession to margraviate, 44; founds Lutter, 118
Bernhard I (d. 1011), second Billung duke in Saxony, 28, 44, 55, 57, 94, 95; Saxons' spokesman to Henry II, 100
Bernhard II (d. 1059), third Billung duke in Saxony, 57
Bernhard of Plötzkau, count (d. 1147), 115
Bernward, bishop of Hildesheim (993–1022), 11, 63, 94; and foundation of Steterburg, 66; farewell advice to Otto III, 79
Berthild, daughter of Aeddila, 56, 58
Berthold, Luitpolding duke of Bavaria (938–47), 54
Berthold of Schweinfurt, margrave of Bavarian Nordgau, 34, 38, 45, 55; in Thietmar's memorial, 46
Berthold, son of Margrave Liuthar of Northern March, 120
Beumann, H., 81–2, 86, 114
Bibra, Count Billing's monastic foundation, 23
Billing, count, vassal of Henry, Otto I's brother, 23–4
Billungs, Saxon noble family, 4, 28, 31, 65, 69, 100, 119; calamities of, 57
Birten, battle (939), 17, 84, 87
Blankenburg, counts of, Siegfried II and Poppo, 119
Böddekken, nunnery, 63

Börde, country west of Magdeburg, 2, 41, 42
Bohemia, 17, 58
Boleslas II (d. 999), duke of Bohemia, 44, 45, 89
Boleslas Chrobry, Polish duke and king (d. 1025), 40, 89, 100, 101
Boleslas III, duke of Poland (d. 1138), 94
Borghorst, nunnery, 69, 70; foundation of, 66; processional cross, 50, 71
Bote, Konrad, his *Saxon Chronicle*, 39
Bremen, 106; diocese of, 115
Brandenburg, 44, 89
Brun, bishop of Verden (962–76), 12
Brun, bishop of Augsburg (1006–29), brother of Henry II, 31
Brun of Querfurt, biographer of St Adalbert and missionary: lament for Otto I, 35; letter to Henry II (1008), 79
Brun, historian of Saxon rising against Henry IV, 46, 79, 121
Brun, Liudolfing *dux*, killed (880), 11, 124
Brun, Otto I's brother, archbishop of Cologne (953–65), and duke of Lotharingia, 10, 14, 53, 88–9, 96; quasi-regal position, 17; warns Liudolf against followers, 29; charisma, 86–7
Brun, count, enemy of Bishop Bernward of Hildesheim, 11
Brun of Arneburg, count (d. 978 in France), 58
Bruning, vassal of Duke Eberhard (937), 18
Brunones, descendants of Duke Brun (d. 880), 12, 28, 33
Brunshausen, nunnery, later moved to Gandersheim, 63
Brussels, Royal Library's MS. with Corvey version of Thietmar's *Chronicon*, 38, 41
Burchard II, bishop of Halberstadt (1059–88), 121
Burkhard II, duke of Suabia (d. 973), 54
Burgundy, kingdom of, 15, 16, 110
Byzantium, 16, 102, 107; emperors, 93; embassies from 17, 104

Capetians, relative security of, 107
Capo Colonne, battle (982), 58
Carinthia, 37, 103, 104
Carolingian: empire, 104; political strategy, 110; treasure and relics, 88
Carolingians, 4, 20, 47, 78, 79, 81, 105, 110; Saxons remain loyal to, 3; admonished by bishops, 78; government compared to Ottonians', 102–3
Cathwulf (775), 79
Charlemagne, 5, 7, 15, 37, 52, 77, 80, 81, 87, 92, 98, 110; peace treaty with Saxons (?), 6; *magnanimitas*, 36; descendants, 50; ruthlessness towards nephews, 85–6

Charles the Bald, 5, 14
Charles III, Carolingian emperor, set aside (887), 3, 15
Charles the Simple, West Frankish Carolingian king, 7
Charles, duke of Lower Lotharingia, brother of King Lothar, 16
Chazars, 102
Christina, daughter of Liudolf and Oda, abbess of Gandersheim, 53, 54–5
Chronicon Episcoporum Ecclesie Merseburgensis, (Merseburg Episcopal History), 113, 114
Chutizi, Slav *pagus*, 115
co-heredes, 24, 41, 70, 115; importunity of, 62, 63, 68,
Cologne, 27, 41, 65; Otto I's court at (965), 27, archbishop of, 24, 98; prelates, nobles and *ministeriales* of, 117
conflict theories, 28–9
conflict and unity, 105
Conrad I, East Frankish king (911–18), 7, 81; death and *discidium regni*, 27
Conrad II, emperor (1024–39), 38, 49, 52, 57, 62, 79, 93, 99, 111, 122
Conrad, count (d. 948) of the Conradine family, 28, 124
Conrad the Red, duke of Lotharingia (d. 955), Otto I's son-in-law, ancestor of the Salians, 9, 20, 27, 29, 36, 37, 38, 85, 86, 95
Conrad, son of Henry IV, 112
Conradines, family of King Conrad I, 9, 15, 28, 81, 84–5, 111
Constance, bishopric, 65
Cordoba, embassies from, 104
Corvey, 4, 5, 61, 65; number of monks at, 71; *Traditiones*, 51, 61
Corvey Annals, 24
Crawford Library, 114

Daleminzi, Slav people, 3, 5, 19
Danes, 3, 86; *see also* Vikings; pirates, 89
Dedi, count, 17, 18, 20, 28
Dedi, count (d. 1009) of Wettin family, 40, 56, 57, 99, 116, 119
Dedi, killed at Laar (938), 28
Dedi of Gutenswegen, father of Archbishop Gero of Magdeburg, 116
Derlingau, East Saxon *pagus*, 11, 120
Dietrich, royal chaplain, son of Margrave Liuthar of Northern March, 120
Dietrich, margrave of Northern March (d. 985), 34, 40, 44, 45, 56, 99, 118
Dietrich, son of Count Dedi: receives father's fiefs, 57; takes over the Eilenburg, 59
diplomata (royal): of protection for nunneries, 68; sacral aura of, 103

divisio regnorum (806), 86
Dodicho, Westfalian count (d. 1020), 59
Dortmund, 17; Synod of (1005), 50
Dornburg, royal Christmas courts held at, 90
Drogo, illegitimate Carolingian, 14
Drübeck, nunnery, 37, 68, 69
Dyle, battle of (891), 5, 6

East Frankish kings: Carolingian, 5, 6, 15, 84; post-Carolingian, 109
East Frankish kingdom, 3; rise of undivided kingship in, 15; and West Frankish ideas on royal power, 78
East Saxon: leading families' role, 111; princes' rising (1073), 83; warrior nobles unpaid, 32
East Saxony, 11, 37, 52, 59, 116, 117, 120; wealth of, 63; bad years (994–5), 89; number of royal stays in, 104
Eberhard, brother of King Conrad I, Frankish duke, 14, 18, 28
Edgar, king of Wessex, 93; charter for the New Minster, 106
Edith, wife and queen of Otto I, 2, 19, 42, 53, 75
Edward the Martyr, king of Wessex, 106
Eila, Thietmar of Merseburg's aunt, 45, 55
Eilenburg, Wettin fortress, 56, 57
Einhard, 5, 6, 36, 52, 81, 110
Einsiedeln, 19, 37
Ekbert, abbot of Tegernsee, 79–80
Ekbert, count, brother of Count Wichmann the Younger, 12, 18, 21, 34, 44, 56, 57
Ekbert, count of Brunswick, 97
Ekbertines, Saxon noble family, 4
Ekkard, son of Liudolf, 11
Ekkehard, margrave of Meissen (d. 1002), 18, 55, 100, 121; offends Sophia and Adelheid, 49; candidate for kingship (1002), 94
Ekkehard, son of above, margrave of Meissen (d. 1046), 40; vassals kill the Wettin Dietrich, 57; feud with uncle Gunzelin, 101
Ekkerhardines, family of, margraves of Meissen, 56, 57; clash with Thietmar of Merseburg, 101–2
Ekkehart IV's *Casus Sancti Galli*, 30
Elbe, river, 1, 2, 3, 5, 41
Elten, nunnery, 50, 60, 66, 69
Emma, abbess of Hilwartshausen, daughter of Aeddila, 56, 68
Emma, wife of Count Liudger Billung, 57
Engern, 10, 12, 63
England: Anglo-Saxon, government compared to Ottonians' 106; Norman, 37; demography of ducal families, 51
equilibrium upheld by conflict, 30; *see also* conflict theories

Erdmann, C., 78
Eresburg, 14, 87
Erfurt, 2
Erich, conspirator (941), father of Bishop Hildiward of Halberstadt, 33, 39
Ernst, Frankish noble, follower of Liudolf (954), 37
Ernst, duke of Suabia (1015–30), 38
Erwin, father of Hatheburg, 12
Eschwege: royal *curtis*, 54; nunnery, 64
Essen: nunnery, 53, 54, 71; treasures, 50
Esico of Ballenstedt, 111
Eurasian steppes, peoples of, 102
Evans-Pritchard, E. E., Frazer Lecture, 102
Ezzo, count palatine, husband of Mathilda, Otto II's daughter, 52, 54

familiaritas regis, 79
Fischbeck, nunnery, 56, 65, 69
Folcmar, bishop of Utrecht (976–91), 18, 56
Francia, 90; Otto I grants forfeited lands in, 37
Frankfurt, 9
Franks, 4, 6, 102, 111; monastic foundations for women, 64; as dominant people, 104, 110
Fraxinetum, Saracen colony, 30
Frederick Barbarossa, emperor, 111–12
Frederick, archbishop of Mainz (937–54), 32, 85
Frederick, Wettin count (d.1017), 56; leaving three daughters, 57, 59
Frederick, burgrave of Magdeburg, brother of Thietmar of Merseburg, 115, 119–20
Freckenhorst (diocese of Münster), nunnery, 63
Friderun, daughter of younger Wichmann, foundress of Kemnade, 56, 65, 68
Fulda: Annals, 3; Regensburg Continuation of, 3, 5; necrologium, 57, 58; *Traditiones*, 51; Widerad, abbot of (1063), 97

Gandersheim, nunnery, 27, 60, 68, 71, 89; St Mary in the Upper Town, Benedictine convent founded by Abbess Gerberga, 66, 71
Gebhard, of the Conradine family, 28
Gebhard, count (d. 1075), father of Lothar of Süpplingenburg, 119
Gerberga (d. 969), daughter of King Henry I and Mathilda, 53, 54
Gerberga (d. 1001), daughter of Duke Henry I of Bavaria, abbess of Gandersheim, 18, 26, 54, 66
Gerbstedt, nunnery, 68, 71
German aristocracy, family structures of, 50–1
Germanic continuity, 75, 80

Germany, 10, 109, 112; kingship, 93; *principes*, 96; eleventh-century strains in, 107
Gernrode, nunnery, 23, 25, 66, 69, 71–2, 98; cult of St Cyriacus, 72
Gero, archbishop of Cologne (969–76), 24, 98
Gero, archbishop of Magdeburg (1012–23), 40, 41, 116, 117
Gero, margrave (d. 965), 13, 14, 15, 20, 22, 24, 25, 28, 32, 33, 34, 72, 98
Gero, margrave, son of Margrave Thietmar, 70
Gero (of Alsleben), count 45, 69; executed after judicial duel (979), 99
Geseke, nunnery, 60, 68
Giebichenstein, castle in Neletice, 24; as prison, 95
Gisela, empress, wife of Conrad II, 111
Gisela, wife of Henry the Wrangler, Duke of Bavaria, 18
Giselbert, duke of Lotharingia (d. 939), 17, 52, 54, 84, 109
Giselher, archbishop of Magdeburg (981–1004), 40, 66
Gluckmann, M., 102
Godehard, bishop of Hildesheim (1022–38), 64
Godesti, abbess of Herford and Metelen, 61, 66
Godfrey, Count of Verdun, 55
Godila, wife of Margrave Liuthar, 41, 43, 52, 55, 72, 120
Goslar: Henry IV's courts at, 97
Grauss, F., 81
gravitas, 53
Gregory VII, pope (1073–85), 82, 97, 107, 112
Grone, Ottonian *curtis*, 60
Gross-Rottmersleben, 42, 113
Günther, margrave of Merseburg (d. 982), 18, 58
Gunther, monk and porter of St Emmeram, Regensburg, 85
Guntram, count, condemned (952), 36
Gunzelin, margrave of Meissen (1002–9), 100–1
Gutenswegen, 34, 39, 40, 41, 114, 115, 116, 122–3

Hadmersleben, nunnery, 67
Hadwig, daughter of Duke Henry I of Bavaria, 53, 54
Hahn, G., translator of Thietmar, 34
Halberstadt: see of, 27, 33, 63, 64, 117, 118; *History of the Bishops of*, 61
Haldensleben, 45, 118; Alt-Haldensleben, 117–18

Haldensleben, comital family; enemies of Walbeck family, 45, 118; lands at Santersleben, 118–19, 122

Hamburg-Bremen, archbishopric, 31, 64

Harzburg, 46, 83; royal chapel defiled in, 93

Harzgau, Saxon *pagus*, 121–2

Hatheburg, first wife of King Henry I, 12, 60

Hathui, daughter of Henry I and Mathilda, married to Duke Hugh the Great, 53

Hathui, daughter of Count Wichmann the Elder, first abbess of Gernrode, 22, 25, 50, 52, 55, 72, 98

Hathui, abbess of Heeslingen, 89, and cf. 69

Hed, count, founder of Heeslingen, 69

Heeslingen-Zeven, nunnery, 65, 67, 69

Heeslingen, Thietmar of Merseburg's *curtis*, 41, 115

Heinemann, O. v., 115

Heiningen, nunnery, 65, 69, 71

Helmarshausen, monastery, 70

Helmburg, foundress of Fischbeck, 56, 60, 65

Henry I, king, 5, 14, 16, 17, 19, 27, 30, 31, 45, 52, 53, 55, 60, 62, 65, 68, 69, 72, 81, 87, 90, 96; enmities in Saxony, 10–13; orders his house (929), 15, 26

Henry II, king and emperor, 19, 30, 31, 36, 40, 46, 47, 50, 52, 54, 67, 70, 75, 79, 80, 90, 94, 95, 99, 103, 104, 106, 107, 109, 120, 121; diploma for Kemnade, 68; grants of nunneries by, 69; and Whitsun as court festival, 99–100; and Margrave Gunzelin, 101

Henry III (1039–56), king and emperor, 52, 58, 70, 79, 82, 97, 106, 107, 117, 120

Henry IV (1056–1106), king and emperor, 13, 46, 52, 79, 93, 107, 109, 111, 112, 117, 119, 120; flight from the Harzburg, 83; minority 96–7, 98

Henry V, king and emperor, 111–12

Henry (I), duke of Bavaria, Otto I's brother, 12, 13, 20, 23, 26, 28, 29, 32, 43, 53, 58, 84, 86, 87, 95; Otto's enemy in Saxony, 14–19

Henry (II) the Wrangler, duke of Bavaria (d. 995), 12, 17, 18, 19, 26, 29, 43, 44, 54, 55, 89, 90, 95

Henry the Lion, 112, 119

Henry the Proud, duke of Saxony, 119

Henry of Schweinfurt, 31, 95, 96

Henry, count, of Stade family (d. 976), 27, 35, 46, 94

Henry, count, of Stade family (d. 1016), 57–8

Henry, count, brother of Thietmar of Merseburg, 115, 120, 121

Henry, L., 51

hereditas, 60; of sons, 59; of nuns, 69

Herford, nunnery, 55, 63, 71; *Sancta Maria ad Crucem*, satellite convent founded by Godesti, 66

Heribert, archbishop of Cologne (999–1021), 70, 120

Hermann Billung, duke in Saxony, 11, 12, 21, 22, 25, 33, 35, 55, 56; liturgical reception in Magdeburg, 94

Hermann (d. 949), of Conradine family, duke of Suabia, 19, 28, 36, 46, 53

Hermann, margrave of Meissen (1009–*c.*-32), 40, 100; feuds against uncle Gunzelin, 101

Hermann of Salm, 121; election to kingship (1081), 83

Hermann of Lerbeck, 122

Hessi, Saxon noble family, 4, 58–9, 63

Hezilo, bishop of Hildesheim (1054–79). 97

Hildesheim: see of, 19, 50, 63; Annals, 110

Hildiward, bishop of Halberstadt (968–96), 33, 38, 39, 43, 89, 98

Hillersleben, nunnery, 64, 65

Hillersleben, counts of, 117, 118

Hilwartshausen, nunnery, 56, 60, 64, 65, 69, 70

Hincmar, 78, 79

Hlawitschka, E., 124

Hodo, margrave, 25, 43

Hohenaltheim, Synod of (916), 84

Hohenstaufen, 96

Hollingsworth, T. H., 51, 57

Holtzmann, R., editor of Thietmar, 34, 40

Holy Lance, 80, 84, 88, 100

Hrotsvitha of Gandersheim, 16, 17, 19, 20, 38, 47, 84, 85, 96

Hugh, illegitimate Carolingian, 14

Hugh the Great, West Frankish *dux*, 12, 22, 35, 53, 88

Hungary, 104

Ida, wife of Liudolf, 19, 53; position at Otto I's court, 20

Ifriqiya, 104

Ilsenburg, forged charter for, 121

Imma, countess, co-foundress of Kemnade, 56, 65, 68

Immedings, Saxon noble family, 12

Ingelheim, 9, 32

Irmgard, marchioness of Plötzkau, 119–20

Isingrim, bishop of Regensburg, 85

Italy, 12, 15, 26, 29–30, 35, 38, 53, 58, 96, 104, 110, 112

James, M. R., 113

John Rylands Library, Manchester, 113, 114, 121

John XII, pope (955–63), 23, 24

John XIII, pope (965–72), 30, 90

Jonas, bishop of Orleans (d. 843); *De Institutione Regia*, 78–9

Judith, wife of Duke Henry I of Bavaria, 29, 53, 72

Kalbe, nunnery destroyed by Slavs (983), 64, 65
Karl, son of Charlemagne, 86
Karlmann, brother of King Pippin, 29
Karlmann, brother of Charlemagne (d. 771), 29, 85
Karlmann, son of Charles the Bald, 14
Katlenburg, counts of, 94
Kaufungen, nunnery, 64
Kemnade, nunnery, 56, 65, 68, 69
Kern, F., *Kingship and Law*, 82
Kiev, 104
kingship: no longer divisible, 15, 47, 105; itinerant, 103–4; a *ministerium*, 78, 82, 84
Koledizi, Slav *pagus*, 25
Königslutter *see* Lutter
Krüger, Sabine, 124
Kunigunde, empress, wife of Henry II, 50, 52
Kunigunde, of Stade comital family, Thietmar of Merseburg's mother, 41, 58, 62, 115

Laar, fortress in Westfalia, 28
Lammspringe, nunnery, 63
Lampert of Hersfeld, 83, 97, 121
Laurent, M., translator of Thietmar, 34
lay nobility, vicarious piety of, 66, 92–3
Lech, battle (955), 23, 26, 77, 111
legatio, permanent command on Saxon frontier, 11, 13, 32, 34
Lenzen, battle (929), 13, 34
Lévy, C., demographer, 51
Lex Saxonum, and women, 50, 58, 59, 61
Libri, G., 114
Libri Memoriales, and family structures, 50, 51
Liudgard, daughter of Liudolf, ninth-century East-Saxon *dux*, 3
Liudgard (d. 953), daughter of Otto I, 53
Liudgard; abbess of Elten, 50, 66, 68
Liudgard, daughter of Margrave Ekkehard I of Meissen, wife of Werner of Walbeck, 72, 115, 119, 120
Liudger, count, brother of Duke Bernhard I, Billung, 55, 57
Liudger, count, vassal of Bishop Arnulf of Halberstadt, 121–2
Liudolf, bishop of Osnabrück, 10
Liudolf, ninth-century East Saxon *dux*, 2, 52, 54, 55
Liudolf, duke of Suabia, Otto I's son by Edith, 9, 12, 18, 29, 35, 37, 38, 53, 58, 86, 95, 105; influence in eastern Saxony and rising, 19–21; death in Italy, 26
Liudolfings, 2, 3, 7, 10, 15, 26, 27, 28, 46, 60, 63, 82, 88–90, 99, 102, 104, 106, 110, 124; Bavarian branch of, 17, 18, 19, 67, 121; and uprisings, 29; infant mortality among, 52; longevity of women, 52–4, and see table; personal inviolability, 85–7
Liudprand of Cremona, bishop, historian, 16, 17, 40, 85, 88, 96; *Antapodosis*, 35, 54, 84, 86–7
Liutbert, archbishop of Mainz (863–89), 5
Liutbirg, anchoress, her *Vita*, 59
Liuthar, monk, in the Aachen Gospels, 78, plate II
Liuthar, Thietmar of Merseburg's great-grandfather, 34
Liuthar, Thietmar of Merseburg's grand-father, chapter 3, pp. 43, 55, 95, 113, 114, 118, 123
Liuthar, margrave of Northern March, Thietmar's uncle, 41, 43, 44, 45, 46, 52, 55, 62, 72, 116, 119, 121, 122; interests in Cologne, 120
Liutizi, heathen Slav people, 79
Lothar I, Carolingian emperor, 3
Lothar, king of Italy (d. 950), 20; married to Adelheid, 53, 55
Lothar, West Frankish Carolingian king (954–86), 16
Lothar of Süpplingenburg, 94, 116; diploma for Lutter, 118; buried there, 119; called Liudger, 122
Lotharingia, 37, 53, 90, 105; Lower Lotharingia, 12, 86; Upper Lotharingia, 103, 104
Louis the Pious, Carolingian emperor, 2, 3, 15, 86, 110
Louis the German, East Frankish Carolingian king, 3, 4, 5, 15
Louis the Child, East Frankish Carolingian king (900–11), 7, 15
Louis the Younger, East Frankish Carolingian king (876–82), 2, 3
Louis IV, d'Outremer, West Frankish Carolingian king (936–54), 35, 53, 54
Luitpoldings, Bavarian ducal family, 15, 96
Lüneburg, St Michael, monastic foundation of the Billungs, 12, 22, 28; *necrologium*, 57, 58
Lutter, nunnery, 118, 119, 122

Magdeburg, royal *curtis*, fortress, *civitas* and district, 1, 2, 34, 35, 42, 114, 116, 117; courts held at, 20, 99, 101; Ottonians there on Palm Sundays, 90
Magdeburg, St Maurice, monastery and arch-bishopric, 1, 2, 23, 24, 26, 33, 40, 42, 52, 61, 64, 70, 90, 94, 103, 120; Otto I's earliest diploma for, 1, 2, 116

Magdeburg: St Sebastian, 116; *Unser lieben Frauen*, canonry, 117
Magdeburg Annals, 38, 94
Magdeburger Schöppenchronik, 39
Magyars (Hungarians), 13, 23, 81, 90, 102
Mainz, 9, 50, 64, 86; Rhine-Frankish dioceses of province, 64–5; council at (888), 84; Pontifical (*c.* 960), 77, 78
Malacin (Eisdorf), 115
Malmédy, 97
Marcswith, foundress of Schildesche, 56, 65
Marienthal, Cistercian monastery, 114
Mathilda (d. 968), Henry I's wife and queen, 10, 12, 14, 16, 26, 47, 53, 55, 62, 65, 72, 75, 87, 90; biographies *see Vita Mathildis*; favours Henry against Otto, 28; founds Nordhausen, 67; rebellious nephews, 21, 22; regal attire, 85
Mathilda, Otto I's daughter (d. 999), abbess of Quedlinburg, 27, 44, 49, 53, 72, 87, 89; monastic foundations, 66
Mathilda, daughter of Otto II and Theophanu, 27, 52, 54
Mathilda, abbess of Essen, daughter of Liudolf and Ida, 53
Mathilda, daughter of Hermann Billung (d. 1008), 55
Meginzo, killer of Thangmar (938), 87
Meibom the Elder, H., antiquary, 34, 39; his *Walbeckische Chronike,* 113, 122
Meinwerk, bishop of Paderborn (1009–36), 59–60, 61, 69; his *Life* by monk of Abdinghof, 60, 114
Meissen, fortress and bishopric, 13, 19, 40, 64; march of, 25
Memleben, monastery, 93
Merseburg, 12, 17, 18, 64, 77, 100, 101, 115, 122; Henry II's 'home' in Saxony, 19; march of, 25; see of, 31, 41; *necrologium*, 58, 87
Meschede, 28, nunnery, 50, 69
Metelen, nunnery, 70
Miesco I, Polish duke, 22, 25, 43, 44, 89
Miracles of St Wigbert, Hersfeld, 84
Mistui, Obotrite prince, joins Henry the Wrangler (984), 44
Modus Ottinc, 26
Möllenbeck, nunnery, 63
Monreburg, fortress, 120
Morawians, 3, 5
mothers as heiresses of their sons, 59–60
Münster, see of, 63
Mulde, river, 5, 19, 101

Nadda, Saxon priest, his *Life of St Cyriacus*, 72
Neletice, Slav *pagus*, 23, 24

Neuenheerse, nunnery, 63, 67
Niederaltaich: abbey 83; Annals, 83
Nienburg, abbey, 70
Nordgau, 37
Nordgermersleben, 42, 113
Nordhausen, nunnery, 65, 67, 93
Nordthüringau, East Saxon *pagus*, 1, 2, 42, 43, 45, 115, 117, 120, 121, 122
Northeim, counts of, 94
Northern March, margraviate of, 34, 40, 41, 44, 99
Nottuln, nunnery, 63, 67

Obotrites, Slav people, 3, 4, 22, 44; *subreguli*, 21
Oda (d. 913), wife of Liudolf, 52, 53, 54, 55
Oda, Henry I's sister, 3, 53, 124
Odilo, abbot of Cluny (994–1049), author of the *epitaphium* of empress Adelheid, 49
Ödingen, Westfalian nunnery, 70
Ohre, river, 41, 115
Oldenstadt, nunnery, 65, 67
Olvenstedt, estate of Archbishop Walthard near Magdeburg, 61
Osnabrück, 12
Otto, East Saxon duke (d. 912), father of Henry I, 3, 11, 52, 53, 55
Otto I, emperor, 1, 9, 11, 12, 13–15, 16–22, 23–9, 32–8, 39, 42, 43, 44, 45, 46, 47, 52, 53, 54, 56, 60, 65, 66, 70, 72, 79, 81, 86, 90, 94, 98, 105, 106, 109, 110, 114, 116, 118, 124; contemporary judgment, 35; and clemency, 36, 87, 111; and Nordhausen, 67; diploma for Meschede, 69; confesses sins for all, 77; his eyes, 83; 'potestas a Deo ordinata', 84–5; letters, 103
Otto II, emperor, 10, 18, 24, 25, 26, 27, 35, 38, 43, 44, 47, 52, 53, 55, 58, 94, 99, 101, 105, 116; summoned to Italy, 29–30; diploma – for Hilwartshausen, 68, for Alsleben, 71
Otto III, emperor, 9, 11, 17, 19, 27, 30, 43, 44, 47, 50, 52, 53, 55, 62, 79, 80, 90, 103, 109, 116, 121; grant to sister Sophia, 54; and ransom of Stade family, 58; diploma – for Vitzenburg, 65, for Elten, 68, for Ödingen, 70; Gospel Book at Aachen, 75, 78, plate III; campaigns against Slavs as child, 88–9
Otto, duke of Suabia and Bavaria, son of Liudolf, 26, 44, 53
Otto of Northeim, 83
Ottonian: coronation *ordo*, 77, 78; historiography, 16, 17, 49, 84; renaissance, 73; 'system', 106
Ottonian empire: paucity of institutions, 102–5; anomalies in make-up of, 110–11

Ottonians (Saxon royal family), 14, 16, 19, 20, 27, 31, 36, 42, 78, 87, 91, 92, 93, 94, 96, 100, 101, 103, 104–7, 111; Slav bodyguards of (?), 32; use of marriages, 45; births of children, 55; acquisition of nunneries, 68–70; masters of prelates, 79; sacrality, 84; *regalis disciplina*, 85; gifts of relics by, 88; churches and palaces, itinerary, 90; and Western consanguinity, 124

Paderborn, bishopric, 31, 59, 60
Paris, Council of (829), 78
Pfäfers, *Liber Memorialis* of, 19, 50
Piasts, Polish dynasty, 88
Pippin, king (d. 768), 110
Pippin the Hunchback, son of Charlemagne, 77, 85–6, 87
Poeta Saxo, 5–7
Pöhlde, 90, 94
Pomarius, Johannes, 39
precariae, 60, 69

Quedlinburg, royal palace and foundation for women, 44, 53, 55, 63, 65, 67, 71, 89, 93; royal Easter courts at, 32, 90–1
Quedlinburg Annals, 5, 9, 33, 35, 44, 89, 104, 110
Querfurt, nobles of, 122; *see also* Brun of

Radbod, bishop of Utrecht (899–917), his *Life* 96
rade, 59
Ragenold, count of Roucy, 54
Ratold, illegitimate son of emperor Arnolf, 15
Ravenna, 33
Recknitz, battle (955), 23
Redarii, Slav people, 11, 13
Reepsholt, 70
regalis disciplina, 85, 106
Regensburg, 18, 21, 85; St Emmeram, monastery, 85, 96
Reginars of Hainault and Louvain, 109
Regino of Prüm, canonist, historian, 15–16, 110
regnum Teutonicum, 46, 104
Reichenau, abbey, 33; *Liber Memorialis* of, 50
Reichskirche, 80, 105–6
Reichsvolk (ruling people), 46, 110–11
Reinhard, bishop of Halberstadt (1107–23), 71
Reinhilde of Beichlingen, kidnapped by Count Werner, 62
relics, to strengthen lordship, 87–88
Ricbert (also called Ippo), uncle of Margrave Liuthar, 121–2

Ricdag, East Saxon noble, 63
Ricdag, margrave of Meissen (d. 985), founder of Gerbstedt, 71
Richenza, empress, 119
Richer of St Remi, historian, 35
Robert the Pious, Capetian king, 54
Rohr, 44
Romanus, son of Constantine Porphyrogenitus, 17
Rome, 94, 99, 102, 103, 105
Rothgard, abbess of Hilwartshausen, Bernward of Hildesheim's aunt, 56, 60
Rudolf II, king of Burgundy (912–37), father of empress Adelheid, 88
Rudolf of Fulda, 4
Rudolf of Rheinfelden, 112
Ruodlieb, 72–3
Ruotger, biographer of Archbishop Brun of Cologne, 10, 17, 21, 26, 29, 35, 84, 86, 96, 105, 106

Saale, river, 3, 19, 23, 101
Saalfeld, 16, 17, 20
Sachsenspiegel, Landrecht, position of women as heiresses, 59, 61
St Emmeram, 80, plate IV
St Gallen, abbey, 19, 30, 33; *Liber Memorialis* of, 50
St Maurice, warrior saint, relics of, 88
St Udalrich, bishop of Augsburg (923–73), 77, 80
St Ursula, cult of, 88
Salian kings and emperors, 27, 71, 78, 79, 80, 96, 101, 106, 111, 112, 122; and infant mortality, 52; houselands of, 93; nobles alienated from, 107
Sallust, 81
Salz, on the Frankish Saale, 6
Salzburg, archdiocese of, 65
Sandersleben (Anhalt), 117
Santersleben, 34, 39, 40, 41, 114, 116, 122–3; later history of, 117–19
Saracens, campaign against (982), 53, 58
Saxon Annalist, 5, 35, 38, 39, 68, 94, 115, 116, 119, 120
Saxon: followers of Henry the Wrangler, 18, 43; fortresses, 17, 18; Hessengau, 60; *Reich* (Empire), 1, 51, 79, 92, 111; Schwabengau, 117; writers, 110
Saxon aristocracy, 13, 44, 47, 49, 51, 52, 57, 107; marriage alliances of, 45–6; in *Libri Memoriales*, 50; women's expectations of life, 56–7; endowment of nunneries, 64; family burials of, 93; role in making Henry II king, 100; and Ottonian court, 104
Saxon nobles, 18, 19, 33, 38, 43, 46, 72,

110–11; losses in wars, 58; estranged from kings, 70, 101, 107, 109

Saxons, 3, 5–7, 14, 19, 21, 25, 26, 36, 46, 56, 100, 102, 104, 111

Saxony: Carolingian, 2, 4, 6, 11, 46, 65; Ottonian and post-Ottonian, 3, 9, 10, 13, 14, 23–5, 27, 29, 31, 32, 36, 44, 46, 47, 58, 71, 83, 84, 94, 100, 104, 106, 110, 117; battlefield of Henry's attacks on Otto I, 17–22; comital constitution, 4, 6; domestic character of Ottonian rule in, 33, 111; Ottonian building in, 90; legal custom, 61; Conrad II's welcome in, 49; monastic endowments for women in, 63–64, 65

Scapendal, 113

Schakensleben, 122

Schaumburg, count of, 118, 122

Schildesche (Westfalia), nunnery, 56, 65, 67, 69

Schlesinger, W., 80

Schöningen, nunnery, 65

Sclavania, 22, 42, 72, 91

Selz, the Empress Adelheid's monastic foundation, 50

senium, 53

Serimunt, Slav *pagus*, 20, 24, 43, 98

Shilluk, nilotic tribe, 102

Siegfried, abbot of Tegernsee, 80

Siegfried, count, 'secundus a rege' (d. 937), 12–13, 14

Siegfried (d. 959), son of Margrave Gero, 22, 52

Siegfried, count (d. 991), Thietmar of Merseburg's father, 41, 43, 55, 62; serves Theophanu, 44–5; his descendants, 119–20

Siegfried, of Stade comital family (d. 1037), 57, 58

Sigebert of Gembloux, writer, 53

Sigebodo, count, brother of Dodicho, 60

Slavs, 4, 5, 28, 32, 51, 89; uprising (983), 9, 44, 64, 111; of Mecklenburg, 86; of Lusatia, 88

Sophia, daughter of Otto II, abbess of Gandersheim and Essen, 49–50, 54, 89, 94; foundress of St Cyriacus, Eschwege, 66

Speyer, 93, 117

Stade, counts, 56, 57–8, 89, 121; at Heeslingen, 69, 115

Stavelot (1071), monks visit Henry IV, 97

Steterburg, nunnery, 65, 66, 69, 71

Stötterlingenburg, nunnery, 65, 67

Suabia, duchy of, 37, 105

Suabians (Alemans), 110, 111

Suitger, bishop of Bamberg (1040–6), later Pope Clement II, 61

Süpplingenburgers, 118, 119–22

Tagino, archbishop of Magdeburg (1004–12), 95, 120

Thangmar, Henry I's son by Hatheburg, Otto I's half-brother, 12, 13, 14, 17, 28, 32, 36, 60; position in Ottonian house, 87

Theodora, Macedonian princess, 107

Theophanu, empress, 44, 49, 53, 55, 89–90

Thietmar of Merseberg (975–1018), bishop and author of the *Chronicon*, 13, 14, 22, 24, 25, 30, 33, 34, 36, 37, 39, 41, 42, 43, 44, 46, 47, 51, 52, 55, 56, 57–8, 61, 62, 72, 79, 87, 94, 98, 99, 100–1, 105, 110, 113–15, 117, 121; Corvey version of the *Chronicon*, 38; compared with other writers, 40; on Otto I at the Lech, 77; on Otto I's visions, 85; on rebellion and kingship, 95–6; tampers with diploma of Otto II, 101–2

Thietmar, margrave, nephew of Margrave Gero, 24, 25, 43, 55, 98

Thietmar, count, brother of Duke Bernhard Billung II, 57; accused of plotting against Henry III, 106

Thionville, Capitulary of (805), 2

Thuringia, 3, 17, 18, 20, 23; Eastern, 24

Thuringians, 3

Tribur: Synod of (895), 46, 78, 84; negotiations at (1076), 83

Trier, archbishop of, 98

Tundersleben, 42, 113, 115

Udo, brother of Duke Hermann of Suabia, 28, 36, 46

Udo, of Stade comital family (d. 994), 57

Ullmann, Walter, 78

uncle-nephew feuds, 20, 101

Ursinus, J. F., translator of Thietmar (1790), 34

Utrecht, see of, 96; Brun sent to, 86–7

Verona, march, of, 17, 20

Vikings (Danes): Elbe raid (994), 57–8; raids against Utrecht, 86, 96

Vita Mathildis prior, 72, 81, 84, 85, 105, 110

Vita Mathildis posterior, 14, 16, 72, 79, 81, 105; on dangers of childbirth, 67

Vitzenburg, nunnery, 65–6

Vreden, nunnery, 49, 69

Walbeck, royal estate and fortress, 19; St Andreas, 66

Walbeck on the Aller, seat of Thietmar of Merseburg's family, 34, 41, 45, 115; collegiate church, 39, 41, 95, 113–16, 123; Thietmar as provost, 120

Walbeck, comital family, 34, 41, 43, 113, 115–16, 120, 121, 122; enmity with house of Margrave Dietrich, 45, 118

Walsrode, nunnery, 65

Walthard, archbishop of Magdeburg (1012), 40, 120; family of, 61, 117
Wazo, bishop of Liège (1042–8), 80
Welf IV, duke of Bavaria, 83
Welfs, heirs of Lothar of Süpplingenburg, 118–19, 122
Wendhausen, nunnery, 63
Werla, 25, 33; assembly of Saxon nobles at (1002), 94
Werner, archbishop of Magdeburg (1063–78), 79
Werner, margrave of Northern March, Thietmar of Merseburg's cousin, 40, 41, 44, 52, 72, 95, 99, 115, 118, 119, 120, 122; kills Count Dedi, 57; kidnaps heiress, 62, 95
Werner, K. F., 124
Wessex, kings and kingdom of, 20, 88, 106–7
Westfalia, 12, 14, 17, 28, 63, 66, 68, 114; nunneries, 69–70; *pagi*, 60
West Frankish: kings, 15, 16, 104, 109; precepts on kingship, 78; centres of culture, 84
Wetter, nunnery, 64
Wettins, 56, 57
Wicfried, bishop of Verdun, 43
Wichmann the Elder, count, Hermann Billung's brother, 11, 12, 52, 55; makes peace with Otto I, 28
Wichmann the Younger, count, 12, 21–2, 23, 25, 29, 34, 55–6, 57, 65
Wichmann, count in Hamalant, founder of Elten, 66

Wichmann III, count, murdered (1016), 57, 120
widows, insecurity of, 62
Widukind of Corvey, monk and historian, 1, 5, 10, 11, 12–13, 14, 16–18, 20, 21, 22, 25, 26, 28, 29, 30, 33, 35, 37, 40, 47, 53, 56, 57, 81, 83, 84, 85, 86, 96, 98, 100, 103, 110–11
Widukindi, Stirps, 10, 12
Wilhelm, Thuringian count, joins Liudolf's rising, 20
Wilhelm, Thuringian count (d. 1003), 44
William, son of Otto I by Slav noblewoman, archbishop of Mainz (954–68), 24, 53, 68; letter to Pope Agapitus II, 25–6
William of Malmesbury, 88
Wimmelburg, nunnery, 65
Wipo, royal chaplain, biographer of Conrad II, 62, 79, 81, 93; and the *archisolium regni*, 98–9
Wolfhere, biographer of Bishop Godehard of Hildesheim, 99
Wolmirstedt, fortress on the Ohre, 41, 45, 115, 119
Wulfhard, 22, 37
Wunstorf, nunnery, 63

Zeitz, bishopric, 64
Zoe, Macedonian princess, 107
Zulus, 102
Zwentibold (d. 900), illegitimate son of the emperor Arnolf, 3, 15, 53

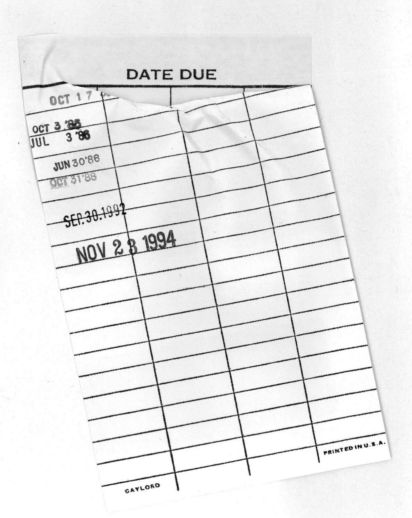

DATE DUE

OCT 17

OCT 3 '85
JUL 3 '86

JUN 30 '86
OCT 31 '88

SEP. 30. 1992

NOV 2 3 1994

PRINTED IN U.S.A.

GAYLORD